Cuisine at home®

VOLUME 6

AUGUST HOME
SPECIAL PUBLICATIONS
2200 Grand Avenue
Des Moines IA 50312
www.augusthome.com

More Than Before

Each year, rather *each issue*, we try give you more recipes, options, and menu ideas. Have we met our goal? Look inside—we've done it! The volumes are jam-packed with ideas for weeknights with the family or entertaining friends on the weekends. And the recipes could not be simpler or easier to understand.

Want even more? Let's talk about our new departments. **Chef At Home:** guest chefs share their world famous recipes. **Faster With Fewer:** fantastic 30 minute or less dishes that even include complete meals. **Cuisine Classes and Techniques:** instructional courses that tell the "hows and whys" from making homemade pasta to roasting chicken. This is followed by plenty of recipes utilizing what you've just learned. Now look inside—there's even more.

Do we look a little bit different than our first issue? Sure ... for the better! We've changed our look, but the easy-to-follow instructions and color photographs are still there. And your "friend in the kitchen" will continue to be by your side in every issue to come.

Can we set the bar even higher next year? You bet. We'll work harder every issue to give you the best cooking magazine we can.

VOLUME 6

Cuisine at home

THE YEAR AT A GLANCE

ISSUE NO. 31

Jan/Feb 2002 Features:

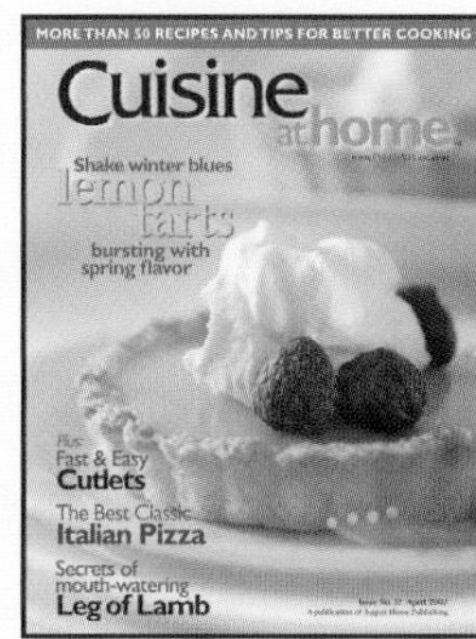

ISSUE NO. 32

Mar/Apr 2002 Features:

ISSUE NO. 33

June 2002 Features:

ISSUE NO. 34

August 2002 Features:

ISSUE NO. 35

October 2002 Features:

ISSUE NO. 36

December 2002 Features:

Cuisine at home®

Please contact us to find out about other *Cuisine at home* products and services:

By Phone: 1-800-311-3995
By Mail: 2200 Grand Avenue, Des Moines IA 50312
By Email: CuisineAtHome@CuisineAtHome.com
Or Visit Our Web-Site: www.CuisineAtHome.com

TWICE AS MANY EASY-TO-FOLLOW RECIPES

Cuisine at home™

Stuffed Pasta
oven-baked cannelloni

Beef Tenderloin
pan-roasted for great flavor

Rich Rich Rich Chocolate Cake
in 6 easy steps

Issue No. 31 February 2002
www.CuisineAtHome.com

Cuisine at home™

Publisher
Donald B. Peschke

Editor
John F. Meyer

Senior Editor
Susan Hoss

Assistant Editor
Sara Ostransky

Test Kitchen Director
Kim Samuelson

Contributing Food Stylist
Janet Pittman

Art Director
Cinda Shambaugh

Assistant Art Director
Holly Wiederin

Graphic Designer
April Walker Janning

Photographers
Scott Little
Dean Tanner

Image Specialist
Troy Clark

Corporate:

Corporate Vice Presidents: Mary R. Scheve, Douglas L. Hicks • *Creative Director:* Ted Kralicek • *Professional Development Director:* Michal Sigel *New Media Manager:* Gordon C. Gaippe • *Senior Photographer:* Crayola England • *Multi Media Art Director:* Eugene Pedersen • *Technology Analyst:* Carol Schoeppler • *Web Content Manager:* David Briggs • *Web Designer:* Kara Blessing • *Web Developer/Content Manager:* Sue M. Moe • *Controller:* Robin Hutchinson • *Senior Accountant:* Laura Thomas • *Accounts Payable:* Mary Schultz • *Accounts Receivable:* Margo Petrus • *Production Director:* George Chmielarz • *Pre-Press Image Specialist:* Minniette Johnson *Electronic Publishing Director:* Douglas M. Lidster • *Systems Administrator:* Cris Schwanebeck • *PC Maintenance Technician:* Robert D. Cook • *H.R. Assistant:* Kirsten Koele • *Office Manager:* Noelle M. Carroll • *Receptionist/ Administrative Assistant:* Jeanne Johnson • *Mail Room Clerk:* Lou Webber

Customer Service & Fulfillment:

Operations Director: Bob Baker • *Customer Service Manager:* Jennie Enos *Customer Service Representatives:* Eddie Arthur, Anna Cox, April Revell, Deborah Rich, Valerie Jo Riley, Tammy Truckenbrod • *Technical Representative:* Johnny Audette • *Buyer:* Linda Jones • *Administrative Assistant:* Nancy Downey • *Warehouse Supervisor:* Nancy Johnson *Fulfillment:* Sylvia Carey, Sheryl Knox, Al Voigt

Circulation:

Subscriber Services Director: Sandy Baum • *New Business Circulation Manager:* Wayde J. Klingbeil • *Multi Media Promotion Manager:* Rick Junkins *Promotions Analyst:* Patrick A. Walsh • *Billing and Collections Manager:* Rebecca Cunningham • *Renewal Manager:* Paige Rogers • *Circulation Marketing Analyst:* Kris Schlemmer • *Associate Circulation Marketing Analyst:* Paula M. DeMatteis • *Senior Graphic Designers:* Mark Hayes, Robin Friend

www.CuisineAtHome.com

editor's letter

Most of our kitchens tend to have a split personality. During the week, the kitchen serves as a survival "pit stop" of sorts—fueling the family machine for a fast-paced week. It's also a social intersection of lives where family members cross paths to eat and chat briefly on their way to meetings, work, or school.

But it's a little different on the weekend. The kitchen takes on a relaxed mood and opens itself up to friendly gatherings and casual conversations, especially when company is over. This room just seems to draw people in like bees to clover. Architecturally, dens and living rooms are obsolete now, and the kitchen and great room have merged into a large, open entertainment complex.

There seems to be plenty of reasons for this architectural and behavioral evolution, too many to list. But the bottom line is that the kitchen is a social focal point of the home—a disarming room that invites participation on many levels: cooking, conversing, spectating, and even learning.

Whatever the reason, the fact is there will always be people in the kitchen when you cook. And that's where homemade pasta comes in. It's a simple but interesting process that gently invites conversation and eventual participation. The best part is that it leads to a substantive result—fresh pasta with incredible flavor and delicate texture.

If you haven't made pasta before, try it soon. It truly is a lot of fun, especially with friends and plenty of wine. You can start off with a pasta as simple as linguine with marinara, but I strongly suggest trying the cannelloni with your new found talent. This is the real thing. The soft texture and powerful flavor are reminiscent of good cannelloni you find in Italy.

So break out the Barolo and call your friends. Winter is the right time to make homemade pasta—specifically classic cannelloni. It's just the thing to warm your home as well as give your kitchen a break from another hectic week.

John

talk to ***Cuisine at home***
Subscriptions, Address Changes, or Questions? Write or call:

Customer Service
2200 Grand Avenue,
Des Moines, IA 50312
800-311-3995,
8 a.m. to 5 p.m., CST.

Online Subscriber Services:
www.CuisineAtHome.com
Access your account • Check a subscription payment • Tell us if you've missed an issue • Change your mailing or email address • Renew your subscription • Pay your bill

Cuisine at home™ (ISSN 1537-8225) is published bi-monthly (Jan., Mar., May, July, Sept., Nov.) by August Home Publishing Co., 2200 Grand Ave., Des Moines, IA 50312.
Cuisine at home™ is a trademark of August Home Publishing Co.

Subscriptions: Single copy: $4.99. One year subscription (6 issues), $24.00. (Canada/Foreign add $10 per year, U.S. funds.)

Periodicals postage paid at Des Moines, IA and at additional mailing offices. "USPS/Perry-Judd's Heartland Division automatable poly". Postmaster: Send change of address to **Cuisine at home**, P.O. Box 37100 Boone, IA 50037-2100.
Cuisine at home™ does not accept and is not responsible for unsolicited manuscripts. **PRINTED IN SINGAPORE.**

table of contents

Issue No. 31 February 2002

departments

features

from **our** readers

tips
and techniques

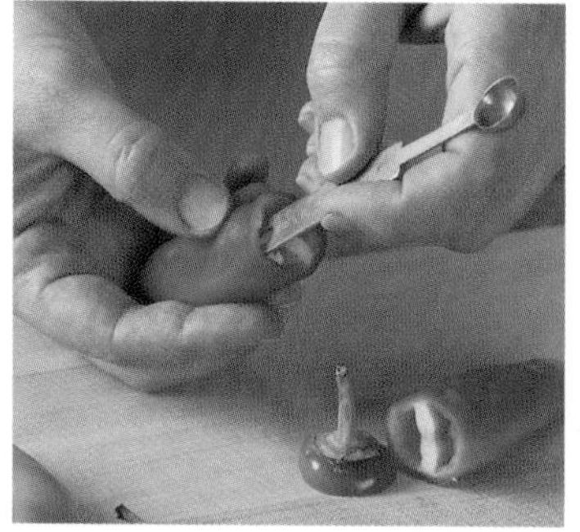

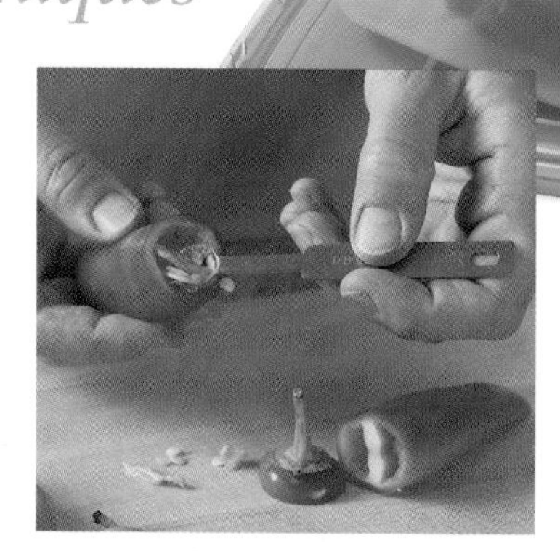

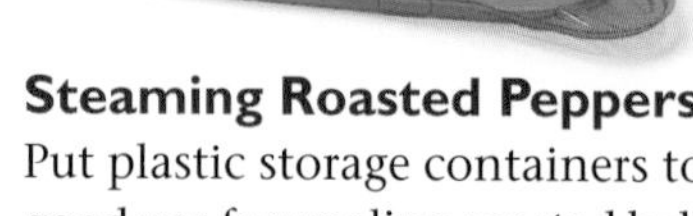

Seeding Small Chiles
Here's a good way to remove seeds from jalapeños and other small chiles for pickling or stuffing, like poppers. First slice off the stem end of the chile. Then use the *flat handle end* of a 1/8 teaspoon stainless steel measuring spoon and slide it down the ribs of the chile. Now turn the spoon around (the bowl end) and scoop out the seeds and ribs. This works like a charm for all but the really small chiles.

Rena Andrews
Dallesport, WA

Steaming Roasted Peppers
Put plastic storage containers to good use for cooling roasted bell peppers. After roasting, place them in a plastic container and seal the lid. When they've cooled, remove the lid and peel as usual. The blistered skins will come off the peppers with ease.

Tim Lavin
Harleysville, PA

No Drip Lid
When keeping soup or stew warm until ready to serve, wrap a clean kitchen towel around the lid and place it back on the pot. The towel absorbs the moisture that collects on the lid, preventing it from dripping onto the food and potentially changing the finished consistency.

Rochelle Himes
Wilmington, DE

Seamless Chicken
Have you had chicken breasts tear when you pound them to tenderize or stuff? Try this tip.

Wet the inside of a gallon freezer bag with a little water. Then place one or two (depending on the size) boneless, skinless chicken breasts inside the bag—no need to seal.

Lay the bag on a work surface and pound the meat to the desired thickness. The water keeps the meat from sticking and tearing, plus there's no mess. Just remove the chicken and throw the bag away.

Tony Stanislo
Cleveland, OH

Rusty Tart Pan Solution #2
In the October 2001 issue of *Cuisine*, a reader asked for a solution to cleaning rusty tart pans. I liked the answer, but I also have a way of preventing the rust. After I'm finished baking, I wash my tart pans and spread them out in a hot oven to dry. This works great for other pans as well.

Jeannie Sammis
Alexander City, AL

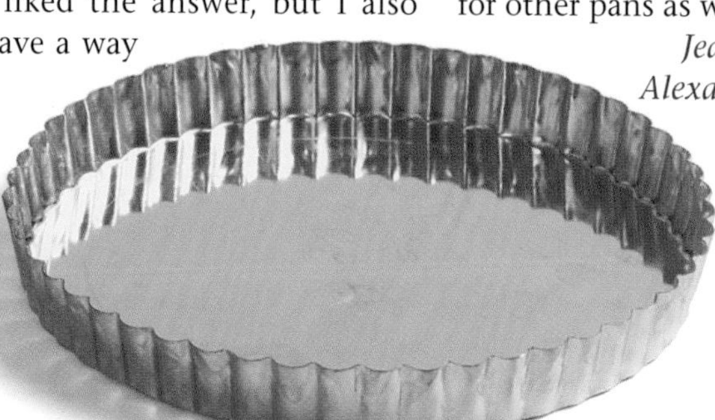

Heart-shaped Cake

Use a square and round cake of equal diameters to make a heart-shaped cake: Split both cakes into layers, then cut the round layers into half-moons and frost both cakes. To assemble, place a half-moon on two sides of the square.

George Berry
Montpelier, VT

Easy Guacamole

When making guacamole, I use a pastry blender to mash the avocados. I can mash them to my desired consistency—chunky or smooth. It's much easier than using a fork. This is great on boiled eggs for egg salad too!

Jackie Mathews
Yucca Valley, CA

Better for Breading

When preparing fish, poultry, or meats for breading, try brushing it with mayonnaise instead of egg. The mayonnaise won't drip like egg does, and it imparts great flavor while helping keep the meat moist. Plus, it improves the "cling" of the breading.

Marion Karlin
Waterloo, IA

Perfect Pancakes

To make perfectly round pancakes, start by making your favorite batter, then put it in a plastic condiment bottle with a wide tip (find the bottles at hardware or grocery stores). Be sure your batter is thin enough to flow through the tip.

Now heat your griddle or pan and start squeezing pancakes! My bottle has a top with a resealable cap—perfect for late-risers or for making just a few pancakes. Just seal the bottle and store it in the refrigerator.

Don Casper
Champaign, IL

Roasting Tomatoes

To make oven-roasted tomatoes any time of the year, slice Roma tomatoes into rounds about ½" thick. Place the slices in a salad spinner, rinse with cold water, then spin! The water and most of the seeds will fall to the bottom.

Preheat the oven to 250° and line a baking sheet with foil. Toss the tomatoes with olive oil, salt, and pepper, then arrange in a layer on a rack. Place the rack on the baking sheet and roast in the oven 6–8 hours, or until they look like big, red raisins.

Susan Anderson
Fairfield, CT

Tip from the Test Kitchen

The secret to cooking perfect pasta? Use a pot big enough to hold four quarts of water for every pound of pasta. Then, before adding pasta, be sure the water is at a rolling boil.

share your tips *and techniques* with *Cuisine at home*

If you have a unique way of solving a cooking problem, we'd like to hear from you, and we'll consider publishing your tip in one or more of our works. Just write down your cooking tip and mail it to *Cuisine at home*, Tips Editor, 2200 Grand Ave., Des Moines, IA 50312, or contact us through our email address shown below. Please include your name, address, and daytime phone number in case we have questions. We'll pay you $25 if we publish your tip.

Email: CuisineAtHome@CuisineAtHome.com

Web address: CuisineAtHome.com

cuisineclass

fresh pasta

Don't be intimidated by the thought of making fresh pasta. With only three ingredients, you can master this technique in short order—plus, it's a blast to make.

Yes, there are hundreds of good dried pastas out there that you can buy, but you want to make your own for two simple reasons. First, the delicate texture and flavor of homemade is impossible to duplicate in commercially produced pastas. And second, just the entertainment value is worth the effort. The ingredients are simple, but when the pasta starts to flow from your machine, it practically commands applause. Making pasta is an easy process to master, but on the other hand, it's almost magical.

Dough

Talk about simple—this dough consists of just three ingredients: flour, eggs, and olive oil.

You've probably heard of pasta made from semolina, a flour made from durum wheat. It's makes a tough dough suited for holding up to the rigors of commercial pasta machines.

But for this pasta, you want a dough that's made from a softer flour. Italians use a fine textured soft flour called "type 00." Italian grocers carry this, but it's simpler to make your own by using all-purpose flour mixed with soft cake flour—about a 5 to 1 blend.

BASIC PASTA

Just a few ingredients produce big results. Fresh pasta is just the ticket for more than flavor—it's great entertainment.

(MAKES THIRTY-TWO 4 X 5" RECTANGLES FOR CANNELLONI)

PULSE IN FOOD PROCESSOR:
2½ cups all-purpose flour
½ cup cake flour

BEAT TOGETHER; ADD:
5 eggs
1 T. extra virgin olive oil

Pulse both flours in food processor to blend.
Beat eggs and olive oil together in a small bowl. With processor running, add egg/oil mixture to flour. Stop processing when the dough forms a ball.

1 Pasta dough will clump in the food processor when it is ready.

2 Knead a little all-purpose flour into the dough so it's easier to handle.

3 Divide dough into quarters, wrap in plastic, and let rest for 15 minutes.

Mixing, kneading & rolling

Mixing

Make your life simple when mixing pasta dough—use your food processor. It only takes about two minutes and cleanup is a snap.

First, blend the flours in a processor. Then, with the machine running, add all the wet ingredients gradually. When the dough begins to form a ball, it's ready. But don't blend it too much—the dough is heavy and could strain your processor's motor.

Knead a little more flour into the dough by hand so it's not too sticky. Now, divide the ball of dough into four pieces as in Step 3. Wrap each piece to keep the pasta moist. Let it rest for 15 minutes so it's easier to work with.

▲*Settings* *The width of the rollers is determined by the settings. The lower the setting number, the thicker the pasta will be.*

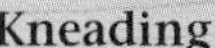

Kneading

Kneading develops a smooth, strong pasta. Since this dough doesn't have the naturally high amounts of gluten that semolina flour provides, it's important to knead it well to make it elastic, soft, and pliable. This kneading process is especially easy when you use a pasta machine.

Once the dough has rested, start kneading. Working with one piece at a time, run it through the machine on the widest setting (that'll be #1). Then fold the extruded dough like you would a letter—in three panels. Place an open end of the folded dough through the machine on the same setting. You can see this in Step 5. Repeat the process about 6–8 times until the dough is smooth as velvet.

If the dough starts to tear, sprinkle it with flour then brush off any excess. Tearing means the dough is too wet and is sticking to the rollers. After kneading, cover each piece with plastic wrap until ready to roll pasta.

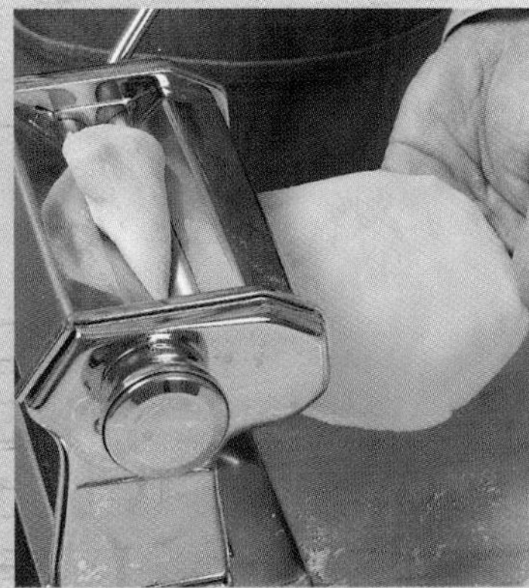

4 The first pass in kneading will produce a rough-textured dough.

5 Fold dough into thirds and pass the unfolded edge through rollers 6–8 times.

Rolling

Once you've finished kneading all the dough, it's time to make the pasta—the magical part. First, dust the rollers on the pasta maker with flour. This prevents the dough from sticking and tearing when rolling.

Now set the machine on #2 and roll the pasta through. Keep rolling and adjusting rollers to the next smaller width. If the dough sticks, dust with flour.

Once you get about halfway through the settings (around #4 or 5), you might want to cut the pasta in half. This simply makes it easier to handle especially if you're rolling by yourself. Once you get to the last setting, stop. Now you can cut the pasta for its specific use (like cannelloni).

Final Thickness

I'm going to get into trouble with this comment, but don't roll pasta to the thinnest setting. I like a little bite to it, so I only go to the *next* to the last setting (#6). But artisan pasta makers always go thinner—so thin you can see through the uncooked sheets!

But if want, don't be afraid to roll the it very thin too. While you might think it will tear, the dough is pretty tough, especially after it's been boiled—it swells a bit and practically doubles in thickness. And this is especially important to think about when making real cannelloni. The idea behind cannelloni is very thin pasta sheets surrounding a very thin layer of filling. You'll see what I mean on Page 9.

6 When rolling pasta, keep it lightly floured to prevent sticking.

7 After setting #4, cut pasta strip in half so it's easier to handle.

cuisineclass

fresh pasta

Cutting & storing

With the dough rolled out, you can easily cut it to make sheets for cannelloni, lasagna, or manicotti. Or you can roll and cut it into strips for pappardelle, linguine, or fettuccine. No matter what, after rolling each strip of pasta, cut and store the sheets right away before they dry out.

▲ Use a pizza cutter to section the pasta strip. For cannelloni, cut 3½ x 5" rectangles.

Cutting cannelloni

The secret to cutting pasta for cannelloni is keeping the squares small. You don't want a big burrito-looking pasta dish that you couldn't eat with *two* appetites.

Cut the strips of pasta into sheets about 3½" wide. They can be 4–5" tall, or as tall as the strip is wide when it comes out of the machine. The height is not real critical—actually, the taller it is, the better since you want multiple layers to form as you roll.

Storing

As you cut the pasta into sheets, you need to store it before cooking. This is not as easy as you might think because fresh pasta is still wet and loves to stick to itself. Cornmeal is the secret.

Take a baking or cookie sheet, and spread it *liberally* with cornmeal. Don't worry about using too much—you can shake most of it off before cooking. The rest will come off while boiling.

Once you've covered the pan with a layer of pasta, sprinkle more cornmeal on top, then cover with waxed or parchment paper. Layer with cornmeal, pasta, and paper until all is stored.

Cooking

Fresh pasta cooks differently than dried pasta does. The bottom line is, it's *fast*. Use plenty of boiling water and cook it about two minutes, until tender but still chewy.

▼ To store, use cornmeal and parchment between layers.

Draining

If you're cooking sheets for cannelloni, dip them in cold water to stop the cooking, then pat them dry—the filling will spread better. But if you're making pasta that's to be sauced immediately (like pappardelle), *never* rinse it after cooking. The sauce will cling better to a starchy surface.

▲ Dry cooked and cooled cannelloni sheets for easier filling.

option

Let's face it. As fun as pasta making is, it does take a little time. If you want to make cannelloni, but don't want to spend the time cranking out pasta, flat lasagna sheets work well (don't use the ones with curly edges). Barilla brand makes flat sheets, and there are a lot of internet sources.

◄ Dried lasagna sheets are an option for fresh pasta.

▲ Boil sheets like any dried pasta then cut into 3½ x 5" rectangles.

Cannelloni

As light as a whisper but loaded with flavor— classic cannelloni will become a family favorite.

Cannelloni is one of those delightful mysteries in food. It has a huge flavor and can be quite filling. But in the same mouthful, it's extremely light—chewing is almost optional. Like a good wine, you can swirl it around in your mouth before it melts down your throat.

So what makes cannelloni so different from many of the other pasta dishes? First, it's made with Italian meats like prosciutto and mortadella for flavor impact. Second, both the pasta and filling are intended to be very thin. When it's rolled up, it's in many layers. And like puff pastry and croissants, multiple thin layers produce a very tender dish.

Finally, cannelloni is baked in béchamel [bay-shah-MEHL], a white sauce made with milk, butter, and flour. Fresh pasta, a flavorful filling, and simple cream sauce—what's not to love?

Classic Cannelloni

Mortadella and prosciutto can be found at most grocers, but there are different qualities and prices. The inexpensive domestic meats work almost as well as imported. (*Makes 32 Cannelloni*)

Prepare; Cut into Rectangles:
1 recipe Basic Pasta Dough, *Page 6* (or packaged option)

Saute in 2 T. Unsalted Butter and 1 T. Vegetable Oil:
1 lb. ground meat (veal, chicken, turkey, or beef)

Add and Saute:
½ cup yellow onion, chopped
1 T. garlic, minced

Deglaze with:
¼ cup dry sherry

Process Meat Mixture with:
2 eggs
1 cup Parmesan cheese, grated
¼ lb. prosciutto, diced
¼ lb. mortadella, diced
¼ cup chopped fresh parsley

Fill Cannelloni. Before Baking, Cover with:
Marinara and Béchamel Sauces, *Page 11*

Prepare pasta as on Page 6. **Saute** ground meat in butter and oil in a saute pan over medium-high heat until browned.
Add onions; cook until softened. Add minced garlic, sauteing only until you smell it.
Deglaze pan with sherry; cook until liquid evaporates.
Process meat mixture and remaining ingredients in food processor. Pulse until it resembles coarse sawdust. Do not overprocess. Cook pasta sheets.
Fill cooked pasta sheets with 1½ T. of filling (spread thinly). Loosely roll sheets, then cover with marinara and béchamel. Bake at 450° for 25 minutes.

Rolling cannelloni

To make classic cannelloni there are a few simple rules, the first being that both the pasta and filling have to be thin. The second rule is that the filling is spread over the entire sheet of cooked pasta—not spooned in a thick line across the middle. Finally, the pasta must be rolled like a carpet for a delicate texture.

What are mortadella and prosciutto?
Mortadella is a type of Italian bologna with cubes of pork fat. Prosciutto is ham that's been seasoned, salt-cured, and air-dried (but not smoked).

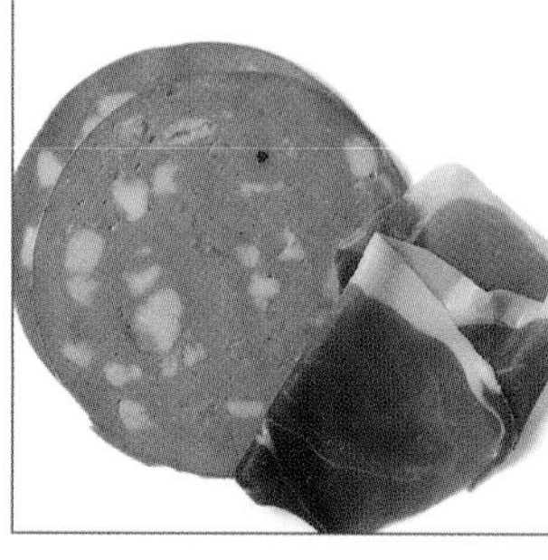

Thin is in

For the best cannelloni, think thin. First, roll out the pasta as thin as possible—the thinner it is, the softer it will feel in your mouth. Then, to make the most of that delicate texture, spread the filling very thin. A big mouthful of meat isn't the goal—rather just flakes of flavor.

Rolling

Before rolling, coat your work surface so the cooked pasta does not stick to it. I use finely grated Parmesan cheese—it works great.

With the filling on the pasta, gently roll it up like a carpet. Then place each tube in a casserole dish that has been lightly sauced on the bottom. Be sure to put the seam side down so that the cannelloni doesn't unravel.

After the cannelloni have been made, spoon your favorite sauce over the top (Page 11), then sprinkle with Parmesan cheese. Bake the cannelloni now, or cover and bake the following day. You can even freeze them just this way.

Baking

Bake the cannelloni uncovered at 450° for about 20–25 minutes, or until Parmesan starts to turn golden and the sauce bubbles.

1 Dust work surface with Parmesan. Lay out pasta sheets; spread each with 1 ½ T. filling.

2 Gently roll pasta. Keep the seam side down so they don't unravel.

3 Place cannelloni in a lightly sauced baking dish. Keep the seam down!

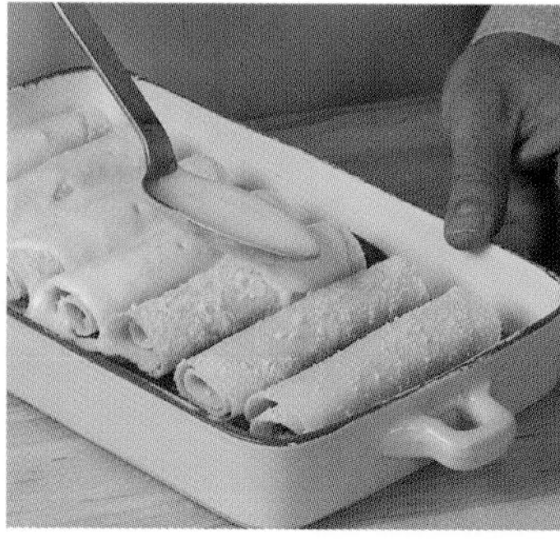

4 Spoon béchamel on top; sprinkle with Parmesan and bake.

options

Spinach and Three Cheese Cannelloni

(Makes 3 Cups)

Saute in 2 T. Olive Oil:
½ cup onion, chopped
1 T. garlic, minced
Add:
1 10-oz. pkg. frozen spinach
Stir in:
1 cup mozzarella, grated
½ cup mild goat cheese
½ cup Parmesan, grated
Salt and pepper to taste
Cover with Sauce; Top with:
½ cup Parmesan, grated

Saute onions and garlic in olive oil until softened.
Add frozen spinach and cook over low heat until water is evaporated.
Stir in the cheeses and add salt and pepper to taste.
Fill according to Classic Cannelloni recipe on preceding page.

Margherita Cannelloni

A refreshing filling but use only béchamel sauce here—it has plenty of tomatoes in the filling.
(Makes 3 Cups)

Seed and Dice:
10 – 12 Roma tomatoes (1 ½ lb.)
Combine with:
1 cup mozzarella, grated
½ cup ricotta cheese
½ cup Parmesan, grated
¼ cup fresh basil, thinly sliced into ribbons
Salt to taste
Cover with Sauce; Top with:
½ cup Parmesan, grated

Seed and dice tomatoes.
Combine tomatoes with cheeses and seasonings.
Fill according to Classic Cannelloni recipe on the preceding page.

cannelloni sauces

Basic and quick, these great-tasting sauces pair perfectly with the delicate flavors of cannelloni.

I like cannelloni served the traditional way—just baked in a béchamel sauce. But that can be pretty rich. So you might want to use a simple marinara sauce on the bottom of the casserole dish.

The acid of the tomatoes offsets the richness of the cream sauce. You might also think about combining equal parts of each sauce to make one terrific pink-colored sauce.

Simple Marinara Sauce

Simple, quick, and fresh tasting. This is a classic marinara.
(Makes 3½ Cups)

Saute in ¼ Cup Olive Oil:
2 cups yellow onion, diced
Add:
1 T. garlic, minced
Stir in and Simmer:
6 cups Roma tomatoes, peeled, seeded, and diced
Process; Add:
¼ cup fresh basil, thinly sliced into ribbons
Salt to taste

Saute onion in oil until softened.
Add garlic; cook 1 minute.
Stir in tomatoes; simmer 10 min.
Process with a hand blender until sauce is smooth and slightly chunky. Finish with basil and salt to taste.

want more info? Visit www.CuisineAtHome.com for a step-by-step photo guide.

Simple Béchamel Sauce

This cream sauce is actually pretty light in consistency. I didn't want anything too heavy to cover up the delicate flavors of cannelloni.
(Makes 3½ Cups)

Melt in Saucepan:
5 T. unsalted butter
Whisk into Butter:
⅓ cup all-purpose flour
Gradually Add:
3½ cups milk (whole or 2%)
When Thickened, Add:
½ t. kosher salt
¼ t. white pepper
⅛ t. freshly grated nutmeg

Melt butter over med.-low heat.
Whisk in flour to make a roux. Cook and stir 2 minutes.
Gradually add milk into roux. Stir constantly to prevent sticking and cook until thick, about 10 min.
When thick, add seasonings.

make it a menu

Although cannelloni is typically a first course item, try pairing it with a salad and serving it as a light dinner or lunch.

Classic Cannelloni *with* Marinara and Béchamel Sauces

Arugula Salad *with* Lemon Vinaigrette

Chocolate Truffles

Arugula Salad with Lemon Vinaigrette

This is as simple as a vinaigrette gets—but don't equate simplicity with blandness. This is flavorful!
(Makes 4–6 Servings)

Wash and Stem:
6 cups arugula or other bitter salad greens
For the Vinaigrette—
Whisk Together:
¼ cup fresh lemon juice
1 T. honey
1 t. garlic, minced
Sea salt and freshly ground pepper to taste
Drizzle in while Whisking:
¼ cup extra virgin olive oil
Toss Arugula with Vinaigrette.
Garnish with:
Parmesan curls

three mushroom ragù with pappardelle

Cold winter nights are made for a long-simmered ragù. This flavorful mushroom ragù will warm your soul, especially if it's tossed with homemade pappardelle.

Let's get something straight from the beginning—this is not a *true* ragù. True ragùs usually contain some form of ground meat and are flavored with pancetta (an Italian bacon), tomatoes, and wine. After hours of simmering, they're often enhanced with cream. Bolognese [boh-loh-NYEH-zeh] is a typical ragù.

But I'm taking some liberty here and calling this fast cooking dish a ragù. While there is no meat here, mushrooms, with their hearty flavor and texture, are an excellent substitute. Many of the ingredients, as well as cooking techniques, are similar to a real ragù.

But what puts this dish over the top is the final addition of a rich Italian cream cheese called mascarpone. Do everything you can to find this cheese to put in your ragù—it's worth every calorie!

Tossing the pappardelle

Italians treat their pasta dishes a little differently than we do. You are probably used to seeing sauces ladled over beds of pasta. In Italy, most sauces are tossed with pasta, and only a little bit is used—not the gargantuan portions we're familiar with. So don't be alarmed that this only makes about four cups of ragù. That's plenty for 4–6 people.

Be prepared to toss the pappardelle with the ragù right away. And after you cook the pasta, don't rinse it! The starch from the unrinsed pasta helps the ragù cling to every strand of pasta.

This dish is rustic so you don't really need a garnish. But if you feel like it, a simple sprinkling of chopped parsley or some Parmesan shavings work great.

Fresh homemade pasta is the best vehicle for the mushroom ragù.

Cutting the pasta

Pappardelle [pah-pahr-DEHL-leh] is a wide pasta noodle (3/4–1") that is perfect for hearty dishes like ragùs or braised meats.

To make pappardelle, prepare and roll the pasta as on Pages 6–7. Roll it to the next to the last setting (*not* the thinnest). Once rolled, sprinkle it liberally with cornmeal or flour and hang it to dry for 10–15 minutes. It'll turn leathery but still quite flexible.

Now sprinkle it again with cornmeal and fold (or roll) it up to prevent sticking. Cut the rolls into widths about 3/4–1". Unroll them and sprinkle again with cornmeal. Either make nests out of them, wrapping them around your hand, or store them flat.

Making ragù

As with all ragùs, this packs a lot of flavor. It begins by sauteing shallots, then the mushrooms in batches. This is so they brown and intensify in flavor, not steam.

Return all the mushrooms to the pan and add sherry to deglaze. Reduce until most of the liquid evaporates. Now add tomatoes, vinegar, and paste. Simmer for 10–15 minutes or until the ragù thickens. Finally, stir in the mascarpone and herbs.

Cook the pasta no longer than 3 minutes in boiling, salted water. Drain it (don't rinse!), add to the ragù, and toss. It may not seem like much sauce, but a slight coating is all you want.

What is mascarpone? *A double or even triple cream Italian cheese that has the texture of soft butter. Most grocery stores carry mascarpone (Italian grocers do for sure).*

1 Roll or fold fresh pasta sheet into very loose cylinder.

2 Cut into 3/4–1" strips. Unfold and sprinkle with cornmeal.

3 Saute mushrooms in batches so they don't steam in their juices.

4 To finish ragù, stir in the mascarpone, herbs, salt, and pepper.

Three Mushroom Ragù

No time to make fresh pasta? Use a pound of dry fettuccine instead.
(Makes About 4 Cups Ragù)
Total Time: 1 Hour

For the Pasta—
Prepare and Roll; Cut:
1 recipe pasta dough, Page 6

For the Ragù—
Saute in 3 T. Olive Oil:
1/4 cup shallots, sliced
8 oz. white mushrooms, sliced (3 cups)
4 oz. crimini mushrooms, sliced (1 1/2 cups)
4 oz. shiitake mushrooms, stemmed, sliced (1 1/2 cups)
Deglaze with:
1/4 cup dry sherry or Madeira
Add and Simmer:
1 can (14 oz.) diced tomatoes with juice
1 T. balsamic vinegar
1 T. tomato paste
Finish Ragù with:
1/4 cup mascarpone
2 T. chopped fresh parsley
1 T. chopped fresh thyme
Salt and pepper to taste
Toss Ragù with:
1 1/4 lb. cooked pappardelle

Prepare and roll pasta dough as on Page 6. Roll or fold floured pasta sheets.
Cut sheets at 3/4–1" intervals to create pappardelle strands.
Saute shallots for ragù in 1 T. olive oil in large saute pan over medium heat. Add 1 T. more oil, increase heat to high, and saute mushrooms in batches until browned. Transfer to a plate. Add more oil to pan, and saute remaining mushrooms. Return all mushrooms back to the pan.
Deglaze with sherry and simmer until liquid evaporates.
Add tomatoes, balsamic, and paste. Reduce heat to low and simmer until thick, 15 minutes.
Finish ragù by stirring in mascarpone, herbs, salt, and pepper.
Toss ragù with cooked and drained pappardelle to coat.

SALT ENCRUSTED *fish*

Cooking fish can be difficult at best. But this ancient technique is still the best way to achieve moist and flavorful fish—everytime.

If there's any food fraught with cooking challenges, it has to be fish. It's either underdone or overdone, and almost *always* makes the house smell fishy. Those are big hurdles to clear.

But this encrusting method makes cooking fish practically foolproof (and odor-free!). The Mediterranean-based technique tackles the difficulties head on by packing a whole fish in a salt and egg white "plaster," then baking it at a high temperature. The salt hardens into a protective shell, insulating the fish from the harsh heat of the oven. The fish cooks gently with more natural moisture staying *inside*—where it's needed the most.

Feel your blood pressure rising just thinking about all the salt? It's okay. The fish's skin acts as a barrier so very little ever touches the flesh. Some will invariably get on the fish but it brushes right off.

There's no need to be nervous about handling a whole fish—I'll show you what you need to know. Just be prepared for an audience to gather! Cracking and removing the salt crust makes for a great show. But if you'd rather have something on a smaller scale, check out the packets with fish and vegetables on Page 20.

Use your hands to combine the salt and egg whites. Pack onto prepared fish.

Encrusting Salt

Pack the encrusting salt on the fish shortly after mixing—wait too long, it will dry out and be hard to use.
(Makes Enough for a 5-lb. Fish)

Combine:
2 boxes (2 lbs. each) kosher salt
6 egg whites

Combine salt and whites in a mixing bowl. It should feel like "sand castle" sand.

Yes, this technique is simple. But it's good to know some details about the salt and how it's used.

The story of salt

Salt has a long history and has been valued for centuries for its preserving qualities and nutritional benefits (it helps balance fluids and promote proper nerve and muscle activity). Salt was so precious that Roman soldiers got it as part of their pay—"sal" (as in "salary") is Latin for salt.

Today, though, salt is taken for granted—so common it's hardly worth talking about. Any grocery store will have several salts to choose from, with table, kosher, and sea salt being typical. Although they each have the same chemical makeup (sodium chloride), they won't all work the same way for encrusting.

The difference has to do with the size of the grains. Tiny grains of table salt don't make good plaster for encrusting. It's too runny and doesn't stick well on the fish. Kosher salt and some sea salts are more coarsely grained so they're perfect for encrusting. And since kosher salt is cheaper than sea salt, it's the obvious choice for this method.

Encrusting the fish

Prepare the Encrusting Salt on Page 14, then rinse the fish and pat it dry inside and out with paper towels. After that, line a large baking sheet with parchment paper—the egg whites in the salt will stick to the pan like crazy and the parchment will help make clean-up a lot easier.

Now make a bed of encrusting salt on the baking sheet. This will protect the bottom side of the fish from the heat of the baking sheet. If the fish is too long to fit across the baking sheet, shape the bed of salt diagonally. Lay the fish on the bed of salt—don't worry if the tail hangs over the side. Stuff the cavity with lemon slices and sprigs of herbs.

Now, firmly pack the remaining encrusting salt over the entire fish. Completely cover all areas, even the cavity and any exposed flesh. These spots will taste saltier than the places protected by the skin, but they'll be fine (think of cured salmon or lox). Bake the fish at 425° for 30 minutes before taking a temperature reading.

1 Prepare salt; pat a ½"-thick bed on parchment-lined baking sheet.

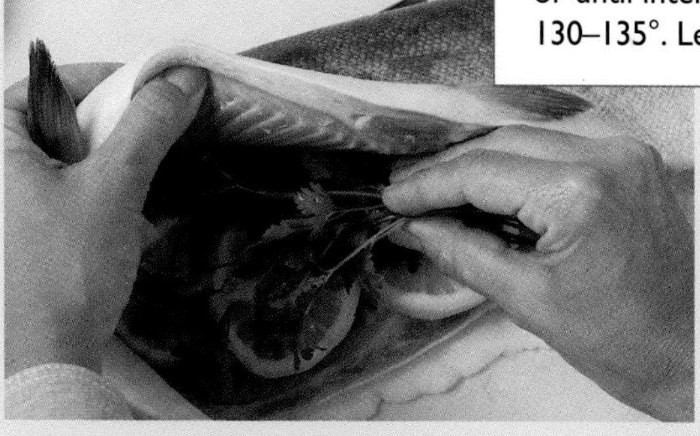

2 Place rinsed, dried salmon on the bed of salt. Stuff the cavity with lemon slices and herb sprigs.

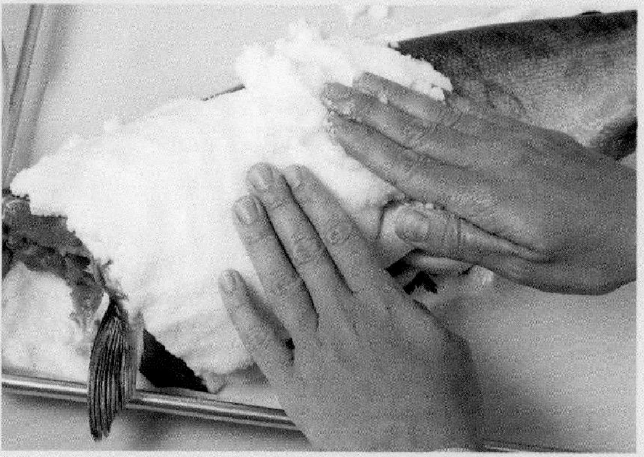

3 Pack the remaining salt on the fish, covering over the cavity and any exposed flesh. Bake salmon at 425° for 30 minutes before taking a temperature reading.

Salt Encrusted Salmon

Salmon is great encrusted, but so are sea bass, snapper, and grouper, Page 17. *No matter what, use only the freshest fish.*
(Makes One 4 to 5-lb. Fish)

Prepare:
1 recipe Encrusting Salt, *Page 14*
Rinse and Pat Dry:
1 whole salmon (4–5 lb.), gutted, gilled, and scaled
Stuff Cavity With:
1 lemon, thinly sliced
1 bunch parsley or thyme
Pack Fish in Salt and Bake.

Preheat the oven to 425°.
Prepare the Encrusting Salt on Page 14; set aside.
Rinse the whole salmon, then pat it dry with paper towels.
Stuff the salmon cavity with lemon slices and herbs.
Pack the fish in the salt mixture and bake a total of 40–50 min., or until internal temperature is 130–135°. Let rest before serving.

Cooking the fish

Yes, encrusting the fish in salt is cool, but this next part is even better. Here are some answers to the more technical questions.

How can I tell if it's done?

Telling when a salt encrusted fish is done can be tough—you can't see, smell, or touch it like you can with other techniques. But one sure bet is to take a few readings of its internal temperature.

How? Insert an instant-read thermometer through the crust into the fish (jab it in there—the crust is *hard*). Take your first reading after the fish cooks for half an hour. A five-pound fish probably won't be done but you'll at least have a clue of where it stands. From there you can gauge how long it still needs to cook.

Take a temperature reading every ten minutes thereafter until it reaches 130–135° (40–45 minutes *total* cooking). A great thing about this method is that the fish can go over by 10 or 15 degrees and *still* be moist—a rarity when cooking fish! Don't bother poking new holes each time. Put the thermometer into the same hole.

Let the fish rest 10 minutes before cracking. It won't get cold. The crust acts as an insulator.

4 Insert thermometer through the crust—it's done at 130–135°.

5 Let fish rest 10 minutes. Crack crust with a heavy, blunt object.

6 Pry off the pieces of salt crust and discard. As you go, brush the salt "dust" off with a pastry brush.

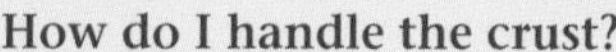

How do I handle the crust?

Use a heavy, blunt object to crack the salt crust. I use the handle of a table knife, but a meat mallet or small hammer works too. Rap it over the entire crust to break—do this in the kitchen, not at the dinner table. Salt will fly!

Now pull off chunks of the crust with your hands. Take care, they're hot. Brush off any residual salt with a dry pastry brush.

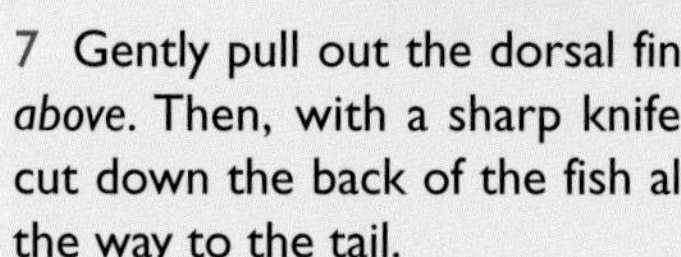

7 Gently pull out the dorsal fin, *above*. Then, with a sharp knife, cut down the back of the fish all the way to the tail.

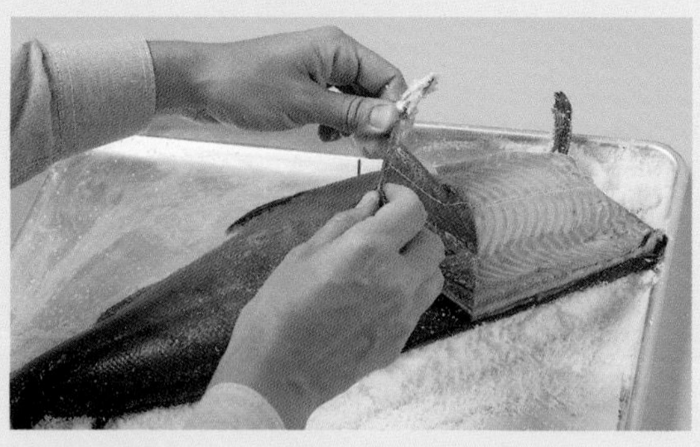

8 To remove the skin, find the the gill plate and use it for something to grasp. Carefully peel back the skin to the tail.

How do I remove the skin?

Pull out the dorsal (back) fin as in the inset photo, *left*. It will come out easily. Then, with a thin-bladed knife, slice down the back of the fish to the tail. You just want to cut through the skin so it peels away easily. The knife *must* be sharp—fish skin is tough.

Now feel for a strip of cartilage at the top of the fish where the head was removed (the gill plate). Grasp the gill plate and use it to help peel back the skin from top to tail—it should come right off. If the gill plate is missing, simply peel back some skin, grasp it, and pull back gently.

Cutting the fish into servings

With the skin removed, the next step is to cut the exposed portion of the fish (the "side") into pieces. First, make a lengthwise cut down the center of the side. The backbone will keep you from slicing into the side underneath. Now slice the side crosswise into pieces two or three inches wide.

Transfer the pieces to a serving platter using a small spatula. The trick is to get under each piece, sliding the spatula along the rib bones to release it. Insert the spatula at the cut down the center (not the outer edges). Then just slide it under the piece of fish toward the outside edge.

Remove the lemon and herbs from the cavity, then gently lift out the rib cage and backbone—some of the bones may stay in the fish. Slice the second side like the first, but look out for the salt!

9 Cut the exposed side lengthwise down the center.

10 Slice crosswise into pieces and remove them with a spatula.

11 Remove lemon and herbs; carefully pull away ribs and backbone. Cut the second side like the first, avoiding salt below. Serve with vinaigrettes, Page 18–19.

options

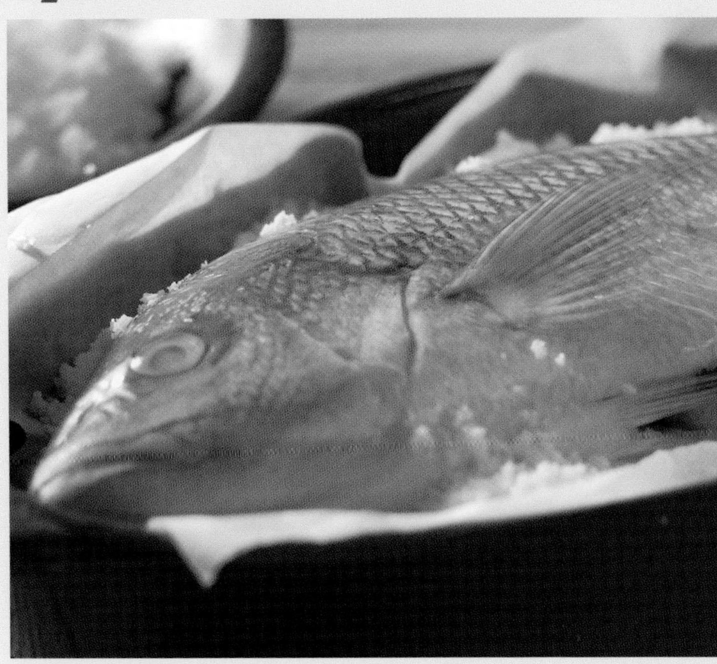

Salmon is ideal for salt encrusting, but there are other fish in the sea. Here are some options for encrusting and what to look for in fresh fish.

In general, most whole fish are great salt encrusted. Other fish to use include sea bass, grouper, trout, tilapia, and yellowtail and red snapper. It should range from two to five pounds (with the head on or off). Larger ones don't always fit in standard ovens!

No matter what you choose, freshness is key. It's best to buy from a reputable, busy market that preferably deals only with seafood. And shop with your senses. *Smell* the store when you walk in and, if you can, smell the fish you choose. Any fishy or "off" odors are a bad sign.

Now *look* at the fish. Are the eyes clear, bulbous, not cloudy? Is the skin shiny and vibrant? And are the fins intact, not torn (indicating rough handling)?

Finally, *feel* the flesh if possible. It should spring back when pressed. Spongy, soft flesh means the fish is past its prime.

vinaigrettes for salmon

Heavy-hitting in flavor (but not in calories), these vinaigrettes are simple, colorful options for eating healthy in the New Year.

menu

Salt Encrusted Salmon with Roasted Red Pepper-Olive Vinaigrette

Sauteed Spinach with Creamy Orzo

Lemon Sorbet

The holidays have come, gone, and left their mark—in *several* places. As usual, the new year finds most of us vowing to turn over a healthier leaf in terms of our cooking and eating habits. But that doesn't mean you're faced with a steady diet of carrot sticks and cottage cheese.

The Salt Encrusted Salmon on Page 14 gets additional flavor, color, and texture with a vinaigrette, *without* the high fat typical of many classic butter-based sauces. These are light, fresh, and versatile accompaniments—as good with a chicken breast as with a piece of fish.

Both vinaigrettes get their primary flavor from fresh fruits and vegetables. In the dead of winter? You bet. The flavor of red bell peppers intensifies after they've been roasted. And citrus is at its best in the winter. In fact, the oranges in the Orange-Avocado Vinaigrette can be substituted using pink grapefruit segments, tangerines, or a combination of different citrus fruits.

www. CuisineAtHome**.com**
Not counting calories? Try a beurre blanc sauce with the salmon.

Basics behind vinaigrettes

These vinaigrettes don't look like the salad dressing vinaigrettes you're accustomed to. The two here resemble relishes or salsas.

But don't let the name trip you up. The idea behind these vinaigrettes and ones for salads is exactly the same: They should enhance the flavor of what they accompany. So don't settle for bottled roasted peppers—take the time to roast them. And look for a perfectly ripe avocado, not over- or underripe. Shortcuts here and there won't do the vinaigrette (or the fish) any good.

You can make the vinaigrettes a few hours ahead of time, but they're best when made shortly before serving (Warning: Do not make the avocado vinaigrette too far ahead or the avocado will turn brown). For the best flavor, serve them at room temperature.

Roasted Red Pepper-Olive Vinaigrette

The peppers should not be roasted to the point that the skin turns "ashy." That tells you the flesh is beginning to cook and turn soft.

(Makes 1¼ Cups)

Roast:

2–3 red bell peppers, peeled, seeded, diced (about 1 cup)

Combine:

Roasted bell peppers
½ cup kalamata olives, pitted, sliced (about 15 olives)
3 T. olive oil
3 T. red wine vinegar
2 T. chopped fresh parsley
1 T. brined capers, drained
1 clove garlic, sliced
½ t. sugar
Zest of one orange, cut into strips
Salt and cayenne to taste

▲Roast peppers over a flame or under broiler until skin blackens.

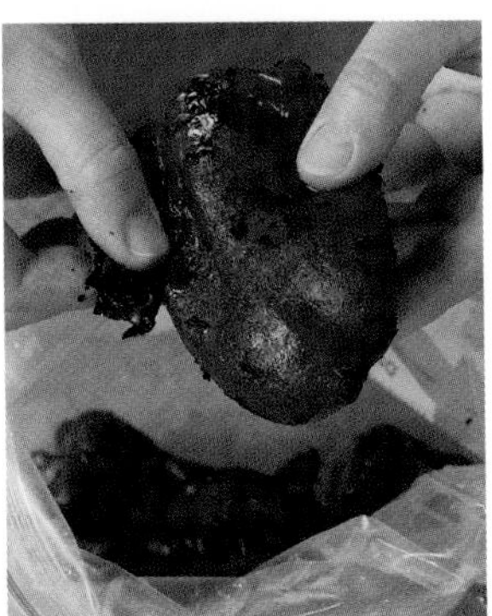

▲After cooling peppers in a bag, peel off charred skin.

Roast the peppers over a gas flame until thoroughly blackened (not ashy). Turn them frequently during roasting. Place peppers in a plastic bag and cool until easy to handle; remove charred areas with your fingers. Cut pepper in half, remove seeds, and dice.

Combine diced pepper in a large bowl along with remaining ingredients; stir gently. Let stand at room temperature at least 30 minutes to blend flavors. Serve with salt encrusted fish.

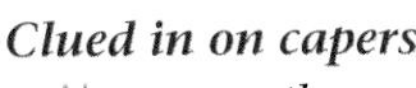

Clued in on capers

Capers are the flower bud of a bush native to the Mediterranean. They come packed in brine or salt—use the brined capers here.

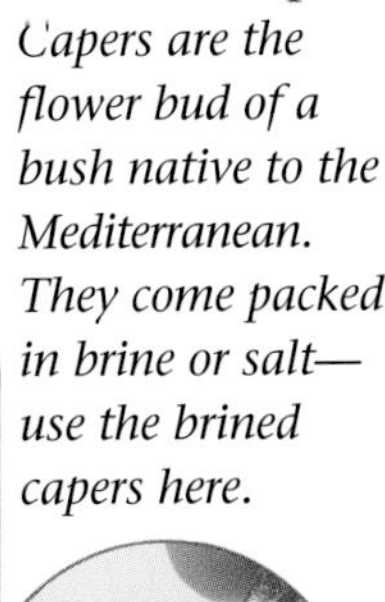

option

Orange-Avocado Vinaigrette

Ripe avocados should give slightly to pressure. To ripen a hard avocado, place it in a closed paper bag for 1–2 days until softened.

(Makes 1¼ Cups)

Peel and Segment:

2 navel oranges

Combine with Orange Segments:

1 ripe (not mushy) avocado, halved, pitted, and diced
¼ cup red onion, thinly sliced
3 T. vegetable oil
3 T. white wine vinegar
2 T. chopped fresh cilantro
1 t. fresh ginger, peeled, minced
½ t. sugar
Salt and black pepper to taste

Peel the oranges by first slicing off the top and bottom of each one to make a flat surface. Remove the peel and white pith with a paring knife cutting from top to bottom following the curve of the fruit.

Over a mixing bowl (to catch juices), remove the segments by cutting on both sides of the membrane on the sides of each segment. Place segments in the bowl.

Combine orange segments with remaining vinaigrette ingredients (use your hands to mix; they're more gentle than a spoon). Let stand at room temperature at least 30 minutes to blend flavors. Serve with salt encrusted fish.

▼Remove peel and pith from the oranges.

▲Cut on insides of membranes to release segments.

packets with fish and vegetables

Salt encrusted packets are a smart, simple, healthy way to cook fish. And they make a great presentation!

Like the idea of salt encrusting but don't want to use a whole fish? You're in luck. These individual packets of fish filets and fresh vegetables are the ticket.

Think of them as a version of cooking *en papillote* [ahn pah-pee-YOHT], or "in parchment." The fish and vegetables steam together so the flavors blend into one great-tasting dish. And baking them in the salt crust means the fish stays moist and the vegetables colorful and a little crisp, even after cooking 40 minutes.

Packets are also great party food. Besides being easy for cooks (assemble them early and chill), they're fun for guests—they can open presents at the table!

Packets with Fish Filets and Vegetables

(Makes 4 Packets; Total Time: $1\frac{1}{2}$ Hours)

For the Vegetables—
Prepare and Combine:

- 1 cup zucchini, cut into thick matchsticks
- 1 cup yellow squash, cut into thick matchsticks
- 3/4 cup carrot, peeled, cut into thick matchsticks
- 3/4 cup tomato, diced (1 tomato)
- 1/4 cup red onion, slivered
- 1 T. garlic, minced (2 cloves)
- Salt and pepper to taste

For the Packets—
Layer, Dividing Among 4 Parchment Sheets:

- Prepared vegetables, *above*
- 4 fresh thyme sprigs
- 4 filets (4 oz. each) salmon, sea bass, halibut, or red snapper
- Salt and pepper to taste
- 4 t. unsalted butter
- 4 thin slices of lemon

Fold Packets; Bake in:

- 1 recipe Encrusting Salt, *Page 14*

Prepare vegetables, slicing the zucchini, squash, and carrot on a sharp bias. Stack the slices and cut into thick matchsticks. Combine with tomato, onion, garlic, salt, and pepper; set aside. Fold four large sheets of parchment crosswise in half.

Layer about 1 cup prepared vegetables in center of each folded sheet of parchment. Top vegetables with a thyme sprig, then a fish filet; season with salt and pepper. Continue layering, placing a teaspoon of butter on each filet, then a lemon slice.

Fold packets to enclose and tie with cotton kitchen string. (Packets may be made to this point and chilled up to 2 hours before baking.) Preheat oven to 425°; spray a large baking dish with nonstick spray. Prepare Encrusting Salt, bury packets, and bake 40–45 minutes. Let packets rest 10 minutes before removing them from the salt.

Good things in small packages

Putting these packets together isn't too tricky, but attention to a few details will ensure success.

Preparing vegetables

Slice the zucchini, yellow squash, and carrot on a sharp bias into $^1/_2$"-thick rounds. Then stack the slices and cut them into thick matchsticks, as in Step 1.

The important thing here is that the zucchini, yellow squash, and carrot are cut fairly small so they fit in the parchment without poking through. Parchment paper is strong, but a few precautions never hurt—if it's torn, you'll get a mouthful of salt.

Parchment paper

You will need four large sheets of parchment paper for this method—16 x 24", give or take, is fine. Fold the sheets in half crosswise before assembling anything on them. This creates a double layer which also helps keep the paper from splitting.

Layering and folding

Place a mound of vegetables in the middle of the folded parchment, then layer the remaining ingredients on top, like in Step 2. To fold, take a look at Step 3 below—bring the long sides of the paper up over the food and fold them together.

1 Prepare vegetables and combine with garlic and seasonings.

Now, gather the paper on sides, join them at the top, and tie the ends together with cotton kitchen string as in Step 4. Tie it tightly so it won't come undone. And look to see that seams haven't opened up at the folds, exposing what's inside. You don't want any salt getting in.

Packing in salt and baking

Mix up a batch of the Encrusting Salt on Page 14, then spray a large casserole or baking dish with nonstick spray (to keep the salt from sticking to the dish). Cover the bottom of the dish with about $^1/_4$ of the salt.

Arrange the packets on the salt, staggering them in the dish if you need to so they fit without crowding. If they're too close they won't cook as evenly. Then pack the rest of the salt around and on top of the packets as in Step 5. The tied portion of the packet will stick out of the salt, but the part with the food inside should be surrounded by it. (You may not have to use all the salt.)

Bake at 425° for 40–45 minutes. Even though the packets are smaller than a whole fish, they cook for the same amount of time. Why? You can't check their internal temperature so it's good to let them cook a little longer. The salt will protect them.

2 Layer all packet components in the center of folded parchment sheets.

Digging for treasure

Let the packets rest 10 minutes before cracking the salt and digging them out. Use a blunt object like the handle of a table knife as in the inset photo below.

Be careful when removing the packets—fish and vegetable juice may have weakened the paper at the bottom. Brush off as much salt as you can and transfer the packet to a serving plate. Then cut the string, open, and serve.

3 To fold, bring long sides of parchment over fish. Fold over once.

4 Gather ends and tie tightly at top with kitchen string.

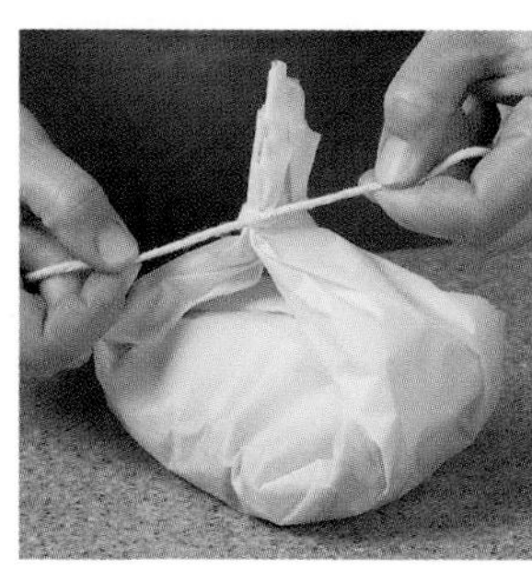

5 Pack salt mixture around packets and bake. After packets have rested, crack the crust and remove carefully.

allabout spinach

Always available and inexpensive, spinach is the one vegetable that you can count on for great flavor and even better color.

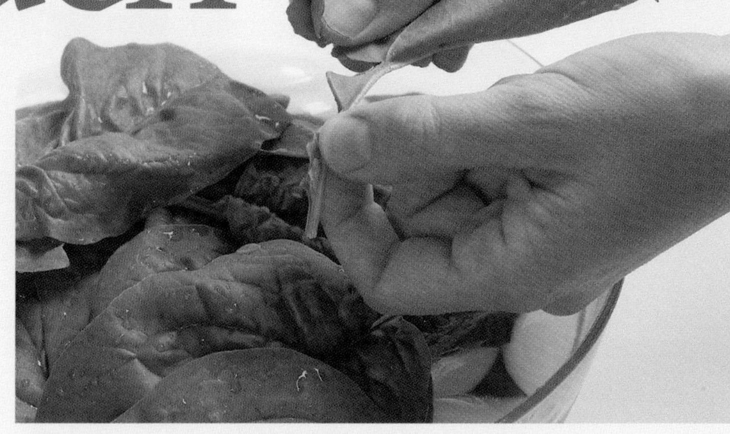

▲To stem spinach, fold the leaf in half at the stem and pull the stem down the length of the leaf. Small leaves can be cooked as they are.

In winter, it's like the produce aisle has headed south—nothing is available, at least not like it is in the summer. Except for spinach. It's *always* available. Maybe that's why so many different cuisines use (and love) it. Italian, Chinese, French, and Indian cooks all take advantage of this reliable vegetable. And so should you.

Buying

Really, the only choice to make when buying spinach is whether to get it prewashed in bags or tied in bundles. The convenience of bags is obvious and I'm not above buying them. But the flavor (and often the quality) of spinach in bundles is sometimes better.

So what should you buy? In the case of spinach, whatever looks best. The leaves should be deep green in color with supple texture, not yellow or wilted. They may be smooth or crinkled, depending on variety, with crisp stems. And no matter what, it shouldn't be slimy (prewashed spinach in bags is prone to this).

The tricky part about buying spinach is knowing how much to get. Frequent spinach eaters know the quantity purchased will be *very* different from that same amount cooked. Generally, 16 cups of loosely packed leaves (about a pound) shrink to about *two cups* sauteed—be prepared if you're cooking for a crowd.

Storing

The shelf life of spinach is short so it must be stored properly to stay fresh as long as possible. Spinach in bags should have little or no moisture inside—that's what turns it slimy. Pick through the leaves, removing any bad ones. Store good leaves loosely in resealable plastic bags in the crisper of the refrigerator for up to three days.

Store spinach by the bundle in the vegetable crisper also, loosely wrapped in a plastic bag. Don't wash it until you're ready to cook—prolonged contact with water also makes the leaves soft.

Cleaning

Spinach in bags is typically dirt-free but bundles of spinach *must* be washed—they're sandy. Wash it in several changes of water. The leaves are clean when there's no sand at the bottom of the sink. It's a pain but this is the only way to know the leaves are clean.

Dry the leaves in a salad spinner or with paper towels, then remove the thick stems, *see photo above*. Stems cook slower than the leaves and can be hard to eat.

Cooking

Spinach is inherently tender and doesn't need much time to cook. One great method is to blanch it in boiling water for literally a second or two, then drain it. This helps eliminate the astringency common to spinach. Then, after pressing out the moisture, the spinach is sauteed just until heated through (see Page 24).

spinach soup

Spinach tends to get lost in most soups, but not this one. Eight cups of spinach and a touch of lemon ensure its presence in this rich treat.

(Makes 8 Cups)
Total Time: 25 Minutes

For the Soup Base—
Simmer:
4 cups low-sodium chicken broth
1/2 cup yellow onion, grated
1/2 cup carrot, grated
1 t. kosher salt, or to taste
1/2 t. freshly ground pepper
1/4 t. freshly grated nutmeg
For the White Sauce—
Melt 6 T. Unsalted Butter;
Whisk In:
6 T. all-purpose flour
Whisk In:
1 cup milk (whole or 2%)
Stir into the Soup Base:
Prepared white sauce
8 cups spinach, stemmed, thinly sliced into ribbons
Off Heat, Add:
2 cups heavy cream
1 T. lemon zest, minced
For the Garnish—
Toast in 2 Teaspoons Unsalted Butter:
1/2 cup sliced almonds

1. For the soup base, simmer broth, onion, carrot, and seasonings in stockpot for 15 minutes.
2. For the white sauce, melt butter in saucepan over low heat; whisk in flour until smooth.
3. Whisk milk into butter mixture, stirring to prevent lumps. Cook 2 minutes to eliminate floury taste. Stir into simmering soup base.
4. Add the spinach to the soup and cook just to wilt, 1 minute. Off heat, add cream and zest.
5. For the garnish, melt butter in a small saute pan over low heat. Add almonds and toast until they begin to brown, about 5 minutes, stirring often. Sprinkle 1 T. almonds over 1-cup servings of soup.

1

2

3

4

5

sauteed spinach

Blanching spinach before sauteing may seem like overkill. But it emphasizes the flavor and texture of this everyday vegetable.

(Makes 2 Cups)
Total Time: 15 Minutes

Wilt; Press Dry:
1 lb. spinach, stemmed (about 16 loosely packed cups)
Saute in 2 T. Olive Oil:
3–4 cloves garlic, thinly sliced
$^1/_4$ t. crushed red pepper flakes
Add and Saute:
Wilted spinach
Salt and pepper to taste
Before Serving, Drizzle with:
Balsamic vinegar

Bring a large pot of water to boil over high heat.

1. Wilt spinach in boiling water. Add it all at once, stir, and drain immediately in a colander—*do not* let spinach sit in the water. Press as much liquid from it as possible, forming it into a disk.

2. To saute, heat oil in a large saute pan over med.-high heat. Add garlic and pepper flakes; saute until garlic turns golden, about 1 minute. Stir constantly.

3. Add the disk of spinach and break it up with a wooden spoon, stirring to coat with oil and garlic. Cook just until heated through, about 1 min. Season with salt and pepper, then transfer spinach to a serving platter.

4. Drizzle spinach with balsamic vinegar before serving.

1

2

3

4

Adding on

With a few additional steps and ingredients, simple spinach recipes are transformed into something bigger *and* better.

Stop with the spinach recipes on Pages 23 and 24 and you'll be doing fine. But these two variations give them a new look.

The sauteed spinach becomes a casual, comforting meal when it's paired with Parmesan-rich pasta. This grown up version of mac and cheese might even get kids to eat their spinach!

And simply adding potatoes and shrimp to the soup turns a light, flavorful first course into something more substantial.

Creamy Orzo with Sauteed Spinach

(Makes About 5 Cups)
Total Time: 30 Minutes

Cook According to Package Directions:
1 cup dry orzo pasta (or other small shape), drained but not rinsed

Combine; Stir into Hot Pasta:
1/4 cup Parmesan cheese, grated
1 egg, beaten
2 T. heavy cream
Salt and pepper to taste

Prepare; Top Pasta with:
Sauteed Spinach, *Page 24*

Garnish with (Optional):
Parmesan cheese, grated

Cook pasta according to package directions; drain but do not rinse.
Combine Parmesan, egg, heavy cream, salt, and pepper in a small mixing bowl while pasta cooks. Stir egg mixture into drained, hot pasta. Cover to keep warm and set aside.
Prepare sauteed spinach as on Page 24, *omitting the balsamic vinegar in the final step.* Transfer pasta to a platter or divide among serving bowls. Top with the sauteed spinach.
Garnish each portion with Parmesan cheese, if desired, and serve immediately.

Shrimp and Spinach Chowder

(Makes 8 Cups)
Total Time: 30 Minutes

Prepare:
Spinach Soup, *Page 23*

Add to Soup Base:
3 cups red potatoes, cut in chunks (about 1 lb.)

Stir in with Spinach:
1/2 lb. medium shrimp, peeled and deveined (about 16)
Tabasco and salt to taste

Garnish with:
Lemon zest curls

Prepare the Spinach Soup on Page 23, *with these changes:*
Add the potatoes to the soup base with the onion and carrot.
Stir in the shrimp with the spinach. Allow the shrimp to cook through, about 3 minutes. Finish with the cream as in recipe on Page 23; omit the lemon zest and toasted almonds. Season the chowder to taste with Tabasco and salt.
Garnish with lemon zest curls.

pan roasted beef tenderloin

Pan roasting is a great technique for thick cuts of meat and fish. It keeps in all the natural flavor and moisture that lean cuts can't afford to lose.

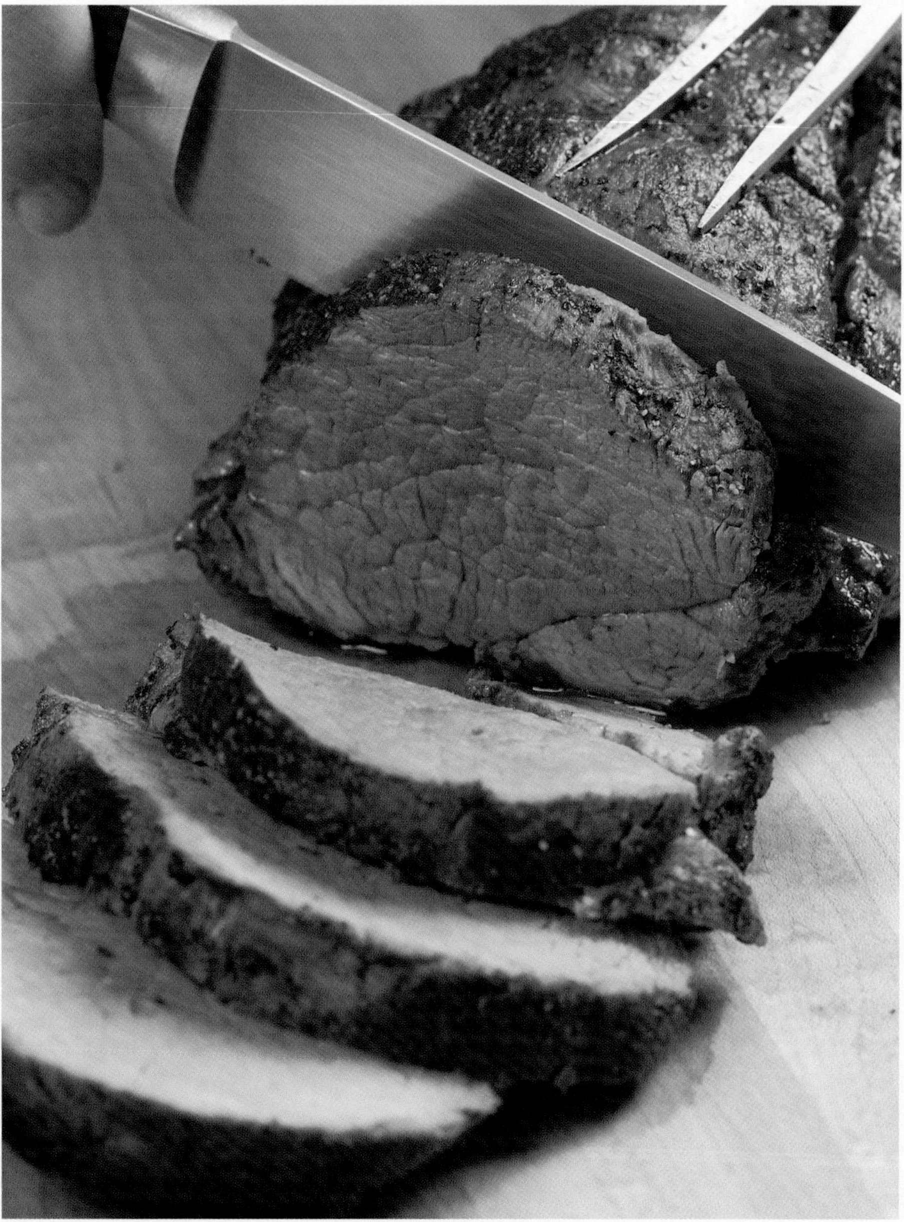

Beef tenderloin is kind of a food chameleon. It's subject to quick and frequent change depending on its environment.

On one hand, it is the most expensive cut of beef, reserved most of the time for special occasions. And yet for all its high stature, beef tenderloin actually plays a fairly unassuming role on the taste charts. So what makes this cut of beef so popular?

First of all, it is, without a doubt, the most tender cut of beef. That's because this muscle rarely gets a workout except to occasionally move the steer's head. The more a muscle works, the more flavor it tends to have.

And second, that tenderness doesn't come from fat. A four-ounce cut only has about 260 calories. But that's the catch—fat usually spells flavor. So tenderloin typically tastes best served with something to make up for its lack of powerful beef flavor.

That's why you have two recipes on Pages 28–31. One is a stroganoff-type sauce with a hit of blue cheese. The other is a hearty barley risotto—a perfect complement to beef.

Pay special attention to the searing and roasting steps. This is one area where tenderloin captures flavor from the browning of proteins and sugars.

Cooking tender meat like this tenderloin requires four steps: trimming, trussing, searing, and roasting. Here's what to do.

Trimming

Tenderloin is surrounded by a thin membrane called silverskin. It lies right next to the meat and has to be removed because it shrinks when heated (rather than melts). If it's not trimmed away as in Step 1, it will cause the tenderloin to curl up into the shape of a quarter moon.

Trussing

Once tenderloin is trimmed, it no longer has any structure (unlike other cuts that are surrounded with fat). You can see this if you look at Step 1 again—the tenderloin starts to flatten out.

You want the meat as round as possible for even cooking and also for a good presentation. Trussing is the key. It's easiest to use individual strings to tie the meat firmly—but not too tight!

Shaping the meat
Use individual pieces of cotton string to truss meat—this helps keep its round shape and insures even cooking. Do not tie too tightly or the string could cut into the meat.

1 Trim the tenderloin of fat and silverskin to prevent curling.

Searing

Once the meat is trussed, rub it with oil, salt, and pepper, then sear it in a hot skillet. As the proteins heat up, they coagulate, releasing a kind of sugar water. And as the water evaporates, the sugar caramelizes (browns), both on the meat and in the pan. This not only looks good on the roast, but also adds plenty of flavor.

Roasting

Tenderloin, like other lean cuts of meat, are best *roasted* at high heat rather than *baked* at lower temperatures. Flavor comes from the browning, not from fat slowly melting into the meat. Roast until the internal temperature hits 130° (medium-rare).

Pan Roasted Beef Tenderloin

Searing then roasting at high heat keeps flavor in tenderloin. Truss it so that the roast cooks evenly and maintains its shape.
(Makes One 3-lb. Roast)
Total Time: 1 Hour

Trim and Truss:
1 3-lb. cut of beef tenderloin
Rub Tenderloin with:
1/4 cup olive oil
1 T. kosher salt
1 T. coarse ground black pepper
Sear, then Roast.

Preheat oven to 450°.
Trim silverskin and fat from tenderloin; wash it and dry well with paper towels. Truss the meat with cotton string at every inch to create a round profile. Heat a large ovenproof skillet over high heat.
Rub meat with olive oil. Then salt and pepper just *before* searing to prevent juices from leeching. This promotes maximum browning.
Sear on all sides until browned, about three rotations, 1 min. each.
Roast in oven 20–30 minutes, turning tenderloin over halfway through cooking for even browning. When temperature reads 130° (medium-rare), remove from oven. Cover the roast with aluminum foil and let rest 10 minutes before cutting into 1 1/2" slices.

2 Sear the meat on top of the stove to start the caramelization process.

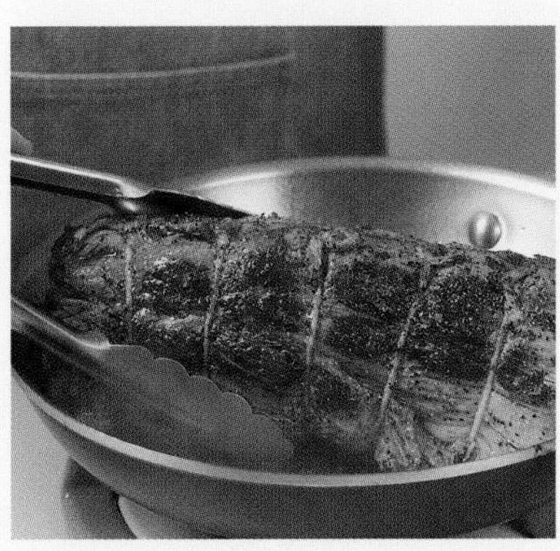

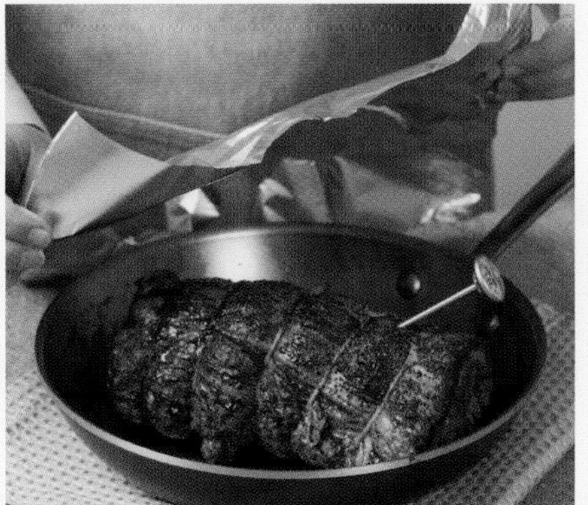

3 Roast meat in oven until internal temperature is 130°. Tent and rest 10 minutes.

4 Look at browning in the pan. You can deglaze with 1/4 cup wine and add to sauce on Page 29.

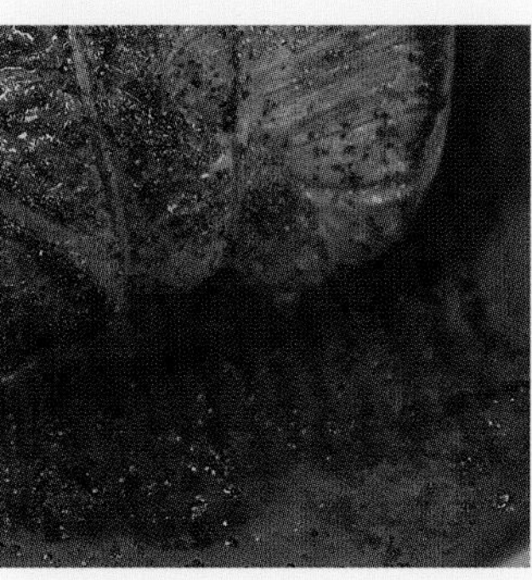

beef tenderloin with Stroganoff Sauce

Beef tenderloin needs a flavorful sauce. Here's one that's simple to make and loaded with flavor. Serve it with herbed new potatoes and you have the perfect Valentine's Day dinner.

menu

Beef Tenderloin with Stroganoff Sauce

Herbed New Potatoes

Vanilla ice cream

Two sauces in one

I'm going to be real honest with you. I had a bit of a dilemma with this stroganoff sauce. It had great flavor and actually wasn't that hard to make. But when I added the sour cream at the end, the beautiful mahogany color of the brown sauce was lost. It tasted great but the good looks were missing—and that's important to us food people.

You make the choice

So here's what you can do. First, make the wine stock, then the brown sauce. The sauce is great just by itself and you can even make it a day ahead.

Then, if you want more of a "stroganoff" sauce, add 1/3 cup sour cream before serving. (Don't boil the sauce or the sour cream will break.) You'll end up with a tan sauce that tastes fantastic but doesn't look great with red meat.

If you don't want to alter the color with sour cream, consider putting the brown sauce over the meat first, then sprinkle some Stilton or blue cheese over the sauce. Strong cheeses like these hold their own against the flavors of the beef and brown sauce. But don't use too much. They are powerful, especially when warmed a little from the sauce.

Just be sure to sprinkle the cheese on the sauce—don't stir. That would discolor it. You want separate little bits of cheese melting in it rather than blending in like the sour cream does.

Accompaniments

Take a look on Page 40—there are several good potato recipes that would be ideal with this dish. Try the herbed potatoes or Hasselbacks. They're simple and won't clash with all the flavors.

1 This is deglazing—loosening the brown bits of food with liquid.

2 This is reducing—evaporating part of the liquid. See the edge?

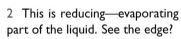

3 Saute mushrooms in batches so they brown instead of steam.

4 Cook roux until light brown. Add stock and simmer to thicken.

Red Wine Stock

A good brown sauce starts with a rich stock. The key is to gently brown everything you put into the sauce, including the onions and tomato paste.

(Makes 1½ Cups)

Saute in 2 T. Vegetable Oil and 1 T. Unsalted Butter:

1½ cups yellow onion, chopped (about 1 large)

Add:

1 T. tomato paste

2 cloves garlic, roughly chopped

Deglaze with:

1 cup dry red wine

Add and Reduce; Strain:

1 can (14 oz.) low-sodium beef broth

Sprig of fresh thyme

Saute onion in oil and butter until lightly brown.

Add tomato paste, cooking until it turns dark. Add garlic and cook for 30 seconds.

Deglaze with red wine, scraping up all the brown bits on the bottom of the pan.

Add broth and thyme; simmer until liquid reduces by half, about 10 minutes. Strain stock before using.

Stroganoff Sauce

(Makes 1½ Cups)

Saute in 2 T. Unsalted Butter and 1 T. Vegetable Oil; Remove:

8 oz. white mushrooms, cleaned and halved

Make a Roux from:

2 T. unsalted butter

2 T. all-purpose flour

Add:

1½ cups Red Wine Stock, *above*

1 T. Dijon mustard

Sauteed mushrooms

Option #1: 1/3 cup sour cream

Option #2: blue cheese

Heat butter and oil in a saute pan over medium-high heat.

Saute mushrooms until barely done and still somewhat white in color. Remove from pan; set aside.

Make a roux in the same pan by melting the butter then whisking in the flour. Cook over low heat until roux browns slightly.

Add wine stock, mustard, and mushrooms. Simmer until sauce thickens. Stir in sour cream, or sprinkle blue cheese over already sauced tenderloin (Page 26).

beef tenderloin with barley risotto

A delightful twist to traditional risotto—make it with barley. This hearty tasting grain pairs perfectly with beef tenderloin.

menu

Pan Roasted Beef Tenderloin with Stroganoff Sauce

Barley Risotto

Sauteed baby zucchini

Barley risotto

If you've made real risotto, you know the commitment of time and attention it requires. The constant stirring to achieve creamy results can be a little disconcerting in the last minutes of any dinner preparation.

But barley risotto is different. It's a snap to make—little stirring or attention is required. You end up with risotto taste and texture but with a unique nutty flavor.

What is barley? *Barley is an ancient grain used for currency, food, and medication. Now this hearty grain is primarily used in beer production.*

Barley

First you need to buy the right kind of barley. No matter what, do not buy instant barley. It will make the risotto soft and gummy. Look for pearled barley. Medium size is best for this dish.

Toasting

Seems most risottos have a one-dimensional flavor until you add something to them like mushrooms, prosciutto, or seafood.

This barley risotto starts out with flavor because it's toasted first. Sauteing the barley until it turns golden gives it great nutty flavor and a *little* color.

1 Toast the barley and wild rice in olive oil—it'll smell like popcorn.

Simmering

So now you have special flavor from toasting. But now, instead of slowly adding broth a little at a time and constantly stirring, it's added all at once.

This is the best part—the minimum amount of attention barley risotto requires. After the wine has reduced, add the broth and cover. The barley simmers unattended until all the broth is absorbed (about 40 minutes).

Finishing

Most regular risottos are finished with butter and Parmesan—this one is no different. Just before serving, gently toss the barley with the butter, Parmesan, and parsley. Don't do it too far ahead or the risotto will get gloppy.

For more character, add your own touch to risotto with the options listed below right.

2 Before serving, stir the Parmesan cheese, parsley, butter, and salt into the cooked barley and wild rice.

3 Gently stir ingredients into risotto so shallots remain intact.

Barley-Wild Rice Risotto

Wild rice isn't rice at all—it's a marsh grass native to the Great Lakes of Minnesota and Canada. Rinse it well before cooking.

(Makes 4 Cups)
Total Time: 1 Hour

Toast in 2 T. Olive Oil:
3/4 cup medium pearled barley
1/4 cup wild rice

Add and Reduce by Half:
1/2 cup dry white wine

Add:
2 cups low-sodium chicken broth
2 cups water
1 cup shallots, peeled, separated into sections

Finish with:
3/4 cup Parmesan cheese, grated
2 T. chopped fresh parsley
1 T. unsalted butter
Salt to taste

Serve with:
Beef Tenderloin and Stroganoff Sauce (made *without* mushrooms)

Toast the barley and wild rice in oil in a large saute pan until barley begins to brown, 5 minutes. **Add** wine and simmer until reduced by half, about 3 minutes. **Add** broth and water; bring to a boil. Cover, reduce heat, and simmer 20 mins. Add shallots and cook 25–30 minutes more, until liquid has completely evaporated. **Finish with** Parmesan, parsley, butter, and salt to taste. **Serve** as a bed for slices of Pan Roasted Beef Tenderloin (Page 26) and Stroganoff Sauce (Page 29).

options

After adding the Parmesan and butter, stir in your choice of:
Chopped fresh tomato
Strips of fresh spinach
Fresh thyme or rosemary

Wares
cheese graters

When it comes to grating hard cheese, all graters are *not* created equal. Don't get stuck with a cheesy model.

When I was a kid, Italian dinner meant spaghetti with a sprinkling of grated Parmesan from a tall, thin green tube. What could be better? Well, fond as I was of those suppers, I eventually learned it really *does* get better.

My passion for Parmesan was ignited by the first waiter who grated fresh Parmesan over my plate. That was cool. Now, those quality chunks of Parmesan and aged Parmigiano Reggiano are available at grocery or specialty stores practically everywhere across the country. But the rub comes in finding grater gratification—a grater that does these great-tasting cheeses justice.

Strand standard

The worth of a grater is ultimately determined by the grated cheese it produces. The cheese strands should be sturdy enough to maintain their identity, both for the sake of texture and flavor. When cheese is good, you want to know it's there and taste it! Fine or wispy strands just don't cut it—the strands melt or disappear on contact with food.

Grater expectations

After the strand test, there are a few other things to consider.

A grater should be comfortable and easy to use. If it requires instructions—probably too fussy.

Then it should be easy to clean and store. Most kitchens can't afford to tie up lots of space for a single-task tool. And graters made up of several pieces are a pain to wash and keep track of.

Model behavior

As with most kitchen tools, the market is loaded with choices. I tested 24 models in five categories.

Rotary: Rotary models allow direct grating over food—with knuckles intact! I tested six versions and found stainless steel models superior to plastic.

Stand: Yes, they do eat up storage space, but I like the multiple surfaces that make these graters multi-task. Some models have metal bottoms to catch cheese—they're more pain than gain.

Flat: Manufacturers have updated the classic flat grater with ergonomic designs and nonstick surfaces. That sounds good, but a basic version beats them all.

Wood: These are the beautiful counter-worthy graters that are available in several styles. I found them all pricey and vain.

Porcelain: Don't get drawn into catalog descriptions of these little white dishes. The circle of sharp porcelain teeth is intended for grating ginger, not cheese.

To purchase a great grater, check your local kitchenware store or see *Resources, Page 43*, for catalog and web information.

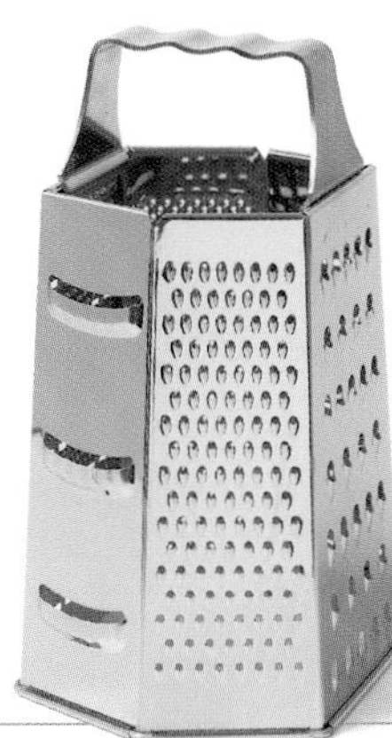

Norpro Six-Sided Stand
$9.99 ★★★★

Here's a stand grater that rates high across the board. It has a sharp, uniform grating surface that yields smooth, long cheese strands. Five other grating options make it a multi-task tool. And cleanup is simple because there's room to reach inside and catch every little hole.

Mouli Grater
$14.95 ★★★★★

The Mouli grater sets the standard for perfect grated Parmesan! At first I was skeptical of the lightweight construction, but long, sturdy, beautiful strands of cheese won me over. The two pieces fit together easily, I never have to worry about shaving my knuckles, and it grates directly over food (either right- or left-handed).

Tower Grater
$12.95 ★★★

This triple surface 9" grater has a rubber ball handle that's comfortable and easy to grasp, and rubber feet that add some stability. But the triangular design short-changes the grating surface area and doesn't allow my hand to reach all the way inside for cleaning. It yields average cheese strands.

OXO Grater
$6.95 ★★

I always like Oxo Good Grips handles. Unfortunately, the rough blade on this grater can't match the comfort of the handle. It grates hard, delivering short, thick cheese strands. The curved grating surface isn't an advantage. It catches only the center of the cheese until it conforms to the rounded blade.

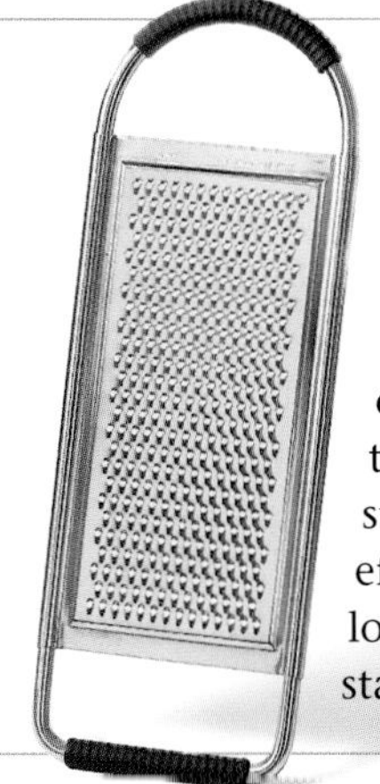

Flat Grater
$10.00 ★★★★

Flat graters have a lot going for them—easy to clean and store, and usually offer two sizes of holes for different tasks. But I like this model's massive surface devoted to one size. Minimal effort turns a cheese chunk into nice long, weighty strands. Rubber grips help stabilize, but it's not entirely slip-proof.

Wooden Box Grater
$49.99 (no stars)

Run, don't walk, from this kind of grater. It looks cool sitting on the counter but that's its only charm. It grates powdery cheese with astronomical difficulty into a needless drawer and it's impossible to clean.

Long Microplane
$11.95 ★★★

No question about it—the Microplane is unsurpassed in grating smoothness and ease, and is very compact for storing. The long grating surface produces lengthy thin strands of cheese—but those strands are *so* thin that the cheese disappears instantly when tossed in a salad! I wouldn't be without my Microplane, but I like it best for zesting.

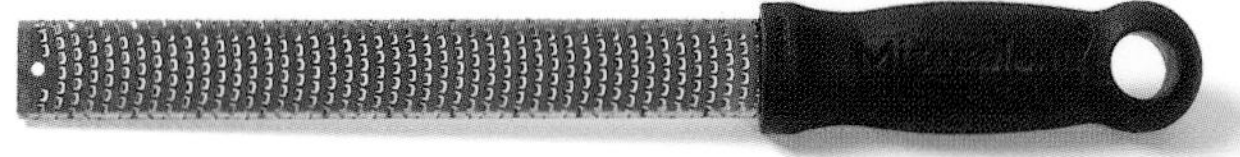

Coarse Microplane
$12.95 ★★★

Microplane has come out with other versions of their patented grating surface. One model even has interchangeable blades for different strand sizes. Like the long Microplane, this one grates like a dream and washes and stores easily. But bigger holes only produce wider strands of very thin cheese that curl up like wood shavings.

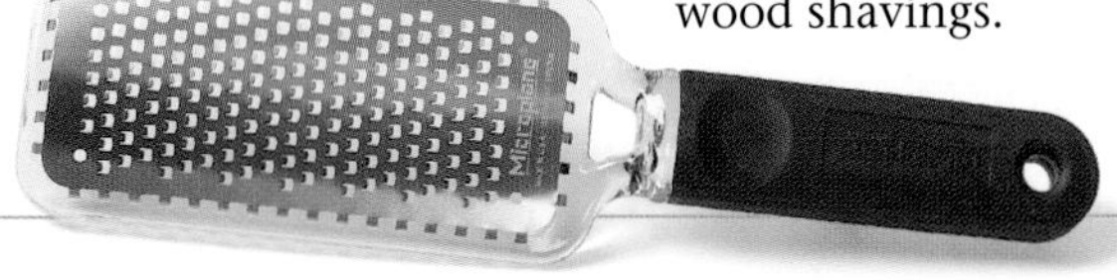

choosing chocolate

Distinguishing among different types of chocolate doesn't have to be hard. A few facts will make it easier for you to buy the right chocolate for the task at hand.

Knowing how chocolate is made and its characteristics will help in choosing it for your recipes.

How chocolate is made

Chocolate is made from cocoa beans. The beans, which contain fat (cocoa butter) and solids, are fermented, roasted, hulled, then ground to make the purest form of chocolate—chocolate liquor. The name is confusing because it's neither liquid nor contains alcohol. This liquor (also known as cocoa solids) is unsweetened chocolate.

To turn liquor into sweet chocolate, ingredients are added. Sugar, lecithin (a soybean-based emulsifier that keeps chocolate from separating when melted), vanilla, and extra cocoa butter may be used to make chocolate of different quality and types.

Quality, types, and storing

The best chocolate has a complex flavor that isn't excessively bitter (a characteristic of beans burned during roasting). It also has a crisp texture and breaks with an audible snap, signifying a high amount of cocoa butter.

Unsweetened chocolate is just solid chocolate liquor. *Bitter-, semi-,* and *sweet chocolate* have varying amounts of liquor and sugar. In general, they can be used interchangeably—the difference in flavor is minor.

Milk chocolate has less liquor than darker chocolate, with milk solids added as well. It's milder and sweeter than dark chocolate.

White chocolate is not true chocolate because it contains no liquor. Instead, it's made from cocoa butter, sugar, lecithin, vanilla, and milk solids. Beware of white confections with no cocoa butter—it's been replaced with solid vegetable fat and is not good for eating or cooking.

Baking chocolate, available in familiar 1-ounce squares, is either unsweetened or semisweet. It's best for recipes where chocolate is one of several ingredients, such as brownies or layer cakes.

Couverture (or "coating" in French) is high grade chocolate, rich in cocoa solids and extra cocoa butter. Confectioners use this for molding and dipping, but it's also fine for recipes (like the cake on Page 35). It's expensive so use it in recipes where the chocolate is dominant. Available from bittersweet to white, you can buy it in bulk from wholesalers, through specialty catalogs, and often in the candy aisle of the supermarket (look for imported European brands at the store).

Keep all chocolate in a cool, dark place (not the fridge or freezer). If the storage temperature fluctuates, a grayish-white "bloom" may appear—either sugar or cocoa butter that's risen to the surface. It doesn't adversely affect taste or performance.

About Nick Malgieri
Mr. Malgieri directs the baking program at The Institute for Culinary Education in New York City (previously Peter Kump's New York Cooking School). Former executive pastry chef at Windows on the World, he learned his craft in Switzerland, France, and Monaco. He is the author of five baking books, most recently ***Chocolate*** *(HarperCollins, 1998) and* ***Cookies Unlimited*** *(HarperCollins, 2000).*

flourless Chocolate CAKE

This cake is not for the faint of heart—it's deeply rich and absolutely, positively chocolate. If you're looking for the perfect Valentine's Day dessert, your search is over.

I love chocolate desserts that are rich, smooth, and really chocolatey. This flourless chocolate cake admirably fills all three requirements. And despite the fact that it is show-stopper delicious and great looking, it's as easy to make as boiling water (and that's how the cake starts).

Beyond that, it's also a great make-ahead recipe. Bake the cake a few days before you need to serve it, and store wrapped in plastic, in the refrigerator. If you need to have a few great desserts in reserve, bake several and wrap and store them in the freezer. Whether chilled or frozen, the cake needs to be brought to room temperature before serving for best flavor and texture.

Cake batter basics

Chocolate, simple ingredients, and easy steps make this cake appealing. Here are the details.

Lessons in liqueur

The chocolate flavor in this cake is enhanced with liqueur—here, it's orange-flavored Cointreau [KWAHN-troh]. You could also use rum, brandy, or other fruit liqueurs, *see sidebar.*

The amount of liqueur in the recipe looks like a lot, but orange or raspberry liqueur is part sugar and part flavoring so the alcohol content is fairly low. (If you use rum or brandy, add just two tablespoons. The alcohol content is higher.)

If you don't want to use alcohol in the cake, add 1/3 cup strong coffee or orange juice instead.

***Liqueurs** are sweetened spirits flavored with oils, extracts, spices, nuts, or fruit like raspberry (Chambord) and orange (Cointreau). Eaux de vie such as Kirsch (cherry) and Poire (pear) are brandies distilled from fruit. Use just 2 T. here—they're higher in alcohol than liqueurs.*

Getting started

First preheat the oven, then prepare the cake pan, buttering the pan with soft (not melted) butter. Put a pat or two of butter in the cake pan, then chop the chocolate and prepare the syrup.

Once the butter softens (after a minute or so), use a crumpled piece of plastic wrap to spread it over the pan bottom and sides. Then cut parchment or waxed paper to fit the bottom of the pan and press it in place. Put the cake pan inside a roasting pan (9 x 13 x 2" high works fine).

To chop chocolate, use a knife or an ice pick to break it into 1/4" pieces. Be aware that the pick will leave divots in the cutting board. Don't use your best board here!

Make a sugar syrup by first placing the water in a 2-quart saucepan, then adding the sugar. Bring the mixture to a boil over medium heat, stirring occasionally to dissolve the sugar crystals. Be sure the syrup comes to a full rolling boil to ensure dissolving.

When the syrup does boil, take it off the heat and add the pieces of butter and chopped chocolate. Shake the pan to coat everything with syrup and let the mixture stand for two minutes.

Nick Malgieri's Flourless Chocolate Cake

This is one of those recipes where the chocolate plays a key role in flavor. Be sure to use the best you can buy.

(Makes One 8" Round Cake)

Total Time: 1 Hour + Cooling

Bring to a Boil:

1/3 cup water

1/2 cup sugar

Off Heat, Add:

1/2 cup (1 stick) unsalted butter, cut into 8 pieces

12 oz. semi- or bittersweet chocolate, chopped into small pieces

Whisk In:

1/3 cup orange liqueur, such as Cointreau, *see sidebar*

6 eggs

Garnish With:

Whipped cream

Fresh raspberries

Preheat oven to 325°; prepare an 8" round cake pan. **Bring** water and sugar to a boil, stirring to dissolve sugar. **Off heat,** add butter and chopped chocolate. Let sit 2 min. to melt; stir to smooth. **Whisk in** liqueur then the eggs, one at a time. Pour batter into prepared cake pan, place it into a roasting pan, then add warm water to the roasting pan. Bake cake 40–45 min. Cool, unmold, and serve with whipped cream and raspberries.

1 Chop the chocolate into small pieces so it melts quickly and thoroughly.

2 Water and sugar should come to a rolling boil so that the sugar dissolves.

3 Let chocolate and butter sit in the hot sugar syrup for 2 minutes to melt.

Baking and serving

Believe it or not, you've just done the hardest part of the recipe. But there are still a few things to do.

Final mixing

After the chocolate mixture sits for two minutes, stir it until smooth, then gently whisk in the liqueur. Add the eggs one at a time, whisking just to blend.

Baking and cooling

Pour the batter into the cake pan (it's *in* the roasting pan) then add $1^1/_2$ cups warm tap water to the roasting pan. Place both pans on the middle rack of the preheated oven and bake about 40 minutes.

A "bain-marie" [bahn mah-REE] or water bath, is important here because it insulates the bottom of the cake pan from the strong bottom heat of the oven. This heat pushes things upward (it's great for souffles) but with a delicate cake like this, it could make the texture coarse. The water bath helps the batter set to a smooth consistency, not one with holes and uneven texture.

The baked cake will be slightly puffed and feel soft when pressed *lightly* in the center with a fingertip (but it should not be liquidy). If a little sticks to your finger when you test it, it's okay.

Remove the roasting pan from the oven (careful—it's filled with very hot water!), take the cake pan out of the water, and cool on a rack for an hour.

Unmolding and serving

Before unmolding, run a paring knife around the inside of the cake pan, then invert onto a platter—the cake should fall right out. If it doesn't, just pass the bottom of the pan over a gas burner or electric stovetop element for a few seconds. This melts the butter between the pan and paper so the cake releases.

Remove the pan, peel off the paper, and cool completely. If serving the cake the same day, do not chill it—the texture and flavor are much better when the cake is room temperature. To serve, simply slice the cake into wedges (see right) and serve with whipped cream and fresh berries.

Advance preparation

To freeze the cake, invert it onto a plate or cardboard circle, double wrap in plastic, and freeze up to a month. Unwrap and defrost until it comes to room temperature—this restores its creaminess and helps release the delicate perfume of the chocolate.

Tips for plating

Smoothing: *If the cake's sides and edges need smoothing, dip a small spatula or table knife in hot water then wipe it dry. Gently smooth any wrinkles or rough edges. Repeat if needed.*

Slicing: *To slice the cake, use a thin-bladed knife also dipped in hot water and wiped dry. "Dip and dry" the knife each time you make a cut so the edges of the slices are smooth.*

4 Whisk in liqueur and eggs. Don't overmix—air holes will form in the cake.

5 Bake the cake in a water bath to help preserve its creamy, dense texture.

6 When cake has cooled, invert it onto a serving platter.

preserved lemons

Need a little "artificial" sunshine to get you through the winter? These preserved lemons just may do the trick.

There's no denying it. Winter is tough. And lemons are cheap right now. Where's the connection? Well, at the risk of being cliché, this is the perfect time to make lemonade. But not *true* lemonade—preserved lemons.

Moroccan cuisine has known the benefits of preserved lemons for ages. It's a staple in their cooking and a common ingredient in slow-cooked tagines [tah-ZHEEHN] or stews.

I know what you're thinking. Lemons and salt just *cannot* taste good together, right? They do, though, and the flavor isn't like anything you've ever tasted—kind of like olives but different. Yes, the sourness is still there, but it's mellowed. And the texture of the lemons softens without breaking down and becoming mushy.

There is one catch: The lemons need to cure a month before using. But don't worry—the April issue will have a recipe for chicken using the rind (yes, the rind!) of these lemons. So the sunshine is a bit down the road, but it's something to look forward to.

PRESERVED LEMONS

The lemons take a month to cure, but will last many more months in the refrigerator.
(MAKES ABOUT 1 QUART)

COMBINE:
10 small lemons, scrubbed, cut from top to bottom (but not all the way through)
1 cup kosher salt

AFTER DAY 6, ADD:
Olive oil to cover

Day 1

Day 2

Small vs. large lemons
Preserve small, thin-skinned lemons. They are typically quite juicy and their size makes them easier to pack in jars. Look for organically grown fruit—the skin will be free from pesticides and chemicals. And scrub off stickers or ink stamps with soap and water.

▲*Pack salted lemons in a clean glass jar. Cover with plastic wrap, close lid, and let stand at room temperature.*

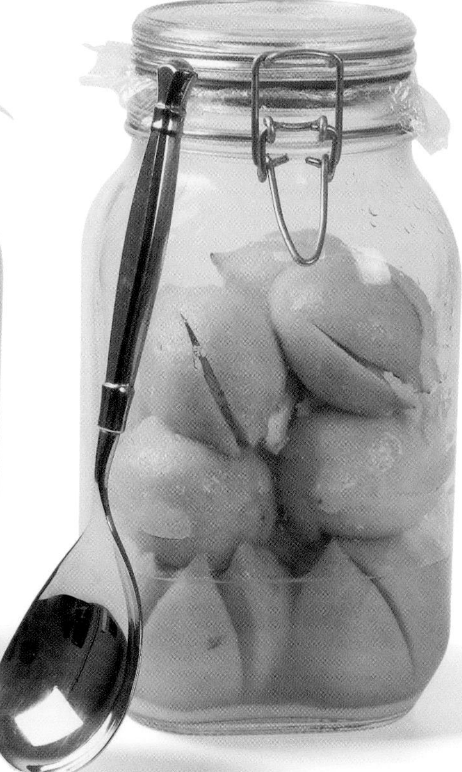

▲*After 24 hours, press lemons with metal spoon to release more juice. Shake jar to help dissolve salt.*

Preserving lemons

The ingredients and procedure are simple, but there are still details you should know.

Ingredients

Lemons, salt, and olive oil are all you need. The lemons should be very fresh with no cuts, bruises, or soft spots. Scrub them well with dish soap, rinse, and dry.

Use kosher salt for preserving. The flavor is mild and it has no additives. Expensive extra virgin olive oil isn't required here—an everyday brand will work fine.

Procedure

Cut the lemons in quarters from top to bottom but not all the way through as in Photo 1. Then pack salt into each lemon, Photo 2. Pry the lemon open one way, add a tablespoon of salt, then open it the other way and add another tablespoon—it's okay if salt falls out. Pack in a clean glass jar.

After they've been packed, press the lemons with a stainless steel spoon to release juices. Let them stand at room temperature, covered, for a week. Follow the "pressing" regime below, top with oil, then chill for a month.

Equipment
Pack lemons in a wide-mouth glass jar (run it through the dishwasher to clean it well). And use a metal (stainless steel) spoon for pressing, not wood or silver. Wood harbors bacteria and salt corrodes silver.

▲*Press lemons and shake jar once a day. After 3 days, they will have compressed to half their size.*

▲*After 6 days, add enough olive oil to cover. Cure lemons in refrigerator for 1 month before using.*

Coming Up...
In the April issue you'll use these lemons in a Moroccan-style dish. But they also add flavor to grilled fish, steamed rice, or sauteed greens.

faster **with** fewer
potato sides

You can't argue with simplicity and these four potato side dishes prove it. Great flavor with a minimum of ingredients and cooking—it doesn't get much better.

Herbed New Potatoes

Feel free to vary the fresh herbs in this dish. Thyme, rosemary, and tarragon are also good.
(Makes About 3 Cups; Total Time: 20 Minutes)

These potatoes are a great side dish for the beef tenderloin on Page 26 or salt encrusted salmon on Page 14.

Steam:
2 lbs. assorted red and white new potatoes, halved (16 potatoes)
Toss Potatoes In:
2 T. unsalted butter, melted
2 T. finely chopped parsley
2 T. finely chopped chives
Salt to taste

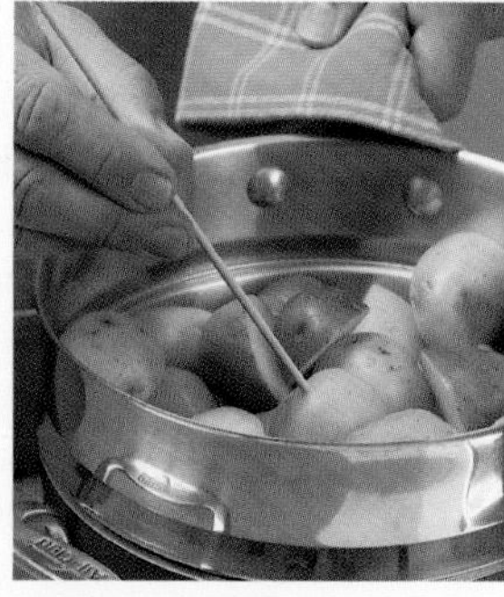

Steam halved potatoes, covered, over boiling water until fully cooked, about 15 minutes. Test potatoes for doneness using a skewer to avoid splitting them.
Toss potatoes with melted butter, herbs, and salt until coated. Serve hot.

"Bravo" Potatoes

This traditional Spanish tapas dish has flavor written all over it. The coarse sea salt at the end adds texture.
(Makes About 3 Cups; Total Time: 30 Minutes)

Fry in 2 T. Olive Oil:
1½ lbs. russet potatoes, peeled, cut into ½" cubes (about 4 cups)
Pulse; Add to Potatoes:
1 can (14 oz.) diced tomatoes, drained
4–5 cloves garlic, sliced
½ t. ground cumin
½ t. sugar
½ t. crushed red pepper flakes
10 dashes Tabasco
Salt to taste
Garnish With:
Drizzle of lemon juice
Chopped fresh cilantro
Coarse sea salt

Serve Bravo Potatoes with fried or scrambled eggs for brunch or a light supper.

In a large nonstick skillet, heat olive oil over medium-high heat until it shimmers.
Fry cubed potatoes in a single layer until browned and partially cooked through, about 10 minutes. Turn once or twice with a spatula, but don't stir too often—they'll brown better if left alone.
Pulse tomatoes, garlic, and seasonings in food processor just to break up tomatoes (do not puree). After potatoes have browned, add tomato mixture and stir to coat.

Reduce heat to medium and cook 5–8 minutes, or until potatoes are cooked through; stir often to prevent scorching. Transfer potatoes to a platter.
Garnish with drizzle of lemon juice, chopped cilantro, and coarse sea salt. Serve warm or at room temperature.

Hasselback Potatoes

These Scandinavian-style potatoes make a simple yet elegant side dish. Plus, they're fun to make!
(Makes 8 Halves; Total Time: 45 Minutes)

The next time you make steak, serve Hasselbacks in place of the usual baked potatoes.

Prepare:
4 medium Yukon gold potatoes, peeled, halved lengthwise, fanned

Process:
1/2 cup white bread crumbs
1/4 cup Parmesan cheese, grated
1 T. olive oil or melted butter
1 t. sweet paprika
Salt to taste

Drizzle Potatoes with:
2–3 T. olive oil

Preheat oven to 450°; oil a large glass baking dish. **Prepare** peeled, halved potatoes, placing each half, cut side down, on a cutting board. Arrange two chopsticks on both sides of potato and thinly slice across. (The chopsticks keep you from cutting through the potato.)

Process crumbs, cheese, oil, and seasonings in food processor; transfer to a shallow dish. **Drizzle** potatoes with oil, carefully bend to separate sections, then roll tops in crumb mixture. Arrange potatoes in baking dish, cover with foil, and bake 30 min. Remove foil and continue baking until crumbs are brown and potatoes cooked, 15 more minutes.

Potato-Tomato Gratin

This is just what you need for cold winter nights when the wind is howling—comfort food at its best.
(Makes One 9 x 13" Gratin; Total Time: 55 Minutes)

This is a nice side dish with roast chicken. But it's also great by itself, served with a green salad.

Saute in 2 T. Olive Oil:
1 yellow onion, thinly sliced

Stir in:
2 T. garlic, minced

Add and Cook:
10 Roma tomatoes, seeded, cut into chunks (1 1/2 lbs.)
2 t. minced fresh rosemary

Layer:
4 russet potatoes, sliced 1/8" thick
Salt and pepper to taste
Tomato mixture
1 cup Swiss cheese, grated

Preheat oven to 450°; spray a large casserole dish with nonstick spray.
Saute onions in a skillet over medium-high heat with olive oil just until soft.
Stir in garlic; cook another minute, just until aromatic.
Add the tomatoes and rosemary. Continue to cook until all moisture is evaporated, about 10 minutes.
Layer half the sliced potatoes in prepared casserole; season with salt and pepper. Now top potatoes with half of the tomato mixture and half the cheese. Repeat layering, ending with cheese. Cover gratin with foil and bake 30 minutes. Remove foil and bake 15 more minutes to brown cheese. Let stand 5 minutes to set the cheese before slicing and serving.

from **our** readers

Q&A
questions & answers

sculpted marzipan ►

WHAT IS MARZIPAN?

What exactly is marzipan and how can I use it?

Mary Mowry
Sherwood, MI

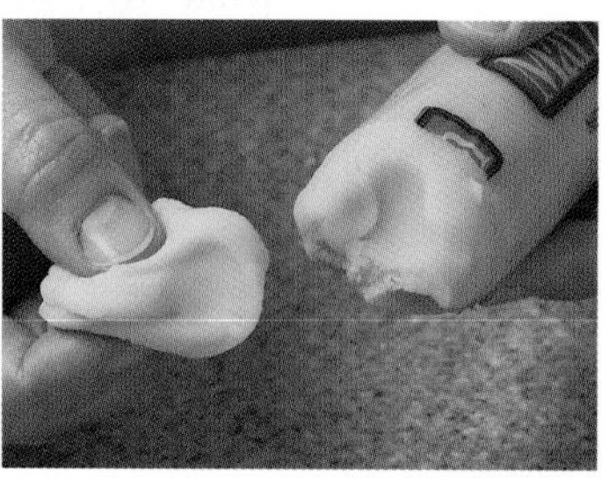

Marzipan is a pliable substance made of almond paste, sugar, and corn syrup or egg whites. It has a strong, sweet almond flavor and a texture that allows it to be rolled and sculpted just like clay.

Pastry shops tint and shape marzipan into beautiful and edible miniature fruits, vegetables, and flowers to top fancy cakes. Or they roll it into a sheet for a perfectly smooth cake covering.

But now that packaged marzipan is available in supermarkets, it's not an art exclusive to pros. A toothpick, knife, and paste food coloring will get you sculpting.

Begin with a simple subject like an apple or tomato. Add a tiny bit of coloring to a piece of marzipan and work it between your fingers until shaping consistency. Roll into shapes and make details with a toothpick. Cut leaves out of flat pieces, then assemble. Marzipan hardens, so store creations in an airtight container until ready to decorate.

PURE VANILLA?

I was surprised to see that my pure vanilla extract contains corn syrup. Why is it there?

Elaine Rutter
Haddonfield, NJ

FDA standards require products titled "pure vanilla extract" to contain 35% alcohol and a specified amount of vanilla beans. They allow (but don't require) the addition of corn syrup, sugar, or several other additives.

Many manufacturers *do* use one of these sweet additives in their pure vanilla extract. Some of them use it to suspend the flavor matter so it doesn't settle to the bottom of the bottle. Others see it strictly as a flavor enhancer that rounds out the flavor of the vanilla. Of course, each brand believes their formula is best.

But pure vanilla extract with no additives *is* available. Read the labels, or order from Penzeys Spices, *see Resources, Page 43.*

MEASURING MUFFIN TINS

I want to make the mini corn muffins in Issue #29. How do I know if I have the right size muffin tin?

Sandy Kruempel
Des Moines, IA

Muffin tin sizes vary widely and that can affect both your baking time and muffin results.

Cups in the tin I used measure 2" in diameter by 1" deep and hold 2 T. batter. To compare your tin volume, measure 2 T. water into a muffin cup. If there's leftover water after filling, your pan is smaller and you need to shorten the baking time and watch closely. If your tin is bigger you'll need to bake a little longer to cook through.

For a nice crown on the top of these muffins, be sure to fill cups to the top with batter.

STORING CHEESE

What's the best way to store cheese?

Gail Sherman
Clark Fork, ID

Unopened cheese of any kind can remain in the original package until you're ready to use it. Here's how to handle the remaining chunk of cheese after the package has been opened.

First wrap the cheese in waxed or parchment paper. Then place in a resealable plastic bag or enclose securely in plastic wrap to protect from circulating air in the refrigerator. The important point is to keep the cheese from direct contact with plastic, which causes it to become moist or slimy and allows mold to grow.

SOFTENING BUTTER

Are there ways to bring butter to room temperature other than letting it sit out?

Beverly Johnson
Tipton, IA

You bet. The microwave makes quick work of it. But the key is to soften the refrigerated butter in small portions on low power. If you microwave a whole stick, it will melt in the middle and still be solid on the ends.

So slice the butter into chunks (tablespoon-sized), then microwave on the defrost setting for 10 seconds at a time, until slightly soft to the touch.

PASTEURIZED CRAB

In Issue #30 you gave a mail order source for Phillips pasteurized lump crab meat. I'm sure I've seen it in a grocery store, but can't remember where. Can you help?

Grace Truman
Oklahoma City, OK

Check out the Phillips website at **www.phillipsfoods.com**.

Click on "Retail Locations" for a national listing of stores that carry the Phillips retail products. You can also order lump crab meat (as well as other Phillips seafood products) online at this company website.

KEEPING UP WITH WOOD

How should I clean and care for my wooden cutting board?

Gabriel O. Ramos
Pico Rivera, CA

First, let's talk about cleaning. The wood should never be exposed to too much moisture, so don't immerse or let it sit in water. Instead, wash your cutting board with a little soap and warm water after each use. Rinse and dry the board immediately.

Second, to care for your board, rub a little mineral oil into the wood with a paper towel whenever the wood looks dry or "thirsty." The mineral oil will keep it hydrated and in tip-top shape. (Yes, this is the same mineral oil your grandmother swore by for tip-top health!) You'll find it in the healthcare products aisle at your grocery or drugstore.

Finally, be sure to store your cutting board away from the oven and dishwasher. Both heat and moisture can damage the wood, causing it to split or warp.

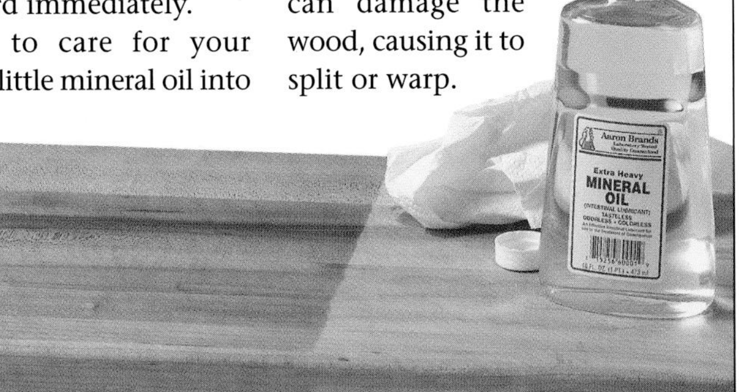

To order a repair and care kit for cutting boards, go to ***jkadams.com*** *(listed under basics), or call* ***(800) 451-6118.***

resources

Chef's Catalog
Norpro Six-Sided Stand Grater,
Item #0838
(800) 338-3232
www.chefscatalog.com

The Chef's Resource
Microplane Long Grater,
Item #40020
Microplane Coarse Grater,
Item #35001
(866) 765-2433
www.chefsresource.com

The Vermont Country Store
Mouli Grater, Item #29163
Tower Grater, Item #36048
(802) 362-8470
www.vermontcountrystore.com

Williams-Sonoma
Flat Grater, Item #77-4033049
(Fine Grater)
(800) 541-2233
www.williams-sonoma.com

Penzeys Spices
Pure Vanilla Extract
(Single Strength)
Item #92151, 4 oz., $7.99
Item #92119, 16 oz., $20.90
(800) 741-7787
www.penzeys.com

Q&A

Do you have a question for *Cuisine at home?*

If you have a question about a cooking term, procedure, or technique, we'd like to hear from you. We'll consider publishing your question in one or more of our works. Just write down your question and mail it to *Cuisine at home*, Q&A Editor, 2200 Grand Ave., Des Moines, IA 50312, or contact us through our email address shown below. Please include your name, address, and daytime phone number in case we have questions.

Email: CuisineAtHome@CuisineAtHome.**com**
Web address: CuisineAtHome.**com**

grand**finale**

chocolate truffles

Chocolate Truffles

Store truffles in airtight containers in single layers between sheets of parchment or waxed paper. Chill for up to a week; freeze for up to a month.
(Makes 25–30 Truffles)

Melt in Double Boiler:

4 oz. good-quality bittersweet chocolate, chopped small
4 oz. good-quality semisweet or milk chocolate, chopped small
6 T. unsalted butter, cubed
2 t. instant coffee granules dissolved in 3 T. warm water

Off Heat, Stir in; Chill:

1 egg yolk (optional)
1 T. liqueur of your choice (optional)

Scoop Chocolate Mixture into Truffles. Roll Truffles in:

Unsweetened cocoa powder
Toasted, finely chopped pecans or almonds
Finely chopped sweetened coconut

Melt both chocolates, butter, and instant coffee mixture in a double boiler set over simmering water. Stir with a rubber spatula until chocolate and butter are melted and smooth, about 5 min.

Off heat, stir in the optional egg yolk (for smoother truffles) and liqueur (for added flavor). Pour chocolate mixture onto a parchment-lined baking sheet or a large plate. Cover with plastic wrap and chill until firm, at least one hour.

Scoop cold chocolate mixture into truffles using a #100 scoop, melon baller, or small teaspoons. Don't roll them between your hands to make them smooth—they're meant to be rough-looking. Place truffles directly into any of the coatings and roll them around until completely covered. This is easiest if you place the coatings in shallow plastic containers with lids. Then, after scooping 5 or 6 truffles, cover the container and shake it gently until the truffles are coated.

ORE THAN 50 RECIPES AND TIPS FOR BETTER COOKING

Cuisine at home™

www.CuisineAtHome.com

Shake winter blues lemon tarts bursting with spring flavor

Plus:

Fast & Easy Cutlets

The Best Classic Italian Pizza

Secrets of mouth-watering Leg of Lamb

Issue No. 32 April 2002
A publication of August Home Publishing

Cuisine at home™

Publisher
Donald B. Peschke

Editor
John F. Meyer

Senior Editor
Susan Hoss

Assistant Editor
Sara Ostransky

Test Kitchen Director
Kim Samuelson

Contributing Food Stylist
Janet Pittman

Art Director
Cinda Shambaugh

Assistant Art Director
Holly Wiederin

Graphic Designer
April Walker Janning

Photographers
Scott Little
Dean Tanner

Image Specialist
Troy Clark

Corporate:

Corporate Vice Presidents: Mary R. Scheve, Douglas L. Hicks • *Creative Director:* Ted Kralicek • *Professional Development Director:* Michal Sigel *New Media Manager:* Gordon C. Gaippe • *Senior Photographer:* Crayola England • *Multi Media Art Director:* Eugene Pedersen • *Web Server Administrator:* Carol Schoeppler • *Web Content Manager:* David Briggs *Web Designer:* Kara Blessing • *Web Developer/Content Manager:* Sue M. Moe *Controller:* Robin Hutchinson • *Senior Accountant:* Laura Thomas • *Accounts Payable:* Mary Schultz • *Accounts Receivable:* Margo Petrus • *Production Director:* George Chmielarz • *Pre-Press Image Specialist:* Minniette Johnson *Electronic Publishing Director:* Douglas M. Lidster • *Systems Administrator:* Cris Schwanebeck • *PC Maintenance Technician:* Robert D. Cook • *H.R. Assistant:* Kirsten Koele • *Office Manager:* Noelle M. Carroll • *Receptionist/ Administrative Assistant:* Jeanne Johnson • *Mail Room Clerk:* Lou Webber

Customer Service & Fulfillment:

Operations Director: Bob Baker • *Customer Service Manager:* Jennie Enos *Customer Service Representatives:* Eddie Arthur, Anna Cox, April Revell, Deborah Rich, Valerie Jo Riley, Tammy Truckenbrod • *Technical Representative:* Johnny Audette • *Buyer:* Linda Jones • *Administrative Assistant:* Nancy Downey • *Warehouse Supervisor:* Nancy Johnson *Fulfillment:* Sylvia Carey, Sheryl Knox, Albert Voigt

Circulation:

Subscriber Services Director: Sandy Baum • *New Business Circulation Manager:* Wayde J. Klingbeil • *Multi Media Promotion Manager:* Rick Junkins *Promotions Analyst:* Patrick A. Walsh • *Billing and Collections Manager:* Rebecca Cunningham • *Renewal Manager:* Paige Rogers • *Circulation Marketing Analyst:* Kris Schlemmer • *Associate Circulation Marketing Analyst:* Paula M. DeMatteis • *Senior Graphic Designers:* Mark Hayes, Robin Friend

www.CuisineAtHome.com

talk to ***Cuisine at home***
Subscriptions, Address Changes, or Questions? Write or call:

Customer Service
2200 Grand Avenue,
Des Moines, IA 50312
800-311-3995,
8 a.m. to 5 p.m., CST.

Online Subscriber Services:
www.CuisineAtHome.com
Access your account • Check a subscription payment • Tell us if you've missed an issue • Change your mailing or email address • Renew your subscription • Pay your bill

Cuisine at home™ (ISSN 1537-8225) is published bi-monthly (Jan., Mar., May, July, Sept., Nov.) by August Home Publishing Co., 2200 Grand Ave., Des Moines, IA 50312.
Cuisine at home™ is a trademark of August Home Publishing Co.

Subscriptions: Single copy: $4.99. One year subscription (6 issues), $24.00. (Canada/Foreign add $10 per year, U.S. funds.)

Periodicals postage paid at Des Moines, IA and at additional mailing offices. "USPS/Perry-Judd's Heartland Division automatable poly".
Postmaster: Send change of address to **Cuisine at home**, P.O. Box 37100 Boone, IA 50037-2100.
Cuisine at home™ does not accept and is not responsible for unsolicited manuscripts. PRINTED IN SINGAPORE.

editor's letter

Seems most of us are staying a little closer to home lately. That's not all bad. It probably does each of us some good to occasionally tighten our "lifestyle" belts just a notch. Maybe that includes a little less dining out and a tad more cooking in. It's not only a budget reality check but could be just the opportunity we need to bring us closer to our family and friends.

What better way to bring all this together than an old fashioned holiday dinner to celebrate the coming of spring. And there's nothing that says spring dinner more definitively than leg of lamb. Unfortunately, roasting a leg isn't like throwing a steak or burger on the grill—it's not a natural talent that lies dormant until awakened in spring. Roasting a whole leg is a learned skill in which knowledge begins at the market and ends at the dinner table when carving.

And speaking of skills ... Pamela Sheldon Johns joins us in the kitchen this issue to bake the perfect pizza. Most of you know that wine and olive oil are tightly regulated by governments in many European countries. Well, guess what? In Italy, so is pizza. In 1998, the Italian government imposed strict guidelines regulating the way real Italian pizza should be made. Pamela shares her knowledge and skills of this process so you can make authentic pizza too. But don't worry about not having all the right equipment or ingredients. She makes allowances for most of these shortcomings and still puts out a pizza that most Italians would be proud to serve.

No matter what you make in this issue, you have to finish with the lemon tart. So refreshing and clean tasting—it's like taking a big bite of spring. But what really puts things over the top are the tartlets with macaroon crust. Senior Editor, Sue Hoss, knows her desserts. Even the experiments gone awry were worth every calorie!

Perfectly roasted leg of lamb seasoned with fresh oregano and rosemary, braised white beans with pancetta, fresh asparagus, and lemon tartlets with coconut crust—with a menu like this, who needs to go out? See ... tightening our "lifestyle" belts, isn't so tough.

table of contents

Issue No. 32 April 2002

departments

features

from **our** readers

tips *and techniques*

Tip from the Test Kitchen *If you don't have a meat mallet or other utensil to make cutlets, pound them out using a rolling pin (one without handles works the best). But be careful—the meat can turn to mush if hit too forcefully.*

Removing Tomato Paste

Here's a helpful idea for getting tomato paste out of the can. Open both ends and remove one lid. Extract the paste by carefully pushing on the other lid with your thumbs (watch out for the can edge!). You'll get every bit.

Jason S.T. Deveau
Guelph, Ontario

Melon Baller Mushrooms

To hollow out mushrooms for stuffing, use a melon baller. First remove the stem, then scrape out the gills and a little from inside the cap (mix this in with the stuffing). It makes a nice shape with lots of space for good stuff!

Carol Obrecht
Sun Lakes, AZ

Steaming Asparagus

To steam asparagus, set a large soup can (with top and bottom removed) upright in a small stockpot. Add an inch of water to the pot and bring to a simmer. Tie asparagus in a bundle with kitchen string, then stand it (tips up) inside the can. Cover with a heat resistant bowl and steam.

Cheryl Hobbs
Willow Grove, PA

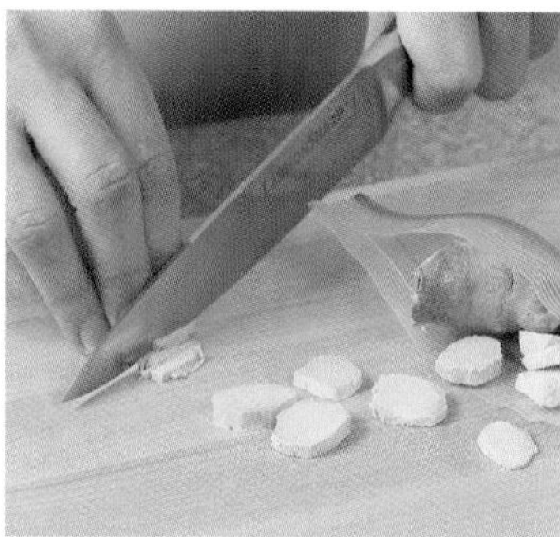

Ginger Ready

I store fresh ginger in the freezer so it keeps longer. Thinly slice the ginger into "coins," freeze them on a baking sheet, then transfer to a plastic freezer bag.

Leona Blackbird
Salt Lake City, UT

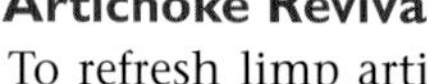

Artichoke Revival

To refresh limp artichokes, simply re-cut the stems, then stand the artichokes in a bowl or glass of cold water and chill. Change the water daily and they will keep for days. This also works with asparagus spears and broccoli.

Linda Tucci
Garden City, NY

Double Duty Egg Wash

To "glue" seeds on home baked bread, use a double dose of egg white wash. Before baking, brush the risen dough with egg white and top with the seeds. Then, five minutes before the bread is done, brush it with egg white again and finish baking. The seeds stick (even when sliced) and the bread shines!

Lorna Balian
Watertown, WI

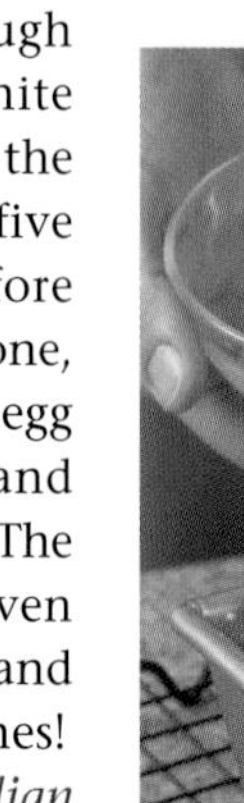

Accordion-style Bacon

To freeze bacon, accordion-fold a large piece of foil, lay strips of bacon between the folds, then wrap in freezer wrap or a resealable freezer bag. This way, you won't have to thaw out a whole package if you need just a slice or two.

Cheryl Hobbs
Willow Grove, PA

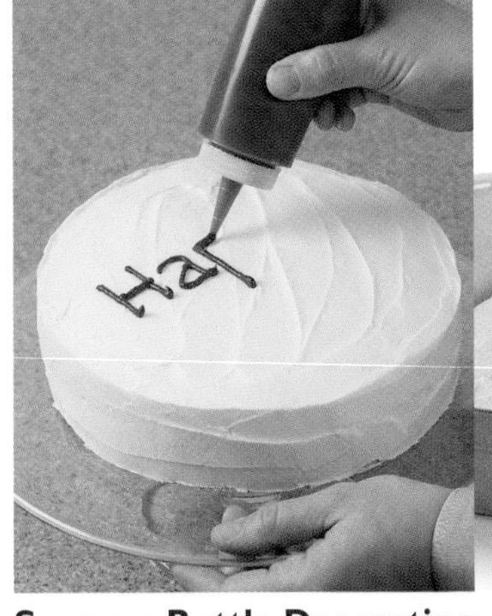

Squeeze Bottle Decorating

I keep frosting in squeeze bottles for designing and decorating cakes and cookies. It's less messy and decorating is much easier. Keep bottles of frosting on hand, refrigerated, for last minute decorating—just warm the bottle under water until squeezable.

Demetra Derro
Willow Grove, PA

Rectangular Rise

When making a yeast dough for stromboli or sweet rolls, I let it rise in a rectangular or square pan. Then as the dough rises, it takes the shape of the pan. And that makes rolling out and shaping the dough into a rectangle much easier.

Susan Martinez
Fairfield, CT

Zesting Frozen Fruit

If I have extra citrus fruit, I store it in a plastic freezer bag and freeze it whole. That way, when I need zest for a recipe, I just use one of the frozen fruits.

Ann Castelli
Chicago Heights, IL

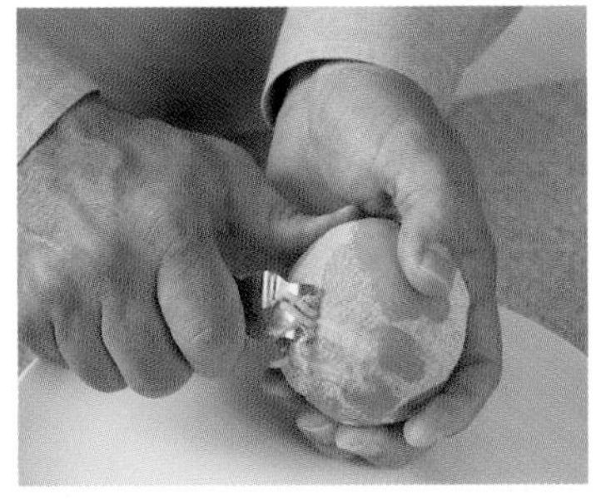

Parchment Paper Pizza

To easily transfer pizza from a peel to a stone, simply form the dough on a piece of parchment paper and add toppings. Place the pizza (on parchment) on a peel and transfer to a hot stone. After baking 5–10 minutes, carefully pull out the parchment and finish baking the pizza on the stone. This also keeps cornmeal from burning on the stone and in the bottom of the oven.

Francis Arnold
Burton, OH

Pepper Stand

To easily stuff bell peppers and keep them upright during baking, arrange and then bake them in a Bundt, tube, angel food, or muffin pan (spray with nonstick spray first). The peppers stay upright, freeing your hands for assembly.

Linda S. Randall
Cleveland, OH

share your **tips** *and techniques* with *Cuisine at home*

If you have a unique way of solving a cooking problem, we'd like to hear from you, and we'll consider publishing your tip in one or more of our works. Just write down your cooking tip and mail it to *Cuisine at home*, Tips Editor, 2200 Grand Ave., Des Moines, IA 50312, or contact us through our email address shown below. Please include your name, address, and daytime phone number in case we have questions. We'll pay you $25 if we publish your tip.

Email: CuisineAtHome@CuisineAtHome.com

Web address: CuisineAtHome.com

cuisineclass

perfect cutlets

Fast, easy, and good-tasting. Cutlets show their versatility using different meats in an infinite array of recipes.

While most cutlet recipes are pretty simple, the key to success begins with the cutlet itself. It can't be too thin or too thick, nor can it be cut just any way. For the best cutlets, they have to be cut correctly and then pounded to the right thickness.

If the cutlet is too thin, the meat can dry out by the time the outside is browned to a presentable finish. On the other hand, if the meat is too thick, the exterior could overbrown (even burn) by the time the meat finishes cooking.

Besides the right thickness, most cutlets should be cut *against* the grain. Short muscle fibers are more tender and less likely to constrict and buckle when cooked over high heat.

Slicing: Slice your own cutlets since you don't know the cut or quality of pre-packaged ones.

Pork: Use loin. Trim it well and slice across the grain. Each slice should be about 1/2" thick before pounding.

Chicken: While some cooks cut breasts in layers for cutlets, this is almost impossible to do to a consistent thickness. Cut in half and pound gently.

Turkey: I use tenderloin that I've sliced on the bias for nice large cutlets. Again, keep them in that 1/2"-thick range.

Pork: Slice loin across the grain about 1/2" thick before pounding.

Chicken: Use the breast and remove tenderloin. Cut in half.

Turkey: Slice the turkey tenderloin on the bias. When cut this way, these 1/2" slices tend not to fray when cut and flattened.

The Perfect Cutlet

Many cutlet recipes direct you to simply slice the meat to the desired thickness—pounding is not necessary. Perhaps that may be true, but I still like to use a mallet to pound the cutlets to an even 1/4" thickness.

First, not all of us can always cut an even slice. It may be thicker at the top and taper off at the bottom. That unevenness is especially noticeable on a chicken breast that tapers naturally.

Pounding can take care of the unevenness on most meats. And while these cuts of meat are naturally tender, flattening breaks down some of the tougher connective tissues to make the cutlet even more tender.

Covering

Before flattening the cutlets, cover them with plastic for better shaping and cleanup.

To help hold shape and prevent splattering, cover meat with plastic wrap.

Plastic wrap: Use a plastic wrap that is as thick as possible to prevent tearing. Regular wrap is okay but can tear after two or three cutlets. Freezer wrap is much better since it's thicker, stronger, and can hold up longer.

Shaping: This may be a slight stretch but think of a pair of stockings. Although they are sheer, stockings hold a leg's shape by displacing pressure evenly. The same thing happens with the plastic wrap. As the mallet hits the meat, the pressure is slightly displaced and less traumatic, preserving the cutlet's smooth appearance.

Gently pound pieces with glancing blows until cutlet is 1/4" inch thick.

Pounding

There is an art to pounding out a cutlet—it's not just waling away at a piece of meat. The secret is gentle, glancing taps.

After covering, gently pound the meat with the flat side of your mallet (there's no point in using the waffled tenderizing end). Strike the meat with glancing movements until the cutlet is about 1/4" thick. This motion will preserve the meat's smooth appearance and when cooked, the 1/4" thick cutlet will be golden brown on the outside and remain moist on the inside.

MALLETS

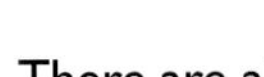

There are all types of mallets. Some have handles which provide leverage, others are palm held for good control. And some are flat and heavy, up to eight pounds. No mallet? Try a sturdy bottle wrapped in plastic.

Chicken Piccata

If you like fresh lemon, tender chicken, and a quick recipe, then this classic Italian dish will fit perfectly on your dinner plate.

online extra

Looking for a side dish?
Try our Sauteed Spinach at **www.CuisineAtHome.com** for a step-by-step recipe.

Because cutlets are lean and only cook for a few minutes, they produce no natural drippings to create a foundation for a sauce. So any sauce you serve with cutlets will be made with ingredients other than pan drippings. But that's not all bad. A splash of white wine and a blast of lemon make a quick, sassy sauce that packs plenty of flavor to accompany these cutlets.

Coating: There are plenty of ways to coat cutlets. Like escallops (a very thin type of cutlet), they can be lightly dusted with flour, or even simply seasoned before being sauteed. But my favorite is to use Japanese panko bread crumbs as shown with pork cutlets on Page 10. They make a crisp crust that browns perfectly.

No matter what method you prefer, the final cutlet should be slightly golden for looks and taste. If I'm not coating cutlets with panko, I always prefer to dust them lightly with flour. Just a little bit acts like an emulsifier (binder) which makes the sauce look and feel richer by thickening it slightly.

Chicken Piccata

This piccata is so rich that one breast half can serve two people. Turkey tenderloin also makes a great substitute.

Makes 2 Servings

Season:
4 chicken cutlets, *Pages 6–7*

Saute in:
2 T. vegetable oil

Deglaze with:
1/4 cup dry white wine
1 t. garlic, minced

Add:
1/2 cup low-sodium chicken broth
2 T. fresh lemon juice
1 T. capers, drained
Sauteed cutlets

Finish with:
2 T. unsalted butter
Fresh lemon slices

Garnish with:
Chopped fresh parsley

Season cutlets with salt and pepper then dust with flour, see *Figure 1*. Spray a saute pan with nonstick spray, add vegetable oil, and heat over medium-high.

Saute cutlets 2–3 minutes on one side, see *Figure 2*. Flip the cutlets over and saute the other side 1–2 minutes with the pan covered, see *Figure 3*. Transfer cutlets to a warm plate; pour off fat from the pan.

Deglaze pan with wine and add minced garlic. Cook until garlic is *slightly* brown and liquid is nearly gone, about 2 minutes.

Add broth, lemon juice, and capers. Return cutlets to pan and cook on each side 1 minute. Transfer cutlets to a warm plate.

Finish with butter and lemon slices, see *Figure 4*. Once butter melts, pour sauce over cutlets.

Garnish with chopped fresh parsley and serve.

1 Prepare the chicken for cutlets. Season the cutlets with salt and pepper; dust with flour, shaking off the excess.

2 Saute cutlets over medium-high heat. Be careful of splattering.

3 Flip cutlets over when golden brown on first side. Cover pan with a heatproof plate and cook 1–2 min.

◀*A Tip*
Use a serving platter to cover the pan. This not only puts moisture into the cutlets, but it also warms the platter. Keep covered only about 1–2 minutes.

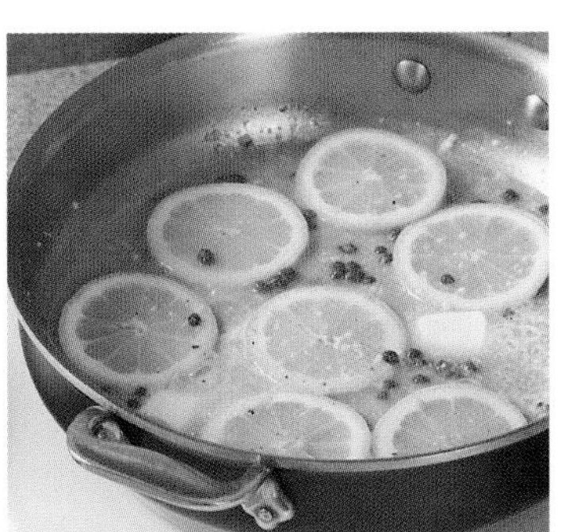

4 Finish sauce with butter and lemon, then pour over cutlets.

option

Chicken Pomodoro

A gorgeous presentation and a delightful fresh flavor. Be sure to deglaze with the vodka off heat.

Makes 2 Servings

Season:
4 chicken cutlets, *Pages 6–7*

Saute in:
2 T. vegetable oil

Deglaze with:
1/4 cup vodka

Add:
1/2 cup low-sodium chicken broth
2 T. fresh lemon juice
Sauteed cutlets

Finish with:
1/2 cup tomatoes, chopped
2 T. heavy cream

Garnish with:
1/3 cup scallions, minced

Season cutlets with salt and pepper then dust with flour.

Saute cutlets in oil. Transfer to a platter; pour off fat from pan.

Deglaze pan with vodka (AWAY FROM FLAME) and cook until vodka is nearly gone.

Add broth and lemon juice. Return cutlets to pan and cook each side 1 minute. Transfer cutlets to a warm plate.

Finish the sauce with tomatoes and cream. Heat through, then pour over the cutlets.

Garnish with scallions.

Pork Cutlet
Japanese style

Japanese cuisine is not all raw fish and rice. Once you taste this pork cutlet, you'll use just about any excuse in the book to make it again—and again.

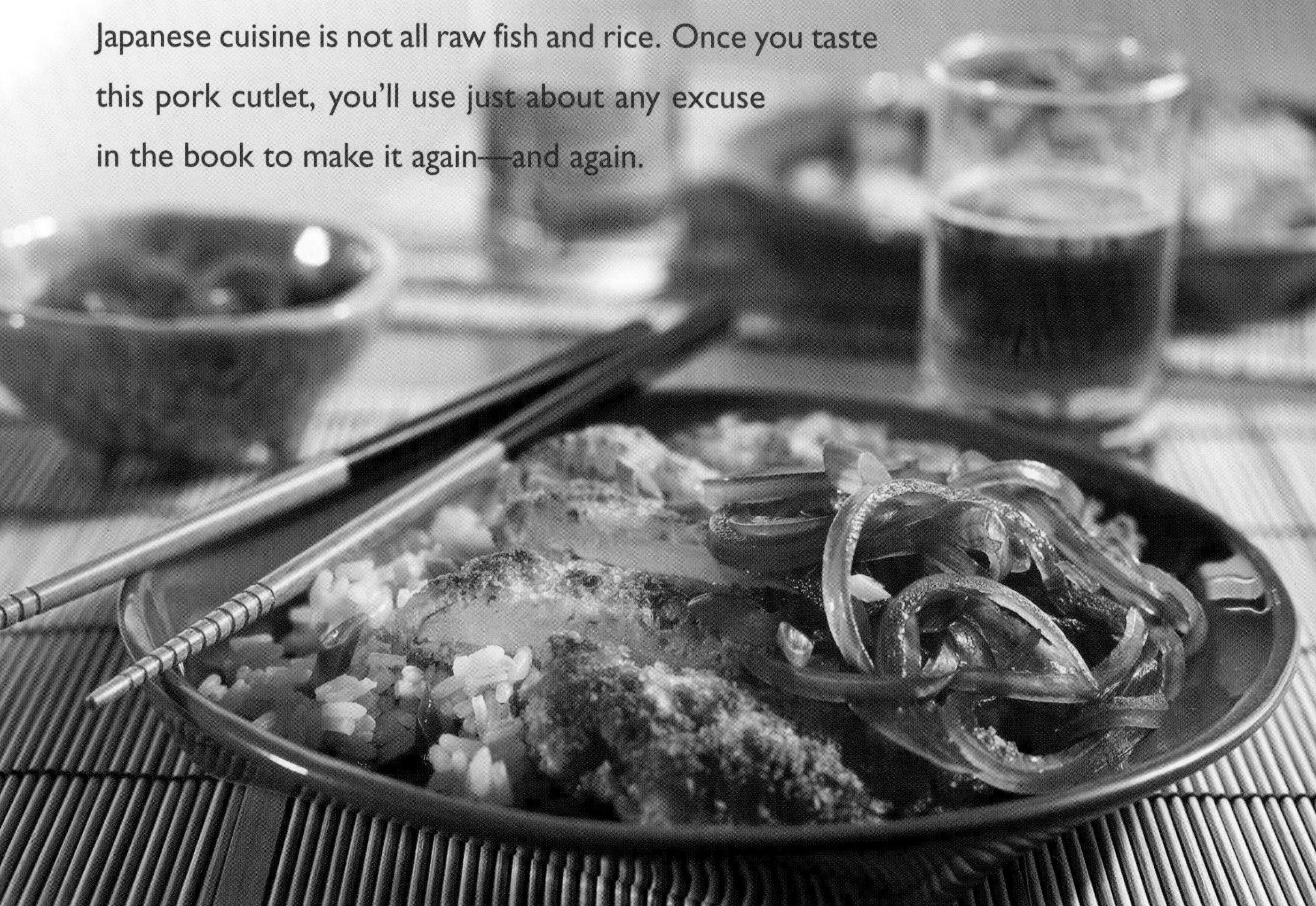

Let's face it. Japanese food conjures up all kinds of scary thoughts for anyone not familiar with the cuisine. Just *thinking* about raw fish can send a lot of people running to the nearest Golden Arches.

But this is one dish that shouldn't intimidate you. It's simply a "chicken fried" pork cutlet served with steamed rice and a lightly sweet onion broth. Nothing scary about that! The dish is called katsudon [KAHT-soo-dohn] and is one of several in the "donburi" family, which literally means "rice bowls." In fact, donburi is Japanese fast food, and once you taste katsudon, you may never care to set foot in a burger-slinging establishment again.

Katsudon is traditionally made with pork, and pounding pork loin into cutlets puts this dish squarely into the fast food category. Prepare cutlets as on Pages 6–7, then bread them following the steps, *right.*

The trouble with ethnic dishes is that they almost always require a few ingredients that most cooks don't have on hand. And there are two here that may require a trip to an Asian market, *see sidebar, right.*

Too impractical? Make katsudon using dry sherry and regular bread crumbs instead of mirin and panko. It'll still taste great, but promise yourself to make authentic katsudon sometime just to compare—as if you need an excuse!

Steps to katsudon

Good katsudon isn't so much about having all the right ingredients as it is about organizing its preparation. Here's how to bring it all together.

First, prepare and pound the pork into cutlets and set them aside. Don't pound the meat too hard or vigorously—you're just thinning it out, not tenderizing it (pork loin is plenty tender already).

Next, cook the rice. It'll probably be done before the cutlets and sauce are, but just keep the pan covered on the back of the stove, off heat.

Now simmer the sauce components until the onions are soft. As they simmer, get the eggs, flour, and crumbs ready for breading.

First dredge cutlets in flour, then follow with egg and panko. "Double bread" them by dipping in the egg and panko once more. This extra coating will really get the cutlets crisp and golden brown.

To fry, heat the oil until it starts to shimmer, but not smoke. It must be at the right temperature (365°) before you start frying. If it's too cool, the cutlets will be greasy and cook slowly. If it's hotter than that, the breading will burn before the meat is cooked. Fry in batches so the cutlets don't crowd the pan and bring down the temperature.

To serve, place two fried cutlets in the simmering onion broth and cook gently for a minute. Transfer to a cutting board, slice, and arrange over some of the rice. Top with broth and garnish with scallions. Repeat with remaining cutlets.

Japanese ingredients
Panko are bread crumbs with a light, coarse texture that's perfect for breading katsudon (or oven-fried chicken). Mirin [MIHR-in] is a sweet cooking wine made from rice and sugar. Both ingredients give katsudon its authentic, unique flavor.

Japanese Style Pork Cutlet

If you don't want to use pork, cutlets made with chicken breast or turkey tenderloins are a great substitute.

Makes 4 Servings; Total Time: 45 Minutes

Prepare:
1/2 lb. pork loin cutlets, see *Pages 6–7*
1 1/2 cups raw medium-grain rice

Simmer:
2 cups yellow onion, sliced
2 cups low-sodium chicken broth
1/2 cup mirin
1/2 cup low-sodium soy sauce
2 T. sugar
4 slices fresh ginger

Bread Cutlets In:
6 eggs, lightly beaten
1/4 cup all-purpose flour
1/2 t. kosher salt
Heavy pinch black pepper
2–3 cups panko crumbs

Fry In:
1/4 cup vegetable oil

Serve Cutlets With:
Prepared rice
Chopped scallions

Prepare pork for cutlets. Cook rice as directed on the package and keep warm until serving.

Simmer onion, broth, mirin, soy sauce, sugar, and ginger in a large saute pan over med.-low heat until onion is soft, 15 min.

Before breading the cutlets, beat the eggs in a shallow dish (like a pie plate), mix flour, salt, and pepper in a second dish, and place the panko in a third dish.

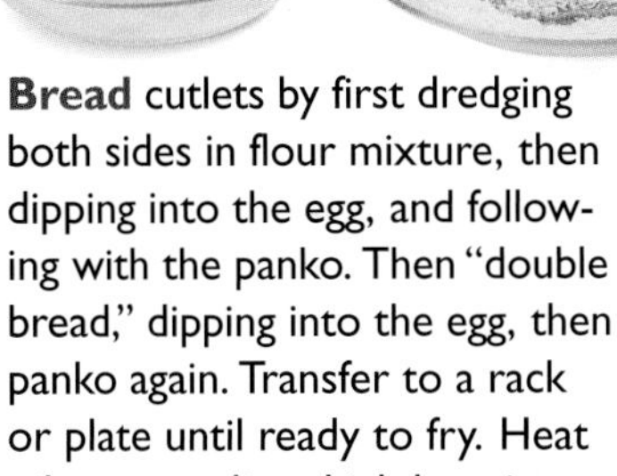

Bread cutlets by first dredging both sides in flour mixture, then dipping into the egg, and following with the panko. Then "double bread," dipping into the egg, then panko again. Transfer to a rack or plate until ready to fry. Heat oil over medium-high heat in a second saute pan.

Fry cutlets in batches, browning on both sides until cooked through, 6–8 minutes total. Transfer cutlets to a cooling rack set over paper towels to drain.

To serve, place 2 cutlets in the simmering broth; cook 1 minute to warm through. Remove and slice cutlets, place on top of some rice, ladle with broth, and sprinkle with scallions.

cuisinetechnique

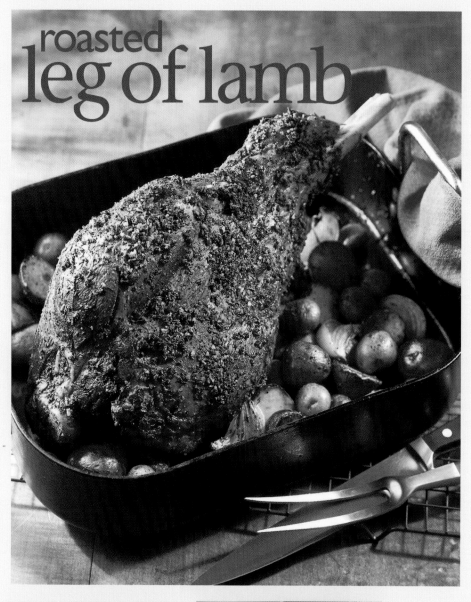

roasted leg of lamb

A mild rub made with fresh herbs and slow oven-roasting make leg of lamb the perfect spring dinner.

Memories of strong-tasting lamb or the fear of handling a leg of any animal (other than chicken) can send most of us running out the kitchen. Well, stop fretting. This traditional spring dinner will put lamb back on the menu.

Steps to roasting

Before you roast, there are four steps to consider. The first is the right cut of lamb. Look at the chart at the far right and you'll see different cuts of lamb leg. The best for this recipe is a "center cut leg roast"—#2. Any parts that can make carving difficult are removed, yet it still looks like a leg (and it fits in the oven).

Trimming: Lamb fat can be strong-tasting so it should be trimmed. Remove all but a thin layer from the leg, *see Figure 1*. This small amount keeps the meat moist while roasting but doesn't impart a bad taste.

Browning: Since you are going to roast the lamb at a moderate temperature (350°), it's best to brown the meat first. This promotes color and provides intense flavor, *see Figure 2*. You can do this in the same pan you'll be using for roasting.

Rub: After browning, apply a rub made of fresh herbs, garlic, and lemon, *see Figure 3*. While you can use your favorite herbs, this is a classic combination that goes especially well with lamb. Before applying the paste, rub olive oil on the meat to make the herb mixture stick better.

1 Trim all but 1/4"-thick layer of fat to moisturize and flavor meat.

2 Brown lamb over high heat for color and a nice crust.

3 Place on rack then coat with oil and herb rub. Cover with foil.

There seems to be a little controversy on just how to cook a leg of lamb—roasting quickly at high heat or slow cooking at a lower temperature. After cooking quite a few legs of lamb, the answer was quite obvious—lower temperatures worked best.

Low temperature

Leg of lamb is a fairly large piece of meat, weighing up to nine pounds. Once the sirloin and part of the shank have been cut off, it still weighs between five and seven pounds.

As a result, it's best to cook the leg at lower temperatures so the connective tissues deep inside the leg can tighten and solidify from the heat. To put it simply, a leg of lamb roasted at a high temperature results in the outside overcooking while the inside remains raw (jiggly and cool). Not good for a leg.

Minutes per pound

5–7 lb. bone-in leg

140° rare	17–20
150° medium	21–24
160° medium-well	24–27

4–7 lb. boneless leg

140° rare	25–29
150° medium	29–32
160° medium-well	32–34

Moisture

I got the best results with a little moisture in the bottom of the roasting pan. I used broth in this recipe. Since young lamb has very little fat in it's muscle structure, this added moisture keeps the meat from drying out. On Page 16 we show you how to get moisture from beans.

Once the leg is done, tent it and let it rest 10 minutes before carving. This allows the meat's interior juices to flow to the drier portions on the outside of the roast.

Herb-Roasted Lamb

If there's any leftover lamb, make the "tostadas" on the Back Cover.

Total Time: 2–3 Hours

For the Herb Rub—

Combine:

- 1/4 cup finely chopped fresh rosemary
- 1/4 cup finely chopped fresh oregano
- 1/4 cup finely chopped fresh parsley
- 1/4 cup garlic, minced
- 1 T. lemon zest, minced
- 1 T. kosher salt
- 1 T. black pepper

For the Lamb—

Trim; Brown in 2 T. Olive Oil:

4–8 lb. leg of lamb, bone-in

Coat Lamb with:

Olive oil

Herb Rub, *above*

Add to Roasting Pan:

2 cups chicken broth

Combine herbs, garlic, zest, salt, and pepper for rub.

Trim lamb of fat, leaving a thin layer, *see Figure 1*. Heat oil over high heat in roasting pan; brown lamb on all sides, *see Figure 2*. Remove lamb; set aside until cool enough to apply rub, *see Figure 3*. Preheat oven to 350°.

Coat lamb with olive oil and Herb Rub. Cover loosely with foil and roast for 1 hour, *see Figure 4*. Remove foil; rotate pan. Finish roasting, *see chart at left*.

4 Roast at 350° for 1 hour. Remove foil; rotate pan. Finish roasting, *see chart above*.

buying lamb

Because it's fed mainly grain, domestic lamb tends to have a milder flavor than imported lamb. Buy the second one down, a *center cut leg roast*. This gives you the leg "look" as well as the meatiest parts. It's also easy to handle before and after roasting, making carving a snap.

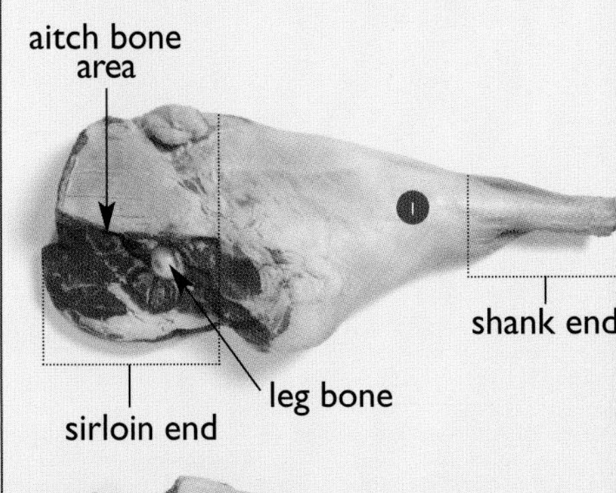

▲ *1) Whole leg: includes full sirloin and shank end. It's best to have aitch bone (hip) removed for easy carving.*
2) Center cut leg roast: sirloin end and aitch bone removed. Lower part of shank is also removed.
3) Rump portion: sirloin and entire shank removed making a uniform shape for evenly cooked meat.
4) BRT (boned, rolled, and tied): boneless leg of lamb. Perfect for grilling when untied and marinated.

roasted lamb
with braised white beans

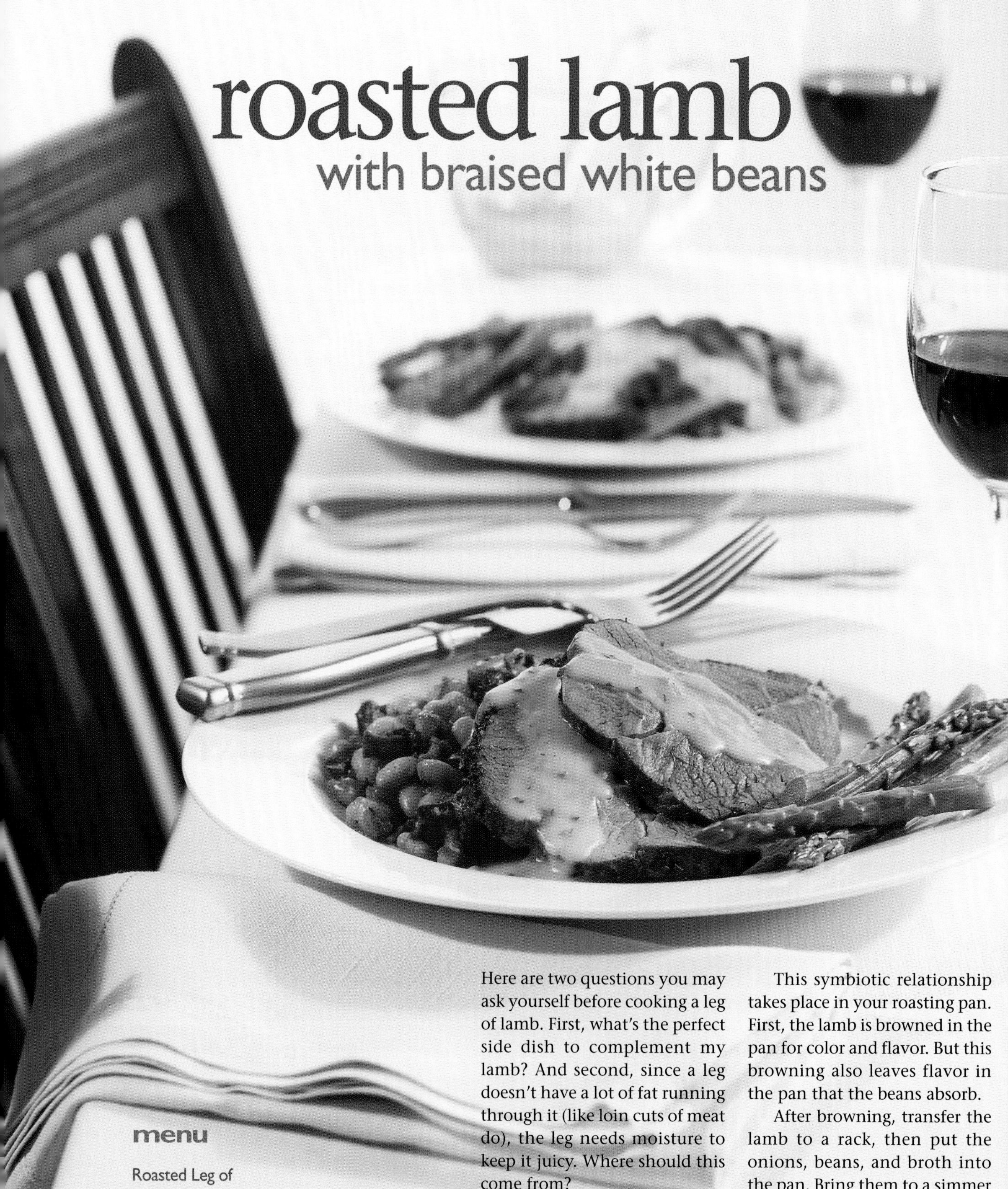

menu

Roasted Leg of Lamb with White Beans and Chardonnay Sauce

Roasted Asparagus

Lemon Tart

Here are two questions you may ask yourself before cooking a leg of lamb. First, what's the perfect side dish to complement my lamb? And second, since a leg doesn't have a lot of fat running through it (like loin cuts of meat do), the leg needs moisture to keep it juicy. Where should this come from?

The answer is simple—Great Northerns beans. The lamb and beans work in harmony. Not only do they pair well for flavor, but they conveniently take the same amount of time to cook.

This symbiotic relationship takes place in your roasting pan. First, the lamb is browned in the pan for color and flavor. But this browning also leaves flavor in the pan that the beans absorb.

After browning, transfer the lamb to a rack, then put the onions, beans, and broth into the pan. Bring them to a simmer (right on the stove), place the lamb over the beans, and roast as usual. The beans add moisture to the lamb as they braise, while juices from the lamb drip into the beans. Pretty neat system!

Preparing the beans

Before cooking dried beans, it's best to soak them overnight to soften their outer shell. This allows plenty of time for the bean's starch to soak up water.

Soaking methods

There are two ways to soak beans: overnight or with a quick-soak method. I've tested this repeatedly and have come to one conclusion—soak them overnight. Dried beans (especially white or year-old beans) need long soaking. This gives the bean's starches plenty of time to absorb water for full softening. Once heated, the starches no longer absorb but constrict.

In the same roasting pan you used to brown the lamb, saute the onions and pancetta, *see Figure 1*. The onions should release enough moisture to loosen the flavorful bits of lamb left from browning—just like deglazing. Add the drained, soaked beans to the pan and immediately stir in *cold* chicken broth, *see Figure 2*.

Cold Broth: The trick to cooking dried beans is adding cold liquid, never hot. Heat constricts starches, making it almost impossible to soften them no matter how long they're cooked—especially white beans.

Roasting: Bring beans to a simmer, then position the lamb (on a rack) over them, *see Figure 3*. Lightly tent the pan with foil, then roast the lamb and beans for an hour. Add tomatoes to the beans, *see Figure 4*, and stir in a little liquid (broth or water) if necessary.

Cook the lamb and beans, uncovered, until done, 1–1 1/2 more hours. Allow the leg to rest, tented, for 10 minutes before carving.

Roasted Lamb with White Beans

If the beans are still slightly firm when the lamb is done, simmer them on the stove while the lamb is resting.

Makes One 4–8 lb. Leg and 6 Cups Beans; Total Time: 2–3 Hours

For the Lamb—

Trim:

4–8 lb. leg of lamb, bone-in

Coat with:

Olive oil
Herb Rub, *see Page 13*

For the Beans—

Saute in 2 T. Olive Oil:

1 yellow onion, chopped
1/2 cup pancetta, diced

Add:

1 lb. white beans, soaked, drained, and rinsed
4 cups low-sodium chicken broth, cold

Add:

2 cups tomatoes, chopped

Trim lamb and brown as shown on Page 12.

Coat the leg of lamb with olive oil and Herb Rub. Preheat oven to 350°.

Saute onion and pancetta in roasting pan over high heat until soft, *see Figure 1*.

Add the soaked white beans and broth, *see Figure 2*. Bring beans to a boil and place lamb on roasting rack over beans, *see Figure 3*. Cover loosely with foil; roast 1 hour.

Add tomatoes to beans, *see Figure 4*, then finish roasting lamb, uncovered, to desired doneness, *see chart, Page 13*.

1 Brown lamb; saute onions and pancetta in oil in roasting pan.

2 Add beans; stir in cold broth and bring mixture to a boil.

3 Position lamb over beans. Cover loosely with foil and roast.

4 After 1 hour, remove foil. Stir in tomatoes. Rotate pan and finish roasting without foil.

cuisinetechnique

Carving lamb

Allowing the roast to rest plus a few simple carving steps will put beautiful leg of lamb slices on your platter.

1 After resting 10 minutes, slice a small section from bottom of roast. This will steady the roast when slicing other side.

2 With the meatiest part facing up, cut slices against the grain, leaving them attached at the bone.

3 Turn the knife parallel to the bone and release the slices in a sawing motion.

4 Turn leg over and carve smaller slices from the other side.

There are two traditional carving techniques used to carve leg of lamb. One slices the lamb lengthwise—parallel to the bone. It's the technique most often used in cookbooks, but I have no idea why. The slices are long and sinewy because you're cutting *with* the grain of the meat.

Once you start cutting this way, you'll quickly realize that the well-done outside pieces are loaded with herb rub while the rarer, interior cuts have none of the flavorful crust. There are just too many disparities in the slices for a nice presentation.

But there is a better way—slice the lamb perpendicular to the bone like you would a ham. The slices are all uniform in flavor, appearance, and doneness.

Carving

The leg has a meaty side where most of the nice slices come from. If you have a hard time figuring which part that is, use a skewer to probe for the bone.

Once you find that chunk of meat, flip the roast over and slice a flat place off the other side, *see Figure 1*. This keeps the roast steady while you carve nice slices from the other side.

Now, carve the meaty portion into thin slices by cutting perpendicular to the bone, *see Figure 2*. Once those are cut, carve along the bone to remove the slices, *see Figure 3*. They'll fall off the bone easily so you can make a beautiful presentation on a platter.

Chardonnay sauce

Chardonnay sauce is as quick as it is colorful. Perfect for all types of spring recipes, from grilled vegetables to roasted meats.

There are two reasons to make this sauce. First, it doesn't need meat drippings for good flavor. And second, this sauce is versatile—it can go on roasts, fish, or even vegetables. The base is made from chardonnay and chicken broth. After reducing, it's thickened with a paste called beurre manié [burr mahn-YAY].

Beurre manié is a quick sauce thickener made from equal parts butter and flour. Unlike a roux, it is not cooked.

Put equal parts soft butter and flour in a bowl and mix to a paste with a fork (or your hands). Then whisk a little paste into the simmering sauce base until it's the thickness you want.

Makes 2 Cups
Total Time: 15 Minutes

For the Beurre Manié—
Combine:
2 T. unsalted butter, softened
2 T. all-purpose flour
For the Chardonnay Sauce—
Boil:
1 1/2 cups chardonnay
1 1/2 cups low-sodium chicken broth
1/2 cup shallots, diced
Whisk in:
1 T. Dijon mustard
Add:
Beurre manié
Stir in:
1 T. minced fresh parsley
Season with:
Salt and cayenne to taste

Combine butter and flour with a fork or fingers to form a paste; set aside.
Boil the chardonnay, broth, and shallots in a saucepan over medium-high heat. Reduce by half (1 1/2 cups), 8–10 min. Strain reduction through a fine mesh strainer into a clean saucepan.
Whisk in Dijon; bring to a boil.
Add beurre manié by tablespoons, whisking constantly, until sauce thickens. Boil 1 minute to cook out the "starchy" taste from the flour.
Stir in parsley off heat.
Season with salt and cayenne.

make it a menu

Mashed potatoes are a natural with lamb. The mustard sauce is actually more of a brown sauce.

Roasted Leg of Lamb with Mustard Sauce*

Sauteed Spinach with Garlic

Horseradish Mashed Potatoes

Lemon Tartlets

Horseradish Mashed Potatoes

Can't remember when you bought that jar of horseradish? Buy a new jar—its pungency fades with age.

Makes 6 Cups
Total Time: 25 Minutes

Cook and Rice:
3 lbs. russet potatoes, peeled, cut into 1 1/2" chunks (about 7 cups)
Simmer; Add to Potatoes:
1 1/2 cups whole milk
4 T. unsalted butter
Stir in:
2 T. jarred horseradish
Salt to taste

online **extra**

***Want more info?** Visit www.CuisineAtHome.com for the *Mustard Sauce* recipe and color photo guide.

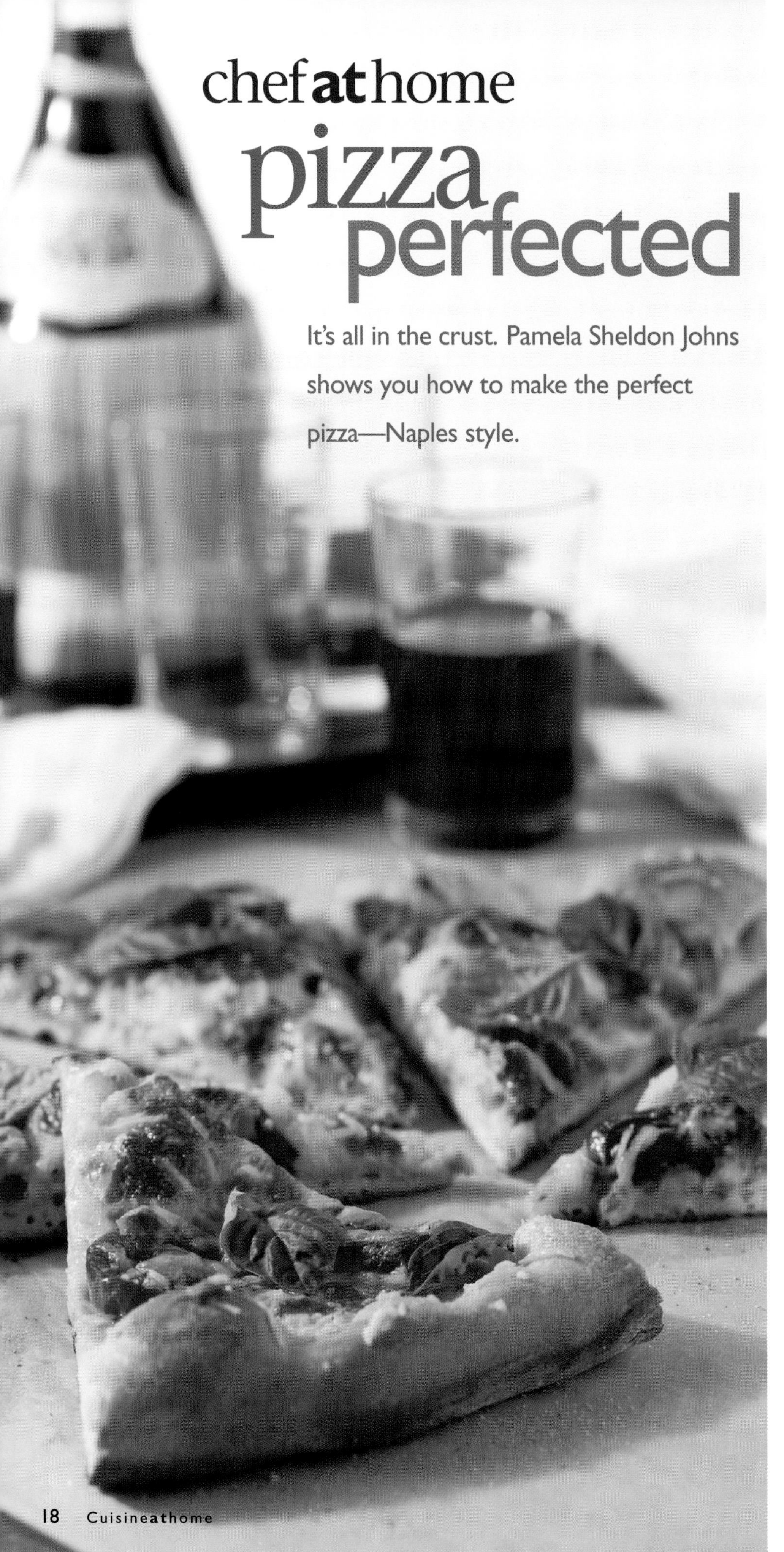

chef**at**home

pizza perfected

It's all in the crust. Pamela Sheldon Johns shows you how to make the perfect pizza—Naples style.

There's no denying it—the crust makes the pizza. So what makes a good crust, and is it the same as a real Italian pizza crust?

I turned to Pamela Sheldon Johns for the answers. Pamela not only lives in Tuscany but has also written *Pizza Napoletana*, a terrific, in-depth cookbook on authentic Italian pizza.

Pamela explained that pizza is taken so seriously in Naples that the same type of controlling board which regulates wine has been established to do the same for pizza. This denomination of controlled origin (DOC) is very specific about the ingredients in pizza dough and its rising time.

The dough is made from just four ingredients: soft flour, water, salt, and yeast. It's kneaded for 30 minutes then left to rise for four hours. After this first rise, it's shaped into smaller balls and allowed to rise another two to four hours. The dough should not be disturbed until it's ready to be shaped into a pizza. Only then can it be stretched by hand—never by a machine.

About Pamela Sheldon Johns
Pamela lives full-time in Tuscany writing cookbooks and managing Poggio Etrusco, her olive oil-producing farm and agriturismo. Some of her many books include Pizza Napoletana, Gelato, *and* Pasta! *which are published by Ten Speed Press.*

See ***www.FoodArtisans.com*** *for more information about her cookbooks, culinary workshops in Italy, and week-long apartment rentals at Poggio Etrusco.*

Now most of us don't have soft Italian flour, nor do we have the six to eight hours required to let it rise. So Pamela suggested this quicker, crustier dough for our American tastes. (On Page 20, she shares her recipe for authentic Neapolitan pizza dough.)

Flour: When we first made the classic pizza, I noticed how soft the crust was. Pamela said the flour we were using was soft "00" Italian flour. You can approximate it using three parts all-purpose flour to one part cake flour.

She did concede that, for a popular modification, you can use a high-protein bread or semolina flour in place of cake flour for a crisper crust. That's what we're doing in this recipe.

Yeast: Yeast is a living entity. To make sure it is alive, you need to "proof" or *prove* it's active. While Pamela rarely uses sugar (it is not allowed according to DOC rules), she did add it here. By feeding sugar to the yeast, activation is accelerated, requiring less time to rise.

She warns, however, that by forgoing the slower rise, the dough tends to lose some of the rich, deep flavor that develops slowly over time.

1 Combine warm water with yeast and sugar; stir and proof.

2 Add oil to yeast mixture, then add to flour mixture. Knead for 10 minutes.

3 Let dough rise until doubled in bulk, about one hour.

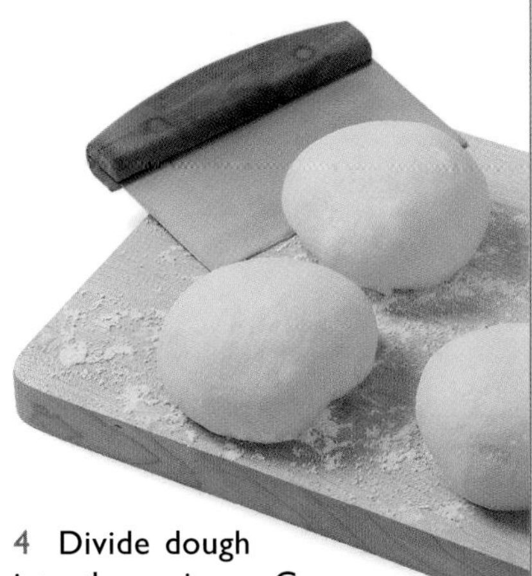

4 Divide dough into three pieces. Cover with plastic wrap and let rise.

Basic Pizza Dough

You can knead this dough by hand but I suggest using a stand mixer instead.

Makes Three 10–14" Pizzas
Total Time: 2 Hours

Combine:
1 1/2 cups warm water (105–115°)
2 T. sugar
2 1/4 t. active dry yeast (one 1/4-oz. packet)

Mix:
3 1/2 cups all-purpose flour
1/2 cup bread flour
1 T. kosher or sea salt

Add to Yeast Mixture:
3 T. extra-virgin olive oil

Pour Yeast/Oil Mixture into Flour and Knead.

Combine water, sugar, and yeast. Proof until foamy, about 5 minutes, *see Fig. 1.*
Mix flours and salt in bowl of heavy-duty stand mixer fitted with dough hook.
Add oil to yeast mixture.
Pour yeast mixture into flour mixture and knead on low speed for 10 minutes (or the same amount of time if kneading by hand). Dough will be elastic and slightly sticky, *see inset, Fig. 2.*

Place dough in a lightly oiled bowl, turning to coat. Cover with plastic wrap and let rise in a warm place until doubled, 1 hour, *see Fig. 3.*

Punch dough down and divide into three pieces; shape into balls and place on a floured work surface, *see Fig. 4.* Lightly brush dough with oil, cover completely with plastic wrap and let rise another 45 min. Meanwhile, preheat oven to 550° with stone on lowest rack.

Equipment

Both a pizza peel and stone will help deliver great results. The peel ferries the pizza to and from the oven, and a porous stone creates a crispy crust. The stone should be preheated for at least 30 minutes on the lowest oven rack.

Plenty of kneading and a long rise deliver the type of crust that Neapolitan pizza is known for.

Kneading: You could knead this dough by hand, but use a stand mixer if possible. Not only does the DOC allow it, they suggest it. "And so do I!" says Pamela. That's because authentic Neapolitan pizza dough (see recipe at right) is kneaded for 30 minutes. Make sure your mixer is powerful enough to complete the task without overheating.

Rising: There's no doubt about it—pizza dough derives its flavor and texture from a long, slow rise. The DOC stipulates the first rise last at least four hours. Then the dough is divided into softball-sized portions and allowed to rise another two to four hours.

Pamela acknowledges that this kind of time is hard to find. So her basic dough recipe increases the yeast to shorten the rise time, includes sugar and oil, and is kneaded just 10 minutes. She assures that these concessions do not sacrifice flavor.

Shaping: The dough should remain undisturbed until you're ready to shape it. With that said, take a ball of dough and using your fingers, pat it out from the center to the edge, *see Fig. 5.* Leave the edge a bit thick so it puffs when baked.

Stretch it further, lifting it by the edge and working your way around the circle, *see Fig. 6.* For thinner, crisp crust, use a rolling pin to flatten the dough into a larger circle, *see Fig. 7.* Once shaped, assemble your pizza.

5 Place risen ball of dough on a lightly floured work surface. Flatten by pressing it from the center out with fingertips.

6 Grab the dough near the edge and rotate the round, allowing dough to stretch as you turn.

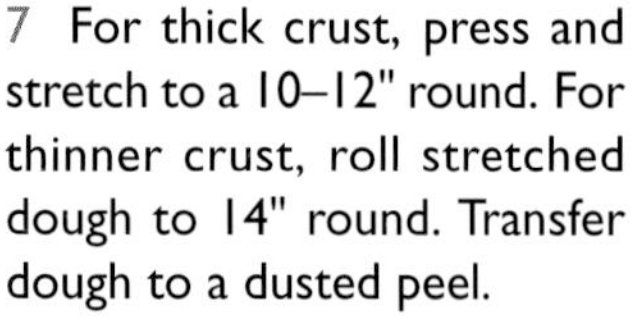

7 For thick crust, press and stretch to a 10–12" round. For thinner crust, roll stretched dough to 14" round. Transfer dough to a dusted peel.

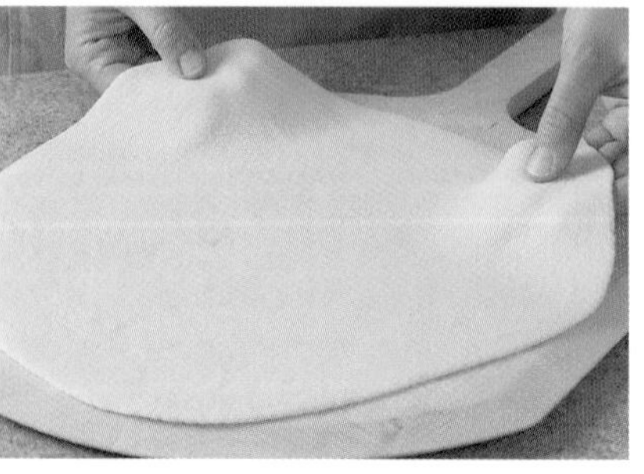

Authentic Neapolitan Pizza Dough

Pamela thought it would be a good idea to give "pizza purists" the true Neapolitan dough as governed by the UNI (the governmental agency that regulates arts, goods, and services in Italy).

Neapolitan Dough

This dough takes 6–8 hours but it's the real deal.

Makes Four 8" Pizzas

Combine:
- 1 1/2 cups warm water (105–115°)
- 1 t. active dry yeast (half of a 1/4-oz. package)

Mix with:
- 3 cups all-purpose flour
- 1 cup cake flour
- 1 T. sea salt

Add Yeast Mixture; Knead.
Cover and Let Rise.
Shape into Pizza Crusts.

Combine water and yeast. Proof until foamy, 5–8 min. **Mix** flours and salt in bowl of a heavy-duty stand mixer fitted with dough hook. **Add** yeast mixture to flour and knead at low speed 30 minutes. Shape dough into a round, place in a lightly oiled bowl, and turn to coat. **Cover** bowl with plastic wrap; let dough rise 4 hours in a warm place. Punch down, divide into 4 pieces, and shape into balls. Brush lightly with oil, cover completely with plastic wrap, and let rise another 2–4 hours. **Shape** by pressing fingertips into dough, leaving edge puffy to create a rim. Grasp rim with hands, working your way around the circle. As dough dangles, it stretches while edge stays plump.

margherita. pizza

With three ingredients, this is probably the simplest (*and best*) pizza you'll ever build!

The story of Margherita pizza is a colorful one. In 1889, Queen Margherita visited Naples. In her honor, a bread maker dressed up his flatbread to reveal the Italian colors—red tomatoes, white mozzarella, and green basil. Suffice it to say, it was a big hit and the rest is history.

Now, governmental guidelines (DOC) require that true Margherita pizza use these same three ingredients (but *only* buffalo mozzarella). It also mandates rising times for dough and wood-burning ovens for baking.

While this recipe wouldn't pass Italian regulations, it comes pretty close and still tastes great. This version uses fresh or low-moisture mozzarella instead of buffalo. And a pizza stone in your oven is a good substitute for a wood-burning oven.

The first choice for tomatoes are fresh Romas. But Italian cooks agree that canned tomatoes are an acceptable substitute when fresh tomatoes aren't in season.

▲*Spread tomatoes over pizza dough and top with slices of mozzarella.*

▲*Before baking, drizzle extra-virgin olive oil over the pizza.*

Margherita Pizza

Tomatoes, mozzarella, and basil make authentic Margherita pizza.

Makes One 10–14" Pizza
Total Time: 15 Minutes

Shape:
1 portion of Basic Pizza Dough, *Pages 19–20*

Assemble Pizza with:
3/4 cup Roma tomatoes, coarsely chopped or sliced 1/4" thick*
3–4 oz. mozzarella, thinly sliced
Sea or kosher salt to taste
Extra-virgin olive oil

Bake; Brush with:
Extra-virgin olive oil

Finish with:
8 fresh basil leaves, whole or chiffonade (thin strips)

**You may also use 3/4 cup drained canned, diced tomatoes.*

Preheat oven and stone to 550°.
Shape dough, pressing and stretching it into a 10–12" round (or rolling with a rolling pin into a thinner 12–14" round). Lift dough onto peel that's been dusted with cornmeal or flour.
Assemble pizza with tomatoes, leaving a 1" margin around the edge; top tomatoes with cheese and sprinkle with salt. Drizzle olive oil in a spiral motion from the center of the pizza to the outer edge.
Bake assembled pizza on preheated stone and bake 5–8 minutes, or until the edges and cheese are golden brown. Slide peel under pizza to remove. Brush crust edges with oil.
Finish with fresh basil, slide pizza onto a cutting board, slice, and serve.

pizza toppings

These *Cuisine Custom Toppings* can make even ready-made crusts score a perfect 10.

BBQ Chicken Pizza

Store-bought rotisserie chicken and BBQ sauce make this easy.
Makes One 12" Pizza

Toss Together:
2 cups cooked chicken, diced
1/2 cup purchased BBQ sauce
Shape Dough; Brush With:
Extra-virgin olive oil
Kosher or sea salt to taste
Assemble Pizza With:
1 cup fontina cheese, grated
Prepared BBQ chicken
1/2 cup tomatoes, chopped
1/2 cup red onion, thinly sliced
Bake; Brush Crust With:
Extra-virgin olive oil
Garnish With:
1/4 cup coarsely chopped cilantro

Toss chicken with BBQ sauce.
Shape pizza dough; brush with oil and sprinkle with salt.
Assemble pizza, topping it first with cheese then following with the chicken, tomatoes, and onion.
Bake as on Page 21. Brush crust edges with olive oil.
Garnish pizza with cilantro and serve immediately.

Potato-Sausage Pizza

The Swiss cheese and potato combination make this pizza unique.
Makes One 12" Pizza

Shape Dough; Brush With:
Extra-virgin olive oil
Kosher or sea salt to taste
Assemble Pizza With:
1 cup Swiss cheese, grated
1 cup fresh spinach leaves
2 cups red potatoes, unpeeled, sliced, cooked
2 cups cooked Italian link sausage, cut into 1/2"-thick rounds
Bake; Brush Crust With:
Extra-virgin olive oil
Sprinkle With:
Crushed red pepper flakes

Shape pizza dough; brush with oil and sprinkle with salt.
Assemble pizza, topping it first with cheese then following with a layer of spinach, cooked potato slices, and sausage.
Bake as on Page 21. Brush crust edges with olive oil.
Sprinkle with red pepper flakes and serve immediately.

Mesclun Pizza

Pizza and salad in one! A bottled vinaigrette on the salad is fine too.
Makes One 12" Pizza

For the Vinaigrette—
Combine:
2 T. balsamic vinegar
2 T. extra-virgin olive oil
1 t. garlic, minced
1/2 t. sugar
Salt to taste

For the Pizza—
Shape Dough; Brush with:
Extra-virgin olive oil
Kosher or sea salt to taste
Assemble Pizza with:
1/2 cup mozzarella or provolone cheese, grated
1/4 cup Parmesan, grated
3 Roma tomatoes, thinly sliced
Bake; Brush Crust with:
Extra-virgin olive oil
Toss with Vinaigrette; Top Pizza with:
3–4 cups mesclun (baby salad greens)
Sprinkle with:
1/4 cup goat cheese, crumbled

Combine vinaigrette ingredients and set aside.
Shape pizza dough; brush with oil and sprinkle with salt.
Assemble pizza with cheeses and tomatoes.
Bake as on Page 21. Brush crust edges with olive oil.
Toss vinaigrette with greens then arrange on top of pizza.
Sprinkle crumbled goat cheese over the greens and serve.

Pizza with Chicken and Roasted Red Pepper Cream Sauce

Move over tomato sauce—this rich red pepper sauce is a nice change of pace. You may want to continue the Southwestern theme with black beans, sour cream, or lime-grilled shrimp.
Makes One 12" Pizza

For the Red Pepper Sauce—
Reduce:
2 cups heavy cream
Roast and Puree:
1 red bell pepper
Blend with:
Reduced cream
Salt to taste

For the Pizza—
Shape Dough; Brush with:
Extra-virgin olive oil
Kosher or sea salt
Assemble Pizza with:
Red pepper sauce
1 cup white cheddar, grated
1 cup frozen corn kernels, thawed
2 cups cooked chicken, diced
4 jalapeños, seeded, sliced into rings
Bake; Brush Crust with:
Extra-virgin olive oil
Garnish with:
1/4 cup scallions, minced

Reduce cream by half in small saucepan over med.-high heat, 10 minutes.
Roast bell pepper; cool, peel, seed, and chop. Place pepper in blender and puree until smooth.
Blend pepper puree with cream and salt to taste.
Shape dough; brush with oil and sprinkle with salt.
Assemble pizza, topping it with some pepper sauce then following with cheese, corn, chicken, and jalapeños.
Bake as on Page 21. Brush crust edges with oil.
Garnish with scallions.

chicken with preserved lemons

Will winter ever end? Eventually. But until it does, this chicken stew will help ease you out of hibernation. Its exotic flavor is sure to lift your spirits.

This is a weird time of year. Spring flowers tempt us in stores but are still a long way from our gardens. We *want* to eat like it's summer, but how can we if the grill's buried under snow?

Well, this chicken with preserved lemons may be the hit you need heading into winter's homestretch. It has the look and feel of good winter food—warm and "stew-y." But the *flavor* will convince you that spring isn't far off.

What's so special about the flavor? It's the preserved lemons. They're soft, salty, and indispensible in Moroccan cuisine (this dish is similar to traditional stews of Morocco). Nothing can replicate the lemons' flavor and texture, but in Issue 31 and on our web site are step-by-step directions to make them. Try it—it's simple and worth the time. Their flavor is really incredible.

In Morocco, they would serve couscous with this stew, but this version takes a different approach—couscous dumplings! They're simple and familiar, yet unique enough to be intriguing.

Getting started

The first step to this dish is marinating the chicken. There's not much to it, but here are a few things to keep in mind.

First, consider how long the chicken is going to marinate. You want to be sure it sits for at least an hour, but the flavor of the whole dish will increase exponentially the longer it can go. Overnight is great, but I've even taken it as long as two days—and that chicken was *really* good.

Second, it's best to use chicken thighs and legs rather than breast meat. Dark meat stays moister during the long cooking time ($1^1/_2$ hours). White meat dries out when cooked that long. If you want to use breasts for the legs or thighs, you can. Remove them after 30 minutes of cooking (leave the other pieces in for the duration), then add them back to warm through at the end.

Third, leave the skin on the chicken and use bone-in pieces. The skin carries the flavors of the marinade into the cooking liquid, and also adds richness to the sauce. The bones add body.

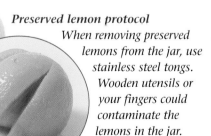

Chicken with Preserved Lemons, Olives, and Spices

Couscous Dumplings make a unique accompaniment to the chicken. But pita bread, steamed rice, and even mashed potatoes are good too.

Makes 4–6 Servings; Total Time: $2^1/_2$ Hours + Marinating Time

Combine and Marinate:
3 lbs. chicken thighs and legs
1/4 cup olive oil
1/4 cup honey
2 T. lemon juice
1 T. sweet paprika
1/2 t. ground ginger
1/2 t. crushed red pepper flakes
1/4 t. turmeric
6 cloves garlic, chopped

Layer; Sweat:
2 cups carrots, thinly sliced
2 cups yellow onion, diced
2 cups Roma tomatoes, diced
1 t. whole cumin seed
1 cinnamon stick

Add and Simmer:
Chicken and marinade
Salt and pepper to taste

Scatter Chicken with:
12 kalamata olives, pitted
1 preserved lemon, pulp removed and rind thinly sliced, *Page 26*

Add, If Necessary:
Up to 1 cup water

Cook:
Couscous Dumplings, *Page 27*

Garnish with:
1 preserved lemon, pulp removed and rind thinly sliced, *Page 26*
1/4 cup fresh cilantro leaves

Combine chicken with oil, honey, lemon juice, spices, and garlic in a resealable plastic bag. Chill and marinate at least one hour or overnight.

Layer vegetables in a large saute pan then sprinkle with cumin seed and cinnamon stick. Cover and sweat over medium-low heat until juices are released, 25 minutes (do not brown).

Add chicken and its marinade; season with salt and pepper. Replace lid slightly askew (so steam can escape) and simmer 45 minutes. Flip chicken pieces over and lightly season again with salt and pepper. Replace lid (still askew) and cook until chicken is very tender, 45 more minutes.

Meanwhile, pit olives then slice preserved lemons as described on Page 26; set aside. Prepare dumpling batter as on Page 27 and set aside.

Scatter the olives and half of the sliced lemons over the chicken; simmer, uncovered, 5–8 minutes. Transfer chicken to a platter and cover with foil to keep warm.

Add up to 1 cup of water if necessary for the dumplings to simmer.

Cook dumplings as on Page 27.

Garnish chicken and dumplings with preserved lemon rind and cilantro.

Preserved lemon protocol

When removing preserved lemons from the jar, use stainless steel tongs. Wooden utensils or your fingers could contaminate the lemons in the jar.

online **extra**

Want to make preserved lemons? For the recipe and step-by-step photos, visit www.CuisineAtHome.com

Simple stewing

Moroccan cooks call this type of dish a tagine [tah-ZHEEHN], referring to the cone-shaped clay vessel it's cooked in. But in American kitchens, this is a stew—with three simple steps.

▲Since there's no oil in the pan, take care not to burn the vegetables as they sweat—stir them often.

Sweating

As a cooking term, "sweating" sounds odd, but it's a way to cook vegetables without adding color. Browning *does* make food taste and look good, but it's not desirable here. The flavor it would impart won't be very noticeable (the stew has lots of flavor as it is). And "pristine" vegetables give the dish its vibrant color.

To sweat, cook the vegetables, covered, over medium-low heat. As juices are released, steam forms—this moisture helps prevent browning. But watch out. The vegetables still can scorch.

▼Arrange the chicken over the vegetables. It may be a tight fit—overlap the pieces slightly if needed.

Stewing

After sweating, place the chicken on top of the vegetables, pour in the excess marinade (since it'll boil, there are no worries about contamination from the chicken), and season. Cover the pan, but this time place the lid slightly askew so steam can escape. Stew the chicken 45 minutes, turn the pieces over, cover (again, askew), and continue stewing until the meat nearly falls off the bone.

Finishing

Add the olives and strips of pre served lemon rind. Simmer th stew, uncovered, to blend the fla vors. Stop right here, or kee going with the dumplings, *righ*

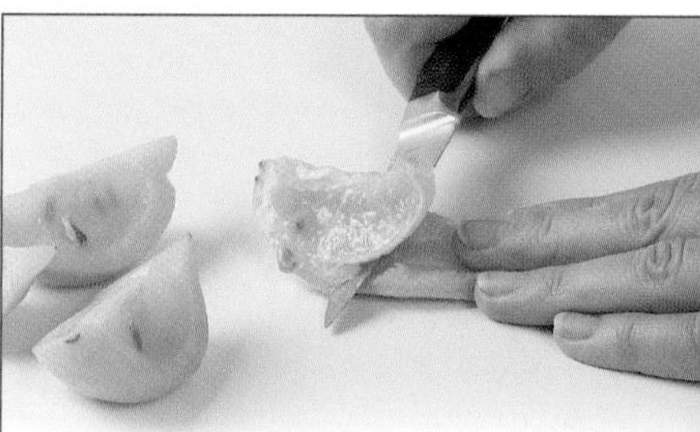

Preparing the lemons

To prepare the preserved lemons, rinse them in warm water to remove oil and salt. Slice into quarters, scrape out the pulp with the back of a paring knife, then discard the pulp (it's very salty). Now thinly slice the rind into strips.

After cooking $1\frac{1}{2}$ hours, add the olives and rind of one preserved lemon to the stew; simmer briefly. ►

couscous dumplings

It's not often that dumplings come along with all the right qualities. But these have them—light, fluffy, and flavorful.

There's *nothing* wrong with plain old chicken and dumplings. But since the stew on Pages 24–26 takes a Moroccan turn, it's logical the dumplings follow.

These drop dumplings are unique because they have couscous [KOOS-koos] in them (along with sugar and spices common in Morocco). Couscous is actually a type of pasta shaped into tiny grains. It usually comes precooked and dried, and must be steamed before eating. But don't bother with that here—the couscous will soften as the dumplings steam in the sauce.

To make the dumplings, remove the chicken from the pan, transfer it to a plate, and cover with foil to keep warm. Now add up to a cup of water to the sauce so the dumplings have enough liquid to simmer properly.

Drop heaping tablespoons of batter into the sauce—be sure to keep them small! If big, the outside will overcook and fall apart before the center is done. And don't let the sauce boil too hard or the dumplings may disintegrate.

Couscous Dumplings

These dumplings are slightly sweet—perfect with the spiciness of the chicken.

Makes About 18 Dumplings
Total Time: 15 Minutes

Mix Together:

3/4 cup all-purpose flour
1/2 cup dry instant couscous
1 T. sugar
2 t. baking powder
1/2 t. kosher salt
1/4 t. ground cinnamon
1/4 t. ground ginger

Cut In:

2 T. cold unsalted butter, cubed

Whisk Together; Stir In:

1/3 cup milk
1 egg

Drop Batter into Sauce.

Cover and Steam.

Mix dry ingredients together in a medium bowl.

Cut in butter with a pastry blender until the size of peas.

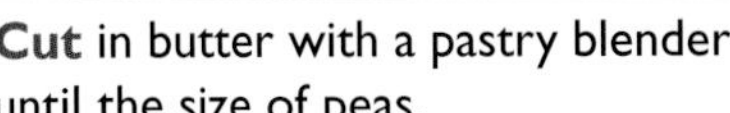

Whisk egg and milk in a bowl; stir into dry ingredients. Transfer chicken to a plate; cover. Add water to sauce.

Drop batter into *barely* simmering sauce using a small scoop or by tablespoonfuls.

Cover and steam dumplings for about 8 minutes. Don't peek *too* often, but monitor the heat so sauce doesn't boil too vigorously.

Angel hair pasta with preserved lemons

The possibilities are practically endless when you have preserved lemons on hand—these pastas are case in point.

It's amazing how one ingredient can make the difference between good and great food. These pasta dishes taste fine without preserved lemons, but their flavor really takes off when the lemon is in there too. Once you understand what these lemons can do for your cooking, you'll be glad you have them.

The pasta with broccoli is quick, clocking in at under an hour from start to finish. For a more substantial dish, try the recipe with bacon and scallops. Scallops are a great addition to pasta dishes because they cook so quickly, but be careful not to *overcook* them as they reheat in the sauce.

Angel Hair Pasta with Preserved Lemons and Broccoli

Other pastas you can use include linguine and thin spaghetti. And do not leave off the bread crumb garnish! It adds great texture.

Makes 4 Cups; Total Time: 45 Minutes

For the Garnish—

Toast in 1 T. Olive Oil:

1 cup coarse bread crumbs (made from a hearty-style French bread)

Toss Crumbs with:

Chopped fresh parsley

For the Pasta Sauce—

Saute in 1 T. Olive Oil:

3 T. shallots, minced

1/2 t. garlic, minced

1/4 t. crushed red pepper flakes

Add and Reduce:

1 cup dry white wine

3/4 cup low-sodium chicken broth

1/2 cup heavy cream

Pepper to taste

Combine:

1 preserved lemon, pulp removed, rind diced, *Page 26*

3 T. Parmesan cheese, grated

For the Pasta—

Cook:

1/2 lb. dry angel hair pasta

Add to Pasta Water and Cook:

1/2 lb. broccoli florets

Toast bread crumbs in olive oil in a small skillet until golden brown, tossing frequently. Transfer to a small bowl.

Toss crumbs with parsley.

Saute shallot in oil in a large skillet over medium heat. Cook just until soft, about 5 minutes (do not brown). Add garlic and pepper flakes; saute 1 minute.

Add wine and broth; increase heat to medium-high and simmer until reduced by 1/3, about 7 minutes. Add cream and simmer 2–3 more minutes until slightly thickened.

Combine lemon rind and Parmesan in a large mixing bowl.

Cook the pasta as directed on the package.

Add broccoli to the pasta water when pasta has 2 minutes left to cook. Drain pasta and broccoli (don't rinse) then add to the lemon rind and cheese. Pour sauce over pasta and toss to coat. Sprinkle with bread crumb garnish and serve.

◄ *Stir shallots often to prevent browning. Otherwise the sauce will turn dark.*

Add cream ► and reduce. The sauce is supposed to be a little bit thin, not too thick.

▲*Don't rinse the pasta after draining. The starch on it helps the sauce cling.*

Adding on

Pasta with Preserved Lemons, Scallops, and Bacon

*Smaller bay scallops may be used here, but cook them just 3–4 minutes **total**. Shrimp are also good in this dish.*

Makes 4 Cups; Total Time: 50 Minutes

Saute and Drain:

1/4 cup bacon, diced

Sear:

12 sea scallops (about 1/2 lb.)

Prepare:

1 recipe Pasta Sauce, *left,* omitting the olive oil

1/2 lb. dry angel hair pasta, omitting the broccoli florets

Add to Sauce:

Reserved bacon and scallops

Toss Pasta with:

1 preserved lemon, pulp removed, rind diced, *Page 26*

3 T. Parmesan cheese, grated

Garnish with:

Chopped fresh chives

Saute bacon in a large skillet over medium-high heat until crisp. Drain on a paper towel-lined plate.

Sear scallops in drippings 3 minutes per side until golden and nearly cooked through; set aside with bacon. Pour off all but 1 T. drippings.

Prepare sauce as described in the recipe at left. Cook pasta as directed on the package and drain (don't rinse).

Add bacon and scallops to sauce and simmer 1–2 minutes, or until heated through.

Toss drained pasta with preserved lemon and cheese. Pour sauce over pasta; toss to coat.

Garnish with chopped fresh chives.

Cook bacon until crisp to render all the fat.▼

▲*Scallops sear best over high or medium-high heat.*

allabout lentils

Lentils are not glamorous, but there's a lot lurking behind their unassuming nature. It's time to pay homage to this humble bean.

There is a group of foods that rests solely on its nutritional merits. These foods may not look beautiful or be anything you crave, but they stay in the food chain rotation because of their redeeming health attributes.

For me, lentils used to be in this category, but not anymore. They won't win any beauty contests, but they *should* be taken seriously for their flavor, not to mention the glowing nutritional stats that go with them (high protein and fiber, low fat).

Varieties and characteristics

Lentil varieties are characterized mainly by size and color. The most common in the States is the pea-sized, olive-colored "USA regular," *below center* (also labelled "brown" or "green" lentils). If there is one variety in stores, this is the one you'll find. They are inexpensive and can be used in a myriad of ways, from soups and stews to veggie burgers. Avoid them for salads, though—they can turn to mush quickly.

French green lentils (also called lentilles du Puy), *below left,* were once only imported from France and relegated, by and large, just to restaurants. But now they're cultivated domestically and are a lot easier to find in markets, especially natural food and gourmet stores. French green lentils are smaller and rounder than brown lentils, dark green on the outside and streaked with black. They hold their shape well and are perfect in salads or soups where the lentils should remain whole for looks.

Red lentils (which turn gold when cooked) come in a couple of shapes and sizes. The red chief, *below right,* is the most typical, similar in both size and shape to brown lentils. The petite crimson is smaller and cooks faster than red chief, but use them interchangeably.

Grocery stores don't always carry red lentils so look at natural food, gourmet, or ethnic stores first. These lentils cook quickly and don't hold their shape well—they are best used in soups, purees, or stews.

Cooking

Lentils are cooked just like dried beans, but they have the upper hand in terms of speed. Lentils don't need presoaking like beans do, and cook in as little as 10–15 minutes (red) or up to 30–40 (brown and French green). Not bad since beans can take hours.

Before cooking, sort lentils to remove stones or clumps of dirt. Spread them on a baking sheet and sift through them with your fingers. You may not find much, but it's best to be on the safe side.

Lentils nearly triple in volume as they cook. Use plenty of water for even cooking—a 3:1 water-lentil ratio is a good benchmark (any excess can be drained off after cooking). And avoid salting the water. It toughens the skin so the lentils won't soften.

sloppy joe lentils

Don't think the words "vegetarian" and "burger" belong together? Then close your eyes and take a bite of this sandwich—yes, meatless can actually taste great!

Lentil Sloppy Joes

These Sloppy Joes also make a good stand-in for baked beans.
Makes 2½–3 Cups
Total Time: 40 Minutes

Sort and Cook:
1 cup brown lentils

Saute in 1 T. Vegetable Oil:
1 cup yellow onion, chopped
1 T. garlic, minced

Add:
1 cup ketchup
1/4 cup pure maple syrup
1 T. prepared yellow mustard
1 T. apple cider vinegar
1/8 t. ground ginger
Tabasco to taste
Salt and pepper to taste

Stir in:
Cooked lentils

Serve Sloppy Joes with:
Toasted whole wheat buns
Pickles
Green leaf lettuce
Red onion rings

Sort through lentils, picking out stones or debris. Cover and cook lentils with 2½ cups water in a medium saucepan over medium heat until tender but not mushy, 30–35 minutes. Drain lentils and set aside.
Saute onion in oil in a saute pan over medium-high heat until soft, 8 minutes. Add garlic and saute until fragrant, 1 minute.
Add ketchup, syrup, mustard, vinegar, ginger, Tabasco, salt, and pepper. Simmer until thick and darker in color, 8–10 min.
Stir in lentils and simmer 2–3 minutes to warm through.
Serve Sloppy Joes on buns with pickles, lettuce, and onions.

lentil tabbouleh
with pitas and feta mayonnaise

A new take on a classic salad—tabbouleh with lentils! Packed with herbs and vegetables, this is a perfect springtime lunch.

Lentil Tabbouleh Salad with Pitas and Feta Mayonnaise

Use the romaine leaves and pitas to scoop up bites of salad.
Makes About 3 Cups
Total Time: 45 Minutes

For the Lemon Dressing—
Whisk:
1/4 cup lemon juice, strained
1/4 cup extra-virgin olive oil
Salt and pepper to taste
For the Salad—
Cook:
1/2 cup French green lentils
Mince:
2 cups packed parsley
3/4 cup packed cilantro
3/4 cup packed mint leaves
Combine Lentils with:
Lemon Dressing, *above*
Minced herbs
1 cup grape tomatoes, halved
1 cup cucumber, seeded, diced
1/4 cup red onion, diced
For the Feta Mayonnaise—
Blend:
1/4 cup mayonnaise
1/4 cup feta cheese, crumbled
1 clove garlic, chopped
Lemon juice to taste
Pinch sugar
Assemble Salad with:
Romaine lettuce leaves
Toasted pita triangles with Feta Mayonnaise
Olive oil and pepper

Whisk lemon juice in a small bowl while slowly drizzling in oil. Season dressing with salt and pepper and set aside.
Cook lentils, covered, in 1 1/2 cups water in a heavy saucepan. Simmer until tender and most of the water has evaporated, 25–30 minutes. Drain lentils and transfer to a bowl.
Mince herbs in a food processor fitted with a steel blade.
Combine warm lentils with dressing, herbs, tomatoes, cucumber, and onion. Let salad sit at room temperature for 15 minutes to develop flavors.
Blend ingredients for Feta Mayonnaise. Lightly oil pitas and toast under broiler. Cut into triangles; spread with mayonnaise.
Assemble salad with lettuce leaves and toasted pitas for scooping. Garnish pitas with a little bit of olive oil and freshly ground pepper before serving.

◄*Brush one side of pitas with oil. Toast under broiler, oiled side up, for 1 min. Cut into triangles.*

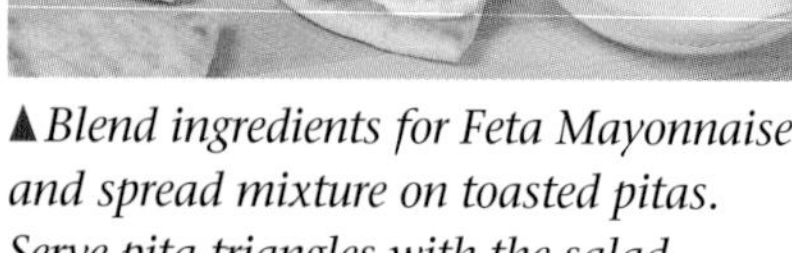

▲*Blend ingredients for Feta Mayonnaise and spread mixture on toasted pitas. Serve pita triangles with the salad.*

◄*Place lettuce leaves on serving plate and top with some of the lentil salad.*

curry-lentil soup

This Indian-inspired soup has three things going for it—simplicity, speed, and super flavor.

Curry-Lentil Soup

Curry powders vary in spiciness—use more or less depending on how hot you prefer your soup.
Makes 4 Cups
Total Time: 30 Minutes

Saute in 2 T. Melted Unsalted Butter:
1 yellow onion, finely diced

Add and Saute:
2 T. garlic, minced
2 T. fresh ginger, peeled, minced
1 T. curry powder
½ t. crushed red pepper flakes
Pinch of sugar

Add and Simmer:
4 cups vegetable broth
½ cup red lentils
Juice of 1 lime

Stir In:
¼ cup heavy cream
Salt to taste

Garnish With:
¼ cup sweetened, shredded coconut, toasted
¼ cup dry roasted peanuts, coarsely chopped
2 T. scallions, coarsely chopped
2 T. coarsely chopped fresh mint leaves

Saute onion in melted butter in a large saucepan over medium heat, 3–5 minutes.
Add garlic, ginger, curry powder, red pepper flakes, and sugar; saute about 1 minute.
Add broth, lentils, and lime juice. Simmer, uncovered, until lentils are soft, 15–20 minutes. Remove soup from heat.
Stir in cream and salt.
Garnish soup with coconut, peanuts, scallions, and mint.

wares
kitchen shears

From opening a package to cutting up a fryer, a good pair of shears may be one of the most important tools you have in the kitchen. So which one is best?

Kitchen shears are kind of a personal thing. After all, people use them for different purposes and every hand fits them in a different way. So unlike testing products based solely on results, testing kitchen shears put us into subjective territory.

We tested 17 pairs of kitchen shears ranging in price from $3 to $50. Since you're seeing only the top eight performers, count on all of them to be good quality shears that'll provide years of reliable service. You won't go wrong with any of them. But I will point out their strengths as well as a few possible pitfalls. Then you make the decision which pair will work best for you and your kitchen.

Shear force
Cutting apart a chicken is one of the toughest tasks in the kitchen. But a good pair of shears should be able to cut through small bones with ease.

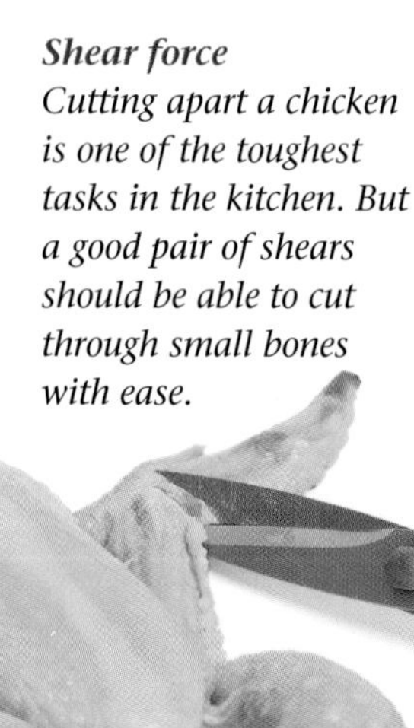

Shear criteria

A good pair of shears should be made of stainless steel, comfortable, and capable of accomplishing most cutting tasks in the kitchen. Expect them to tackle everything from string to cardboard, pastry dough to parchment, and flower stems to small chicken bones.

Shear details

Here are a few particulars to increase your shear knowledge.

Serrated: Some shears have a serrated blade. Its purpose is to grab and hold what you're cutting—especially helpful for slimy items like fish and chicken.

Types: Shears are made either by forging or stamping—both methods are effective. Forged are shaped through a process of pounding and molding a hunk of steel. Stamped shears are produced by stamping and cutting from sheets of steel.

Dishwasher safe: While many models boast "dishwasher safe," most companies do not actually *recommend* it. Treat shears just like knives—handwash and dry thoroughly.

Sharpening: Since shear blades are thicker than knife blades, they should keep an edge longer (our test-kitchen Henckels still haven't needed sharpening after five years!). But if sharpening is necessary, take them to a professional knife sharpener.

Warranty: The only test that couldn't be completed is the test of time. But since good shears usually carry a lifetime warranty, I tend to believe manufacturers are confident of durability.

Bells & whistles: Many shears boast extras like jar and bottle cap openers, or a screwdriver tab. Don't be too impressed. Most of the time, these additions are just for show and are often inadequate. But I do like that some of them come apart for cleaning.

Shear ratings & sources

The shears are rated on a scale of 0–5 stars, with 5 being the highest. Buy them at your local kitchenware store or see Resources, Page 42.

LamsonSharp Forged
★★★★

price: $29.99

These traditional shears are as sturdy as they come. They're forged, heavy, and quite capable of handling any kitchen task. A handy "breakaway" feature means they come apart easily into two pieces for thorough cleaning. Asymmetrical handles are reminiscent of Grandma's sewing scissors, and a serrated blade makes clean cuts despite the stiff opening and closing.

KitchenAid
★★★★

price: $31.99

Lightweight but sturdy, these shears open and close smoothly, making precise cuts. The long, pointed tips are able to puncture and nose their way into chicken and fish. Although the blades are sharp, it took extra effort to cut through chicken bones. Because of the type of stainless steel the blades are made from, KitchenAid actually *recommends* dishwasher use.

Chicago Cutlery Insignia
★★★½

price: $19.99

Chicago Cutlery makes good all-around shears with a serrated blade and poultry notch to help hold and cut through bones. They have ample, smooth handles, and swiftly separate into two pieces for easy washing. The opening and closing is a little stiff, but they cut decently. Available in department and kitchenware stores.

Henckels Twin Lissi
★★★★

price: $39.95

Exceptionally smooth cutting action and very sharp tips top the plus column for these sleek shears with a fine serrated blade. They emerge triumphant from even the tough stuff—bones and rose stems. Thin black fiberglass handles cover steel that runs through the handle but offers little cushion for fingers. A word of caution: Handles come together so close they can pinch fingers.

Joyce Chen
★★★★

price: $19.95

Lightweight but mighty, these little scissors cut *everything* with ease. Their design, pairing a long handle with short blades, provides surprising leverage to cut tough stuff (bones and rose stems). Flexible, spacious handles assure comfort for both right- and left-handers and accommodate even thick fingers. While more than capable, they still seem more like scissors than shears.

Wüsthof Come-Apart
★★★

price: $19.99

The best part of these shears is their come-apart feature. They disassemble in one simple move and yet never fall apart when cutting. The serrated blade opens and closes a little tight, but does an adequate cutting job. Wüsthof also makes Grand Prix shears, but since they cost more and don't disassemble, these are a better value.

Henckels Blue Dot
★★★★★

price: $15.99

Henckels has two similar lines—simply put, the blue dot and the red dot. Red dot is the original, traditional line made in Germany, while blue is their aptly named *value brand* that's made in Japan. While manufacturing processes differ, both are made with the same quality materials and requirements.

Now here's the good news. Henckels has succeeded in producing value shears that operate as well as the original red dot and maybe better! The blue dot has a roomy, comfortable handle, a serrated blade that cuts as smooth as butter, and the same lifetime warranty as the red dot. Henckels is right—these *are* a value. The Henckels Blue Dot is one good pair of shears. The reasonable price is just a bonus.

Henckels Red Dot
★★★★

price: $24.99

lemon TART

This dessert has everything going for it—true lemon flavor, great textures, and a fresh look. And did I mention that it's easy?

With the lack of seasonal fruits at hand for dessert making this time of year, it's important to have a lemon tart recipe in your repertoire. And let me tell you, this is the one you want to have.

What makes this tart special? Balance. Nothing about it tips too far one way or the other. Take the filling—it's the first place the balance can get out of whack. It's either too sweet, too eggy, too firm ... you get the idea. But not here. Now, I'll admit that I prefer a tangy lemon filling in a tart, and this is definitely tangy (it's a *lemon* tart, after all). For a more subdued filling, make it with half orange juice. But don't add more sugar to straight lemon juice—that will mess up the texture.

And if the filling's texture is off, you won't notice the crisp almond crust underneath. It's great against that smooth filling and you don't want to miss it.

So with the filling and crust in harmony, this tart is darn near perfect. But some whipped cream won't throw things off *too* much!

Making the crust

The high proportion of fat to flour makes this crust "short"—tender, crumbly, and forgiving to mix and roll. For best results, keep these things in mind.

Cubing butter
Small cubes of butter incorporate into the dough quickly and with the least amount of melting. First cut the stick of butter in half lengthwise, then cut those two halves lengthwise in half. Now slice across the sticks for cubes.

Mixing

A food processor mixes this dough quickly. Add the butter all at once and pulse just until it's the size of peas. If mixed too much, the dough will become oily and hard to roll.

How much water to add is a bit of a judgment call. The air and flour humidity can fluctuate, making it tricky to give you *exact* water quantities. The dough should hold together when pinched, but not be sticky. Start with the minimum amount of ice water, then gradually increase it as needed.

Chilling

It's critical to chill the dough, both after mixing and before prebaking. It'll roll out more easily, and won't be as apt to sink down the sides of the pan when baked.

Rolling

As you roll, lightly flour the work surface to prevent sticking. Flip and turn the dough a lot in the early stages of rolling to keep sticky spots from forming. And don't worry if the edges crack a little. Just pinch them together.

Roll the dough into a 14" circle, fold it into quarters, transfer to a tart pan, then unfold. Lift the edges of the dough, tucking it into the pan where the bottom meets the sides (try not to stretch the dough or it may shrink excessively when baked). Trim excess dough by rolling the rolling pin on top of the pan, then gently press the dough against the sides of the pan. Freeze until firm.

Prebaking

Prebake the dough in the lower third of the oven until golden on the edges and bottom. The crust can be either hot or cool when the lemon filling is added.

Lemon Tart with Almond Crust

Makes One 9" Tart
Total Time: 1 Hour + Chilling

For the Almond Crust—
Process:
1 cup all-purpose flour
1/3 cup sliced almonds
1/4 cup sugar
1/4 t. kosher salt
Pulse in:
6 T. unsalted butter, cold, cubed, *see box, left*
1/2 t. almond extract
Add; Pulse to Blend:
3–5 T. ice water

For the Lemon Tart Filling—
See Page 38

Process first four ingredients in processor fitted with steel blade until they resemble coarse sand. **Pulse** in butter and extract until butter is the size of peas. **Add** ice water; pulse to incorporate (add more water 1 T. at a time if dough seems dry). Dump dough onto a sheet of plastic wrap, form into a disk, wrap, and chill for at least 30 minutes before rolling out.

Preheat oven to 425° with rack in lower third; spray a 9" tart pan with removable bottom with nonstick spray. Roll out dough, place it in the pan, trim, then freeze. Prebake in lower third of oven 20–25 minutes, or until golden brown. Reduce heat to 325°.

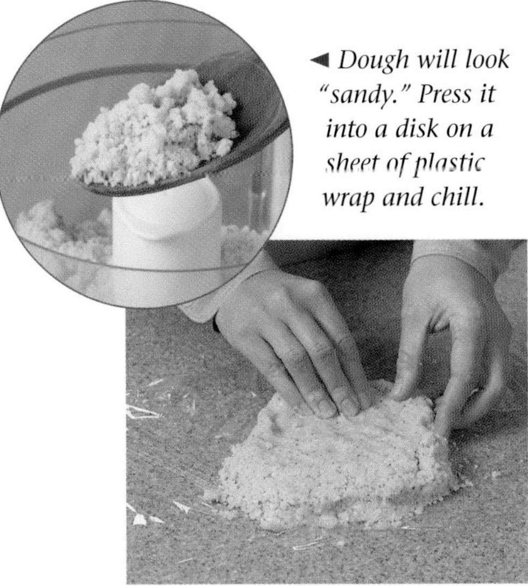

◄ *Dough will look "sandy." Press it into a disk on a sheet of plastic wrap and chill.*

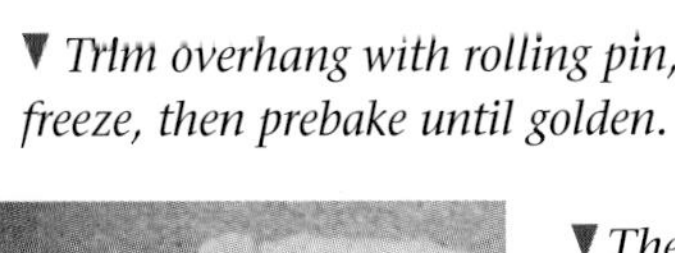

▲ *A bench scraper helps lift and move the rolled out dough to the pan.*

▼ *Trim overhang with rolling pin, freeze, then prebake until golden.*

▼ *The sides may slip a little during baking—it's okay.*

Filling and finishing

This filling adheres to the "less is more" philosophy. Because of that, the flavor is pure lemon and the texture is smooth as silk. Here's how to bring everything together.

Making the filling

One reason for the filling's incredible smoothness has to do with how it's cooked. For the best results, keep these things in mind.

First, use a nonreactive saucepan (by that, I mean one with a stainless steel interior). Otherwise, the lemon juice will react with the material (say, aluminum) and discolor. Be sure the pan has a heavy bottom and sides as well for the best heat diffusion. That will help the eggs set gently.

▼ *Shortly into cooking, the filling will be thin and liquidy.*

▲ *But it only takes about 10 min. for it to thicken properly.*

Second, cook the filling just until it thickens to a consistency of loosely whipped cream. This does not take very long—about 10 minutes. As it cooks, stir constantly with a rubber spatula, scraping the sides and bottom. And don't let the filling boil or the eggs may scramble (although the sugar and acidity of the lemon juice will help limit that).

Maybe the most critical step when making the filling is straining it. This removes the zest and any cooked bits of egg for a silky texture.

▲ *Straining the filling ensures its texture is super-smooth.*

Baking

The tart is baked briefly to just *barely* set the filling in the crust. Test it for doneness by lightly touching the center with your fingertip—it should jiggle, and some filling may stick to your finger. If the filling is firm or "bouncy," it's overdone.

Lemon Tart Filling

Gently cooking the filling will help achieve the silky texture you want. Stir constantly as it cooks.
Makes About 2 Cups

Whisk:
3 whole eggs
3 egg yolks
1 cup sugar
3/4 cup fresh lemon juice, strained (4–5 large lemons)
2 T. lemon zest (3 lemons)
Pinch salt

Add:
6 T. unsalted butter, cubed

Whisk eggs, yolks, sugar, lemon juice, zest, and salt together in a large saucepan.

Add the butter and cook over medium-low heat, stirring constantly. Cook until filling thickens slightly but is pourable, 8–10 min. Strain filling through a fine mesh strainer into the prebaked crust.

Bake tart at 325° until filling is just set, about 10 min. Cool tart before removing the sides and transferring to a serving platter.

Don't worry too much if this happens—the tart will taste fine, but the texture will be a bit firm.

Slicing and serving

Be sure the tart cools completely before removing it from the pan and slicing. I know you'd like to dig right in, but if you do, the filling will be too soft and the tart won't slice neatly.

As an added bonus, this can be made, chilled, then served the next day—or even frozen! I can attest to the fact that it tastes great straight from the freezer, but for the best flavor, it really should come to room temperature first. If you're garnishing it with berries, *right*, wait to do so until shortly before serving.

Adding on

You'll know that spring has sprung when you serve a lemon tart with strawberries. Here's how to put an elegant (but simple) "pastry shop" spin on this tart.

First, rinse and hull two pints of small, ripe, red strawberries. Now slice them by standing each one on its stem end, then cutting the berry from tip to stem end into four or five thin slices.

Arrange the slices around the baked, cooled tart, starting at the outside edge and spiraling to the center. As you go around, overlap the slices slightly, using any small pieces to fill in any gaps.

Finally, mix 3 T. apricot jam with 1 T. water and warm the mixture briefly in the microwave. Carefully glaze the berries with apricot jam before serving.

lemon tartlets with coconut crusts

Makes 8 Tartlets
Total Time: 1 Hour

Process in Food Processor:
2 cups sweetened, shredded coconut
1/2 cup sugar
Blend In:
2 egg whites
Fill Crusts With:
1 recipe Lemon Tart Filling, *Page 38*

Process coconut and sugar until coconut is minced.
Blend in egg whites. Press mixture into well-greased 4" tartlet pans with removable bottoms. Bake at 325° for 25–30 min., or until golden. Remove from pans. Prepare tart filling as on Page 38.
Fill each crust with 1/4 cup filling, bake for 7 minutes, and cool.

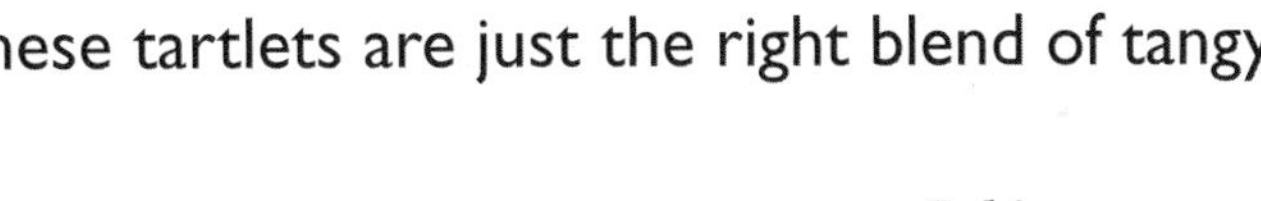

Lemon and coconut—a match made in heaven.
These tartlets are just the right blend of tangy and sweet.

Press 3 T. coconut mixture into each heavily greased tartlet pan. ►

▲Halfway through baking, press crusts down with a spoon. Return to oven and bake until golden.

▲While they're hot, carefully remove crusts from pans and remove bottoms.

With a few simple steps, you could be serving this charming spring dessert. Here's what to do.

Making the crusts

Use a food processor to make the crust mixture. The processor is the only thing that can properly pulverize the coconut. Plus, it makes mixing a breeze.

You'll need eight 4" tartlet pans with removable bottoms for this. Don't use *anything* else—the crusts stick and will be impossible to remove from other pans without breaking. Spray them *generously* with nonstick spray and place on a baking sheet.

Use your fingers to press the coconut mixture evenly on the bottom and sides of the pans. Moisten them with water periodically to prevent sticking.

Baking

Bake the tartlets in the lower third of a 325° oven. Halfway through baking, take the tartlets out of the oven and press them with the back of a teaspoon (egg whites make them puff). Return to the oven; bake until golden.

Removing and filling

Unmold the crusts while hot, *before* adding any filling (the crusts get stickier as they cool). First, loosen the sides with a knife, then carefully push the base plate up to release the rim. Slide a spatula underneath to loosen the plate. One or two crusts may break—these are the cook's treat!

Place the crusts on a parchment-lined baking sheet, fill with lemon filling, *Page 38*, and bake briefly to set. Cool and serve.

faster **with** fewer
Asparagus

Simple is best when it comes to preparing this staple of the season. These easy recipes show off the king of spring vegetables.

Asparagus, Chicken, & Mushroom Stir-fry

With or without the chicken, this is a perfect weeknight meal.

Makes About 4 Cups; Total Time: 25 Minutes

Prepare:
1 lb. asparagus, trimmed, cut into 1" pieces
8 oz. shiitake mushrooms, stems removed, sliced
4 oz. chicken breast, thinly sliced
1 T. fresh ginger, peeled, minced
3 garlic cloves, thinly sliced

Combine:
3 T. brown sugar
3 T. lime juice (1 lime)
2 T. low-sodium soy sauce
1 t. chili garlic sauce
1 t. cornstarch

Stir-fry in:
1 T. vegetable oil

Serve with:
Steamed white rice

Prepare first five ingredients, keeping the chicken separate.
Combine sugar, lime juice, soy sauce, chili garlic sauce, and cornstarch in a bowl (crush cornstarch lumps with your fingertips to dissolve). Heat oil in a large nonstick skillet over medium-high heat until it shimmers.
Stir-fry chicken in the hot oil for 1 min., stirring constantly. Add asparagus, mushrooms, garlic, and ginger; stir-fry another 4 minutes, stirring constantly to prevent the garlic and ginger from burning. Add the soy sauce mixture to the vegetables and simmer 1 minute, or until sauce reduces and thickens slightly.
Serve the stir-fry with steamed white rice.

Ham and Asparagus Sandwiches

These open-faced sandwiches are nice for brunch, served with fresh melon or a mixed green salad.

Makes 6 Sandwiches; Total Time: 25 Minutes

Blanch:
3/4 lb. asparagus spears, trimmed

Blend:
1 cup mayonnaise
3 T. orange juice
2 t. garlic, minced
2 t. sugar
1/4 t. kosher salt
1/8 t. cayenne

Assemble Sandwiches with:
6 slices (1/2" thick) French bread
2 T. unsalted butter, softened
6 oz. thinly shaved smoked ham

Cool blanched spears in ice water. Remove promptly—don't soak them.

Preheat broiler to high with rack 2" from heat.
Blanch asparagus in boiling water for 4 minutes, or until cooked but still slightly crisp. Cool in ice water and drain.
Blend the mayonnaise, orange juice, garlic, sugar, salt, and cayenne together in a small bowl.

Assemble sandwiches by spreading one side of bread slices with butter. Arrange bread on a baking sheet, buttered side up; broil just until toasted, 1 minute. Flip bread over and spread each slice with about 2 teaspoons of the mayonnaise mixture. Top with slices of ham, more mayonnaise, and spears of asparagus. Spread asparagus with more mayonnaise then broil sandwiches until mayonnaise turns golden, about 2 minutes. Rotate pan once or twice during broiling to prevent burning. Serve immediately.

"Caesar" Asparagus

Just like the classic salad but made with roasted asparagus. Serve warm or at room temperature.

Makes About 3 Cups; Total Time: 25 Minutes

Toss Together; Roast:
1 lb. asparagus spears, trimmed
1 cup hearty French bread, cut into 1" cubes
3 T. extra-virgin olive oil
Salt and pepper to taste

Blend:
1/4 cup fresh lemon juice, strained
2 T. Parmesan cheese, grated
1 t. garlic, minced
1 t. Dijon mustard
1 t. sugar
1/2 t. Worcestershire sauce
1/4 t. anchovy paste (optional)

Drizzle In:
1/4 cup extra-virgin olive oil

Garnish With:
Grated Parmesan cheese

Roast asparagus and croutons at the same time. When done, transfer to a serving platter.

Preheat oven to 425° with a rack set in the lower third. **Toss** asparagus and bread cubes with oil, salt, and pepper; spread in a single layer on a baking sheet. Roast until asparagus is cooked but still bright green and croutons are toasted, 6–8 minutes. **Blend** together the lemon juice, Parmesan, garlic, mustard, sugar, Worcestershire, and anchovy paste while the asparagus is roasting. **Drizzle** in the olive oil, whisking constantly. Transfer roasted asparagus and croutons to a serving platter, then drizzle with dressing to taste (you may not need all of it). **Garnish** with grated Parmesan before serving.

Asparagus Bundles with Hot Prosciutto Dressing

These bundles make a good side dish to roasted chicken. They're best served immediately out of the broiler.

Makes 4 Bundles; Total Time: 25 Minutes

Find prosciutto (a salt-cured Italian ham) in Italian markets. Smoked ham may be substituted.

Blanch:
1 lb. asparagus spears, trimmed

Saute in 1/4 Cup Olive Oil:
1/2 cup prosciutto, sliced (2 oz.)

Add and Reduce:
1/2 cup apple cider vinegar
1 T. shallot, chopped (1 shallot)
1 T. honey

Top Bundles with; Broil:
2 oz. fresh mozzarella, sliced

Preheat broiler to high with rack 2" from heat. **Blanch** asparagus in boiling water for 4 min., or until cooked but still slightly crisp. Cool in ice water; drain. Arrange in 4 bundles on a baking sheet. **Saute** prosciutto in oil until crisp and "frizzled." **Add** vinegar, shallot, and honey. Cook over medium heat until dressing thickens, about 5 minutes. **Top** asparagus with a slice of mozzarella; broil to melt cheese. Spoon hot dressing over and serve.

from **our** readers

Q&A
questions & answers

PASTA SHEET SOURCE
I made the cannelloni with fresh pasta from Issue 31 and loved it. I'd also like to try the purchased pasta sheet option for days I'm short on time, but I don't have access to Barilla. Is there a mail order source?

Michael Emley
Garden City, KS

You can order Barilla flat lasagna sheets from My Brands Inc. Six boxes cost $13.14, plus shipping. A box contains about 16 sheets, each measuring 6½ x 3½".

A. G. Ferrari sells flat lasagna sheets that are made in Italy (Gragnano Sfoglia brand). A package of about 30 sheets (6¾ x 3¼") sells for $3.65, plus shipping. Note that imported Italian pasta is thicker than American-made and takes longer to cook.

See Resources on Page 43 for ordering information.

ALUMINUM SAFETY
You featured aluminum bakeware in Issue 30. Is aluminum safe to cook and bake in?

Jo Borntreger
St. Joseph, MO

Despite persistent rumors to the contrary, there is no health safety issue surrounding the use of aluminum bakeware. The FDA has repeatedly assured the public that aluminum does not contribute to Alzheimer's or other diseases. Neither aluminum cookware or bakeware has been deemed unhealthy to use.

However, the Cookware Manufacturers Association has always recommended that aluminum cookware not be used to *store* foods—particularly acidic foods such as tomato sauce. Off tastes can develop when acidic food comes into contact and reacts with aluminum over a lengthy period of time.

FALLEN ANGEL (FOOD)
Will my chiffon and angel food cakes fall out of one of those new slick-surface (nonstick) pans when they hang upside down to cool? Or should I just let them cool upright?

Lois Heric
Sparks, NV

I understand your concern. It would seem that a slick nonstick pan might easily send a cake flying south. But we gave it a try in the absolute slickest pan we could find and had no problem with it falling out whatsoever.

Don't cool these types of cakes upright. Because of their airy structure, they'll settle and shrink. Cooling them upside down allows them to stretch.

CLEAN MACHINE
In Issue 31 of Cuisine at home, *I learned how to make pasta. But how should I clean my pasta machine?*

Ron Walker
San Francisco, CA

Always follow the machine manufacturer's instructions. But if you don't have the instructions available, here's what to do.

Use a dry pastry brush (or any brush that's for kitchen use only) to thoroughly sweep flour out of the rolling mechanism. If a piece of pasta is stuck in a gear, poke it out with a bamboo skewer.

The most important thing is to *never* wash the machine with water. Since the stainless steel rollers cannot be reached for thorough drying, the gears will rust and ruin the machine. Just wipe the outside with a cloth.

CONFUSING TERM
What does "fricassee" mean?

Cindy Pollock
Sioux Falls, SD

A fricassee is a thick, chunky stew, usually made with chicken. But it's difficult to give a definite procedure for cooking the chicken. Some recipes insist the meat should *not* be browned before simmering, creating a light-colored stew. Others call for initial browning which adds darker color to the stew.

BENDABLE BAKING

I've seen the new bendable baking pans in cookware stores and catalogs. What are they made of and can I really bake in them?

Petra Amstad
New York, NY

Originally used only in professional kitchens, these flexible nonstick baking "molds" are now available in sizes and shapes targeted for home bakers.

Made of silicone, they withstand high oven temperatures, bake evenly, and yet immediately stop the baked goods from cooking further after removing from the oven. Because they're pliable, molds should be placed on a baking sheet so they're easy to get in and out of the oven. Unmolding is simple—just twist!

Molds available include varying sizes of cake rounds, muffin, mini-muffin, and loaf. Some styles even *fold* for storage!

COFFEE + CHOCOLATE

Why are small amounts of coffee often added to chocolate recipes? Will the recipe suffer if I omit it?

Doreen Townsend
Perry, IA

Adding of small amounts of coffee to chocolate recipes acts as a chocolate *boost*. It enhances and deepens the intensity of the chocolate flavor. If a recipe calls for espresso powder or instant coffee, leaving it out won't affect the outcome of the recipe. But if the recipe requires liquid coffee, you must substitute the same amount of water for the coffee to make up for the loss in liquid.

Of course, any recipe with "mocha" in its title relies on a heavy chocolate-coffee combination. Omitting coffee from a mocha recipe is pointless.

Substitution tip: If a recipe calls for espresso powder, you can substitute it with $1^1/_2$ times the amount of instant coffee.

resources

PROFESSIONAL CUTLERY DIRECT
LamsonSharp Forged shears, Item #1CM201
Henckels Blue Dot shears, Item #1CM203
Henckels Red Dot shears, Item #1CM202
(800) 859-6994
www.cutlery.com

CHEF'S CATALOG
Wüsthof Come-Apart shears, Item #2094
(800) 338-3232
www.chefscatalog.com

COOKING.COM
Henckels Twin Lissi shears, Item #160096
Joyce Chen, Item #143492
(800) 663-8810
www.cooking.com

FANTE'S KITCHEN WARES SHOP
KitchenAid shears, Item #8939
(800) 44-FANTE (443-2683)
www.fantes.com

MY BRANDS INC.
Barilla lasagna sheets (six 9-oz. boxes), Item #07680-8515589
(888) 281-6400

A. G. FERRARI FOODS
Gragnano Sfoglia lasagna sheets, Item #3299
(877) 878-2783
www.agferrari.com

SEMI- VS. BITTERSWEET

What's the difference between semisweet and bittersweet chocolate? Can they be used interchangeably?

Lorraine Thomas
Caracas, Venezuela

Both bittersweet and semisweet chocolate contain chocolate liquor (essence of the cocoa bean) and sugar. But bittersweet has more chocolate liquor, giving it a stronger, more intense chocolate flavor. Depending on availability and your own taste, they can be interchanged as needed.

Baker's brand bittersweet and semisweet chocolate ►

Q&A

Do you have a question for *Cuisine at home?*

If you have a question about a cooking term, procedure, or technique, we'd like to hear from you. We'll consider publishing your question in one or more of our works. Just write down your question and mail it to *Cuisine at home*, Q&A Editor, 2200 Grand Ave., Des Moines, IA 50312, or contact us through our email address shown below. Please include your name, address, and daytime phone number in case we have questions.

Email: CuisineAtHome@CuisineAtHome.**com**
Web address: CuisineAtHome.**com**

grand**finale**

gyro tostadas

Gyro "Tostadas"

This is a great way to use leftover roasted leg of lamb, and it comes together in about half an hour. Roast the lamb over a weekend, then use the extra for these tostadas during the week.

Makes 4 Tostadas; Total Time: 20 Minutes

For the Vinaigrette—
Whisk:
2 T. fresh lemon juice
2 T. red wine vinegar
2 T. extra-virgin olive oil
1 t. garlic, minced
1 t. sugar
Salt and pepper to taste

For the Tostadas—
Saute in 2 T. Chicken Broth:
8 oz. roasted lamb, sliced
½ cup red onion, thinly sliced

Toss Vinaigrette with:
4 cups mesclun (baby salad greens)
12 grape tomatoes, halved
½ cucumber, halved, seeded, and sliced

Divide Among 4 Pitas:
Mesclun salad
Lamb-onion mixture

Garnish Tostadas With:
16 kalamata olives, pitted
¼ cup plain yogurt
¼ cup feta cheese, crumbled
Fresh mint leaves

▲ *Halve cucumber lengthwise, remove seeds, and thinly slice into half-moons.*

Whisk all vinaigrette ingredients together; set aside. **Saute** lamb and onion in broth until heated through. **Toss** mesclun, tomatoes, and cucumber with vinaigrette.

Divide salad among warmed pitas (or broil them as on Page 32); top with lamb mixture. **Garnish** tostadas with olives, yogurt, crumbled feta cheese, and fresh mint leaves.

THE BEST ITALIAN FETTUCCINE ALFREDO...AND MORE!

Cuisine at home™

www.CuisineAtHome.com

Easy to make Champagne Cake with blackberry filling

Plus:

Colorful and Flavorful—Complete Meal

Market Salads

Sizzlin' Summer Steak in 15 minutes

Keep the flavor! Secrets to a

Juicy Pork Chop

Issue No. 33 June 2002
A publication of August Home Publishing

Cuisine at home™

talk to ***Cuisine at home***
Subscriptions, Address Changes, or Questions? Write or call:

Customer Service
2200 Grand Avenue,
Des Moines, IA 50312
800-311-3995,
8 a.m. to 5 p.m., CST.

Online Subscriber Services:
www.CuisineAtHome.com
Access your account • Check a subscription payment • Tell us if you've missed an issue • Change your mailing or email address • Renew your subscription • Pay your bill

Cuisine at home™ (ISSN 1537-8225) is published bi-monthly (Jan., Mar., May, July, Sept., Nov.) by August Home Publishing Co., 2200 Grand Ave., Des Moines, IA 50312.
Cuisine at home™ is a trademark of August Home Publishing Co.

Subscriptions: Single copy: $4.99. One year subscription (6 issues), $24.00. (Canada/Foreign add $10 per year, U.S. funds.)

Periodicals postage paid at Des Moines, IA and at additional mailing offices. "USPS/Perry-Judd's Heartland Division automatable poly". Postmaster: Send change of address to **Cuisine at home**, P.O. Box 37100 Boone, IA 50037-2100.
Cuisine at home™ does not accept and is not responsible for unsolicited manuscripts. **PRINTED IN SINGAPORE.**

editor's letter

What an honor it is to have Lidia Bastianich show us how to cook pasta. Most of us have seen her on television—she has her own show, you know, and maybe you've even been lucky enough to eat in one of her five outstanding restaurants. To put it right out there, she is an all-around successful, high-profile woman.

Now, I'm going to tell you the behind-the-scenes truth about Lidia. On her television show, she comes across as a sweet Italian grandmother who wants to share her family recipes—she's everything you'd imagine an Italian cook to be. Well, that's TV, and we all know the persona is vastly different from the reality, right? The truth is, she's better, if you can believe that. Lidia and her top-rate staff could not have been nicer or more helpful to all of us. She made us feel like we were part of her family.

When we cooked fettuccine Alfredo, it was everything I remembered from Italy—the texture, the flavor, the creaminess. What I couldn't believe was how easily it came together. I don't say this often, but Lidia is magic. And now you can be part of her big family as she shares some of that magic with you.

Another topic that's near and dear to my heart is pork. We've always wanted to cook pork chops with you since the magazine started, but never found the right technique. Since pork has evolved into a meat that's as lean as chicken, a tender, juicy chop is getting harder to come by—there just isn't enough fat to keep it moist. After mixing and matching all the variables, we finally mastered the art of cooking a juicy chop. Now, understanding a few key factors, you'll put out a flavorful chop that's plenty moist and tender.

With Father's Day coming up, you might want to think about combining these two great dishes—the glazed grilled pork chops with a side of Lidia's Fettuccine Alfredo (hold the vegetables!). Yes, it's a bit over the top, but after all, it is his day.

John

table of contents

Issue No. 33 June 2002

departments

features

from **our** readers

tips
and techniques

Tip from the Test Kitchen
A drop of yolk in egg whites will ruin meringues and 7-Minute Icing. To prevent this, separate each egg into a small bowl, then transfer the white to a mixing bowl. Repeat for each egg needed.

Milder Onions

To reduce the strong flavor of onion in salsas and other uncooked foods, chop the onion and rinse it in cold water three times. Let sit in the final rinse water for 30 minutes, then drain and dry. This retains the crispness but eliminates the burn.

Steven Sano
Berkeley, CA

Coffee Treats

When you have leftover whipped cream, place it in a pastry bag fitted with a star tip, pipe it onto a parchment-lined baking sheet, and freeze. Don't feel like piping? Just drop dollops from a spoon and freeze. When frozen, transfer them into a freezer bag. They are great on top of hot chocolate or coffee.

Sarah Hunt
Portland, OR

Perfect Cuts

Use an electric knife to slice through cinnamon roll dough rather than a serrated knife or dental floss. The electric knife doesn't smash or tear the dough like the other methods.

Donald Lowe
Laguna Niguel, CA

Zest At Hand

I always peel the rind off citrus before juicing or using the fruit, and store the rind in a resealable plastic bag in the refrigerator. That way, I have zest on hand even if I don't have the fruit.

Maria del Mar Hausle
Knoxville, TN

Note: Freezing the zest works well too!

Hollowing Tomatoes

I have a great way to hollow out cherry tomatoes: Use a small (1/4 tsp.) metal measuring spoon. First remove the stem, then cut into the tomato with the edge of the spoon. Scoop out the seeds with the bowl of the spoon.

Kathy Roberts
Elmhurst, IL

Grate Butter

When making scones, I grate the butter on the large-hole side of a cheese grater instead of cutting it in with a knife. This makes the whole process easier and less messy. I found that my scones come out better too! Hold the butter by the wrapper to prevent it from melting from the warmth of your hands.

Glen Aby
Santa Clara, CA

Safe Chile Slicing

To prevent painful chile burns while dicing, hold the chile with the tines of a fork and slice it lengthwise in half, *top photo.* Then, holding one of the halves cut side up with the fork, scrape out the seeds and membranes with a spoon, *inset photo.*

Finally, place the seeded chile half cut side down and secure it in place with your fork. Cut thin slices lengthwise then slice across the strips to dice, *bottom photo.*

Karen Oberjohn
Park Hills, KY

Nonstick Strainer

Spray strainers or colanders with nonstick cooking spray before draining starchy pasta or potatoes. No sticking, easy cleanup!

Irwin Jacobson
Las Vegas, NV

Dusting Nuts

Before using chopped nuts to decorate a cake, put them in a sieve and tap out the "dust" (the powdery pieces). The nuts have a cleaner, more professional look, and the dust can be added to cake batters for extra flavor.

Desiree Steinberg
Calabasas, CA

Smashing Garlic

If you have a large amount of garlic to chop, peel the cloves and place them in a resealable freezer bag. Then, with the smooth side of a meat mallet, lightly pound the cloves until they're chopped.

Dee Regilio
Schiller Park, IL

Tea Bag Fishing

I just hate fishing for tea bags that have fallen into the pitcher during brewing. I solved that by tying the bags onto a wooden spoon, then laying the spoon across the pitcher. The bags hang in the hot water and brew the tea. When it's the strength I'm after, I just lift out the bags with the spoon.

Terry Luther
Nashville, TN

Perfect Cake Slices

Store cut cake slices by wrapping parchment or waxed paper strips around each slice. Reassemble the cake, refrigerate or freeze, and remove slices as needed. It's great when preparing for a party.

Colleen Wurtsmith
Cheyenne, WY

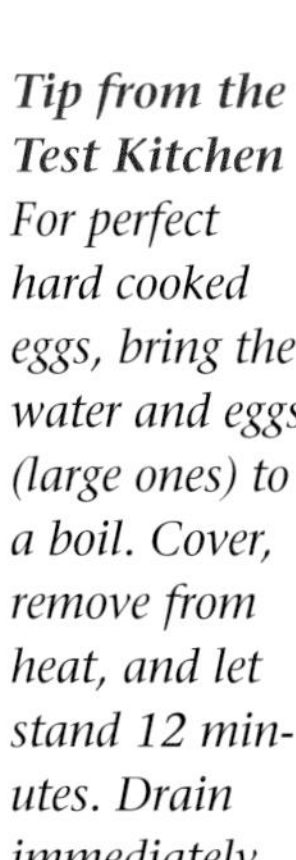

Tip from the Test Kitchen

For perfect hard cooked eggs, bring the water and eggs (large ones) to a boil. Cover, remove from heat, and let stand 12 minutes. Drain immediately and run under cold water to cool quickly.

share your tips *and techniques* with *Cuisine at home*

If you have a unique way of solving a cooking problem, we'd like to hear from you, and we'll consider publishing your tip in one or more of our works. Just write down your cooking tip and mail it to *Cuisine at home*, Tips Editor, 2200 Grand Ave., Des Moines, IA 50312, or contact us through our email address shown below. Please include your name, address, and daytime phone number in case we have questions. We'll pay you $25 if we publish your tip.

Email: CuisineAtHome@CuisineAtHome.com

Web address: CuisineAtHome.com

Roasted Chicken

Roasting a chicken has never been simpler. Here's the no-nonsense way to roast a great-tasting, juicy bird.

A lot of theories claim to be the *best* way to roast a chicken—upside down, super-high heat, brined, slow-roasted. But after trying them (plus a few others), it's nice to know that a basic approach (one oven temperature for one hour) is still the best way.

Unconventional start

That said, there are a few steps I take that aren't typical to roasting a chicken. First, remove the wishbone, *Figure 1*. I always do this with turkey to make carving easy, and it's good to do with chicken too. A chicken wishbone is smaller, though, and trickier to remove. If it breaks as you twist it out, *Figure 2*, don't panic. The two "legs" of the bone are all that really have to come out.

Second, salt the bird then chill it overnight (or even just a few hours) prior to roasting, *Figure 3*. It sounds contradictory—won't salt leech out juices? Yes, but they're reabsorbed, along with the salt. That makes for a deeply seasoned (not salty) bird.

Roasted Chicken

Makes One 3–4 lb. Chicken

Trim and Rinse:
1 3–4 lb. whole chicken

Rub Chicken with; Chill:
Kosher salt

Rinse; Drizzle with:
Juice of one lime
Kosher salt to taste

Trim chicken of excess fat and skin and remove wishbone. Rinse bird, then dry with paper towels.

Rub salt over entire chicken (including the back and inside cavity) that's been placed on a rack set over a baking sheet. Cover with plastic wrap and chill at least 4 hours or overnight. When ready to roast, preheat oven to 450° with oven rack in the center.

Rinse chicken, pat dry, and drizzle with lime juice and salt to taste. Stuff juiced lime inside cavity; loosely tie legs together with kitchen string. Roast chicken 1 hour, rotating pan occasionally. It's done when temperature is 170° in thigh and 160° in breast. Remove from oven, tent with foil, and let rest 15–20 minutes to redistribute juices before carving.

Trimming tip ► *Find wishbone at neck opening. Cut along inside and outside of both "legs." Go behind bones with knife tip; cut down to release at bottom.*

1 Cut around the wishbone, 1/2" deep. Then cut behind the bones.

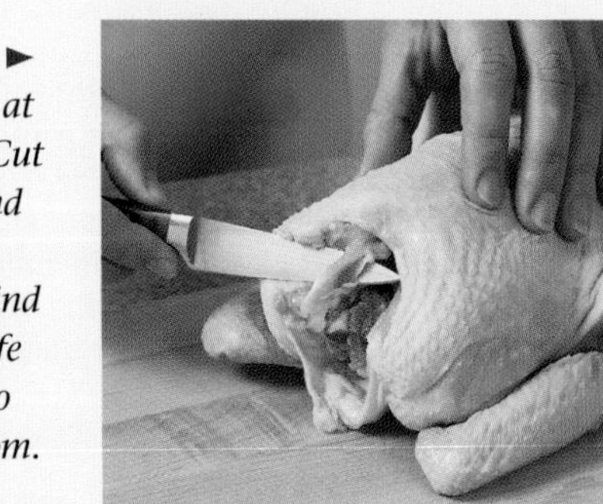

2 Grasp wishbone and twist to remove it. Rinse bird and pat dry.

3 Salt bird inside and out. Place it on roasting rack over baking sheet; chill.

Roasting and carving

Now that the chicken is ready, dinner isn't far behind. Here are some things to keep in mind.

Preparing for roasting

Preheat the oven to 450°. While I prefer the results of roasting at 500° (crispy skin and juicy meat), I'm not crazy about the smoke it creates from burning fat drippings. Roasting at this slightly lower temperature minimizes the smoke (there will be *some*) without sacrificing the qualities I like.

Rinse the chicken inside and out and pat it dry. Squeeze a lime over and inside the bird, stuff the juiced halves into the cavity, and tie the legs together with cotton kitchen string. You just want to keep the legs together for presentation. A formal "full bird" truss binds the bird too tightly, causing uneven roasting.

Lightly sprinkle the chicken with salt to give the skin a slightly crunchy texture and season the drippings. But don't use pepper. It burns at high temperatures like this.

Equipment *A collapsible v-rack lifts the bird so air circulates around it. The low-sided 1/4-size baking sheet promotes browning on the sides.*

Roasting

Place the bird on a roasting rack that's been set in a shallow baking pan. The rack and low-sided pan allow air to circulate around the chicken for faster, more even cooking. The bird won't brown as well on the sides in a larger, deeper roasting pan.

Roast a 3–4 pound chicken 1–1 1/4 hours, rotating the pan halfway through cooking. Don't rely on the juices running clear, or wiggling the leg to indicate doneness—the only way to be sure is to take a temperature.

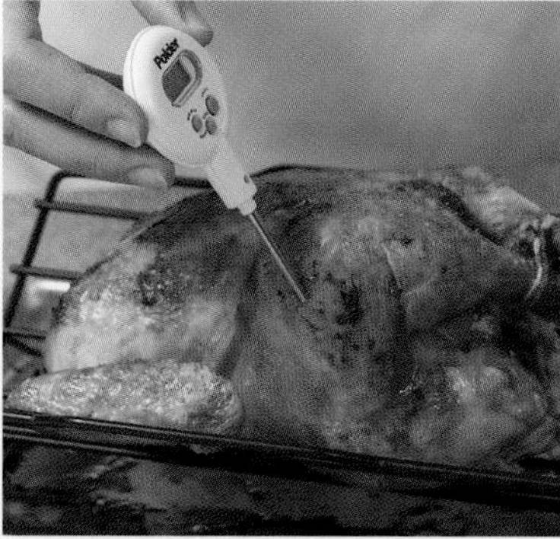

4 Insert thermometer into the thigh running parallel to the thigh bone.

5 Insert thermometer into the thickest part of the breast meat.

Temping

Get a temperature reading in the thigh and breast. First, insert the thermometer deeply into the thigh, running the thermometer stem parallel to the thigh bone, *Figure 4* (don't touch bone or the reading will be too high). Thigh meat is thoroughly cooked at 170°, but may be a bit pink at the bone and joints (the color often fades on contact with air).

Next insert the stem into the thickest portion of the breast, *Figure 5,* again away from bone—breast meat is done at 160°.

So, what if the breast meat is done but the thigh meat isn't? Keep on roasting, but check the thigh temperature every 10 minutes until it hits 170°. Tent the bird with foil and let it rest before carving so the juices redistribute. The temperature will continue to rise five to ten degrees.

Carving

Follow *Figures 6–9* below to see how to carve the chicken into parts—two leg-thigh pieces and two breast sections. The wings can also be cut off and served.

6 Remove leg-thighs by cutting the skin and down through the hip joint.

7 Cut across neck cavity and around sides of breast.

8 Remove the breasts, slicing down sternum and rib cage.

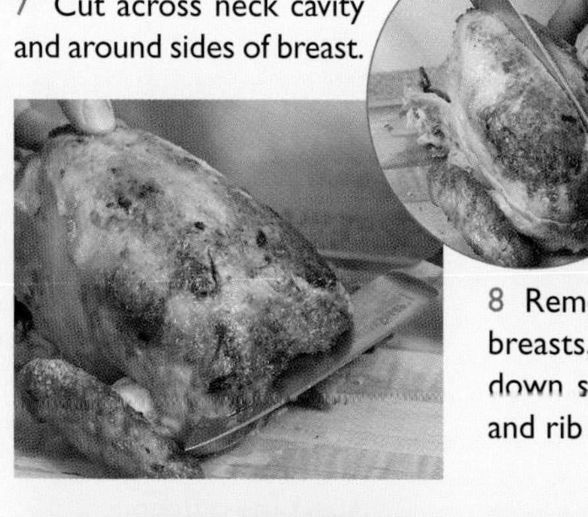

9 Slice both breast portions crosswise and against the grain into 1/2"-thick slices.

Roasted Chicken with pan gravy

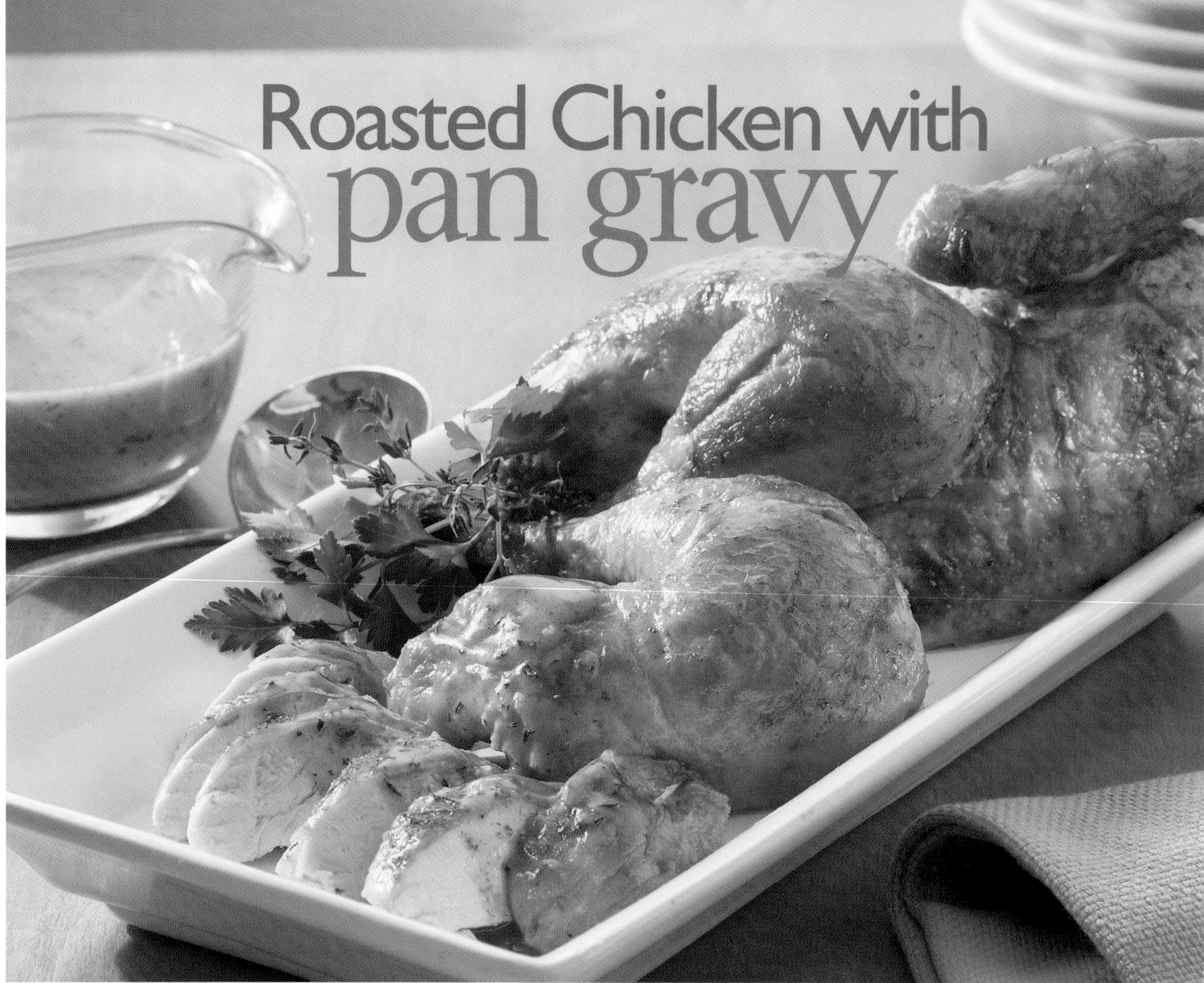

The next best thing to the roasted chicken is the drippings in the bottom of the pan. A simple procedure turns pan drippings into liquid gold.

There's no denying that the pan drippings from chicken make fine gravy. Simple ingredients combined with solid technique equal one of life's great pleasures.

But there are a few things to be aware of. First, since all chickens are different, the amount of drippings may vary—less or more is no big deal and won't significantly affect the outcome.

Second, keep an eye on the drippings as the chicken roasts. They will darken over time (and give the sauce deep brown color), but if they start to get too dark, add some water to the pan. Burnt drippings will give an off-flavor.

Finally, the herb choice is up to you. Thyme, rosemary, tarragon, and chives are all good.

Pan Gravy for Roasted Chicken

Makes About $1^1/_4$ Cups

Saute in 1 T. Chicken Fat:
- 1/4 cup shallots, minced

Deglaze with:
- 1/4 cup dry white wine

Add and Reduce:
- 1 cup low-sodium chicken broth
- Defatted chicken drippings

Combine; Whisk in:
- 3 T. low-sodium chicken broth
- 2 T. all-purpose flour

Finish Gravy with:
- 2 T. unsalted butter
- 1 T. chopped fresh herbs
- Salt and pepper to taste

Roast and rest chicken as on Pages 6–7. For gravy, pour off all but 1 T. fat from roasting pan; defat and reserve the drippings. Place the pan on a burner over medium heat.

Saute shallots in fat until soft.

Deglaze pan with wine, scraping up the browned bits. Transfer to a saucepan.

Add 1 cup broth and the defatted drippings. Bring to a boil over medium heat and simmer 3 minutes.

Combine 3 T. broth and 2 T. flour until smooth. Whisk into boiling broth and simmer 5 minutes until thickened; strain.

Finish with butter, herbs, salt, and pepper to taste.

From drippings to gravy

It's hard to believe, but that crusty stuff on the roasting pan can morph into flavorful pan gravy. Here's how to make magic.

Remove the chicken and rack from the pan, and let the bird rest on a cutting board. Pour the fat from the pan into a bowl and let the drippings (the brown residue) settle to the bottom. Some drippings may be stuck to the pan—that's just fine.

Place the pan on a burner, add some chicken fat, and heat the pan. Saute the shallots until soft, then deglaze the pan with wine, *Figure 1* (you can also use broth or apple juice). Deglazing is imperative because it loosens the stuck-on bits, which in turn give *tons* of flavor and color to the gravy. To finish, transfer this mixture to a small saucepan.

Now, spoon off some of the fat floating on the drippings you poured off earlier, *Figure 2*. It's okay if you can't remove it all. Add the drippings and broth to the saucepan and simmer.

Thicken with a little flour mixed with broth, *Figure 3*. Boil a few minutes to thicken and remove any starchy taste from the flour.

Finally, strain, *Figure 4*, then finish with butter and herbs. Carve the bird, *Page 7*, and serve with gravy.

1 Saute shallots in chicken fat. Deglaze with wine.

2 Spoon fat off pan drippings before adding to saucepan.

3 Thicken the boiling broth with flour/broth mixture.

4 Strain the gravy, then finish it with the butter, herbs, and seasonings.

make it a **menu**

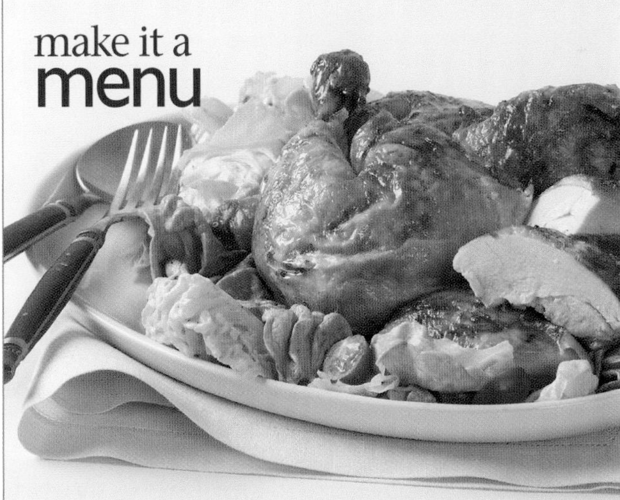

Roasted Chicken with Warm Vinaigrette

Drippings are also a great base for a salad vinaigrette. Follow the first three steps of pan gravy, toss the vinaigrette with tender lettuce, and serve with the chicken.

Makes About 2/3 Cup

For the Vinaigrette—

Saute in 1 T. Chicken Fat:

2 T. shallot, minced

Deglaze with:

1/4 cup sherry vinegar or red wine vinegar

Add:

2 T. sugar

1 t. Dijon mustard

Defatted chicken drippings

Salt and pepper to taste

Drizzle in:

1/4 cup extra-virgin olive oil

For the Salad—

Toss Warm Vinaigrette with:

Bibb lettuce leaves, torn

Halved grape tomatoes

Saute shallot in 1 T. fat as in pan gravy recipe, *left*.

Deglaze with vinegar, scraping up browned bits as in Figure 1.

Add sugar, mustard, drippings, (defat first as in Figure 2), salt, and pepper. Simmer 1 minute; transfer to a cup or bowl.

Drizzle in oil while whisking.

Toss vinaigrette with lettuce and tomatoes. Carve chicken and serve with salad.

▲*Drizzle oil into vinegar mixture while whisking (or use a hand-held blender).*

▲*Toss vinaigrette with prepared lettuce and tomatoes. You may not need it all—serve extra on the side with the chicken.*

The Ultimate Chicken Sandwich

Chicken salad or roasted chicken?—a sandwich lover's dilemma. Until now. With this one, you get the best of both worlds.

Building a better sandwich

Constructing the ultimate sandwich is a minor work of art. Its two main elements (bread and fillings) must be carefully considered to achieve perfect balance. Here are the "specs" for this masterpiece.

The bread

Naturally, the bread needs to taste good, but don't jump to the conclusion that it has to be a rustic, artisan type—those tend to be too crusty and "holey" so the sandwich is hard to eat. Try an inexpensive French or Italian bread with a fine texture (not many holes) and a crust that's sturdy, not jaw-breaking. Any sacrifice in flavor is made up for by brushing the pan drippings on the bread, *Figure 1.*

1 Brush bread with drippings before grilling or broiling.

The fillings

Unlike some deli sandwiches, this one isn't jammed with fillings. But what is there packs a punch—a dark meat-only chicken salad, *Figures 2 & 3,* and juicy slices of breast meat, *Figure 4.* I prefer a fairly spartan chicken salad, just meat and mayonnaise. Adding onion or celery is up to you.

And resist using "fancy" lettuce when assembling these sandwiches, *Figure 5.* There's a time and place for iceberg, and this is one of them.

The Ultimate Chicken Sandwich

Makes 4 Sandwiches

For the Chicken—
Roast:
1 3–4 lb. whole chicken

For the Mayonnaise—
Combine:
1/4 cup mayonnaise
2 t. sherry vinegar or rice vinegar
2 t. sugar
1 t. garlic, minced
Salt and cayenne to taste

For the Sandwiches—
Prepare:
8 slices (1/2" thick) Italian or French bread
1 cup shredded iceberg or romaine lettuce

Roast chicken as on Pages 6–7.
Combine all ingredients for mayonnaise in a medium bowl; chill until ready to use.
Prepare bread and lettuce for sandwiches; set aside.

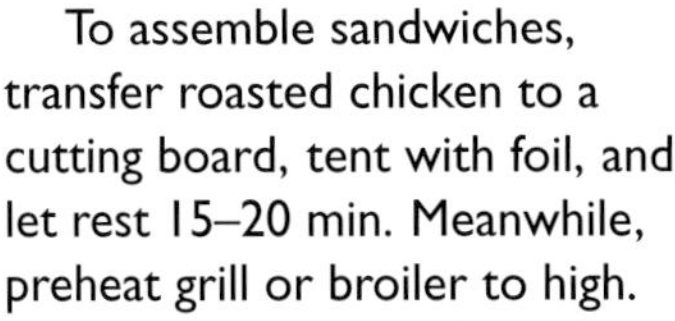

To assemble sandwiches, transfer roasted chicken to a cutting board, tent with foil, and let rest 15–20 min. Meanwhile, preheat grill or broiler to high.

Brush both sides of bread slices with pan drippings, then grill or broil bread on both sides until golden, 1 minute per side.

Once chicken has rested, carve off legs and thighs as described on Page 7; pull the dark meat off the bones. Coarsely chop the meat and combine with mayonnaise mixture. Carve off breast portions from the chicken as on Page 7, and then slice them crosswise and on a sharp bias.

Divide chicken "salad" among four slices of toasted bread and top with some of the shredded lettuce. Place 3 or 4 slices of breast meat on top of the lettuce, and top with a second slice of bread. Cut the sandwich in half and serve.

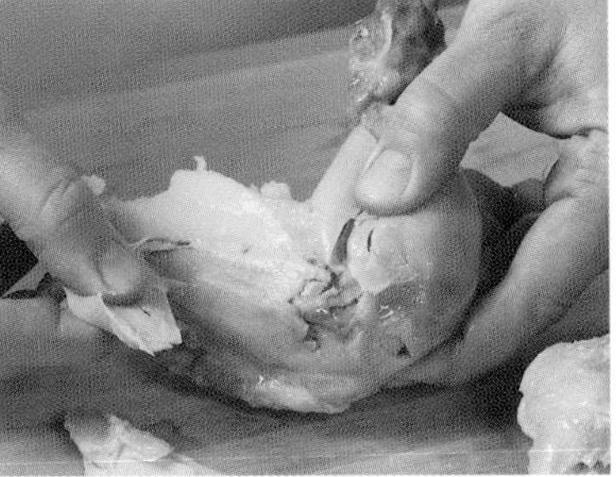

2 Pull the dark meat from the leg-thigh portions and the wings.

3 Coarsely chop dark meat and blend with mayonnaise mixture.

4 Slice breast meat on a bias to achieve larger pieces.

5 Assemble sandwiches with chicken salad, lettuce, then slices of breast meat. Top with second slice of bread, halve, and serve.

market salads

These three salads go way beyond the common side dish. With just a baguette, they could be a complete dinner.

I get to travel around quite a bit, but probably don't do the typical tourist things. Believe it or not, the first thing I always do is head for the coolest grocery stores to look around. It's a thrill to walk around in Dean and Deluca, Whole Foods, Wegmans, Eatzis, Zabar's in New York, or the myriad of other great food stores throughout the country. It's an inspiration to see what these stores serve up and what customers buy. I often use this information for some of the articles in *Cuisine*—like the market salads you're about to make.

We all visit regular grocery stores that get away with selling some pretty boring potato salads, cole slaws, and bean salads. Well, those are what I consider to be market salads, albeit a primal form.

If you're lucky, your grocer goes beyond this tier and makes salads that are as flavorful as they are pretty. But if you're still faced with the dull choice of mustard or mayonnaise-based potato salad, create these market salads. They can be a casual main course or a fancy side dish. They are perfect for a "kicked-back" Sunday summer dinner.

paella salad

Paella Salad

Here's a fun spin-off of the popular Spanish saffron-flavored rice dish. It's made with orzo pasta rather than rice for a better texture and look.

Makes 8 Cups; Total Time: 35 Minutes

For the Salad—

Saute in 2 T. Olive Oil:

- ½ lb. kielbasa, sliced
- ½ lb. large shrimp, peeled and deveined
- 1 T. garlic, minced
- 2 cups red bell pepper, diced

Prepare:

- 4 Roma tomatoes, seeded and sliced into rounds
- ½ lb. dry orzo pasta
- 1 cup frozen peas

For the Vinaigrette—

Warm:

- 3 T. white wine vinegar
- 3 T. fresh lemon juice
- ¼ t. saffron threads, crumbled, or ¼ t. ground turmeric

Whisk in:

- ¼ cup mayonnaise
- 1 t. garlic, minced
- 1 t. powdered sugar
- ½ cup extra-virgin olive oil
- Salt and cayenne to taste

Garnish Salad with:

- ½ cup scallions, chopped

Saute kielbasa over medium-high heat until it begins to brown. Add shrimp and cook until it becomes opaque (about 5 minutes). Add garlic, saute 1 minute then place in large mixing bowl. Saute peppers 3–4 minutes in same pan. Add to mixing bowl.

Prepare tomatoes by seeding and slicing. Cook orzo according to package directions. Just before draining pasta, add frozen peas. Now drain—do not rinse. Combine with kielbasa-shrimp mixture and the sliced tomatoes.

Warm vinegar and lemon juice for the vinaigrette. Crumble in saffron and "steep" 5 minutes. (If you're using turmeric, there's no need to steep.)

Whisk in mayonnaise, garlic, and sugar until combined. Drizzle in olive oil. Season to taste with salt and cayenne. Add vinaigrette to salad ingredients and toss gently.

Garnish with chopped scallions.

◄Saute kielbasa until brown. Add shrimp and cook until opaque. Turn both shrimp and kielbasa frequently to prevent burning.

Cook orzo according to package directions. Add frozen peas to the pasta water just before draining. The peas don't need cooking, just thawing.►

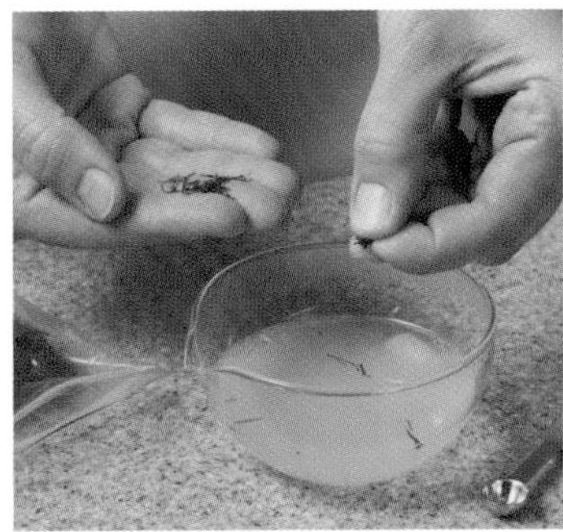

◄Saffron must be warmed to release its flavor and color. If you don't have saffron, use ¼ teaspoon turmeric. It won't have the flavor of saffron but does have the yellow color.

Thai beef salad

Thai Beef Salad

This salad has incredible textures and flavors. It's best eaten shortly after it's made, but you can prepare the components and then toss them together at the last minute.

Makes About 6 Cups; Total Time: 45 Minutes + Marinating

For the Steak—
Marinate; Grill:
1 lb. flank steak
1/4 cup low-sodium soy sauce
1/4 cup rice vinegar
2 T. brown sugar
1 T. toasted sesame oil

For the Vinaigrette—
Combine:
1/4 cup fresh lime juice
2 T. fish sauce (or 2 t. anchovy paste)
2 T. brown sugar
1 T. fresh ginger, peeled, minced
1 t. chili garlic paste
1 t. peanut butter
Whisk in:
1/4 cup vegetable oil

For the Salad—
Prepare:
1 pkg. (3 oz.) ramen noodles, cooked (omit seasoning packet), drained, and tossed with 1 T. toasted sesame oil
1 cup fresh bean sprouts
1 cup cucumber, seeded, cut into half-moons
1 cup grape tomatoes, halved
3/4 cup carrots, thinly sliced
3/4 cup red bell pepper, seeded, diced
1/4 cup shallots, thinly sliced

Garnish with:
1/4 cup coarsely chopped mint
1/4 cup coarsely chopped cilantro
2 T. dry roasted peanuts, chopped

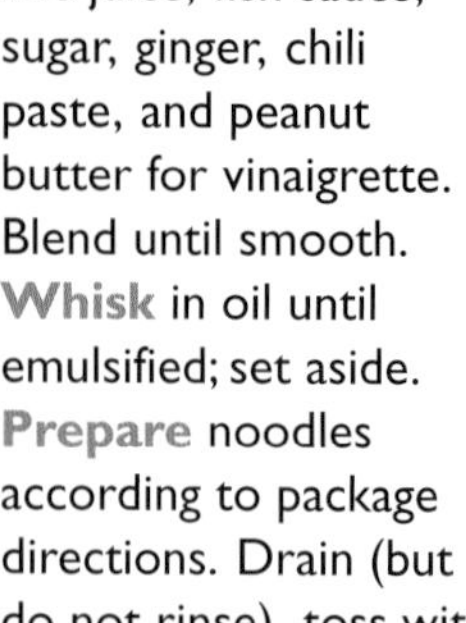

Marinate the steak in soy sauce, vinegar, sugar, and oil for 1–2 hours, chilled.

Combine lime juice, fish sauce, sugar, ginger, chili paste, and peanut butter for vinaigrette. Blend until smooth. **Whisk** in oil until emulsified; set aside.

Prepare noodles according to package directions. Drain (but do not rinse), toss with oil, and set aside. Prepare vegetables and combine with noodles; prepare garnishes and set aside.

Preheat grill to high. Grill steak to medium-rare, 3–4 minutes per side; allow meat to rest 5 minutes before carving. Thinly slice steak against the grain and on a bias, and add it to the vegetables. Toss salad with dressing (you may not need all of it) and transfer to a large serving platter.

Garnish with herbs and peanuts. Serve at room temperature.

Thinly slice steak against the grain and on the bias.▼

chicken niçoise salad

Chicken Niçoise Salad

A little taste of the Mediterranean that's perfect for all seasons. Don't shy away from the anchovy paste—it makes the vinaigrette distinctive without imparting a fishy taste.

Makes About 6 Cups; Total Time: 45 Minutes

Anchovy paste *is a blend of mashed anchovies, vinegar, and spices that comes in a tube. Added in the right amount, it provides depth to dressings and sauces.*

For the Salad—

Boil:

- $1\frac{1}{2}$ lbs. small red potatoes
- 4 large eggs

Blanch:

- $\frac{1}{4}$ lb. green beans, stemmed

Saute in 1 T. Olive Oil:

- 2 boneless, skinless chicken breast halves, seasoned with salt and pepper

Prepare:

- 1 pint grape tomatoes, halved
- $\frac{1}{2}$ cup niçoise or kalamata olives, pitted and halved

For the Vinaigrette—

Whisk Together:

- $\frac{1}{4}$ cup fresh lemon juice
- 2 T. minced fresh tarragon
- 1 T. shallot, minced
- 1 T. Dijon mustard
- 2 t. anchovy paste
- 1 t. honey
- $\frac{2}{3}$ cup extra-virgin olive oil
- Salt and pepper to taste

Boil potatoes until done and hard-cook eggs. Plunge both into ice water to cool; drain. Slice potatoes $\frac{1}{4}$" thick. Chop eggs for garnish and set aside.

Blanch green beans 5 minutes. Plunge into ice water to cool; drain and set aside.

Saute chicken in oil over medium-high heat until cooked through (about 8 minutes per side). Cut into $\frac{1}{4}$"-thick slices.

Prepare tomatoes and olives.

Whisk first six vinaigrette ingredients together in a small bowl. Whisk in olive oil slowly to blend. Season to taste.

Combine potato slices, green beans, sliced chicken, tomatoes, and olives in a large bowl. Drizzle with vinaigrette and toss lightly to coat. Transfer salad to a platter and garnish the top of the salad with chopped egg.

▲*Plunge steamed green beans into ice water to halt the cooking process.*

▲*Slice sauteed chicken breasts against the grain and on the bias into about $\frac{1}{4}$"-thick pieces.*

cuisinetechnique

juicy Pork Chops every time

Just because today's pork is lean doesn't mean it lacks flavor. The right chop, preparation, and cooking method guarantees juicy, tasty results.

For years, pork had a reputation for being a flavorful meat but unfortunately, high in fat. It also, occasionally, carried around a parasite called trichina. Over the last few decades, that's changed.

Now, pork is lean and the parasites are gone. But just because the fat is gone doesn't mean the flavor went with it. Smart purchasing and cooking insures a juicy, flavorful pork chop.

Selection: Good chops begin at the grocery store. First, ask for a center cut rib chop. It cooks evenly since it has only one texture of meat. Most of us are used to a more typical T-bone looking loin chop which has both a sirloin and a tenderloin—these cuts cook differently.

Then ask for one about an inch thick. These can cook fairly quickly without drying out.

And finally, check the color and the fat. Too much of either is not good. Look for a well trimmed chop that is deep pink.

Selections of pork

Rib Chop Ask for additional length of rib bone. Trim the meat and fat away for nice presentation, *see Figure 1*.

Loin Chop Note the round tenderloin next to the loin (separated by the bone). These are two different textures and cook differently.

Boneless Loin Chop No tenderloin or bone. Cooks evenly but lacks the presentation punch of the rib chop.

Chops that are about an inch thick cook quickly. Thicker chops tend to dry out from prolonged exposure to heat.

Pork Chop Brine

This brine is simple. There's no need to add other seasonings since the chops will either be glazed or sauced.
Makes 8 Cups
Total Time: 5 Minutes

Dissolve in One-Gallon Resealable Freezer Bag:
2 cups hot water
1/2 cup kosher salt
1/2 cup brown sugar
Add:
6 cups ice water

Dissolve salt and sugar in hot water. It helps to set the bag inside a large bowl in case of spills or leaks.
Add ice water to brine. This will cool the brine quickly so you to add the pork chops. Seal the bag and refrigerate.

1 For a fancy dinner look, cut the meat and fat off the bone. You don't have to clean it perfectly.

2 Place freezer bag inside a large bowl. Dissolve salt and brown sugar in the bag with hot water.

Brining and cooking

Because pork is so lean, fat does not add the flavor that it used to. Flavor comes from a short brine and limited cooking.

Brining: Much of the pork today comes injected with flavor enhancers and preservatives to maximize shelf life. Additives don't bother me, but some people prefer "natural" meat. Both types benefit from brining—the "natural" much more than the already "enhanced."

This brine is simple. It's nothing more than a large resealable storage bag filled with water, salt, and sugar. Since there are other flavors that will be introduced during cooking, there's little reason to add them to the brine.

First, make sure the salt and sugar are dissolved completely in hot water, *see Figure 2*. Then, cool the mixture totally before adding the pork. Seal the plastic bag and set it in a large bowl, *see Figure 3*. Brine the chops for one to two hours. Just before cooking, dry chops to remove excess brine, *see Figure 4*.

Cooking: Now you're ready to start cooking. But the rules have changed. Pork has evolved into a whole new meat over the last few decades. Since it's fed purely grain, trichina parasites aren't a big health concern now. Older cookbooks stipulated cooking pork to 180° to ensure the elimination of trichina—that also killed the flavor and moisture. Now we know trichina meets its "waterloo" at 137°. We also know that connective tissues begin to constrict at 160°, squeezing moisture out of the meat.

For a tender chop, cook until internal temperature hits about 150°. Then it will rise gradually to 155° while it rests. Don't worry if you see a little pink! It's more than safe to eat.

3 Add ice water to bag. When the water is completely chilled, submerge chops and seal bag.

4 Pat pork dry to remove any residual brine before cooking. Additional salt isn't necessary.

glazed and grilled pork chops

There's only one thing better than a well-cooked pork chop—that's a *grilled,* well-cooked pork chop.

The path to a perfect pork chop: an inch thick, trimmed of fat, brined, and briefly cooked. There's only one way to top this nugget of nourishment and that's to grill it for over-the-top flavor.

Pork is actually a very mild-flavored meat that readily accepts even minimal seasoning. You're not only going to brine this chop, but expose it to a smoky grill that intensifies the flavor.

Grilling an inch-thick chop is anything but a long process. It cooks over direct heat about a total of eight minutes. The final minutes of grilling are done over indirect heat (on the unlit side of the grill). You'll cook it this way so the simple, spicy, sweet glaze applied for the last half of grilling won't burn. Serve these chops with creamed mustard greens—a perfect complement.

menu

Glazed Grilled Pork Chops

Creamed Mustard Greens

Lemon Sorbet

Like any cut of pork, overcooking spells nothing but dried-out trouble. And grilling is no exception. These chops are best grilled like a steak—no more than medium.

Grill marks

People "eat" with their eyes and that's why grill marks are important. It's a technique you should learn for grilling any meat.

To make good marks, think of the chop like a clock. Point the bone towards 4 o'clock, *see Figure 1*. After a few minutes, point the bone to 8 o'clock, *see Figure 2*. Flip and repeat the process.

You can see how nice the grill marks look. But for this recipe, after you flip the chops over, coat them liberally with the spicy glaze, *see Figure 3*.

Indirect Grilling

Because the glaze contains sugar, it burns easily if left over direct heat. So grill the chops half the time over the flame. Then, glaze them (both sides) and place the chops over the side of the grill that isn't lit. Keep the lid down to retain the heat. After 5–6 minutes, the chops will be cooked and ready for the plate.

Glazed and Grilled Pork Chops

Prepare grill so one side has a medium-high fire (direct) and the other side is not lit (indirect).

Makes 4 Servings
Total Time: 30 minutes

For the Glaze—

Combine; Set Aside:
- 1/4 cup lime juice
- 1/4 cup ketchup
- 1/4 cup brown sugar
- 3 T. honey
- 1 T. crushed red pepper flakes

For the Pork Chops—

Trim and Brine:
- 4 1"-thick rib chops, *see Pages 16–17*

Rub Chops with; Grill:
- 1/4 cup olive oil
- 2 t. ground black pepper

Preheat grill to medium-high.
Combine ingredients for the glaze and set aside.
Trim brined pork chops, *see Figure 1* on Page 17.
Rub chops with oil and pepper.
Over heated side of grill, cook chops for 6 minutes making grill marks following Figures 1 and 2. Flip, glaze, and place chops over indirect heat side. Grill 6–8 more minutes (to 150°).

1 Start chops *directly* over medium-high heat with bones facing 4 o'clock.

2 After 3 minutes, turn the bone so it faces 8 o'clock. Grill another 3 minutes. Flip.

3 Glaze the chops and finish cooking for 6–8 minutes on *indirect* side (no flame).

Creamed Mustard Greens

Makes 3–4 Cups
Total Time: 30 Minutes

Blanch:
- 1 lb. mustard greens, stemmed and sliced into ribbons (about 8 cups)

Saute in 2 T. Butter and 1 T. Olive Oil:
- 1 cup onion, finely diced

Add and Reduce:
- 2 cups heavy cream

Add and Saute:
- Blanched mustard greens

Season with:
- Salt and pepper to taste

Mustard Greens: The mildest of the bitter greens. Especially good and colorful with cream.

Blanch mustard greens in a large pot of boiling water for 5 minutes. Plunge into ice water to stop the cooking and to retain color, *see Figure 1*. Drain, spin-dry, and set aside.

Saute onion in butter and olive oil in large saute pan over medium-high heat for 5 minutes.
Add cream and simmer. Reduce until thick, as shown in *Figure 2*.
Add blanched and drained mustard greens, stirring to coat with the cream mixture for 2–3 minutes, *see Figure 3*.
Season with salt and pepper.

pan roasted Pork chops *with bourbon sauce*

Outdoor grilling isn't the only way to cook a good chop. Here's an oven recipe that delivers the flavor in summer or winter.

Pan Roasted Pork Chops with Bourbon Sauce

Makes 4 Servings
Total Time: 40 Minutes

Season and Flour:
4 1"-thick brined rib chops
Brown in:
2 T. olive oil
Remove Chops; Saute:
1 T. garlic, chopped
1 T. shallot, chopped
Deglaze with:
1 1/2 cups chicken broth
1/3 cup bourbon
1/4 cup brown sugar
1 T. apple cider vinegar
Add and Reduce:
2 T. heavy cream
Reserved pork chops

Preheat oven to 425°. **Season** chops with pepper. Dust lightly with flour. **Brown** one side in olive oil over medium-high heat. Turn, cover, and roast in oven for about 10 minutes. **Remove** chops to a warm platter. Saute garlic and shallot in 1 T. drippings over medium-high heat until soft. **Deglaze** pan with bourbon and broth. Add sugar and vinegar; reduce by half. **Add** cream and pork chops to pan and cook for 2 minutes on each side until sauce is thick. Makes 1 cup sauce.

Editor's Note: Be careful when deglazing with liquor. Higher-proof alcohols, like bourbon, can cause a large flame. This can be prevented by diluting bourbon with broth. If you're a showman or like a milder sauce, add the alcohol away from the flame and ignite with a long match. This burns off the alcohol.

Cooking the chops

Pork is a Southern thing. Early explorers introduced hogs to the Southern states as they traveled northward from the West Indies. Later, British colonists, who settled in Virginia, raised them for profit in and around Smithfield. This area is still known for top-quality pork—especially hams.

It seems only natural to pair this pork chop with another Southern product—bourbon. It doesn't take much of this simple bourbon sauce to put these tender chops on a higher level.

Pan roasting

Pan roasting is a perfect cooking technique for thicker cuts of meat and fish.

First, lightly flour the brined chops, *see Figure 1.* This will help them brown and thicken the sauce. Now, brown the chops in a pan that can be fitted with a lid and placed in an oven, *see Figure 2.* When deep brown on one side, turn them over and cover. Put the pan in a 425° oven and roast 10 minutes or to an internal temperature of 150°.

Bourbon sauce

Once the chops are cooked through, remove them to a warm platter. Prepare the sauce in the same roasting pan, *see Figure 3.* When the sauce comes to a boil, add the chops back to the pan so they can reheat and absorb the bourbon and brown sugar flavor, *see Figure 4.* Cook a few minutes until the sauce thickens.

1 Season the chops with pepper only (brine had salt). Lightly dust each chop with flour.

2 Brown chops on one side. Be sure to use a saute pan that has a lid and can be placed in the oven.

3 After roasting in the oven, remove chops and saute shallots and garlic. Deglaze pan and reduce by half.

4 Add the chops back to the sauce to reheat. Simmer to thicken sauce (about 2 minutes).

make it a menu

Stuffed baked potatoes make an excellent side dish. They're not too filling and fit perfectly in the bend of the pork chop bone.

Pan Roasted Pork Chops with Bourbon Sauce

Goat Cheese & Rosemary Stuffed Baked Potatoes

Blanched Mustard Greens

Pineapple Ice Cream

Pineapple Ice Cream

Makes 5 Cups

Whisk Together:
4 egg yolks
3/4 cup sugar
Heat:
2 cups heavy cream
1 cup buttermilk
Stir into Cream Mixture:
1 cup pineapple puree

Whisk together egg yolks and sugar.
Heat cream and buttermilk. Bring to a simmer.
Gradually whisk egg mixture into hot cream.
Reduce heat. Cook for 5–7 minutes until thick. Chill.
Stir puree into chilled custard. Freeze 24 hours.

33 *online* **extra**

Want more info? Visit www.CuisineAtHome.com for a step-by-step guide to Pineapple Ice Cream.

fettuccine Alfredo

A few quality ingredients and simple steps from Lidia put you in the heart of Rome eating Fettuccine Alfredo.

Mario Novak

Star of the 52-part television series, *Lidia's Italian American Kitchen*, and the 39-part public television show, *Lidia's Italian Table*, Lidia Matticchio Bastianich is widely regarded as the "First Lady of Italian cuisine and restaurants in the United States." Born in Istria, a peninsula about 90 miles northeast of Venice, Lidia came to New York in 1958.

Lidia is an acclaimed chef and restaurateur. She is co-owner of five sensational restaurants: *Felidia, Becco,* and *Esca* all in New York, as well as *Lidia's Kansas City* and *Lidia's Pittsburgh*.

While you would think restaurants and television shows would be enough to keep any one person busy, she has also developed her own line of pasta sauces. Called *Lidia's Flavors of Italy*, these sauces are now distributed nationwide.

She's founder of *Esperienze Italiane*, an international tour operator specializing in high-end culinary and cultural tours to Italy.

Lidia has three popular cookbooks. Two share the same name as her television shows, and the third is *La Cucina Di Lidia*.

To say Lidia is an expert is an understatement. No wonder we turned to her to show us how to cook fettuccine Alfredo.

Creamy fettuccine Alfredo

Fettuccine Alfredo, like so many other pastas dishes, has two versions: Italian and American. But the American one never seems to taste the same here as in Italy. It must be the ingredients. Right?

To answer this question and also to find out the art of making real Italian fettuccine Alfredo, I called on Lidia Bastianich. She explained everything anyone needs to know about cooking pasta, *and* her Alfredo is nothing less than pure, perfect Italian!

Cooking pasta: Lidia first showed me the right way to cook pasta. There has to be plenty of boiling water—for this recipe, use three quarts of water for half a pound of pasta. She told me she didn't know where the practice of adding oil to the water came from, but don't do it. It coats the surface of the pasta making it difficult for sauce to adhere.

You should never overcook pasta. Al dente is the term indicating that the pasta will have a slight resistance when bitten. To tell if it's cooked al dente, cut a piece. If you see a small, white dot in the center, it's perfect.

For maximum flavor, add the pasta directly from the boiling water to the cooking sauce and simmer together for a few minutes. The pasta will absorb some of the sauce and the sauce will intensify in flavor.

And finally, don't oversauce. Lidia explained that Italians don't like their pasta swimming in sauce—just enough to coat so the pasta *glides*, not plops, onto the plate.

Fettuccine Alfredo: Besides a great recipe, organization and timing are key to good Alfredo.

Lidia starts by adding pasta to a pot of boiling salted water. When the pasta is five minutes from al dente, she starts her Alfredo sauce. So the sauce does not separate, Lidia adds the cream and broth before the butter melts completely. Once this simmers for 2–3 minutes, she adds the pasta, stirring and simmering a few more minutes.

Lidia removes the pan from the heat and quickly and completely stirs in the yolks. Then she blends in the cheese (high heat can separate the fat from the protein causing the cheese to become stringy). A little seasoning and you've got the perfect Alfredo.

1 Before the butter has a chance to fully melt, pour in the cream and broth.

Lidia's Fettuccine Alfredo

Use most any pasta shape, but Lidia warns to avoid the really small pastas like capellini—the strands will stick together in the sauce.

Makes 4 Servings; Total Time: 20 Minutes

Boil:
3 quarts salted water

Cook:
8 oz. dried fettuccine

Begin to Melt:
4 T. unsalted butter

Pour in; Boil:
2/3 cup heavy cream
1/2 cup low-sodium chicken broth

Add:
Cooked pasta

Off Heat, Add:
2 egg yolks, broken
1/4 cup freshly grated Parmigiano-Reggiano cheese

Season with:
Salt and coarsely ground black pepper to taste

Boil the salted water in a large pot over high heat.
Cook the pasta al dente.
Begin to melt butter in a large saute pan over medium heat.
Pour in the cream and chicken broth before the butter is completely melted, *see Figure 1*. Bring to a boil. Simmer 2–3 minutes.
Add the cooked pasta to the sauce right from boiling water, *see Figure 2*. Stir and cook until sauce turns creamy (2 minutes).
Off heat, add yolks into center of pasta and stir quickly to prevent curdling, *see Figure 3*. Sprinkle with cheese; toss well.
Season with salt and pepper to taste and serve immediately.

2 Add pasta to the sauce and stir to coat.

3 Stir quickly as you add the egg yolks or they'll curdle.

chef**at**home: *Lidia Matticchio Bastianich*

a lighter fettuccine Alfredo

Fettuccine Alfredo is one of those occasional luxury meals. But with Lidia's lower-fat version, you can enjoy this creamy classic without all the guilt.

There's no need to tell you that real fettuccine Alfredo is pretty high in fat. It's one of those special treats to be consumed in moderation—like cake, bacon, or hollandaise sauce.

So when I expressed my concern to Lidia, she didn't hesitate to offer up a lower-fat version—actually, a version with one-third the fat of her regular Alfredo. What's the secret? Ricotta cheese.

Yes, there is still butter and Parmesan cheese, but you can't sacrifice *all* the flavor. At about 15 grams of fat per serving, this tasty version makes a pretty good substitute for the real thing.

Lidia said the cooking technique for this low-fat version is similar to the regular Alfredo. The real difference is in the ingredients. Unfortunately, you don't have the cream and egg yolks to produce a rich sauce. So what do you do? Lidia says the thick, creamy texture comes from an unusual source—ricotta cheese.

Using ricotta was a great idea, but I was concerned about the grainy texture ricotta often has. We decided to try blending the ricotta with the milk and broth to smooth it out. It worked great!

Now my only other concern was if the sauce would get thick enough. Lidia assured me that the finely grated (not shredded) Parmesan cheese would do the trick. She was right again. This reduced-fat version is a viable alternative to authentic Alfredo.

1 Blend the ricotta, milk, and broth in a blender until smooth.

2 Add the ricotta mixture to the partially melted butter and simmer.

3 Off heat, sprinkle in the finely grated Parmesan cheese.

Lidia's Light Alfredo

Makes 4 Servings
Total Time: 25 Minutes

Boil:
3 quarts salted water
Cook:
4 oz. dried fettuccine
4 oz. dried spinach fettuccine
Blend:
1 cup part-skim ricotta
2/3 cup 2% milk
1/2 cup low-sodium chicken broth
Begin to Melt:
4 T. unsalted butter
Add and Simmer:
Blended ricotta mixture
Add:
Cooked pasta
Off Heat, Sprinkle with:
1/4 cup finely grated Parmigiano-Reggiano cheese
Salt and coarsely ground black pepper to taste
Optional:
1 cup scallions, chopped

Boil the salted water in a large pot over high heat.
Cook the pasta al dente.
Blend the ricotta, milk, and broth in a blender until smooth, *see Figure 1*. Set aside.
Begin to melt butter in a large saute pan over medium heat.
Add the ricotta mixture to the pan before the butter is completely melted, *see Figure 2*. Simmer 2–3 minutes.
Add pasta and add to sauce in the pan. Bring the sauce and pasta to a boil, stirring to coat. Cook until the sauce is reduced to a thick, creamy consistency.
Off heat, sprinkle with grated cheese, salt, and coarsely ground black pepper, *see Figure 3*. Toss well and serve fettuccine in warm bowls.
Optional: Stir in chopped scallions for a little added flavor, texture, and color.

Ricotta cheese

In the normal scheme of things, after cheese is made, the by-product is whey. When heated, this nutritious, low-fat liquid turns into ricotta.

Italian ricotta is made from sheep, buffalo, or goat's milk. Most American ricotta is made from cow's milk. It's fairly moist and bland while the Italian versions are dry and nutty-flavored.

Lidia uses part-skim ricotta with good results. Nutritional values vary with brands, but this provides a guideline.

Whole milk ricotta: *About 14 grams of fat per 4 oz. with about 200 calories.*

Part-skim ricotta: *Around 9 grams of fat per 4 oz. and roughly 150 calories.*

Light ricotta: *Drops to as low as 2 grams of fat with 40 calories.*

Fat free ricotta: *Don't bother.*

Alfredo add ins

Use your favorite pasta shape and either of Lidia's Alfredo recipes to create these flavorful, restaurant-style dishes.

Mushroom and Sausage Alfredo

This Alfredo is loaded with woodsy flavors—great in the fall, but good any time of year. Use white button mushrooms if you can't find one of the other types.

Makes 4 Servings; Total Time: 40 Minutes

Cook:
8 oz. dried rigatoni
Brown in 2 T. Olive Oil; Slice:
1/2 lb. Italian link sausage
Add Olive Oil (If Needed) and Saute:
2 cups shiitake mushrooms, stemmed, halved
2 cups crimini mushrooms, sliced
Add:
Sliced cooked Italian sausage
1 T. garlic, minced
Deglaze with:
1/4 cup dry Madeira or dry sherry
Proceed with Alfredo Recipe.
Season with:
2 T. chopped fresh thyme leaves
Salt and black pepper to taste
Garnish with:
Sliced scallions

Cook the pasta al dente.
Brown sausage in oil in a large saute pan over med. heat. Remove from heat, cool slightly, and slice into 1/2"-thick rounds. (If not cooked through, don't worry. It will cook more later.)
Add oil to the pan if needed, and saute mushrooms in batches for 5 minutes, or until lightly browned.
Add the sausage. When it's cooked through, add the garlic and saute just until you can smell it, about 1 minute.
Deglaze with Madeira, scraping to release bits from bottom of pan.
Proceed with Alfredo according to directions on Page 23 or 25, adding the ingredients to the same saute pan.
Season with thyme, salt, and pepper.
Garnish with sliced scallions.

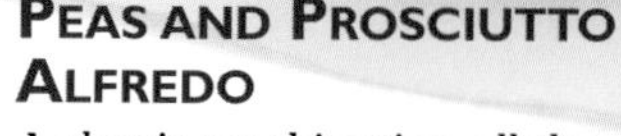

Peas and Prosciutto Alfredo

A classic combination all the way—peas, prosciutto, and cream.

Makes 4 Servings
Total Time: 30 Minutes

Cook:
8 oz. dried thin spaghetti
Sweat in 2 T. Olive Oil:
1/2 onion, thinly sliced
Add:
3 oz. prosciutto, sliced into strips
Deglaze with:
1/4 cup dry white wine
Proceed with Alfredo Recipe.
Add:
1 cup frozen peas
Season with:
Salt and black pepper to taste

Cook the pasta al dente.
Sweat onion in oil in a saute pan until slightly translucent. Do this slowly, covered, over medium heat—you don't want to brown the onion.
Add the prosciutto and increase heat to medium-high. Cook 2–3 minutes.
Deglaze pan with wine, scraping up any browned bits from the pan. Reduce until liquid has evaporated.
Proceed with Alfredo according to directions on Page 23 or 25, adding the ingredients to the same saute pan.
Add peas in the last minutes of cooking to keep them bright green.
Season with salt and pepper.

Chicken and Artichoke Alfredo

Hands down, this was our favorite Alfredo recipe in the test kitchen. Be careful not to brown the pine nuts too much since they're quick to burn.

Makes 4 Servings; Total Time: 45 Minutes

Blanch:
12 asparagus spears, cut in thirds
Cook:
8 oz. dried penne
Saute in 1 T. Olive Oil:
1/4 cup pine nuts
Brown 1 T. Olive Oil (If Needed):
1 lb. chicken breast
Add:
1 T. garlic, minced
Deglaze with:
1/3 cup dry white wine
Proceed with Alfredo Recipe.
Add with Cream:
6 canned artichoke hearts, halved
1 T. minced fresh oregano
Blanched asparagus
Add with Cheese:
Sliced chicken
1/2 cup mild goat cheese, crumbled
1/2 cup roasted red peppers, cut into large chunks
Season with:
Salt and black pepper to taste
Garnish with:
Sauteed pine nuts

Blanch asparagus in boiling water, then plunge into ice water. Remove from water and set aside.
Cook the pasta al dente.
Saute pine nuts in oil in same saute pan you'll make the Alfredo in. Cook over medium heat, stirring frequently, until golden; remove and set aside.
Brown chicken in the same pan (add a little oil if needed). Saute until completely cooked through, 8–10 minutes.
Add garlic and cook briefly, about 1 minute. Don't let the garlic burn.
Deglaze pan with wine and reduce by half. Remove chicken and slice.
Proceed with Alfredo according to directions on Page 23 or 25, *except* add artichokes, oregano, and blanched asparagus with the cream and broth.
Add the sliced chicken, goat cheese, and roasted red peppers when you add the Parmesan cheese.
Season with salt and pepper.
Garnish with sauteed pine nuts.

Seafood Alfredo

The fresh tomatoes and basil combine to make this Alfredo taste like summer.

Makes 4 Servings
Total Time: 40 Minutes

Cook:
8 oz. dried fettuccine
Saute in 2 T. Olive Oil:
12 large shrimp, peeled, deveined
8 sea scallops, halved
Add, Reduce, then Remove Seafood:
1 T. garlic, minced
1/4 cup dry sherry
Proceed with Alfredo Recipe.
Stir in Before Adding the Pasta:
1 1/2 cups Roma tomatoes, seeded and diced
1/4 t. cayenne
Stir in:
Reserved seafood mixture
Salt to taste
Garnish with:
1/4 cup fresh basil, cut into strips

Cook the pasta al dente.
Saute seafood in oil in saute pan over medium-high heat until opaque, 3 min.
Add garlic and sherry; reduce until sherry is evaporated. Remove seafood from the pan and set aside.
Proceed with Alfredo according to directions on Page 23 or 25, *except* stir in tomatoes and cayenne when cream begins to boil. Simmer 2 min.
Stir in the reserved seafood when the cheese is added. Season with salt.
Garnish with strips of fresh basil.

Wares
can openers

The requirements for a good hand-held can opener are pretty simple: to cut open a can quickly and capably, with as little effort as possible. So who meets the standard?

We went through case after case of chili beans to determine the best openers on the market. Starting with 22 name-brand openers, we whittled the finalists down to eight. Among those not making the first cut were some big names, a few gimmicky, "inventive" ones, even an "As Seen on TV" model.

While hand-crank can openers come in a myriad of styles, they all fall into two basic categories: The traditional opener that cuts the lid off *inside* the rim, and the safety lid opener that cuts the lid from the *outside* of the can, on the rim, so the whole lid lifts off.

Traditional openers

Traditional openers are familiar and straightforward to operate. They attach to cans without much thought, and then cut with a gear-driven mechanism, *see right.* The lid is cut off completely, then drops into the can. (To prevent the lid from dropping in, stop just short of finishing the cut, leaving a thin thread of metal.)

Safety openers

Then there are safety lid openers. I became enamored with them the first time I saw the results—smooth-edged, danger-free lids and cans. And the lid fits right back on to store things like dog food. Pretty slick.

Each particular brand attaches to the can a little differently. While they may seem tricky or unfamiliar at first, like most tools, after the first few times it becomes second nature. And because the cutting mechanisms don't come in contact with food, they stay clean and don't accumulate a crusty buildup.

But safety lid openers may not be for everyone. Because they actually cut through the thick rim of the lid, more turning effort is usually required than with a quality traditional opener. And they often cut into a line of glue used on many cans, so that strands of gummy glue stretch and lift as the lid is removed.

And the winner is . . .

Happily there's something for everyone here. As it turns out, openers in *both* categories received our highest rating. And interestingly enough, they were the *most* expensive and *least* expensive of the 22 tested.

Buy these openers at kitchenware stores (prices may vary slightly), or see Resources, *Page 43*, for ordering information.

Cutting mechanisms

Here's a close-up look at the way openers are driven.

▲***Gear-driven:*** *Traditional openers rely on gears (the heavily notched wheels) to move around the can and turn the blade.*

▲***Standard safety lid:*** *Mounting from the top, a notched circle hugs the inner rim and rotates, as the nearly hidden blade cuts into the outside of the rim.*

▲***Rösle safety lid:*** *In a design category by itself, the revolutionary Rösle mounts from the side, with the support arch (shown above) resting on top of the can. It rolls around the can powered by a notched driving gear, while the cutting wheel penetrates the outer rim.*

safety lid

Rösle

★★★★★

price: $34.99

Introduced last year, German engineering produced a safety lid opener that's a cut above the rest. So sleek and compact, it doesn't appear capable of opening anything. But not so! The weighty single handle attaches easily from the side, then moves around the rim with smooth turning action, cutting at a level that usually misses the nasty "glue line." The opener removes the lid by simply lifting up, and carries an incredible lifetime warranty.

Kuhn Rikon Safety Lid Lifter

★★★½

price: $15.95

On the market for three years, Kuhn Rikon offers two top-mounting Safety Lid Lifter models. Both the white plastic and deluxe stainless steel versions are built with identical cutting mechanisms and attach to the can exactly the same. Each carries a two-year warranty.

Their differences are both aesthetic and operational. While the plastic version is considerably lighter in weight and cost, the handsome, well-balanced stainless version edged ahead with a more comfortable turning knob that seems to rotate just a little easier.

The patented Lid Gripper located on the side of each opener looks like a tiny beak. It works as its name implies, grabbing the lid and lifting it off.

That they are not dishwasher safe isn't a serious flaw. The gears never actually come in contact with contents of the can, and stay pretty clean as a result.

price: $24.95

Kuhn Rikon Deluxe Safety Lid Lifter

★★★★

Zyliss Safe 'N Secure

★★★

price: $15.00

Available in transparent (shown) or white, the top-mounting Zyliss attaches easily to the can and cuts into the rim at the point where the lid is welded onto the can. But turning does require some effort. Lid removal is with a beak designed to grab and lift. Zyliss features an impressive five-year warranty and is dishwasher safe. Watch for an improved model on the market within a year.

traditional

Pedrini Ergo Soft

★★★

price: $12.99

Made in Italy, the Pedrini Ergo Soft is sold in several different finishes and colors, but they all share the same cutting mechanism and general design features—like the raised soft-grip handles that are designed to mold to each hand. While certainly capable, the Pedrini turns with considerable effort. This opener is dishwasher safe and boasts a lifetime warranty.

Chantal

★★★½

Elegant comfort marks the Chantal opener. The long, contoured handles are shaped so well they don't *need* any padding. Filled with a nonreactive cement that keeps them in perfect balance, they fit any size hand comfortably. It attaches with ease and rolls masterfully around the can, but doesn't consistently cut the lid off entirely. Dishwasher friendly, it has a lifetime warranty.

price: $24.99

Swing-A-Way

★★★★★

price: $6.99

Since they began manufacturing hand-held openers in 1955, Swing-A-Way has sold over 200 million. And they've done it all with the same original model (#407, *above*) and the newer Comfort Grip (#709, *below*), carrying five-year warranties.

Mechanically identical, both openers attach with a powerful pop, then roll around the can with unmatched ease. While the original model is quite comfortable, the Comfort Grip kicks it up a notch with a chunkier handle that offers more padding. To keep your opener spinning smoothly, wipe with a damp cloth, then dry.

Still made at their factory in St. Louis, it's the most readily available opener on the market. But don't be misled by knock-offs. The name Swing-A-Way is imprinted on every opener. Watch for their upscale Signature line in kitchenware stores soon.

Swing-A-Way Comfort Grip

★★★★★

price: $7.99

allabout

Baked potatoes

Bake a potato and you're not far from an easy dinner or side dish. The question is, what's the best way to do it? Read on.

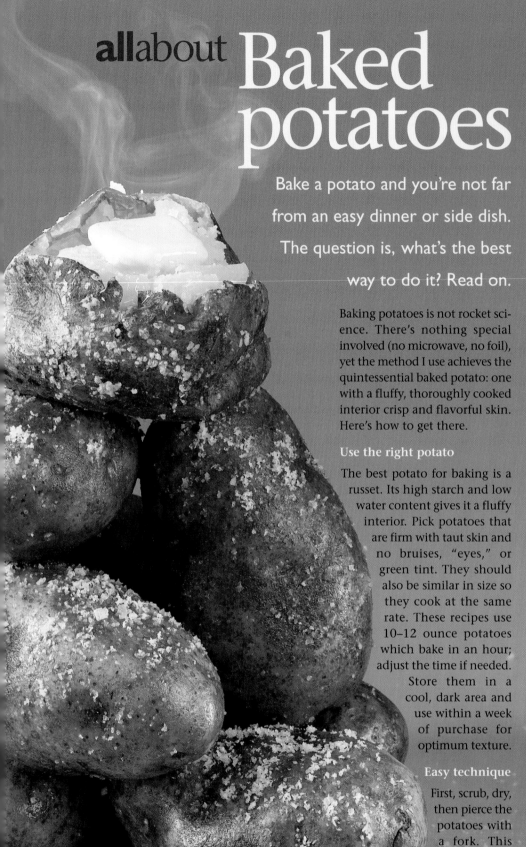

Baking potatoes is not rocket science. There's nothing special involved (no microwave, no foil), yet the method I use achieves the quintessential baked potato: one with a fluffy, thoroughly cooked interior crisp and flavorful skin. Here's how to get there.

Use the right potato

The best potato for baking is a russet. Its high starch and low water content gives it a fluffy interior. Pick potatoes that are firm with taut skin and no bruises, "eyes," or green tint. They should also be similar in size so they cook at the same rate. These recipes use 10–12 ounce potatoes which bake in an hour; adjust the time if needed. Store them in a cool, dark area and use within a week of purchase for optimum texture.

Easy technique

First, scrub, dry, then pierce the potatoes with a fork. This releases steam during baking (for a fluffy interior) and helps prevent them from bursting open.

Then place the potatoes in a sealable plastic bag with a little oil and salt, *see photo above*. Rub to coat with oil then place them directly on the rack of a 450° oven. Forget about microwaving them first to give them a head start—it doesn't do a thing for the flavor and the skin won't get crisp. Same goes for wrapping them in foil. It just steams them.

Bake the potatoes for an hour, or until they're completely soft inside when pierced with a knife or skewer. The skin should be crisp and brittle. Split and serve them quickly, or the skin will soften as a result of steam inside.

The Best Baked Potatoes

Makes 4 Potatoes

Rub with Oil and Salt:

4 medium russet potatoes (10–12 oz. each), scrubbed, dried, and pierced

Preheat oven to 450° with rack in center.

Rub prepared potatoes with oil and salt (doing this in a plastic bag makes the job less messy). Bake directly on the rack for 1 hour, or until tender all the way through when pierced with a skewer.

Remove potatoes from the oven, split, and serve immediately.

baked potato soup

Don't write this off as being too wintery.
Baked potatoes are great any time of year—
and so is this soup.

Baked Potato Soup

You can bake the potatoes the day before making the soup.
Makes 8 Cups
Total Time: 30 Minutes + Baking

For the Soup—
Bake as on Page 30:
4 medium russet potatoes
Saute in 4 T. Unsalted Butter:
1/2 cup yellow onion, diced
Whisk in:
1/4 cup all-purpose flour
Stir in:
2 cups low-sodium chicken broth
2 cups whole milk
4 cups baked potato flesh, lightly mashed
2 T. chopped fresh parsley
Salt and pepper to taste
For the Garnishes—
Toss in 1 T. Olive Oil; Bake:
Skins from baked potatoes, cut into strips
Salt and pepper to taste
Prepare (Keep Separate):
4 strips bacon, diced, sauteed
3/4 cup cheddar cheese, grated
1/2 cup sour cream
1/4 cup chopped fresh chives

Bake potatoes and cool slightly. Scoop out and lightly mash the flesh (reserve skins); set aside. **Saute** onion in melted butter until soft, about 5 minutes. **Whisk** in flour; cook 2–3 min. **Stir** in broth and milk. Cook and stir until thick, 4–5 minutes. Add potato and simmer 5 min.; stir in parsley and seasonings. **Toss** strips of potato skins in oil, salt, and pepper. Roast in 400° oven 15 minutes, or until crisp. **Prepare** remaining garnishes and serve with soup.

Scoop potatoes and lightly mash flesh. Cut skins into 1/4" strips. ►

▲*Roast skins for garnish.*

▲*For soup, saute onion in butter; whisk in flour.*

◄*Stir broth, milk, potato, parsley, and seasonings into onion.*

stuffed baked potatoes

The elegant shape, crisp shell, and flavor options breathe a little new life into these stuffed baked potatoes.

Stuffed Baked Potatoes

Makes 8 Potato Halves
Total Time: 45 Minutes + Baking

Bake:
6 medium russet potatoes
For Milk Mixture, Heat:
$^1/_2$ cup whole milk
2 T. unsalted butter
3–4 garlic cloves, minced
Salt, white pepper, and nutmeg to taste
Prepare Potato Shells; Brush with:
Olive oil
Coarse sea salt
Mash Potatoes, Stir in Milk, and Pipe into Shells.
Drizzle with:
Olive oil
Coarse sea salt

Bake potatoes as on Page 30. **Heat** milk, butter, garlic, and seasonings in small saucepan over medium heat until hot and butter has melted. Remove from heat and set aside; keep warm while preparing the potatoes. **Prepare** potato shells by first cutting a small piece off both ends of 4 hot baked potatoes; discard the ends. (To bulk up the filling, peel the 2 extra potatoes and add them to the mashed potato filling.)

Cut each potato in half crosswise, *Figure 1*, then scoop out the flesh, leaving about $^1/_4$" around sides, *Figure 2*. It's okay if you break through the bottom. Stand the shells in a muffin tin, wide end up. Brush insides of shells with olive oil, sprinkle with salt, and bake at 450° for 15 min., or until crisp and brown. Reduce oven to 425°. **Mash** potato flesh while it's hot using a ricer, *Figure 3*, hand masher, or an electric mixer. Stir in enough of the hot milk mixture to make stiff mashed potatoes. Transfer potatoes to a piping bag fitted with a large plain tip and pipe into shells, *Figure 4*. Drizzle each stuffed potato with a little more oil, sprinkle with salt, and bake 20–25 minutes, or until browned and heated through.

▲*Scoop flesh from halves and bake shells until crisp.*

Placing shells in a muffin tin helps keep them upright. Because potatoes may be lumpy, use a plain tip to pipe, not a star tip (or just spoon potatoes in the shells). Fill shells quite full to keep filling from caving in as they bake. ►

Adding on

◄ *Goat Cheese and Rosemary*

▲*Bacon and Gruyere*

Basil Pesto ▲

Stuffed Baked Potatoes with Basil Pesto

If using purchased pesto, be sure to buy a refrigerated brand—the color and flavor are fresher. Or make your own pesto, below.

Makes 8 Potato Halves

Bake as on Page 30. Scoop and Bake Shells, Page 32:

6 medium russet potatoes

Mash Potatoes with:

Hot milk mixture, *Page 32*

3 T. purchased basil pesto

Bake potatoes, then scoop shells and bake until crisp.

Mash potatoes and mix with hot milk mixture. Stir in pesto, fill shells, and bake according to the recipe on Page 32.

33

online **extra**

Want more info? Visit **www.CuisineAtHome.com** for a step-by-step recipe and photo guide for pesto.

Stuffed Baked Potatoes with Goat Cheese and Rosemary

These potatoes are great alongside a roast pork or lamb. You can use thyme instead of rosemary.

Makes 8 Potato Halves

Bake as on Page 30. Scoop and Bake Shells, Page 32:

6 medium russet potatoes

Mash Potatoes with:

Hot milk mixture, *Page 32*

4 oz. mild goat cheese, crumbled (about ½ cup)

2 t. finely minced rosemary

Bake potatoes, then scoop shells and bake until crisp.

Mash potatoes and mix with hot milk mixture. Add goat cheese and rosemary, fill shells, and bake according to the recipe on Page 32.

Add milk mixture, goat cheese, and rosemary to hot, riced potatoes. ►

Stuffed Baked Potatoes with Bacon and Gruyere

The cheese in the bottom of the shells bakes to a cracker-like texture. You can skip it if you want—but you'd be sorry!

Makes 8 Potato Halves

Bake as on Page 30. Scoop and Bake Shells, Page 32:

6 medium russet potatoes

Saute until Crisp; Drain:

4 slices thick-sliced bacon, diced

Mash Potatoes with:

Hot milk mixture, *Page 32*

Sauteed bacon

¼ cup scallions, minced (white and green parts)

Place in Potato Shells:

½ cup Gruyere cheese, shredded

Bake potatoes, then scoop shells; bake until crisp.

Saute bacon over medium heat until crisp; drain on paper towel-lined plate.

Mash potatoes and mix with hot milk mixture. Stir in bacon and scallions.

Place about 1 T. cheese in the bottom of each potato shell, *right.* Fill shells and bake according to the recipe on Page 32.

Champagne Chiffon Cake
with Blackberry Filling and 7-Minute Icing

If you want a party cake, this is the one to make.
Just look at it—how can you not feel like celebrating?

Three things make this cake so festive: the cake, filling, and icing. Here are the highlights of each component.

The cake

This is a classic chiffon cake, a 1920s invention which uses vegetable oil (not butter) and leavens with baking powder and beaten egg whites. The texture is light and spongy, like angel food but with more body. Its height is mainly from the egg whites, but also from the pan it's baked in and the unusual cooling technique, *see Fig. 3, below right.*

The champagne imparts a distinct flavor, giving the cake a "grown up" taste. If you don't want to use alcohol, substitute orange juice or water.

The filling

Tangy blackberry filling is a perfect contrast to the champagne and citrus in the cake. Even better, it's simple to make because it uses frozen berries.

The icing

The lightness of chiffon cake requires a light icing as well. An old fashioned 7-minute icing is perfect. It matches the cake's texture and gives it a casual, yet finished look, but without the piping hassle of a fancy frosted cake.

Making the cake

Don't let the cake's size scare you. The right tools and techniques will ensure success.

▲*A removable bottom makes it easy to release the cake.*

The proper pan

This cake is baked in a 9 1/2" tube pan with 4" sides, a 14–15 cup capacity, and removable bottom with a tube in the center (it makes the cake look cool *and* helps it bake evenly).

The pan should be made of lightweight, shiny aluminum. If you need to buy one, look at hardware or grocery stores first. Kitchen stores tend to carry heavier pans that have dark interiors which create an overbaked crust.

Avoid nonstick pans. Their interiors are almost always dark and will overbake and toughen the outside of the cake.

Techniques

Beating the egg whites and folding them into the batter are the two primary techniques in making this cake. When beating, it's important that they aren't too soft or too stiff, *Figure 1.* Soft whites won't raise the cake well, and stiff whites will dry it out. Beat just until glossy and hold a firm, stiff (but not dry) peak.

The next challenge is to fold them in so they deflate as little as possible. First, lighten the batter by stirring in a quarter of the whites. Add the rest of the whites and then gently fold them in using an over-under motion with a rubber scraper, *Figure 2.*

When the cake is done, invert it onto a bottle and let it cool completely upside down, *Figure 3*—this helps prevent the cake from falling. Release the sides and tube, *Figure 4,* then split, fill, and ice the cake, Pages 36–37.

1 Beat until whites hold a firm peak when mixer is lifted out.

2 Lighten batter with some of the whites. Fold in the remaining whites until no streaks remain—do not overmix.

3 After baking, immediately invert pan onto a bottle. Cool cake before releasing it from the pan.

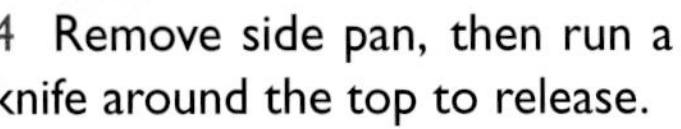

4 Remove side pan, then run a knife around the top to release.

Champagne Chiffon Cake

This cake is great filled and iced, but also good with powdered sugar and fresh berries.

Makes One 10" Cake

Sift Together:

2 cups all-purpose flour
1 1/4 cups sugar
1 T. baking powder
1/2 t. table salt

Whisk In:

1/2 cup vegetable oil
1/2 cup dry champagne (do not substitute white wine)
1/4 cup fresh orange juice
1/4 cup Cointreau or Triple Sec (water may be substituted)
5 egg yolks

Beat:

7 egg whites
1/4 t. cream of tartar

Sprinkle In:

1/4 cup sugar

Preheat oven to 325° with rack in center. Have an ungreased 9–10" tube pan with removable bottom ready.

Sift dry ingredients together in a large mixing bowl. Make a well in the center of the mixture.

Whisk into the well the oil, champagne, juice, liqueur, and yolks until smooth.

Beat whites and cream of tartar on low speed until frothy. Increase speed to medium.

Sprinkle in sugar 2 T. at a time. Beat just until whites are stiff and glossy, but not dry.

Mix 1/4 whites into batter to lighten, then gently fold in remaining whites just until incorporated. Pour batter into pan and bake 1–1 1/4 hours, or until skewer inserted in center comes out clean. Invert cake onto the neck of a bottle and cool completely upside down.

To remove cake from pan, run a knife around the sides and carefully push the bottom out. Use a knife to release the tube portion from the cake.

Assembling the cake

Once the cake is cool and out of the pan, you can either wrap it tightly in plastic wrap and freeze it, or split and fill it (the cake is a little easier to split when frozen). Splitting a cake into layers is tricky at first, but it's a good skill to know. Here's what to do.

Splitting the cake

Place the cake on a work surface—ideally, a decorating stand with rotating base. The bottom of the cake will be sticky so place parchment or waxed paper on the work surface before placing the cake on top of it.

Before actually splitting the cake into layers, you're first going to "score" shallow cuts around its circumference. This is easiest to do if you lean over and get eye level with the cake. "Eyeball" where it divides in half, about two inches from the top (if the cake is four inches tall).

Using a long serrated bread knife, place the blade at that halfway spot and rotate the cake with your other hand, cutting about 1/2" in all the way around, *Figure 5*. Now eyeball and then score each of the halves in two—this is the start of four layers.

Split the cake by slicing through the score marks. Use long strokes of the knife as you rotate the cake around at the same time, *Figure 6*. Don't worry if the layers aren't perfectly even (mine never are), but they should be about an inch thick.

Filling the cake

Set the top three layers aside and place the bottom layer on a serving platter. But first, lay strips of parchment around the platter to protect the plate from icing.

Spread filling on each layer, leaving a 1/4" margin along the outside so it won't swirl into the icing, *Figure 7*. Chill the cake until ready to ice (may be made and filled one day before icing).

Blackberry Filling

The citrus flavor in the cake is great paired with this blackberry filling. Frozen raspberries may also be used, or a combination of the two.

Makes About 2 Cups

Mash Together:

- 1 package (1 lb.) frozen blackberries, partially to fully thawed
- 1/4 cup sugar
- 2 T. dry red wine
- Zest from one orange, minced
- Pinch of table salt

Combine:

- 2 T. cornstarch
- 2 T. fresh orange juice

Mash berries, sugar, wine, zest, and salt together in a mixing bowl. Transfer mixture to a saucepan and bring to a boil over medium heat.

Combine cornstarch and juice in a small bowl, crushing any cornstarch lumps with your fingers. When berry mixture comes to a boil, whisk in cornstarch mixture. Simmer berries for 1 minute, or until thick and the "starchy" flavor is cooked out. Transfer filling to a clean bowl, cover with plastic wrap pressed directly on the surface, and chill until completely cold (filling may be made 1–2 days ahead).

◀*Boil the berry mixture for a minute or two after adding the cornstarch. This will eliminate any starchy taste.*

5 "Score" cake into layers, cutting 1/2" deep all the way around it.

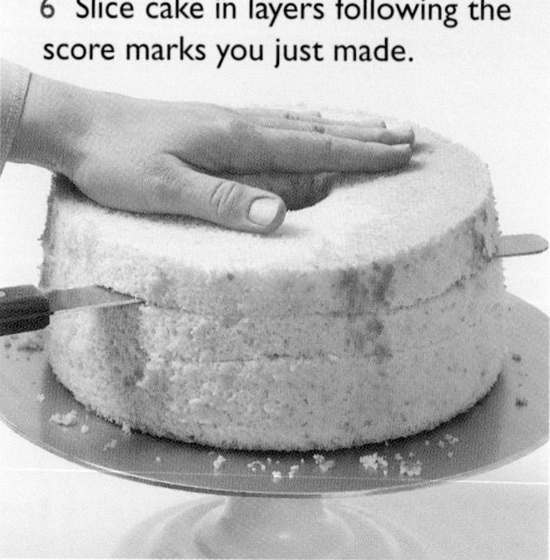

6 Slice cake in layers following the score marks you just made.

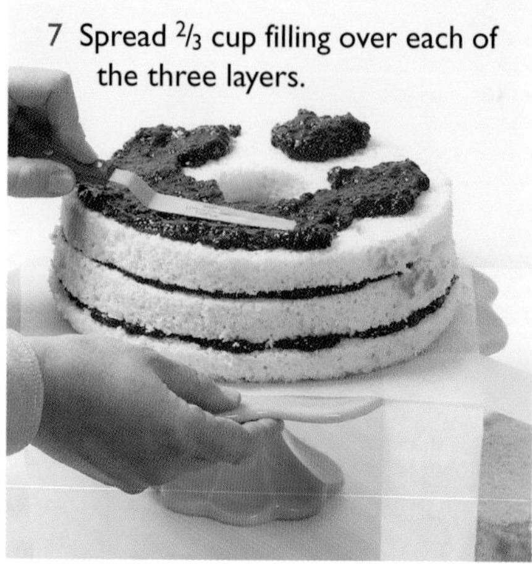

7 Spread 2/3 cup filling over each of the three layers.

This 7-Minute Icing is classic, but there are a few tricks to making and using it. Keep these in mind.

Making the icing

First of all, get everything ready for icing the cake *before* you make the icing. Gather utensils (spatula, spoon) and brush crumbs from the cake's surface, *Figure 8*. The icing sets up quickly and is easiest to use and looks best within minutes of finishing.

As you beat the icing over the water, pay attention to how hot the water is. If you see a lot of steam rising up the outside of the bowl, the water is too hot. That will cause the icing to cook too fast and set before reaching its full volume.

Using the icing

Working quickly, put the icing on the top and sides of the cake in big blobs, *Figure 9* (don't worry about where it lands). Spread with a spatula, being careful not to streak it with filling or crumbs.

Now use the back of a tablespoon to create peaks and curls, *Figure 10*. If the icing starts to turn stiff and doesn't form peaks, stop—it'll still taste great.

To cut the cake, dip a thin-bladed knife into hot water before slicing. Wipe the knife clean as necessary.

7-Minute Icing

Makes Enough for a 10" Cake

Combine:

1 1/4 cups sugar
2 T. fresh orange juice, strained
2 T. fresh lemon juice, strained
1 T. light corn syrup
2 egg whites
1/4 t. cream of tartar
Pinch of table salt

Combine all ingredients in a medium or large metal mixing bowl. Place the bowl over a saucepan of lightly simmering water. (Don't allow the bowl to touch the water. The bottom should be about 1" above the surface.) Beat the mixture with a hand mixer on high speed for 5 minutes, or until the mixture holds stiff peaks when the beaters are lifted out.

Once the desired texture is reached, remove the bowl from the saucepan and continue beating at high speed 2–3 minutes, or until icing is very stiff and slightly cooler to the touch. Use right away or it will stiffen and be hard to spread.

Beat all ingredients over simmering water for 5 minutes.▼

After 2–3 minutes, the mixture turns white and starts to thicken.►

▲*Remove bowl from pan and beat until white, glossy, and stiff.*

8 Brush off excess crumbs with pastry brush before making the icing.

9 Prepare icing. Use immediately, "blobbing" it over the top and on the sides.

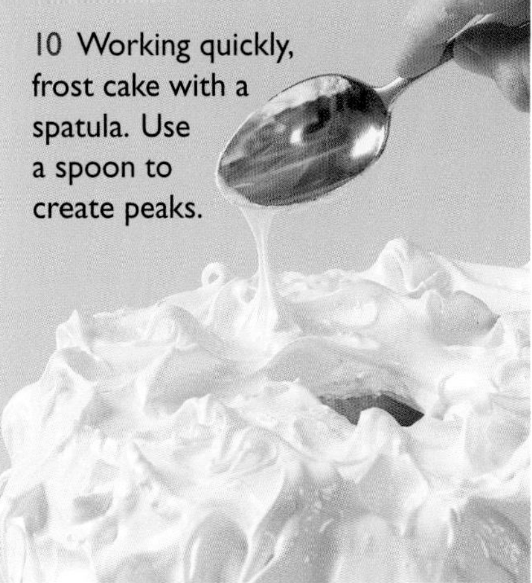

10 Working quickly, frost cake with a spatula. Use a spoon to create peaks.

faster **with** fewer

fiesta summer grill

Sure, time is limited, but dinner doesn't have to be out of a can or the microwave. This quick meal is company-worthy!

Even if you're not short on time, a little natural simplicity and do-ahead preparation puts this meal on the "A" list. But don't let its ease fool you—there's plenty of flavor and eye appeal here. Try these three favorites and see just how easy (and great-tasting) cooking can actually be.

Most of the preparation is done in reverse order. First, make the coffee for the dessert so it can chill. Second, marinate the meat for the main course (you can do this up to four hours before grilling). And finally, prepare the salad just before serving so it looks and tastes ultra-fresh.

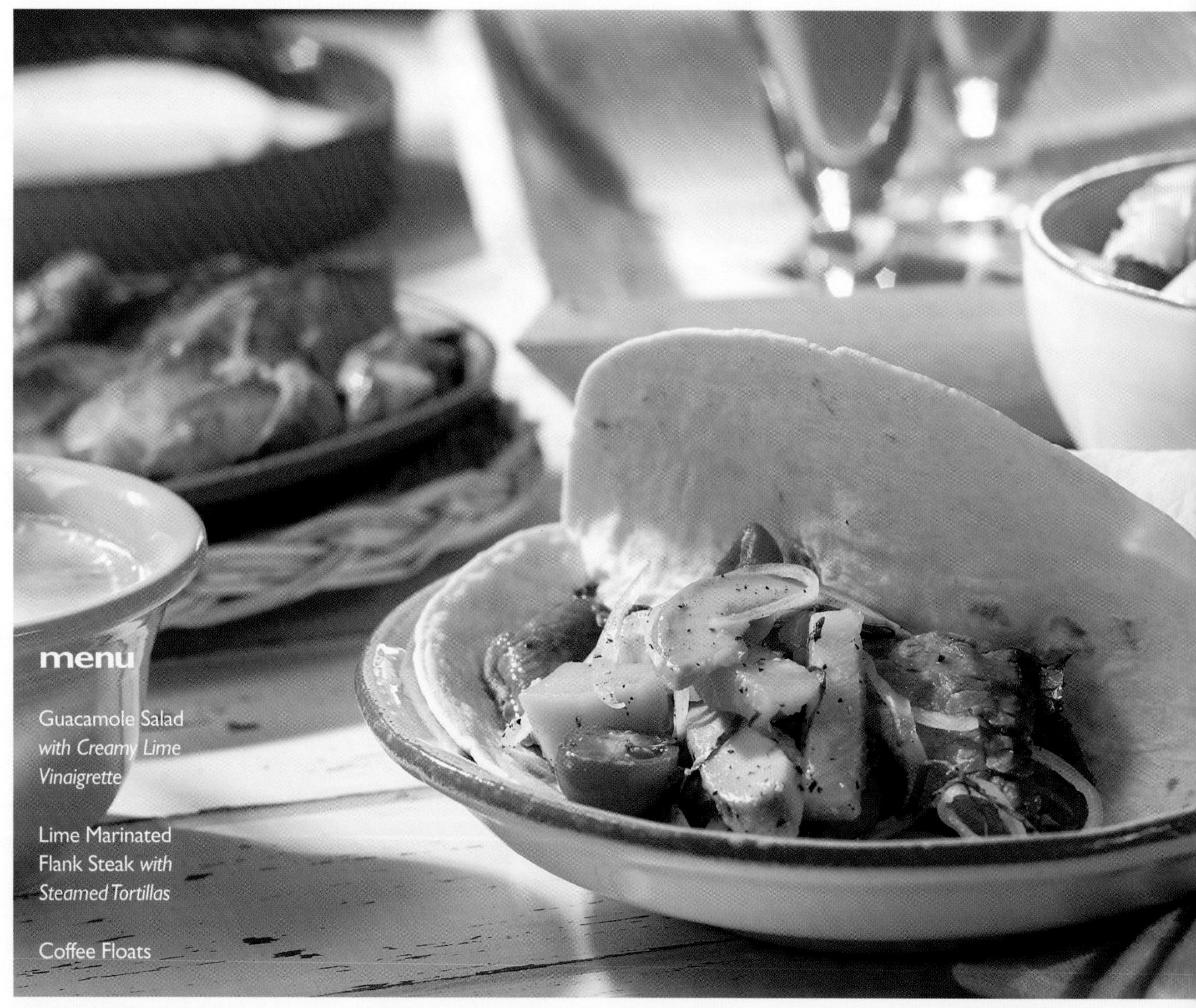

menu

Guacamole Salad *with Creamy Lime Vinaigrette*

Lime Marinated Flank Steak *with Steamed Tortillas*

Coffee Floats

Buying mangoes *Choose blemish-free, golden fruit tinted with red (like a sunset). They should give slightly when pressed—hard ones will ripen at room temperature.*

33

online **extra**

Want more info? Visit www.CuisineAtHome.com for a step-by-step photo guide on dicing mangoes.

guacamole salad

Guacamole Salad

Basil isn't a traditional herb in Mexican cooking, but it tastes terrific in this salad. Be sure the avocado and mango aren't too soft or they'll turn the salad "muddy."

Makes About 2 1/2 Cups
Total Time: 15 Minutes

Combine:
- 1/2 ripe but firm mango, peeled, pitted, and cubed
- 1/4 fresh pineapple, cut into sticks
- 1/2 cup grape tomatoes, halved
- 1/2 cup white onion, slivered
- 3 T. fresh basil, thinly sliced into strips
- 2 T. fresh lime juice
- 1 T. jalapeño, seeded, minced
- 1 ripe but firm avocado, peeled, pitted, and sliced
- Salt and pepper to taste

Serve with:
- Creamy Lime Vinaigrette

Combine all ingredients, tossing gently to blend. I do this on a baking sheet, turning ingredients with a metal spatula to keep them from breaking up. Set aside at room temperature until ready to serve. (Can be made up to 1 hour ahead—don't add avocado until just before serving.)
Serve salad with the Creamy Lime Vinaigrette.

Creamy Lime Vinaigrette

You'll be amazed at the intensity of this simple vinaigrette. Make it up to a day ahead and keep chilled.

Makes 2/3 Cup
Total Time: 10 Minutes

Whisk Together:
- 1/4 cup fresh lime juice
- 2 T. sour cream
- 2 t. sugar
- 1 t. garlic, minced
- 1/2 t. kosher salt
- 1/4 t. crushed red pepper flakes
- 1/4 t. ground cumin

Drizzle in:
- 3 T. vegetable oil

Whisk together first 7 ingredients.
Drizzle in oil slowly, whisking to emulsify.
Serve with salad.

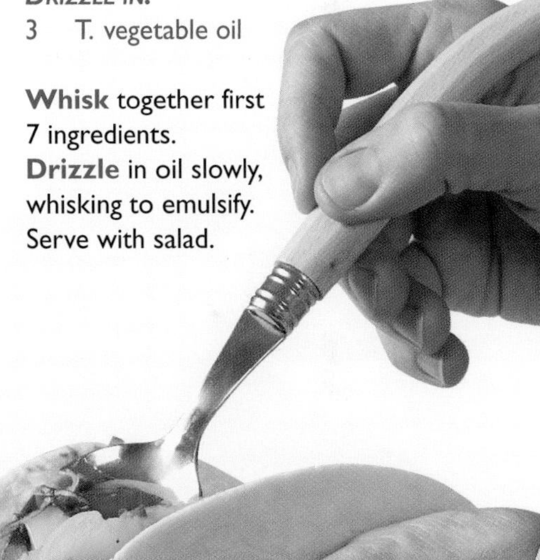

grilled flank steak

Flank steak is perfect for this fast dinner—grill it quickly for the optimum in tenderness and flavor.

LIME MARINATED FLANK STEAK

MAKES ONE 1-LB. STEAK
TOTAL TIME: 30 MINUTES

MARINATE:
1 lb. flank steak, trimmed
3 T. fresh lime juice
2 T. garlic, minced
2 T. olive or vegetable oil
Salt and pepper to taste

SERVE WITH:
Guacamole Salad and Creamy Lime Vinaigrette, *Page 39*
Steamed flour tortillas

Marinate steak in lime juice, garlic, oil, salt, and pepper in a resealable plastic bag for at least 15 minutes or up to four hours (chill steak if marinating for longer than one hour).

Preheat one side of grill to high. Place steak on lit side, cover, and cook to medium-rare, 3–4 minutes per side. Steam tortillas. Let steak rest five minutes, then thinly slice against the grain on a sharp bias.

Serve slices of steak wrapped in tortillas with Guacamole Salad and Lime Vinaigrette.

▲ *Remove steak from marinade; discard marinade. Grill, covered, 3–4 min. Flip and finish grilling.*

▲ *Gauge temperature to ensure doneness. Steak is medium-rare (and at its best) at 120–125°.*

▲ *Wrap tortillas loosely in a damp towel, then wrap in foil. Place packet on unlit side of grill during last 3 minutes of cooking.*

▼ *Thinly slice steak against grain (perpendicular to the arrow). Thin slices mean they will be less tough.*

coffee floats

Coffee Floats

Even if you don't care for coffee, you'll like this. Chocolate and cinnamon transcend coffee's morning image and move it into the realm of an adult milkshake.

Makes 4 Floats
Total Time: 5 Minutes + Chilling

Brew and Chill:
6 cups strong coffee

Pour Coffee Over:
1 pint good-quality cinnamon, vanilla, or coffee ice cream
1/4 cup chocolate syrup

Garnish Floats with:
Chocolate-covered coffee beans, shaved chocolate, or cocoa powder

Brew coffee and chill until cold. **Pour** 1 1/2 cups chilled coffee over 2 scoops ice cream and 1 T. chocolate syrup per float. **Garnish** floats as desired.

from **our** readers

Q&A
questions & answers

TRUFFLES

Can you explain what truffles are (not the chocolate kind)? And is it possible to grow them?

Wendy Spini
Red Bluff, CA

Truffles are a fungus related to mushrooms. Prized for centuries for their pungent, alluring aroma and flavor, they are still one of the most expensive and coveted items in the world.

There are two types of truffles—black and white. Black truffles are considered to be the best, and come primarily from France's Pèrigord region. White (or Alba) truffles, from Italy's Piedmont region, are the next most sought after.

Truffles grow underground around tree roots—typically oak, but also chestnut, beech, and pine. Farmers used to use pigs to sniff out truffles, but now rely on dogs because they aren't as apt to eat the buried treasure once it's been dug up.

Commanding prices of $800–$1500 per pound, it's natural to want to get into the business—but it's not an easy career path. Farmers often inoculate tree roots with spores, but wait *at least* five years before seeing any growth.

Jarred Black Truffles
While not as aromatic or flavorful as the fresh variety, they will give a dish the hint of truffle magic—and at a much more reasonable price than fresh. Find them at gourmet food stores, or order from Angelina's Italian Truffles at ***angelinastruffles.com***

CHAI REPORT

What exactly is chai?

Beth Hagler
Loganville, GA

Chai (pronounce it like "eye" with a ch- sound in front) is a centuries-old beverage with roots in India, Tibet, and Nepal. The word itself means "tea" in many languages, but it has recently become synonymous with a spicy, milky, sweetened tea drink.

In its most basic form, chai is simply tea that's been brewed with aromatic spices. Cardamom is almost always included in the spice blend, but cinnamon, ginger, cloves, and black peppercorns are also common.

In India, where chai has been enjoyed for centuries, milk is added either during or after brewing. Honey or sugar may also be stirred in. Nearly every corner in India has a chai vendor (called chaiwallahs), and every vendor will sell a slightly different chai.

The popular American coffee house version of chai is more of a chai "latte"—spiced tea, blended with sugar or honey, and steamed milk, served hot or cold.

But you don't have to go to a coffee house. There are many products on the market for making chai at home—tea bags, chai latte mixes, liquid concentrates, loose leaf tea with spices, and bottled, ready-to-drink chai.

DEGLAZING

What is deglazing and when is it necessary?

Dina Ciaramella
Reno, NV

Deglazing is a technique used after sauteing meats or vegetables. It's a way to incorporate the flavorful brown residue stuck in the pan into liquid (it's a key step to pan gravy, Pages 8–9).

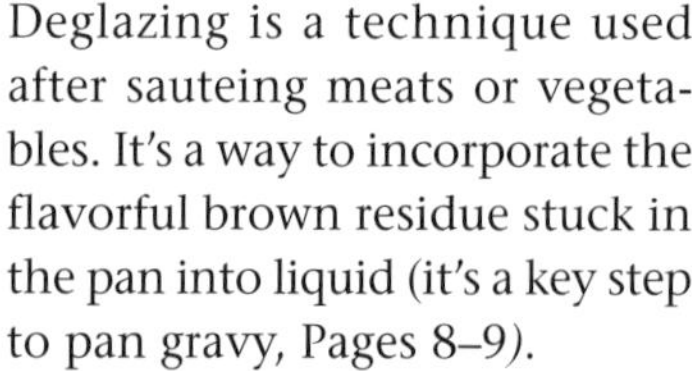

To deglaze, first remove meat from pan (if used), then add a liquid—broth, juice, or wine. Next, scrape up the residue (the liquid loosens it) and simmer. This is a perfect base for a sauce.

Since so much flavor is released by deglazing, it really enhances the flavor of a dish. However, if the residue is burnt or scorched, deglazing should not be done, or that will be the overwhelming taste.

HALF-LINE SPRINGFORM

I have a recipe that calls for a half-line springform pan. Can you tell me what that is?

Julie Klise
Perry, IA

Perhaps your recipe has German roots, because the folks at Kaiser Bakeware report that in Germany the term "half-line springform" refers to a half-size springform pan. They call it half-line to indicate that a recipe can be halved to make a smaller or individual portion in this pan. Here in America, it's usually called a mini-springform pan.

SCOTCH BONNET CHILE

I have a recipe calling for a Scotch bonnet chile, but can't find one. What is a good substitute?

Lynn Alberding
Richland, MI

Scotch bonnet chiles are unique because, besides being one of the hottest chiles on the planet, they have a fruity quality not found in other hot chiles. Unfortunately, Scotch bonnets can be hard to find. Habaneros have a similar fruitiness and make a good substitute. But beware! They are a little bit hotter than Scotch bonnets. Use both with caution.

PIZZA STONES

Can pizza stones really be used at the high oven temperature recommended in the pizza article in Issue 32? Could you give me a source?

Terry Strohman
Des Moines, IA

A good pizza/baking stone must withstand high oven temperatures, even the recommended 550° in the pizza article. Cracking will occur only if there's a hairline flaw or if the stone is made from low-quality clay.

So how can you tell if a stone is of good quality? It should be made from a porous material and be at least $^{1}/_{2}$" thick. And check the warranty. If a company stands behind the stone, they're confident it's going to stand up!

We've never rated stones, but here are some we use and like in the test kitchen.

a) Kitchen Supply Co. offers an impressive lifetime guarantee on their 14 x 16" stone ($25.95). Made from the same firebrick material that's used to line kilns, the underside has "feet" so it stands slightly above the oven rack for easier lifting.

b) FibraMent makes a $^{3}/_{4}$"-thick stone from a porous, patented "fiber cement." Often used in commercial ovens, it can withstand temperatures up to 750°. Their 13 x 17" stone for home ovens comes with a 180-day warranty and costs $35.99.

c) The ceramic Bravo stone sells for $36.95. It's $15^{1}/_{2}$ x $14^{1}/_{2}$", $^{3}/_{4}$" thick, and carries a one-year warranty. With both sides flat, you can bake on either side.

Check local kitchen stores or see Resources, *right*, to order.

Rectangular stones offer ► more space for the size and shape of pizzas than round stones do. Be sure to measure your oven to ensure a good fit.

resources

PROFESSIONAL CUTLERY DIRECT
Chantal Can Opener, Item #2CM205
Rösle Can Opener, Item #2CM204
(800) 859-6994

KITCHEN ETC.
Swing-A-Way Can Openers:
White, Item #120443
Black Comfort Grip, Item #590927
(800) 232-4070
kitchenetc.com

KITCHEN EMPORIUM
Bravo Pizza Stone, Item #VW518
(888) 858-7920
kitchenemporium.com

FANTE'S KITCHEN WARES SHOP
FibraMent Pizza Stone, Item #3350
(800) 443-2683
fantes.com

GOURMET CATALOG
Zyliss Safe 'N Secure Can Opener, Item #ZYL1005
Pedrini Can Opener, Item #PED1002
(877) 445-0005
gourmetcatalog.com

COOKING.COM
Kitchen Supply Co. Pizza Stone, Item #102521
Kuhn Rikon Safety Lid Lifter Can Opener, Item #127224
Kuhn Rikon Deluxe Safety Lid Lifter Can Opener, Item #127231
(800) 663-8810
cooking.com

Henckels Blue Dot Shears
In the last issue of Cuisine at home, *these shears got our highest rating. Order them by phone from Professional Cutlery Direct (they aren't listed on their web site). To order Henckels Blue or Red Dot shears, or the LamsonSharp shears, call* ***(800) 859-6994***.

Q&A

Do you have a question for *Cuisine at home?*

If you have a question about a cooking term, procedure, or technique, we'd like to hear from you. We'll consider publishing your question in one or more of our works. Just write down your question and mail it to *Cuisine at home*, Q&A Editor, 2200 Grand Ave., Des Moines, IA 50312, or contact us through our email address shown below. Please include your name, address, and daytime phone number in case we have questions.

Email: CuisineAtHome@CuisineAtHome.**com**
Web address: CuisineAtHome.**com**

make it a **menu**

Summer Night Dinner

The Market Salads on Pages 12–15 can be eaten by themselves, but sometimes you need a little something warm to satisfy your hunger. These crustless custards are just the ticket. Serve them hot, warm, or at room temperature with your favorite market salad. Just the meal for a summer dinner.

Savory Crustless Custards

Makes Eight 4-oz. Custards
Total Time: 45 Minutes

Whisk Together:
6 eggs
1 1/4 cups half and half
1 cup plain lowfat yogurt
2 T. unsalted butter, melted

Add:
3/4 cup all-purpose flour
1 1/2 t. kosher salt

Stir In:
8 oz. mild cheddar cheese, finely shredded
1/4 cup each chopped fresh parsley and chives

Preheat oven to 425°. Spray eight 4-oz. ramekins liberally with nonstick spray.
Whisk together eggs, half and half, yogurt, and melted butter until well combined.
Add the flour and salt. Stir until there are no lumps.
Stir in the cheese, parsley, and chives. Transfer the mixture to a pitcher (this makes it easier to pour). Fill each ramekin 3/4 full, place them on a baking sheet (to catch overflow), and bake for 30–35 minutes, or until set, puffy, and lightly browned on top. Remove ramekins to a cooling rack and cool for at least 10 minutes before unmolding (they will fall slightly). Gently invert ramekins to unmold. Serve custards warm or at room temperature with a Market Salad of your choice.

▲ *Invert and unmold baked custards onto a clean towel. Flip them over onto a plate.*

MBURGERS DONE RIGHT—JUICY & GRILLED TO PERFECTION

Cuisine at home™

Grill a *Perfect* Steak Everytime!

Plus:

Summer **Sundaes**

3 recipes to **cool** a hot day

Barbecue Ribs

big flavor—**easy** technique

Issue No. 34 August 2002

A publication of August Home Publishing

Cuisine at home™

www.CuisineAtHome.com

talk to ***Cuisine at home***
Subscriptions, Address Changes, or Questions? Write or call:

Customer Service
2200 Grand Avenue,
Des Moines, IA 50312
800-311-3995,
8 a.m. to 5 p.m., CST.

Online Subscriber Services:
www.CuisineAtHome.com
Access your account • Check a subscription payment • Tell us if you've missed an issue • Change your mailing or email address • Renew your subscription • Pay your bill

Cuisine at home™ (ISSN 1537-8225) is published bi-monthly (Jan., Mar., May, July, Sept., Nov.) by August Home Publishing Co., 2200 Grand Ave., Des Moines, IA 50312.
Cuisine at home™ is a trademark of August Home Publishing Co.

Subscriptions: Single copy: $4.99. One year subscription (6 issues), $24.00. (Canada/Foreign add $10 per year, U.S. funds.)

Periodicals postage paid at Des Moines, IA and at additional mailing offices. "USPS/Perry-Judd's Heartland Division automatable poly". Postmaster: Send change of address to **Cuisine at home**, P.O. Box 37100 Boone, IA 50037-2100.
Cuisine at home™ does not accept and is not responsible for unsolicited manuscripts. PRINTED IN SINGAPORE.

editor's letter

For many of us, any time of the year is grilling season. I'm sure some of you have grilled in chilly temperatures, rain, and snow just as I have. But we don't have to endure any of these negative elements now—this is "full contact" grilling season.

And it's not by accident that we have worked with one of the world's foremost authorities on barbecuing and grilling, Steven Raichlen. Oprah called him the "Gladiator of Grilling" and *USA Today* wrote "Where's there's smoke, there's Steven Raichlen."

In search of the perfect steak, we've all dabbled at ways to raise the bar at one time or another. We've tried all the special grill tricks and goofy rituals like 48-hour homemade spice rubs or marinades created from bottled Italian dressing. No more!

Experimenting is over and steak "nirvana" is here as Steven Raichlen shares his 10 steps to perfect grilling. Once you read this article and try his simple methods, you'll never cook a steak with all the gimmicks you've used in the past. As it has with the *Cuisine* staff, I know the Bistecca alla Fiorentina (porterhouse with simple herbs and olive oil) will become a family favorite.

Don't overlook two of summer's other grill favorites—ribs and burgers. The Asian style ribs are easy to prepare because they're precooked in the oven. There's no lingering for hours over a smoker that requires constant poking, prodding, and babysitting. And of course, summer wouldn't be the same without the aroma of burgers on the grill. But there's more to it than just throwing ground beef over a fire. Learn all the tips and techniques starting on Page 6 so you can become a true burger meister.

There are plenty of recipes in this issue to maximize summer's pleasures. Some are quick, others cooling, but most just taste like summer—fresh and outdoorsy. It's a special time of the year where everything seems to be at its best. Enjoy summer.

table of contents

Issue No. 34 August 2002

departments

features

from our readers

tips and techniques

Tip from the Test Kitchen
If you don't have a citrus zester, you can use a vegetable peeler or paring knife for zesting. Simply peel or slice the colored portion of the citrus, slice it into strips, and chop into pieces.

Clever Cubes

When there are more herbs in the garden than you can use, try freezing them. Place the herbs (basil, parsley, rosemary, etc.) in a food processor with 1 cup water and puree. Pour the mixture into ice cube trays and freeze. Pop the cubes into freezer bags for storage. The cubes can be used in stews and soups all year.

And if citrus is on sale, stock up! Zest the fruit, then juice it. Place the zest and juice into ice cube trays and freeze. Store the cubes in freezer bags. Each cube roughly equals a citrus half.

Helen Smith
Albany, OR

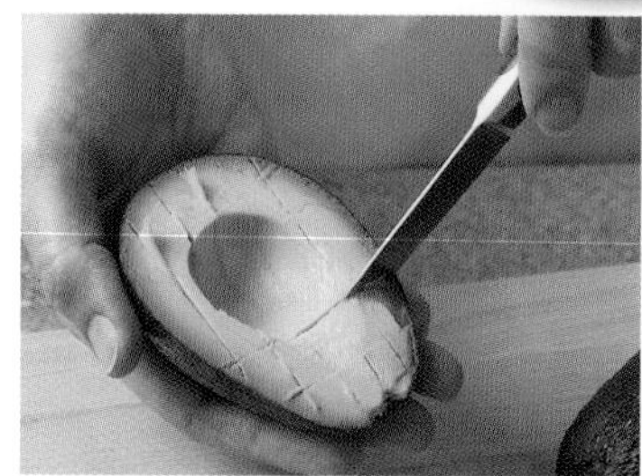

Avocado Dicing

Cut an avocado in half and remove the pit. With a paring knife, make long slits the length of each avocado half, being careful not to cut through the skin. Turn the avocado and make small slits crosswise making a cube pattern.

Bend the avocado half and push out the cubes or scoop them out with a spoon. This can be used with the types of avocados with heavy, dark skin.

Grace Stevens
San Mateo, CA

Double Duty Muffin Tin

Our family regularly gets together for picnics and cookouts. Instead of having all those condiment bottles on the table, I put the burger and hot dog toppings in the wells of my muffin tin. It can be placed out of the way at the end of the table.

Brenda Lawyer
Jefferson, IA

Easy Thawing

There's an easy way to store ground meat so that it will thaw faster when you're ready to cook it. Put one pound of ground meat into a large resealable freezer bag and then flatten it like a pancake. It stores better and thaws in half the time.

Audrey Devaty
North Olmsted, OH

Great Combination

Instead of boiling two pots full of water to cook corn and potatoes, cook them together in one pot with a steamer basket. Simply cut the potatoes (not necessary if using new potatoes) and corn into roughly the same size pieces. Place them in a steamer basket inside a large pot with a small amount of water. The corn and potatoes will cook much faster and be less soggy! Plus, there will only be one pot to clean.

Cynthia Waltho
Ham Lake, MN

Key Lime Squeeze

To juice those tough little Key limes, I use my garlic press. Cut the limes into quarters, place into the press, and squeeze. The press also traps the seeds.

Kara Burkhardt
Centreville, MD

Cake Dome

How do you store the remainder of a decorated cake without ruining the frosting? Carefully place it under a large bowl.

Sally Ives
Mesa, AZ

Spray For Ease

Before unmolding a congealed dessert or salad, lightly spray the serving plate with water. It will be easier to move around and center on the dish.

Audrey Devaty
North Olmsted, OH

Flavored Pie Dough

When making pie dough or tart shells, I add citrus zest, chopped nuts, minced candied ginger, or fresh herbs (mint, basil, lavender, tarragon, or dill). The "extras" give the dough wonderful texture, and the added flavor enhances the final pie or tart.

Maria del Mar Hausle
Knoxville, TN

Wasp Deterrent

To distract those uninvited wasps at your next picnic, place a small amount of honey in a shallow can or dish. Place the container away from the table and traffic. The wasps will be attracted to the honey and forget all about what you're serving.

Miguel Lopez
El Paso, TX

Grilling corn *Peel back the heavy outer husks and the interior husks. Remove the silk and return husks to cover corn. Soak ears in cold water for an hour. Grill corn over medium-high heat about 20 minutes, rotating 1/4 turn every 5 minutes.*

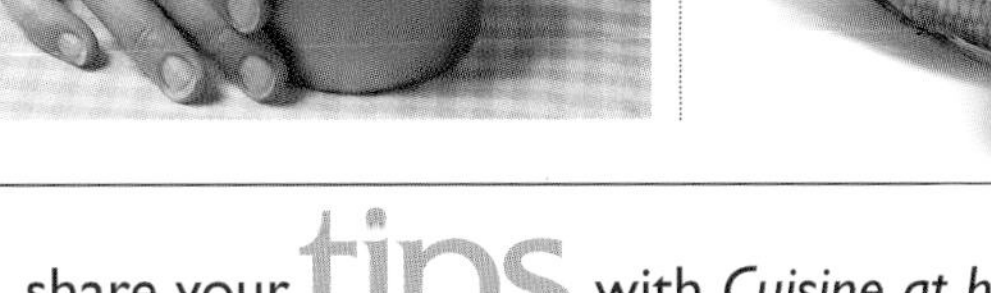

"Grate" Nuts

When you need ground nuts for a recipe, try using your hand-held cheese grater. It works like a charm and the job gets done in no time. And you don't have to bother with cleaning the electric coffee grinder to do it.

Ron Kramer
Bedford, MA

Storing Holders

Store your corn cob holders by sticking them into a gum eraser. That way you won't prick your fingers storing them haphazardly.

Drew Himes
Vienna, Ohio

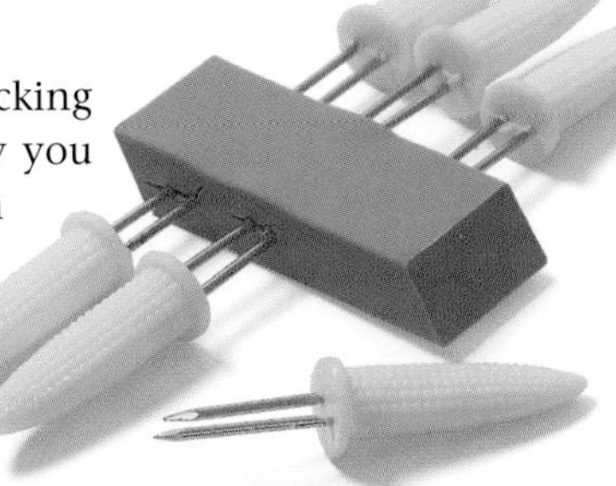

share your **tips** *and techniques* with *Cuisine at home*

If you have a unique way of solving a cooking problem, we'd like to hear from you, and we'll consider publishing your tip in one or more of our works. Just write down your cooking tip and mail it to *Cuisine at home*, Tips Editor, 2200 Grand Ave., Des Moines, IA 50312, or contact us through our email address shown below. Please include your name, address, and daytime phone number in case we have questions. We'll pay you $25 if we publish your tip.

Email: CuisineAtHome@CuisineAtHome.com

Web address: CuisineAtHome.com

the art of the hamburger

Odds are, the first thing on the grill this barbecue season will be a burger. Here's how to get summer off to a great start.

Revered and worshiped, hamburgers are arguably the glory of grilling. A great one is pure and simple ambrosia—beefy in taste and texture, juicy, flavored by fire and a good dose of salt and pepper. The bun is toasted and condiments are generous (so are the napkins for wiping juices dripping through your fingers). Absolutely *nothing* beats it.

Unfortunately, too many burgers wind up as burnt offerings to the grill gods—tough, overcooked, and shrunken to the point that they're dwarfed by the bun. No amount of ketchup or mustard can save them.

But this summer it'll be different. That's because each step to the perfect hamburger is mapped out right here—buying the meat, shaping and sizing the patties, and then grilling them perfectly. It's not rocket science so forget about wacky techniques like forming the meat around ice cubes, or poking holes in the center of the patties. But there is an *art* to the hamburger. And after this quick lesson, you'll be eating a burger masterpiece too.

The fine art of the burger requires a few simple techniques. Here's what you need to know.

The right beef

You have a few choices when buying ground beef—chuck, round, sirloin, and plain "hamburger." The biggest difference between them is their fat content. No, ground sirloin is not pulverized sirloin steak! Sirloin *may* be in there, but it's just trimmings from cutting sirloin steaks. According to industry standards, ground sirloin has about 10% fat. Chuck and round have 15–20% fat, and hamburger has up to 30%.

Surprisingly, a lot of fat is *not* a good thing when it comes to a grilled burger. There needs to be some to keep the meat moist, but excessive amounts cause shrinking and scorching. Ground chuck is my choice—it has great beefy flavor and just enough fat to be juicy without being greasy.

Seasoning

Burgers can be seasoned two ways: from the outside with salt and pepper on the surface, or from the inside by mixing the meat with seasonings *before* shaping. For the best all-around flavor, by all means, season from the inside.

Now, I expect to hear from grilling gurus about the salt leaching out juices. They may be right, but if the patties aren't shaped too far ahead, it's not a problem.

Use your hands to blend the meat with salt and pepper, *Figure 1*. They're gentle and that will make for a more tender burger.

Shaping

One of my pet peeves is a bun that's too big for the burger. So I measure the bun's diameter, then shape the patties about 1/2" larger. Fussy? Maybe, but the grilled burger fits the bun like a glove.

You just used your hands to mix the meat, but for shaping use a fork, *Figure 2*. Overworking the meat while shaping is typical, and a compressed patty shrinks a lot and makes the burger tough. "Forking" helps prevent that.

Finally, aim for a patty that's 3/4" thick, *Figure 3*. The burgers won't take too long to cook, or be so thin that they overcook and dry out. They won't get lost in all the condiments, either.

Grilled Hamburgers

Shape the burgers up to 30 minutes before grilling. Form each on a piece of parchment or wax paper for easy transfer to the grill.

Makes Four 6-oz. Patties
Total Time: 30 Minutes

Combine, Shape, and Grill:
1 1/2 lbs. ground chuck (85% lean)
1 t. kosher salt
1 t. freshly ground pepper
Top Each Burger with:
1 oz. sliced cheese, *optional*
Toast:
4 buttered hamburger buns
Serve with:
Easy Burger Toppings, *Page 11*

Preheat grill to medium-high. Clean grates, then oil lightly.
Combine meat, salt, and pepper in a large bowl; toss gently with your hands to mix—work quickly and with a light touch, handling the meat as little as possible. Shape into patties 3/4" thick and 1/2" larger than the diameter of the hamburger buns. Grill burgers, *Page 8*, until they register 160° on an instant read thermometer.
Top burgers with cheese, if desired, *Page 8*.
Toast buns, *Page 8*.
Serve with burger toppings of your choice, *Page 11*.

1 Gently blend the salt and pepper into the ground meat with your hands.

2 Use a fork to shape the burgers—it won't compress the meat. Form them on pieces of parchment.

3 A thickness of 3/4" is ideal. A 4 1/2" wide, 3/4"-thick patty will require close to 6 ounces ground meat.

grilling burgers

Perfectly seasoned and shaped burgers aren't worth their buns if they end up like charcoal briquets. Here's how to grill them to perfection.

The art of grilling

For hamburgers worth dreaming about (and drooling over) long after the grill heads south for the winter, follow these simple rules.

The grill: The temperature of the grill should be hot, but not so high that the outside of the burgers burn before they cook through—medium-high is good. Preheat the grill for at least 20 minutes, clean the grates, then oil them as Steven Raichlen does in the steak article, *Page 29*.

Grilling: Lightly spray the surface of the burgers with nonstick spray before slapping them on the grill, *Figure 4*. Place them, sprayed side down, on the grates and peel off the paper. Now lightly brush the other side of the burgers with oil, close the lid, and cook for 3–4 minutes, undisturbed (4–5 minutes for the turkey and pork burgers). Resist the urge to open the grill and press on the burgers with a spatula—that squeezes out juices.

Now flip them, top with cheese if desired, *Figure 5*, close the lid, and cook 3–4 more minutes (4–5 for turkey and pork). When they hit an internal temperature of 160°, they're done.

And don't forget to toast the burger buns in the last minute of cooking, *Figure 6*!

4 Spray burgers lightly with nonstick spray before grilling. Oil the other side after peeling off paper.

5 After cooking the first side, flip burgers and top with thin slices of cheese. Close lid and continue cooking until done.

6 Just before burgers are done, place buttered buns on grill to toast—keep an eye on them!

burger combos

All-American
Beef burger, Cheddar cheese, Chowchow

Summer Sizzler
Beef burger, Boursin Butter, Tomato Relish

turkey burgers

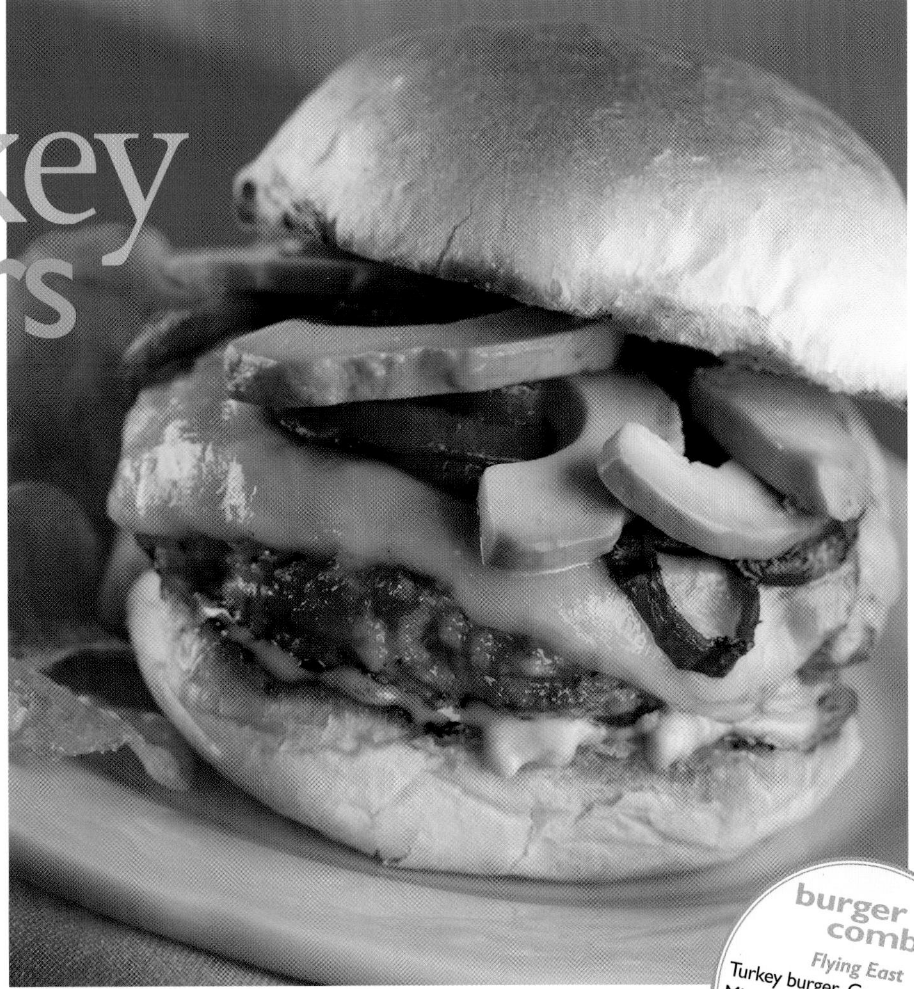

I know you're thinking, "Turkey burgers are so *dry*." Not these! Give them a try and taste for yourself.

A dismal history of Thanksgiving turkeys has most of us convinced there's only one way to get it—dried out. The thought of grilling something so "moisture challenged" is pretty dubious.

But the key is to combine two types of ground turkey: all breast meat and regular ground turkey (made from both dark and white meat). Besides enhancing the overall flavor, a blend gives the meat some much needed fat (moisture). This burger isn't as lean as one made with straight turkey breast, but the added flavor and juiciness more than make up for the extra calories.

It's still fairly lean, though, so be sure the grill grates are really clean so the burgers don't stick. Oil the grates and burgers extra well for good measure too.

Let's face it—turkey is mild, and a flavor kick from outside sources never hurt (why else is there gravy and cranberry sauce at the holidays?). This burger gets its boost from barbecued onions, spicy mayonnaise, and avocado (bacon isn't bad, either!).

Turkey Burgers with BBQ'd Red Onions

Makes Four 6-oz. Patties
Total Time: 30 Minutes

Combine, Shape, and Grill:
1 lb. ground turkey breast
$\frac{1}{2}$ lb. ground turkey
1 t. kosher salt
1 t. freshly ground pepper

For the Onions—
Grill:
4 $\frac{1}{2}$"-thick slices red onion
$\frac{1}{4}$ cup purchased barbecue sauce

Top Burgers with:
Sliced Monterey Jack cheese

Toast:
4 buttered hamburger buns

Serve with:
Chipotle Mayonnaise, *Page 11*
Sliced avocado

Preheat grill to medium-high. Clean grates, then oil lightly.

Combine ground turkey meats, salt, and pepper in a mixing bowl, tossing gently with your hands. Shape into four $\frac{3}{4}$" thick patties, *Page 7*. Coat patties with nonstick spray before grilling, *Page 8*. Grill 4–5 minutes.

Grill onions while burgers cook. Brush onions with barbecue sauce and cook until soft, 8–10 minutes. Turn often, brushing with additional sauce.

Top burgers with cheese after flipping, *Page 8*. Grill to 160°, 4–5 more minutes.

Toast buns during the last minute of grilling, *Page 8*.

Serve burgers with mayonnaise, onions, and avocado.

burger combos
Flying East
Turkey burger, Cucumbers with Mint Vinaigrette, mango chutney
Ruffled Feather
Turkey burger, brie, prepared cranberry relish

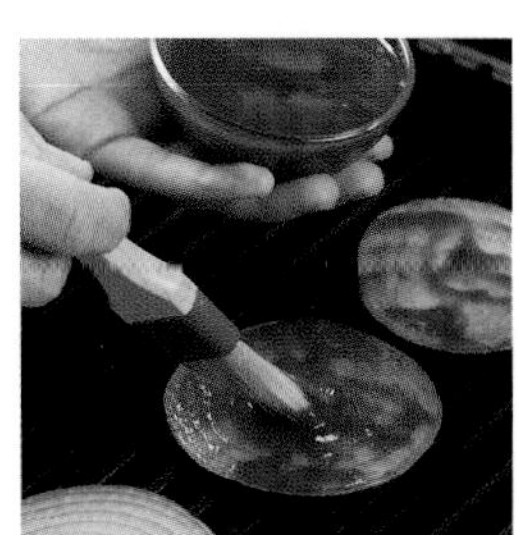

▲*Brush slices of onion with barbecue sauce often during grilling.*

pork burgers

An interesting change from regular hamburgers, these pork burgers will add a new dimension to your grilling repertoire.

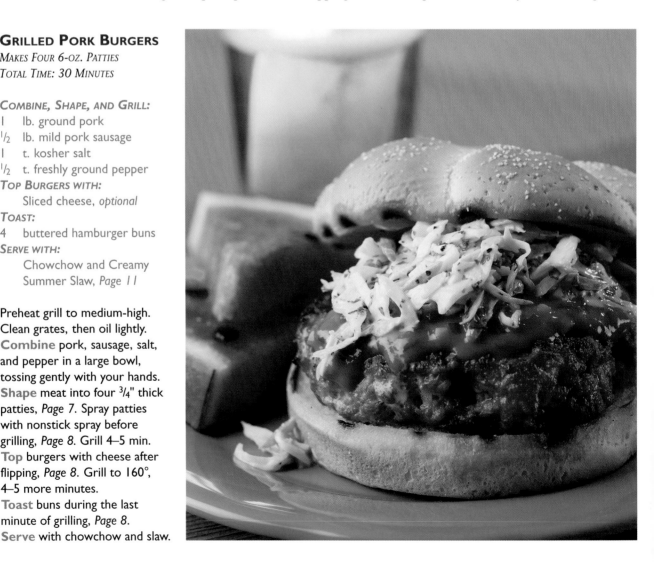

burger combos

Hog Heaven
Pork burger, Boursin Butter, Sun-dried Tomato Mayo

The Razorback
Pork burger, provolone cheese, BBQ'd Onions, Tomato Relish

A burger made of ground pork isn't as odd as you might think—just imagine it's flattened-out bratwurst! Loaded up with chow-chow and coleslaw, you may give up beef burgers altogether.

Like the turkey burgers, these are a combination of two ground meats: sausage and plain pork. The spices in the sausage give the plain pork a little more flavor. I use a mild sausage, but if spicy is more your thing, use hot sausage. Do not, however, use *all* sausage. It tastes too "breakfast-y."

Pork is a staple in the South, so this burger is outstanding with toppings from the region. Coleslaw is, of course, the South's salad of choice, and this Creamy Summer Slaw is perfect here (or with a platter of fried chicken).

This chowchow is a unique blend of several condiments in one—it's *addictive*! (Unlike other chowchows, this isn't cabbage-based.) Try it on hot dogs too.

Grilled Pork Burgers

Makes Four 6-oz. Patties
Total Time: 30 Minutes

Combine, Shape, and Grill:
1 lb. ground pork
1/2 lb. mild pork sausage
1 t. kosher salt
1/2 t. freshly ground pepper
Top Burgers with:
Sliced cheese, *optional*
Toast:
4 buttered hamburger buns
Serve with:
Chowchow and Creamy Summer Slaw, *Page 11*

Preheat grill to medium-high. Clean grates, then oil lightly. **Combine** pork, sausage, salt, and pepper in a large bowl, tossing gently with your hands. **Shape** meat into four 3/4" thick patties, *Page 7*. Spray patties with nonstick spray before grilling, *Page 8*. Grill 4–5 min. **Top** burgers with cheese after flipping, *Page 8*. Grill to 160°, 4–5 more minutes. **Toast** buns during the last minute of grilling, *Page 8*. **Serve** with chowchow and slaw.

easy burger toppings

Sun-dried Tomato Mayonnaise

Makes About 1/2 Cup
Total Time: 10 Minutes

Blend:
1/2 cup mayonnaise
2 t. sun-dried tomatoes packed in oil, minced
1 t. sugar
1 t. Italian seasoning
1 t. fresh lemon juice
Minced garlic to taste

Blend all ingredients in a small bowl. Refrigerate 30 minutes before serving so flavors can develop.

Boursin "Butter"

Makes About 3/4 Cup; Total Time: 5 Minutes + Chilling

Blend:
1/4 cup Boursin cheese
1/4 cup cream cheese, softened
1/4 cup Monterey Jack cheese, finely shredded
2 T. Parmesan cheese, grated

Blend all ingredients in a bowl. Shape into a cylinder, wrap in plastic, and chill until firm. Slice into rounds and place on burgers as you would cheese.

Chipotle Mayonnaise

Makes About 1/2 Cup
Total Time: 10 Minutes

Blend:
1/2 cup mayonnaise
1 t. sugar
1 small chipotle chile, minced
1/2 t. adobo sauce (from canned chipotles)
Juice of half a lime

Blend all ingredients together in a small bowl. Let sit at least 30 minutes before serving so flavors can develop.

Fresh Tomato Relish

Makes 2 Cups
Total Time: 10 Minutes

Combine:
4 Roma tomatoes, seeded and diced (about 2 cups)
1/4 cup scallion, sliced
1 T. balsamic vinegar
1 t. brown sugar
Salt and black pepper to taste

Stir in:
2 T. thinly sliced basil

Combine tomatoes, scallion, vinegar, brown sugar, salt, and pepper in a bowl. Let stand at room temperature for at least 30 minutes so flavors can blend. **Stir in** the basil just before serving.

Creamy Summer Slaw

Makes About 3 Cups
Total Time: 10 Minutes + Chilling

Whisk Together:
1/4 cup mayonnaise
2 T. apple cider vinegar
2 T. sugar
2 t. prepared horseradish
Salt and pepper to taste

Toss with:
4 cups shredded cabbage
2 T. chopped fresh parsley

Whisk mayonnaise, vinegar, sugar, horseradish, salt, and pepper together in a large bowl. **Toss with** cabbage and parsley. Chill until ready to serve, at least 30 minutes.

Chowchow

Makes About 1 1/2 Cups
Total Time: 15 Minutes + Chilling

Simmer:
1/2 cup prepared yellow mustard
1/4 cup ketchup
1/4 cup purchased barbecue sauce
2 T. maple syrup

Stir in:
3/4 cup red onion, minced
1/2 cup sweet pickle relish, drained

Simmer mustard, ketchup, barbecue sauce, and syrup in a small saucepan over medium heat. Cook 2–3 minutes, then cool to room temperature. **Stir in** onion and pickle relish. Chill chowchow until ready to serve.

Fresh Tomato Relish
Creamy Summer Slaw
howchow
hipotle Mayo
Sun-dried Tomato Mayo
Boursin Butter

the secret to easy grilled ribs

Use your oven to make spareribs juicy and tender. Then grill them quickly to deliver knock-out outdoor flavor.

So, you're going to buy ribs?

There are two choices—baby back and spare. True rib enthusiasts will tell you there is only one—spare. I agree.

Baby Backs

From the loin rib section. Real baby backs are from a young pig and weigh about a pound. If they weigh more than that, they're *not* baby backs.

Spareribs

These 13 ribs are also called "3 and down" because they weigh 3 pounds or less. Note the hump at top. This is the breast plate and feather bones. Remove and grill with ribs.

Good ribs are an art form. To do them right, most hardcore rib cookers smoke them for hours in a carefully controlled 200–225° outdoor smoker. This makes a great rib, but the attention this process requires can be too time consuming. So what do you do when you want to eat a few ribs without the fuss? Oven-roast, then give them a quick grilling.

By slow-roasting the ribs first in an oven, you ensure this tough cut will be tender. Then, for that outdoor flavor, finish them on the grill with your favorite sauce.

Choosing Ribs: Serving good ribs begins with picking the right ones. Advertising has convinced us that baby back ribs are the only ribs to buy. They're okay, but for texture and flavor, the sparerib is the clear winner. Here's why.

Picture the side of a pig and draw a line dividing the top from the bottom. Tender loin cuts run along the top but lack flavor since they don't get much exercise. Baby back ribs come from this area and are simply an extension of pork chops. They are hardly even ribs and usually have nothing to do with younger pigs.

Now, picture the lower half of the pig. This is where the ribs are located that protect all the breathing parts. These ribs are exercised constantly making the surrounding meat flavorful. You know how flavorful bacon (pork belly) is. It's a close neighbor. So, without a doubt, for the most flavorful ribs, buy spareribs.

Trimming and docking ribs

You first have to trim the ribs to remove the tough membrane and bony ends of the ribs.

Trimming: You can do this yourself or have the butcher do it for you. It's not hard.

To start, trim the little piece of flap (skirt) from the sinew side of the ribs, *Figure 1*. You can grill this along with the ribs.

Next, cut off the breast plate and flexible feather bones that form the rounded part of the ribs, *Figure 2*. You can leave them, but for a uniform look, cut them off. This is called St. Louis style.

All ribs have a sinewy membrane that won't melt away when cooked. This has to be removed. Grab the corner of this membrane with a paper towel and slowly pull it away from the bones, *Figure 3*.

Finally, trim any unusually fatty areas and dock between the bones, *Figures 4* and *5*. You're now ready to apply a rub.

1 Remove the skirt flap from the sinew side of the ribs. This can be grilled.

2 Cut off the breast plate and feather bones. This can be grilled.

3 Remove the sinewy membrane by pulling with a paper towel.

4 Trim some of the unnecessary fat from the ribs.

5 "Dock" the meat between the bones for extra flavor.

Rub and roasting ribs

Season the ribs with your favorite rub, cover with foil, and let them sit for about an hour. Longer exposure to the rub isn't necessary since most of the flavor will penetrate the ribs in the first hour. Besides, the rub will continue to flavor the meat while cooking for several hours.

Double check the foil to make sure it fits snugly around the pan. Now, slow-roast the ribs in a 250° oven for about two hours. This isn't an exact science so check the ribs after $1^1/_2$ hours. You want the meat to pull away from the bone, *Figure 8*. Now, you're ready to grill.

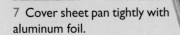

6 Apply the rub using your hands.

7 Cover sheet pan tightly with aluminum foil.

8 These ribs roasted for 2 hours. The meat has pulled away from the bones and the fat has rendered. Roasting may take longer.

asian lime ribs

Pork and Asian flavors naturally go together. The refreshingly light tastes of ginger and lime make this a perfect summer dinner.

Once you taste this Asian Lime sauce, you'll want to put it on everything (just not the sundaes on Page 34!). What's interesting about this sauce is its complexity—sweet, tart, spicy, full-bodied, yet light-tasting. It has several layers of flavor. But perhaps the best thing about Asian Lime sauce is it's not hard to make—no cooking required.

The rub is simple to make as well. You should have most of these spices in your pantry. If you don't, make it easy on yourself. Go to your grocery store and buy *five spice powder*—it'll be sitting with the rest of the spices. It is almost the same as the rub recipe except it has star anise and fennel—both add a nice touch of flavor.

After the ribs have been rubbed and roasted, you're only 15 minutes away from eating some mighty fine barbecue.

Grilling: Before you heat up the grill, you'll need to coat it with a nonstick spray. This sauce has sugar in it and tends to stick to the grate when the sugar melts from the heat.

Simply lift up the grate and spray it thoroughly. You can also rub the grate with an oil-soaked paper towel. Whatever you do, just don't spray the grate while the flame is on—it'll flare up and could back up into the can.

Now, preheat the grill to medium-high. Coat the ribs with sauce and place on the grill. When they begin to develop a little black char on them, flip and brush again with sauce, *Figure 1*.

Repeat this process at least twice so that the ribs become well glazed and nicely charred, *Figure 2*. This will take only about 15 minutes.

With the ribs grilled, you are ready to serve. On a cutting board, hold the rack vertically and cut between bones, *Figure 3*. Serve with chilled mint cucumbers and plenty of extra sauce for dipping.

What is hoisin sauce? *[Hoy-sihn] is a sweet and spicy sauce made from soybeans, garlic, and chile pepper. Widely used in Chinese cooking, it's readily available in most grocery stores.*

1 Slather sauce over ribs each time you turn.

2 When the outside of the ribs begin to char, they are ready.

3 Allow ribs to rest for 10 minutes. Hold the rack vertically on a cutting board. Cut the ribs between the bones.

Asian Lime Ribs

Serve plenty of sauce on the side for dipping the ribs.
Makes 26 Spareribs

For Rib Rub—
Combine; Rub on Two Racks of Spareribs:
2 T. ground cinnamon
2 T. kosher salt
2 T. black pepper
1 T. ground cloves
1 T. ground coriander

For the Asian-Lime Sauce—
Stir Together:
3 T. ginger, coarsely chopped
2 T. garlic, coarsely chopped
3/4 cup rice vinegar
1/2 cup low-sodium soy sauce
1/2 cup ketchup
1/2 cup chopped fresh cilantro
1/3 cup fresh lime juice
1/3 cup brown sugar
1/4 cup hoisin sauce
2 T. dark sesame oil
1 T. crushed red pepper flakes

Grill; Serve with:
Cucumber Salad
Asian-Lime dipping sauce

Prepare two racks of spareribs as on Page 13.
Combine ingredients for rub and apply to ribs. Cover and refrigerate for 1 hour. Roast according to instructions on Page 13.
Stir together ingredients for sauce. Brush on roasted racks of ribs before grilling.
Grill over medium-high heat a total of 15 minutes. Serve ribs with Asian-Lime Sauce and chilled mint cucumbers.

make it a menu

Keep it light and refreshing. This cooling summer menu can bring down the temperature on even the hottest August day.

Asian Lime Spareribs

Cucumbers with Mint Vinaigrette

Lemon Sorbet

Cucumbers with Mint Vinaigrette

Even if you're not a fan of cucumbers, you must try this. It's the perfect palate cleanser between bites of each spicy rib.
Makes 4 Cups

Puree in Blender:
10–15 fresh mint leaves
1/4 cup sugar
1/4 cup rice vinegar
2 t. fresh ginger, chopped
1/2 t. crushed red pepper flakes
Toss with:
1 English cucumber, thinly sliced (about 4 cups)

Puree in blender the mint leaves, sugar, vinegar, ginger, and red pepper flakes.
Toss with thinly sliced cucumber. Serve chilled.

▲ *Use English cucumber sliced thinly on a mandoline. The rough, green peel is attractive.*

rub and sauce options *for ribs*

Sure you can buy rubs and sauces, but you won't find any as good as these. A Carolina vinegar sauce and a southwestern chipotle sauce are sure to please.

Now that you know some of the basics to easy ribs, a little understanding of barbecue rib lingo is in order.

Ribs are served either *dry* or *wet*. Dry ribs are served only with the rub on them—sauce is on the side. Wet ribs are brushed with sauce as they cook, and additional sauce is served with them. Although much messier to eat than dry ribs, I prefer wet ones. I like the way the sauce slightly chars on the grill.

For these two sauces, the rub is the same. It's a good, generic rub that can be used on most any rib (even the Asian ribs).

The Orange-Chipotle Sauce is both hot and sweet. Neither the orange or chipotle flavors are overpowering but tend to pleasantly linger after you swallow.

And the Vinegar BBQ Sauce isn't a true North Carolina sauce. While vinegar is the predominant ingredient, the little bit of sugar and ketchup counteracts its harshness.

One rub—two sauces

Barbecue started out in the 1600s using nothing but a vinegar sauce. Over the years, ingredients like tomatoes and sugar were added as they were cultivated or imported.

Eastern North Carolina has kept to this tradition of serving barbecue with a vinegar and pepper dip. While interesting, I need a little more body and a little less harshness, so I added tomatoes and sugar. I simmer it for about 30 minutes to smooth out the flavors.

Since both of these sauces have sugar in them, be sure to watch the ribs closely as they grill. They can burn easily.

Basic Rib Rub

Makes Enough for Two Racks of Pork Spareribs

Combine and Rub:

2 T. kosher salt
2 T. black pepper
2 T. chili powder
1 T. paprika
1 T. ground oregano
1 T. dried thyme

Combine all dry ingredients. Rub onto racks of spareribs. Cover and refrigerate for 1 hour before roasting, *see Pages 12–13*. Grill following procedure shown on Page 15.

Orange-Chipotle Sauce

You should be able to find canned chipotle peppers in the international section of your grocery store.
Makes Enough for Two Racks of Pork Spareribs

Saute in 2 T. Vegetable Oil:

1 cup yellow onion, chopped

Add and Simmer:

2 T. garlic, minced
1 cup ketchup
1 cup orange marmalade
3/4 cup apple cider vinegar
1/2 cup brown sugar
1/4 cup prepared yellow mustard
1/4 cup fresh lime juice
3 chipotle peppers

Off Heat, Stir In:

1/4 cup fresh cilantro, chopped

Saute onion in oil until softened. **Add** garlic, ketchup, marmalade, vinegar, sugar, mustard, lime juice, and peppers. Simmer until sauce slightly thickens, about 30 minutes. **Off heat, stir in** chopped fresh cilantro and stir.

Vinegar BBQ Sauce

If you're interested in more of an authentic eastern North Carolina sauce, eliminate the ketchup and sugar from this recipe. Use as a dip rather than a sauce.
Makes Enough for Two Racks of Pork Spareribs

Simmer:

2 cups apple cider vinegar
2/3 cup ketchup
1/2 cup brown sugar
1 T. fresh lemon juice
1 T. Worcestershire sauce
1 t. dry mustard
1 t. black pepper
1/2 t. kosher salt
1/2 t. cayenne

Simmer all ingredients over a medium heat for 30 minutes, or until slightly thickened. Brush on ribs before grilling and baste with sauce as they grill. Serve extra sauce on side.

make it a menu

Sweet tea is a must. Mix 1 1/4 cups sugar to 1 gallon hot tea. Chill. Serve over ice with mint and lime.

Grilled Spareribs with Orange-Chipotle or Vinegar Sauce

Lime–Cilantro Slaw

Iced Sweet Tea

Lime-Cilantro Slaw

Makes 6 Cups

For the Lime Mayonnaise—
Stir Together:

1/3 cup mayonnaise
1/4 cup fresh lime juice
3 T. sugar
1 t. dry mustard
1/2 t. kosher salt

For the Slaw—
Combine:

8 cups green cabbage, shredded
1/4 cup chopped fresh cilantro
Lime Mayonnaise

Stir together ingredients for Lime Mayonnaise.
Combine cabbage, cilantro, and Lime Mayonnaise. Refrigerate slaw 1–2 hours to develop flavor.

34

online **extra**

Want another sauce? Visit www.CuisineAtHome.com for the recipe for a South Carolina Mustard Sauce.

allabout

Sweet Corn

You've been waiting all winter for it—the return of fresh sweet corn. Start shucking and put the pot on to boil!

Right now, vegetable gardeners everywhere are doing anything legal to shed the surplus of zucchini, tomatoes, and cucumbers currently ruling their lives. But no one on the receiving end of desperate gardeners *ever* gets sweet corn. That's different—it's a treasure just for the growers.

But there's still plenty of it to go around, typically spilling from truck beds at farmers markets and roadside stands. So here's information on the sweet corn that's available, how to buy it, and then dealing with it at home.

Types of corn

Corn varieties are lumped into two categories. *Field* (or dent) corn is for animal feed, processed foods (like cornflakes), and oil.

Sweet corn is eating corn, and there are three types you may find, all with varying sugar contents. *Standard* (or heirloom) is the lowest in sugar; *super-sweet* is at the other end of the scale. *Sugar-enhanced* falls in between.

Unfortunately, it's hard to tell which is which unless you know varietal names. Your best bet is to buy from local farmers—they're likely planting super-sweet or sugar-enhanced.

Selecting

The key to picking out good corn isn't so much a matter of what it looks like, as how long it's been since it was harvested. The second those ears are pulled off the stalks, sugar in the corn begins to convert to starch. And once the sugar is gone, so is a lot of the flavor and delicate texture. Buy corn with a plan in mind—like for dinner that night!

There are a few physical clues to good corn. Take a look at the photos, *right*, for telltale signs of the perfect ear.

Cooking

Corn is best simply cooked and served—shuck, boil, then butter! Cook it in plenty of water, about a gallon for four ears. Don't salt the water—it toughens the kernels. Some people add sugar to the water for sweetness, but the corn doesn't need it. And most importantly, *do not* overcook it. Fresh sweet corn should be cooked and on your plate in no more than five minutes.

Choosing sweet corn

▲*Look for silk that's pale in color, a little sticky, and brown at the very tips.*

▲*The tops of the ears should feel filled in with kernels developed right to the ends.*

▲*The cut should be fresh, moist, and free of spots. Old cuts take on a rusty look.*

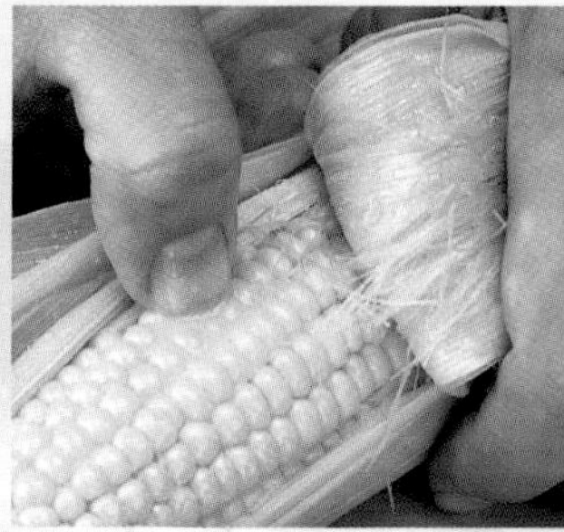

▲*Ripe kernels release a milky juice. An overripe ear is dry and tough.*

summery corn soup

Summery Corn Soup

Making stock takes time, but it's worth it. The extra flavor from the corn cobs is the key to this soup.

Makes 8–10 Cups
Total Time: About 2 Hours

For the Corn Stock—

Cut Kernels from:

10 ears sweet corn, husked (approx. 5 cups kernels)

Sweat in 2 T. Vegetable Oil:

1 large yellow onion, chopped
1 large leek, chopped
4 cloves garlic, smashed

Add and Simmer; Strain:

10 cups cold water
8 corn cobs, halved
5 yellow tomatoes, diced
2 cups corn kernels

For the Soup—

Simmer:

6–8 cups Corn Stock
2 large tomatoes, large dice
1 summer squash, large dice
1–2 canned chipotle chiles in adobo sauce, thinly sliced
Remaining corn kernels
Salt to taste

Serve with:

Scallions, cut into 2" pieces
Sliced avocado
Chopped fresh cilantro
Lime wedges

Cut kernels from husked corn. **Sweat** onion, leek, and garlic in oil until softened. **Add** water, corn cobs, tomatoes, and 2 cups kernels; simmer $1\frac{1}{2}$ hours. Strain stock, pressing on vegetables to extract juices; discard vegetables. **Simmer** corn stock for soup with remaining reserved corn, tomatoes, squash, and chiles for about 20 minutes. Salt to taste. **Serve** each bowl of soup with scallions, avocado, cilantro, and a wedge of lime.

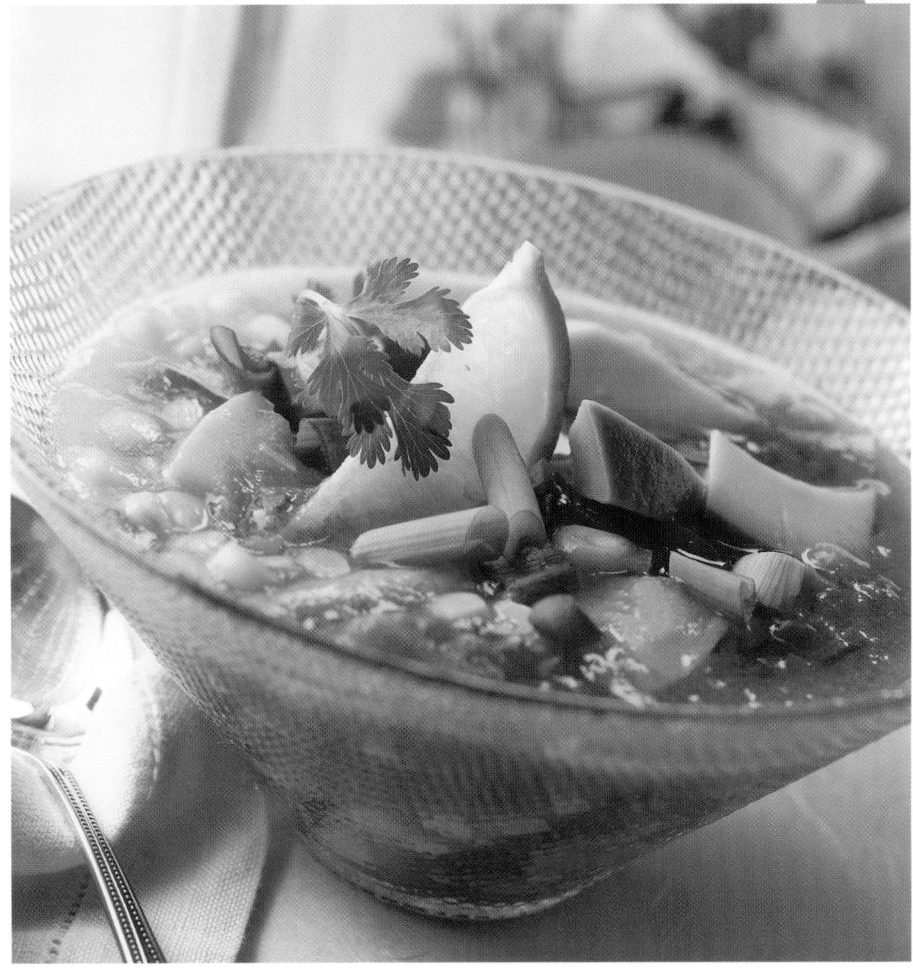

◄ Pour stock through a strainer and press the vegetables to extract all of the juices.

◄ Add tomatoes, squash, chipotle chiles, and reserved corn to simmering stock. Season to taste.

add ins

Add prior to serving:

2 cups roasted, chicken breast, shredded
1 cup cooked black beans
1 cup Monterey Jack cheese, grated, OR fresh Mexican *queso fresco*, crumbled

fresh creamed corn

Creamed Corn

Makes 5 Cups
Total Time: 20 Minutes

Cut Kernels From:
8 ears sweet corn, husked (approx. 4 cups kernels)

Puree:
About 2 cups reserved corn kernels
1/2 cup half and half

Melt:
1/4 cup unsalted butter

Add and Simmer:
Remaining corn kernels
Pureed corn mixture
2 cups heavy cream
1/2 cup half and half
1/8 t. cayenne
Salt to taste

Cut kernels from ears of corn. Using the back of the knife, scrape the cob to extract the milk. Divide corn into 2 batches.
Puree 2 cups corn in a blender with half and half.
Melt butter in a saute pan over medium-high heat.
Add remaining corn kernels, pureed corn mixture, cream, half and half, cayenne, and salt to taste. Simmer until thickened, 6–8 minutes.

◄*To remove kernels, stand cob upright. Carefully cut straight down along the cob.*

Scrape the cobs with the back of the knife to release the "milk." ►

▲*Puree 2 cups kernels in a food processor with half and half.*

34 *online* **extra**

Another corn idea? Visit www.CuisineAtHome.**com** for a recipe and easy steps.

corn stuffed tomatoes

Corn Stuffed Tomatoes

Makes 4 Tomatoes
Total Time: 45 Minutes

For the Tomatoes—
Prepare:
4 firm, medium tomatoes
For the Filling—
Blanch and Cool:
2 cups fresh corn kernels (cut from 4 ears)
Combine:
Blanched corn
$\frac{1}{4}$ cup red bell pepper, diced
3 T. mayonnaise
3 T. scallion, minced
3 T. thinly sliced basil leaves
1 T. fresh lemon juice
1 T. sugar
Salt and cayenne to taste
For the Topping—
Pulse:
1 slice French bread, cubed (enough to make $\frac{1}{2}$ cup crumbs)
Add and Pulse:
1 T. olive oil
1 T. chopped fresh parsley
Minced zest of 1 lemon
Serve with:
Fresh mesclun

Preheat oven to 400°.
Prepare the tomatoes by cutting off the tops and hollowing out the seeds and pulp with a spoon. Leave $\frac{1}{2}$"-thick wall of flesh around the inside of the tomato so sides don't collapse when baked. Discard pulp or reserve for another use. Invert tomatoes onto a plate to drain briefly while preparing the filling.
Blanch corn kernels for the filling in boiling water for 3 minutes. Drain and cool.
Combine the corn, bell pepper, mayonnaise, scallion, basil, lemon juice, sugar, salt, and cayenne in a medium bowl. Season the cavities of the tomatoes with salt and black pepper, then fill with a generous $\frac{1}{4}$ cup of the corn filling (amount will vary depending on size of tomatoes). Arrange tomatoes in a glass or ceramic baking dish.
Pulse the bread cubes for the topping in a food processor fitted with a steel blade. Process just until bread is coarse crumbs—not too fine.
Add the oil, parsley, and zest; pulse to combine. Top each tomato with about 2 T. of the crumb mixture and pat into place. Bake 15–20 min., or until crumbs are crisp. Don't overcook or tomatoes will collapse.
Serve with fresh meslcun.

◄Hollow out the tomatoes with a small spoon. Take care not to break through the skin.

Pat a generous amount of the crumb mixture on the tomatoes before baking. ►

salad dressings *revived*

thousand island

Tired of balsamic and honey-mustard vinaigrettes? Taste what you've been missing with these revived classics.

No wonder mainstream dressings have been steamrolled in recent years by trendy vinaigrettes. The bottled stuff we were raised on were no great shakes. But these classics put the bite back into salads.

Today's Thousand Island dressing is miles from what was created by a fishing guide's wife at the turn of the 20th century. The "islands" (flavorful bits of onion, relish, and egg) have been all but wiped out over time. But in this recipe they're back—a tribute both to flavor and the dressing's home in the island-rich lake area of upstate New York.

Serve with:

Sliced vine-ripe tomato
Thinly sliced sweet onion
Sliced cucumber
Parsley sprigs

Thousand Island Dressing

Serve this dressing on crisp greens, with seafood, or as a "special sauce" on burgers.

Makes About 1 1/2 Cups
Total Time: 15 Minutes

Combine:

- 1/2 cup mayonnaise
- 2 T. ketchup
- 2 T. red bell pepper, finely diced
- 1 T. sweet pickle relish
- 1 T. red onion, finely diced
- 1 T. minced fresh parsley
- 1 t. fresh lemon juice
- 1 t. prepared horseradish
- 1 hard-cooked egg, chopped
- Salt and pepper to taste

Combine all ingredients in a small bowl. Chill at least an hour before serving for flavors to develop. Keeps for one week.

▲*Layer slices of tomato, sweet onion, and cucumber on a platter. Tuck parsley sprigs all around for garnish and great flavor—don't be afraid to eat them too! Drizzle with Thousand Island and sprinkle with coarsely cracked black pepper before serving.*

green goddess

What ever happened to green goddess? This classic deserves a curtain call.

Green goddess was the rage in the 1920s after it was created at the Palace Hotel in San Francisco. It was named for the stage play, *Green Goddess*, showing in town at the time, and served to the play's star, George Arliss.

But for whatever reason, the dressing vanished years ago—it shouldn't have. Its herby-ness is good drizzled over bitter greens, but *perfect* with seafood and fish.

Green Goddess Dressing

If tarragon is too strong for you, use two tablespoons chopped fresh basil—it's not classic, but tastes great. Do, however, use anchovy paste!

Makes 1 Cup; Total Time: 15 Minutes

Process in Blender:

- 1 cup mayonnaise
- 1/4 cup chopped fresh parsley
- 1/4 cup scallion, chopped
- 2 T. sour cream
- 2 T. white wine vinegar
- 1 1/2 t. chopped fresh tarragon
- 1 t. anchovy paste
- 1 t. Dijon mustard
- White pepper to taste

Process all ingredients in a blender until creamy. Chill at least an hour before serving for flavors to develop. If too thick to pour, thin with a little milk. Keeps for one week.

▲*Carefully pull away leaves from the heads of endive.*

Serve with:

- Poached, chilled shrimp
- Leaves of Belgian endive
- Slices of avocado
- Cubes of mango

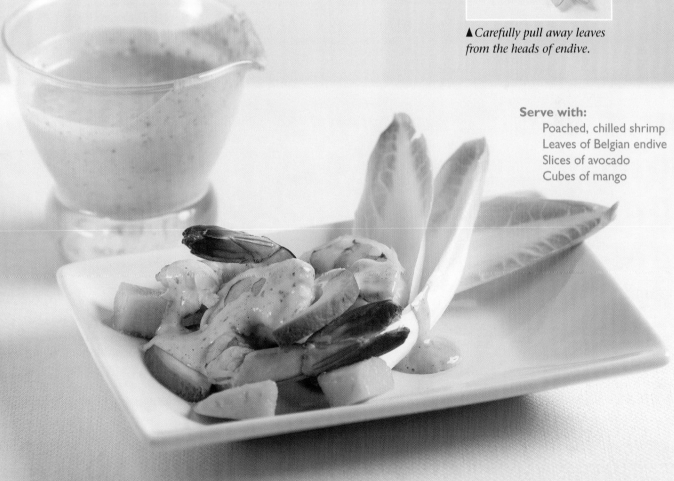

salad dressings *revived*
red french

Where did French dressing as we know it come from? Not France! This "red" version isn't like other French dressings—it's better!

"Real" French dressing is *not* the sweet, syrupy version seen on most salad bars. Nor is it similar to the orange "western" dressing popular in the '50s. French dressing is merely oil and vinegar—a vinaigrette!

So what happened? It's hard to say, but over time something clearly got lost in translation. This French is just meant to improve on what we know—and it does. Serve this over iceberg, spinach, or romaine.

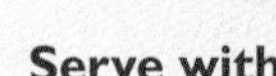

Serve with:

Grilled romaine halves
Slices of grilled rustic bread

French Dressing

Exemplary on its own, this dressing is even better paired with blue cheese dressing on Page 25!

Makes About 1 Cup
Total Time: 15 Minutes

Whisk Together:

- 1/4 cup ketchup
- 1/4 cup honey
- 2 T. yellow onion, grated
- 2 T. apple cider vinegar
- 2 T. fresh lemon juice
- 2 T. vegetable oil
- 2 T. water
- 1 T. tomato paste
- 1/4 t. celery seed
- Salt and pepper to taste

Whisk all ingredients together in a small bowl. Chill at least an hour before serving for flavors to develop. Keeps for one week.

▲*Lightly brush romaine halves with oil and sprinkle with salt; brush slices of rustic bread with oil. Grill both over medium-high heat until lightly charred on both sides, 3–4 min. Serve lettuce with dressing and bread for each person to tear into "croutons."*

blue cheese

Blue cheese is the king of dressings, and this is one you must make. Period.

I have plenty of beefs about store-bought dressing, but it's blue cheese that really gets me going. Why does it taste so bad? And where's the blue cheese? Make this version and you'll never go back to the bottle. No way.

It's rich stuff, but you can scale back with lowfat mayonnaise and sour cream. Avoid fat free, though—they're flavorless and pointless.

Blue Cheese Dressing

The cheese is the star here, so use the best you can find—Maytag is exceptional. Steer clear of the pre-crumbled stuff. It tastes stale.

Makes 1 Cup; Total Time: 10 Minutes

Whisk Together:

1/2 cup mayonnaise
1/2 cup blue cheese chunks
1/4 cup sour cream
1 t. Worcestershire sauce
1 t. fresh lemon juice
1/2 t. dry mustard
1/2 t. sugar (or to taste)
Salt, pepper, and Tabasco to taste

Whisk all ingredients together in a small bowl. Chill at least an hour before serving to allow flavors to blend. If too thick, thin out with a little milk. Keeps for up to one week, chilled.

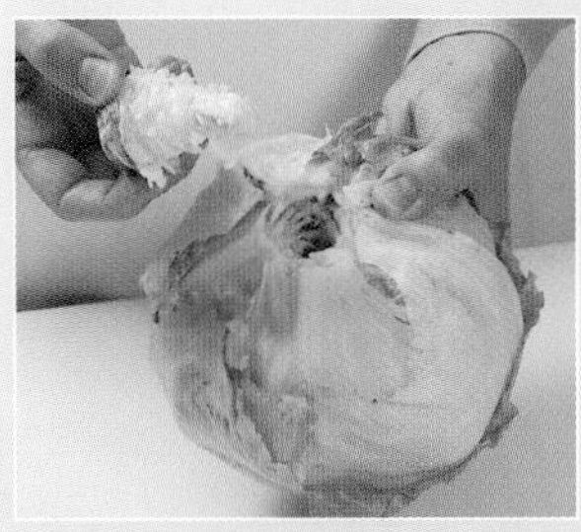

▲*Remove the core by hitting the head (on its core) against the work surface. The core comes right out.*

Serve with:
Iceberg lettuce wedges
Halved grape tomatoes

Wares
salad spinners

Let's face it, salad spinners are bulky to store and kitchen shelf space is at a premium. So a spinner must be worthy of its high-rent storage.

A good salad spinner is an invaluable tool that saves a lot of time and effort. It quickly washes and then *really* dries lettuce, so dressing can stick to the leaves. But all spinners are not created equal. There are a lot of flimsy models available that aren't even worth their low price.

To find the best models, we launched into testing 15 spinners. They break down into two main categories—sink models and self-contained models. Both types consist of a bowl, a colander, and a lid containing the spinning mechanism.

Sink model

These models have openings in both the lid and bowl bottom. This allows fresh water to run over the greens in the colander as it spins, then escape into the sink. After washing, the leaves are spun dry. While this rolls the washing and drying into one step, the process can be awkward because it *must* take place in a sink and there's just no room to work. Unfortunately, all but one of the models tested were cheap and inferior, so don't bother.

Self-contained model

With this kind of spinner, greens are washed in the colander, then the colander is placed into the solid bowl to spin dry. Because the water collects in the bowl, no sink is needed. We found the process easier and tidier with these spinners.

Spinning mechanisms

Spinners are set in motion with a variety of mechanisms: lever, pull-cord, pump, or crank. All are right- and left-hand user friendly, and largely a matter of preference.

Winning spinning

We've narrowed the 15 contestants to six quality finalists. Buy the one that feels the best for you at kitchenware stores, or see Resources, *Page 43*, to order.

Not just for lettuce

While washing and drying greens is its primary task, a spinner is multi-functional. Use the colander as a strainer, or to clean and dry berries and other vegetables.

▲*Berries need gentle handling, so spin them only briefly to dry.*

▲*A spinner easily cleans and dries the small leaves on herbs.*

Pedrini

price: $19.99

★★★★★

Form and function come together beautifully in this 3½-quart Italian-made spinner that's available in four colors. Definitely the most comfortable crank model tested, the large knob is easy to grasp and turns effortlessly, producing dry greens. A great combination of ease, style, drying power, and price, this model carries Pedrini's standard (but incredible) lifetime warranty.

Oxo Good Grips

price: $24.99

★★★★½

Ergonomically inclined, Oxo's pump spinner is operated by pressing a large plunger with the palm of the hand. It's easy to use and does a good job drying greens. Especially notable is the automatic brake button that brings spinning to a halt, and a retractable handle for storage. On the downside, the pump extends into usable bowl space and the lid has a tendency to hold onto the colander.

Copco Turbo

price: $17.99

★★★

The 5-quart Copco Turbo has a patented lever spinner mechanism that moves with ease from side to side fueling the spinning action. However, the lever tends to squeak and the lid must be aligned precisely with the colander or the lever can't engage the gear to start spinning. It does a decent job drying the greens, is dishwasher safe on both the top and the bottom racks, and has a one-year warranty.

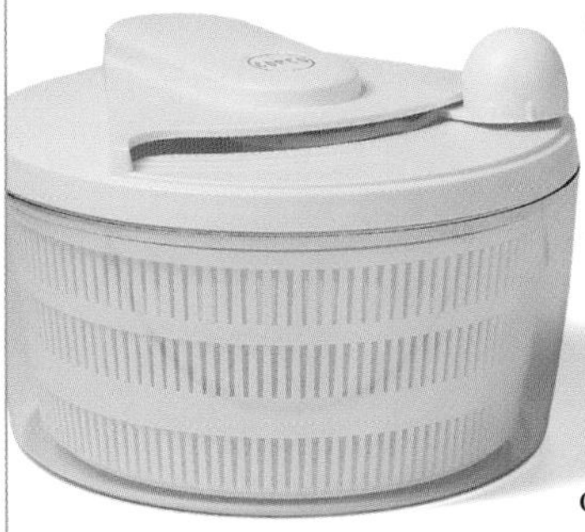

Emsa Salad Shower Plus

price: $24.95

German-produced Emsa makes a sink model of substance. It carries a five-year warranty and works by pulling a 23-inch ribbon that automatically retracts, like a yo-yo. With each pull, the basket spins powerfully, alternating directions, then stops with a jerk. Ribbon is made of sturdy parachute silk; it soils but washes easily with dishwashing soap. It comes with a berry basket insert for gentle spinning.

Zyliss

price: $19.99

Made in Switzerland, the Zyliss string-pull mechanism operates by pulling a 21-inch nylon cord, then letting it retract—like starting a lawn mower, but, of course, easier! Speed is determined by how hard the string is pulled and each pull spins the basket in alternate directions, so water is literally thrown off. Top rack dishwasher safe, the Zyliss adds a useful storage lid, and has a five-year warranty.

Tupperware Spin 'n Save

price: $34.99

This hip-looking spinner from Tupperware does a *very* good job drying leaves. It gets up plenty of speed and then spins for a long time. The downside is the handle's small turning circumference. It's a bit of a chore to get started, and then the bowl shakes as it spins. Although a little pricey, this 4-quart spinner comes with a handy storage lid, an impressive lifetime warranty, and is top rack dishwasher safe.

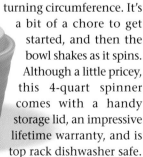

grilling the perfect steak

Steak. One simple word that spells a heap of pleasure. Tender and juicy on the inside, and cooked to perfect doneness is the mark of a master.

Journalist, cooking teacher, syndicated columnist, and multi-award winning author, Steven Raichlen is one of the world's foremost authorities on barbecuing and grilling. He's written ***The Barbecue Bible*** *(1.2 million copies sold) and* ***How to Grill****.*

As a columnist, he is read monthly by 15 million people. His TV appearances include Oprah, The Today Show, Food Network, and CNN. See his website at ***barbecuebible.com****.*

I've always heard of Steven Raichlen. Even have most of his books in my library. But to tell you the truth, I never thought I needed to read how to grill a steak. My steaks have always been pretty good and like most guys, we're born with a kind of sixth sense—the outdoor grilling sense. It just comes natural to us.

Then there was a Raichlen revelation. After listening to Steven's steps to the perfect steak, I followed his instructions exactly. My steaks were unbelievably good—especially the difficult-to-cook thicker steaks.

So Steven is passing this information on to you. We will discuss his 10 simple steps to grilling and then show you how to grill two different kinds of steak. One is the ubiquitous and popular strip steak and the other is a thick, special occasion porterhouse.

These two steaks require different grilling techniques because of their thickness. Follow the rules closely and you'll become a certified grill master. And be sure to treat yourself to the porterhouse on Page 32—it is truly special.

Raichlen's rules for grill set up

Unfortunately, a lot of confusion surrounds choosing and grilling the perfect steaks. Many people have less than optimal success. Over the years, Steven has developed 10 simple steps for grilling the perfect steak.

Choose the right steak

The high dry heat of grilling requires a relatively thin, tender cut of beef. The best candidates are listed in the adjacent box.

Build the right fire

Steak needs high heat to sear the meat and form a crust. But to cook a thick steak (porterhouse or rib), you also need a moderate heat zone to finish cooking the meat without burning it. For this, Steven uses a two-zone fire.

To build a two-zone fire in a charcoal grill, rake the coals into a double layer on one side of the grill and a single thick layer in the center. To gauge heat, hold your hand four inches above the grate and count. You'll be able to hold your hand over a hot zone for 2–3 seconds and the moderate zone for 5–6 seconds.

For a gas grill, simply turn one side on high and the other side on medium.

types of steaks

Rib-eye

Also known as Delmonico or shell steak. Juicy and well marbled. Fat gives it flavor and makes it *almost* impossible to ruin.

Rib steak

A bone-in rib-eye. Thicker than conventional rib-eye (2–3 inches). You get the richness of prime rib and the smoky crust from grilling.

Strip steak

New York, Kansas City, and top sirloin are all names for this steak. Lean, meaty, and firm textured. Should be 3/4 to 1 inch thick.

Fillet mignon

Lean and tender—you can literally cut through it with a fork. Flavor is subtle to almost bland.

Porterhouse

Two steaks in one: a firm strip sirloin and a succulent tenderloin attached by the T-bone. Should be 1 1/2 to 3 inches thick. Serves 3.

T-bone

Similar to porterhouse but closer to center of steer. This makes for bigger sirloin but smaller tenderloin. Thinner than porterhouse.

Sirloin steak

Rich, red, and meaty. Flavorful but tends to be tough. Slice thin for tenderness.

Flank and Skirt steak

From the underbelly of steer. Highly flavorful but tough and stringy. Cook medium rare and slice thinly against grain.

Practice good grill hygiene

The mark of a pro is a steak with a handsome crosshatch of grill marks. To achieve this, the grill grate must be properly cleaned and greased. To clean the grate, preheat the grill to high, then scrub the grate with a stiff wire brush. It's much easier to clean when hot.

To oil the grate, fold a paper towel into a small pad, dip it in vegetable oil and draw it across the bars of the grate with tongs.

Season to taste

Steven says to keep the seasoning simple: coarse salt (kosher or sea) and freshly ground pepper. Coarse salt crystals dissolve more slowly than table salt, giving you crunchy little bursts of flavor. Porterhouse, rib-eye, fillet, and strip are best with this seasoning.

Sirloin and flank steaks do well with Asian seasonings like ginger, garlic, and soy sauce. Skirt steak shines with Latino flavors like cumin, cilantro, and lime.

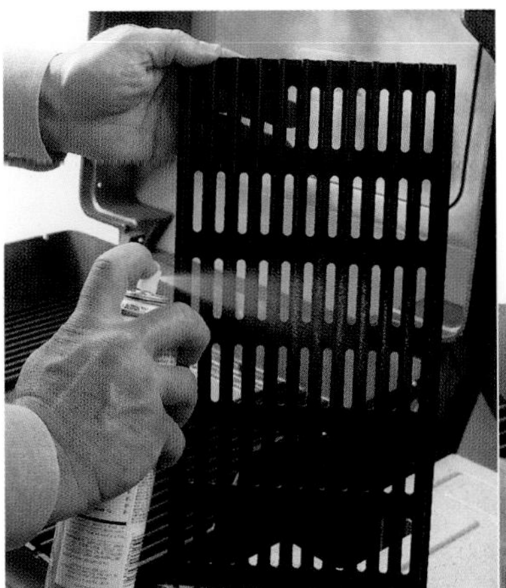

You can grease the grate by coating it with nonstick spray before turning on the heat.

If you don't spray, use a folded paper towel. Dip it in oil and draw it across grate using tongs.

Keep the seasoning simple: coarse sea or kosher salt and freshly ground black pepper.

Raichlen's steps to grilling steaks

Know when and how to turn

Arrange the steaks on the grate at a 45 degree angle to the bars of the grill grate. Grill for about 2 minutes, then rotate each steak 90 degrees. This makes the nice crosshatch grill marks. You'll know to flip the steaks when you see tiny beads of blood form on the top (after 4–6 additional minutes for a 1-inch thick steak, and 8–10 minutes for a 2-inch steak).

Don't overcook it

The greatest challenge to grilling steak is knowing when it's done. The best way to test for doneness is the "poke" test, *see box at right.* When grilling a really thick steak (such as a porterhouse or rib steak), you may want to use a thermometer. Insert it through the side and not from the top. This will give you an accurate reading. For medium-rare, the temperature should read between 140–145°. But remember, large steaks continue cooking even after they come off the grill.

Turn, don't stab

The proper way to turn a steak is with tongs or a spatula. Never stab the meat with a carving fork unless you want the flavor-rich juices left on the coals.

Never desert your post

Grilling steaks demands constant attention. Once they hit the grate, stay with them. This isn't the time to answer the phone or make the salad dressing.

Don't forget the fat

Like the polish on a mahogany table, a steak needs a drizzle of olive oil or pat of butter to bring it to perfection. Anointing steak with fat, rounds out the flavor and keeps the meat succulent. This is a good time to reseason the meat with salt and pepper.

Let it rest

All steaks need to rest a few minutes before serving. The high heat of grilling tends to dry out the meat. Transfer steak to a platter and wait 3 minutes. The juices will return to the meat as it sits.

Just a few final tips. Don't bother bringing raw steaks to room temperature. Steak houses don't, neither should you. And finally, try to flip the steaks only once. They'll be much juicier.

For handsome crosshatch grill marks, arrange the steaks on the grate at a 45 degree angle. Press to sear marks.

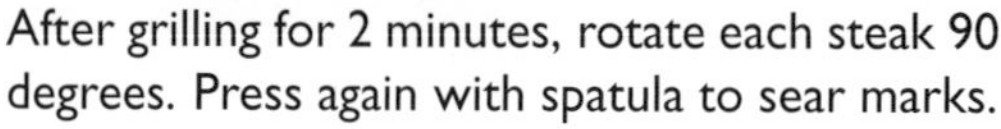
After grilling for 2 minutes, rotate each steak 90 degrees. Press again with spatula to sear marks.

testing for doneness

Poke Test
Knowing when a steak is ready to come off the grill can be challenging. Poking the top of the steak is the best indicator of doneness.

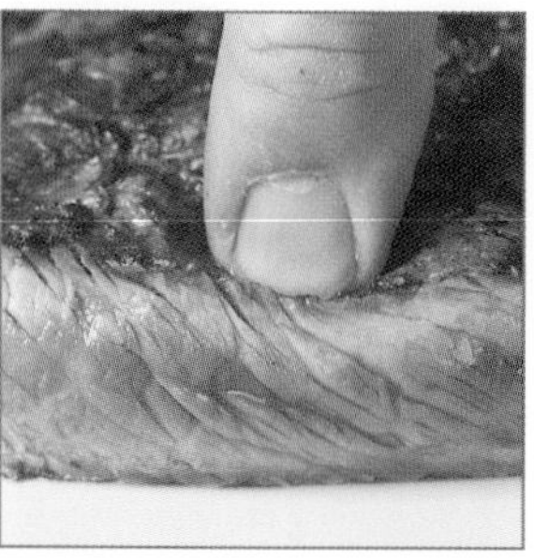

Rare
The steak will feel soft to touch. The meat is red in the center and warmish-hot.

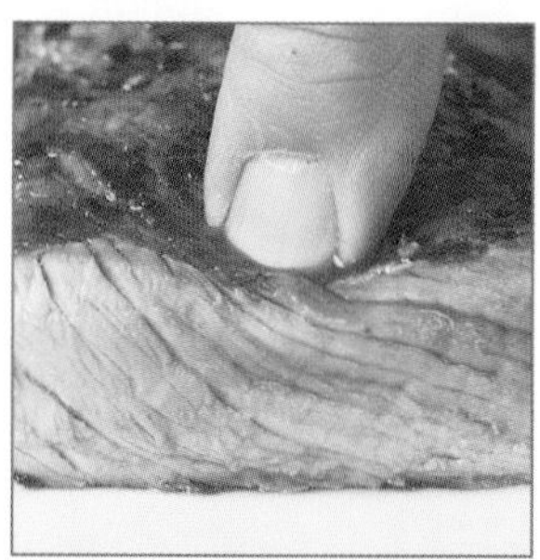

Medium-rare
The steak will be gently yielding. Meat is pinkish-red in the center and hot.

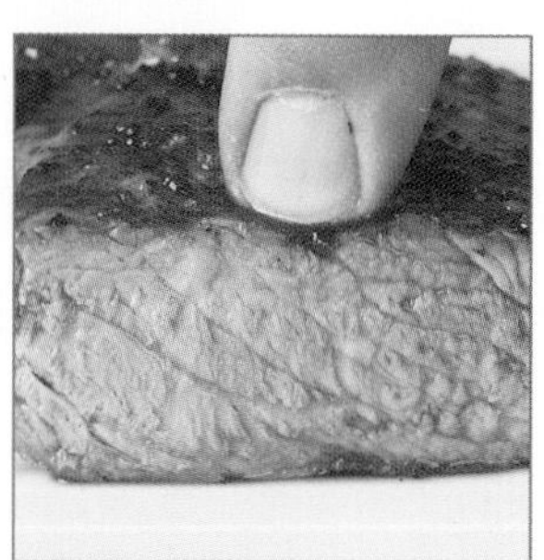

Medium
The steak will yield only slightly. The meat will be pink and hot.

the perfect steak

High heat, simple seasonings, and herbed butter—these are the beginnings of the perfect steak.

Cooking a strip steak (known as a New York or Kansas City strip) encompasses most steak grilling techniques. Only thick steaks like a 2-inch porterhouse or rib steak are cooked differently.

Most steaks should be cut 3/4 to 1-inch thick. At this thickness, they can be cooked directly over the hot part of the grill.

As the grill heats, add wood chips or a foil pouch of chips to create smoke. Brush grate with oil so steaks won't stick.

Now put the heavily seasoned steaks on the grill at a 45 degree angle, and cook 2 minutes. Press the steaks with a spatula to sear marks on their surface. Rotate the steaks 90 degrees and continue grilling for 2–4 minutes.

Turn the steaks and repeat this same process. Try to keep the grill lid closed during cooking.

When done, transfer steaks to a platter to rest for 3 minutes. While they sit, do as the French do and top each steak with tarragon butter. Rub the butter over the top of each steak.

New York Strip Steaks with Herb Butter

Makes 4 Steaks
Total Time: 15 Minutes + Chilling

For the Herb Butter—
Cream:
4 T. salted butter, room temperature
1 1/2 T. finely chopped fresh tarragon *or* herb of choice
1/2 t. lemon zest, finely grated
1/4 t. freshly ground black pepper
Few drops of lemon juice
Season and Grill:
4 8–10 oz. New York strip steaks (3/4–1" thick)
Coarse salt and freshly ground black pepper

Cream butter, herbs, zest, pepper, and juice; mound in center of plastic wrap square. Roll into cylinder, twisting ends of plastic to seal; chill until firm. **Season** steaks liberally, then grill. Top with 1/2"-thick slice of Herb Butter and rest 3 minutes.

Porterhouse steak
Bistecca alla Fiorentina

The noble porterhouse deserves to be draped only in the finest olive oil and freshest herbs. This is a steak that will be long remembered.

Gorgeous picture down below, isn't it? I've got news for you—it tastes even better than it looks!

I've always been a fan of rib-eye steaks because they're easy to cook and packed with flavor. Now that I know how Steven Raichlen grills a thick Florentine porterhouse, I'm a convert, as is as the whole *Cuisine* staff. Try this and you will be too.

Bistecca alla Fiorentina is one of the most celebrated dishes in Tuscany. It's a well marbled, two-pound porterhouse from prized Chianina cattle.

It's hard to find Chianina beef here, so Steven adds a few fresh herbs to pop up the flavor. As you'll see, he also adds olive oil which is one of his grilling rules. Use the very best for great results.

Grilling a thick porterhouse

A porterhouse should be cut thick—between $1^{3}/_{4}$ and 2 inches. It should also weigh in at a hefty two pounds. This can easily serve three people. What's nice is that when you slice it, *Figures 4 and 5*, each person can enjoy meat from both the flavorful sirloin and the tender fillet.

Two-zone heat

Prepare the grill with two-zone heat as on Page 29. Place steaks over high heat and sear for two minutes. This creates initial hatchmarks and forms a crust on the outside, *Figure 1*.

Next, move the steaks to the moderate heat zone and grill an additional 8 minutes, *Figure 2*. Be sure to rotate the steaks 90 degrees when you move them to the moderate zone. This creates the nice crosshatch grate marks. Repeat the process for the other side.

Seasoning

Here's where the real flavor comes in. Prepare a platter with fresh garlic, sage, and rosemary. Add grilled steaks and olive oil. As the steaks rest, turn them often so the meat is coated with the herb-infused oil, *Figure 3*. This is eating at its best!

Porterhouse Steak Florence Style

The key to cooking extra-thick porterhouse steaks is using a two-zone heat. Fresh herbs and good olive oil are the finishing touch.

Makes Two 2-lb. Steaks
Serves 6 to 8

Season and Grill:
2 2"-thick porterhouse steaks
Coarse salt and freshly ground black pepper

Strew Platter with:
2 cloves garlic, finely chopped
1 T. fresh rosemary, chopped
6 fresh sage leaves, torn

Finish with:
½ cup extra-virgin olive oil

Carve and Serve.

Preheat grill, setting it up using a two-zone heat.

Season steaks generously with coarse salt and freshly ground black pepper. Grill over the two-zone heat.

Strew a large platter with chopped garlic, rosemary, and sage leaves. Arrange the grilled steaks on top.

Finish by pouring olive oil over the steaks. Turn a few times to coat with garlic, herbs, and oil. Let steaks rest and marinate for 3–5 minutes. Turn them frequently so the flavored oil coats the steaks completely.

Carve the sirloin and fillet sections by cutting crosswise into ¼"-thick slices. Spoon the flavored oil over slices and serve.

1 Place steaks at 45 degree angle over high heat; sear 2 minutes.

MODERATE HEAT

2 Rotate steaks 90 degrees. Grill over moderate zone 6–8 minutes.

3 When done, let steaks rest for about 5 minutes in good olive oil and fresh herbs.

4 Cut the sirloin and the smaller fillet away from the T-bone.

5 Slice sirloin and fillet crosswise. Serve with flavored oil spooned over meat.

cool ice cream sundaes

Talk about a perfect match—summertime and sundaes. They're the ultimate dessert for eating out on the porch, watching the lightning bugs and dying embers from the grill.

Ice cream sundaes have a lot going for them. For one thing, they hold universal appeal. Show me someone who doesn't like sundaes and I'll show you a person a few scoops short of a pint. Second, they're *easy*—hardly any cooking is involved. Then after that, it's a do-it-yourself job in terms of putting them together!

Above all, the toppings make the sundae, so here are a couple of things to bear in mind. First, since the toppings are the star, it's not crucial to use a premium ice cream. Covering them with sauces make quality a fairly moot point. Buy a decent ice cream, of course, but don't feel like the name should be "big."

Second, since the sauces are *the* deal here, take time to make them. Store-bought doesn't hold a candle to homemade. Each can be made ahead, chilled, and rewarmed in a microwave or double boiler. And they should be warm when they go on the ice cream to contrast against the cold. A piping hot sauce would melt the ice cream on contact.

But do you want to know the *best* thing about these sauces? Try sneaking a spoonful from the fridge, at midnight, when no one is watching. It's pure heaven.

34 *online* **extra**

Want to make your own vanilla ice cream? Visit www.CuisineAtHome.com for a recipe and easy steps.

black forest sundaes

Chocolate wafers: These thin chocolate cookies are sort of like Oreos without the icing inside. Chocolate graham crackers or cubes of brownies work fine too. ►

Bing Cherry Sauce

If using fresh bing cherries, take care not to simmer the sauce too long—otherwise the cherries will become mushy.

Makes About 2 Cups; Total Time: 15 Minutes

Simmer:
- 1 lb. fresh or frozen Bing cherries, pitted
- $\frac{1}{3}$ cup sugar
- $\frac{1}{4}$ cup apple juice
- 2 T. dry red wine
- 1 T. fresh lemon juice
- Pinch salt

Combine; Whisk in:
- 2 T. apple juice
- 1 T. cornstarch

Simmer cherries, sugar, $\frac{1}{4}$ cup apple juice, wine, lemon juice, and salt in a heavy saucepan over medium heat.

Combine apple juice and cornstarch in a small bowl until smooth. Whisk into boiling cherry mixture and simmer until thickened, about 3 minutes. Cool sauce at least 10 minutes before serving.

Hot Fudge

Dutch process cocoa creates a dark, deep sauce, but regular cocoa works too. Don't boil too long or the fudge will turn grainy.

Makes About $1\frac{1}{2}$ Cups; Total Time: 15 Minutes

Combine:
- $\frac{3}{4}$ cup sugar
- $\frac{3}{4}$ cup heavy cream
- $\frac{1}{2}$ cup unsweetened Dutch process cocoa
- 1 t. espresso powder
- Pinch salt

Combine all ingredients in a heavy saucepan. Bring to a boil over medium-high heat, stirring constantly. Boil 3 minutes, stirring, then remove from heat. Let sauce cool at least 10 minutes before serving.

Black Forest Sundaes

Layer:
- Hot Fudge Sauce
- Vanilla ice cream
- Bing Cherry Sauce
- Crushed chocolate wafers

Top with:
- Lightly sweetened whipped cream
- Chocolate cookie halves

1 ◄*Pour a good tablespoon of warm fudge in the bottom of each sundae glass. Top with 2–3 scoops of ice cream.*

2 ◄*Drizzle ice cream with warm cherry sauce, then sprinkle with crushed cookies.*

3 ◄*Finish with more fudge and cherry sauces, a dollop of whipped cream, and cookie halves. (Cherry on top—optional!)*

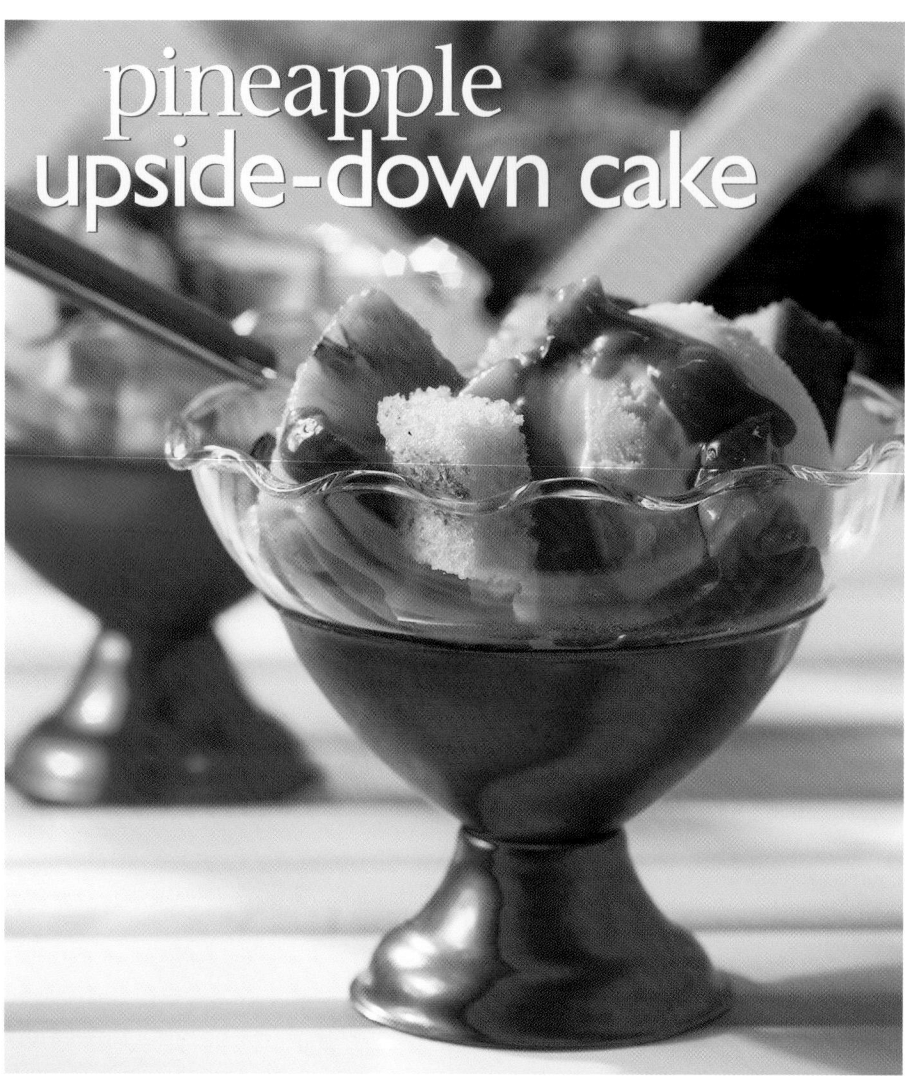

Caramel Sauce with Mixed Nuts

Cook the syrup until it looks like iced tea. Less than that, the flavor lacks depth. Longer, it's bitter.

Makes About 1 1/2 Cups
Total Time: 15 Minutes

Combine:
1 cup sugar
1/4 cup water
1 t. fresh lemon juice
Carefully Add:
1/2 cup heavy cream
1/4 cup (4 T.) unsalted butter
Stir In:
1 cup salted mixed nuts, coarsely chopped

Combine sugar, water, and lemon juice in a heavy saucepan. Simmer over medium heat until sugar dissolves, then increase heat to high. Boil, swirling pan, until syrup is iced tea-colored, 10–12 min. Remove from heat. **Carefully add** cream a little at a time while whisking—it'll bubble violently so stand back from the pan as you do this. When bubbling subsides, add butter and whisk until smooth. **Stir in** the nuts. Cool sauce 15–20 minutes to thicken.

Pineapple Upside-Down Cake Sundaes

Grill or Broil:
Rings of fresh pineapple, sprinkled with sugar (1 ring per 2 sundaes)
Slices of purchased pound cake (1 slice per 2 sundaes)
Layer:
- Caramel Sauce with Mixed Nuts
- Vanilla ice cream
- Cubes of grilled pineapple
- Cubes of grilled pound cake

Grill pineapple and pound cake over medium heat until lightly charred. Cut each into cubes and set aside.

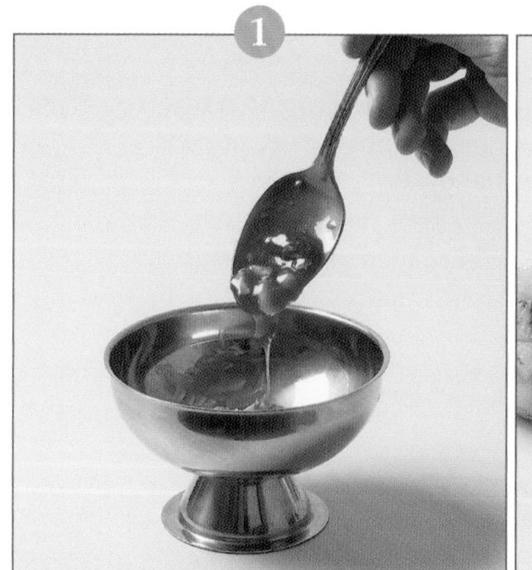

▲*Pour a couple of tablespoons of warm caramel sauce into each dish.*

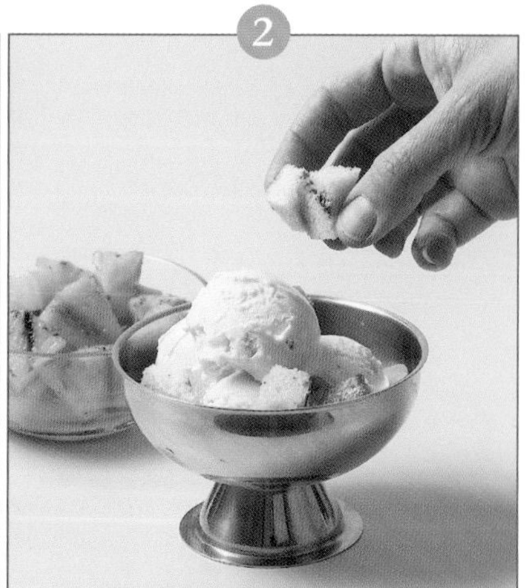

▲*Now top with scoops of ice cream, pineapple, cake, and more caramel sauce. Serve immediately.*

peanut butter and jelly

PB&J Sundaes

Layer:
- Peanut Butter Sauce
- Raspberry Crush
- Vanilla ice cream
- Coarsely crushed graham crackers
- Chopped toffee peanuts or Beer Nuts (their saltiness is great against the sweetness)

▲*Layer warm Peanut Butter Sauce in a dish. Top with ice cream, then crushed graham crackers, and Raspberry Crush. To finish, sprinkle with coarsely chopped toffee peanuts.*

Chambord [sham-BORD] is a sweet, raspberry based French liqueur. It enhances the flavor of the crush, but may be left out if unavailable.

Peanut Butter Sauce

Makes About 2½ Cups
Total Time: 15 Minutes

Boil:
1 can (12 oz.) evaporated milk
1 cup sugar
1 T. light corn syrup
Pinch salt

Whisk in:
⅔ cup peanut butter
3 T. unsalted butter
½ t. vanilla extract

Boil milk, sugar, corn syrup, and salt in a saucepan over medium-high heat, stirring often. Simmer until it reaches 225° on an instant read thermometer, 10–12 minutes. Remove from heat. **Whisk in** remaining ingredients until smooth. Let stand 10 minutes before serving.

Raspberry Crush

Makes About 1 Cup
Total Time: 15 Minutes

Combine:
1½ cups fresh or frozen unsweetened raspberries (if frozen, do not thaw)
2 T. sugar
1 T. Chambord, *see sidebar,* or dark rum, *optional*
Pinch salt

Combine all ingredients in a small bowl and let stand at room temperature for at least 30 minutes (slightly longer if berries are frozen). Lightly mash berries with the back of a spoon to crush and release juices. Take care not to "overcrush"—a few whole berries will give the sauce a nice texture.

faster **with** fewer

easy stir-fry dinner

Grilling isn't the only way to cook in the summer. This stir-fry dinner has you in and out of the kitchen (and eating!) fast.

Yes, we love to cook, but a quick meal is always welcome. This stir-fry dinner is just the ticket. Most of the ingredients can be prepared ahead and chilled until you're ready to cook. Then when it's time to heat the wok, cooking time is minimal. A bonus—it's a dinner nice enough for a party.

You can take some creative liberties with the recipes too. Chicken can be used in the stir-fry in place of the shrimp. And if you don't want to assemble salad wraps, serve the noodles on beds of lettuce. Finally, terrific summer fruits are everywhere now—use what strikes you for the dessert.

menu

Glass Noodle Salad Wraps

Shrimp and Plum Stir-Fry

Summer Fruit in Ginger-Mint Sauce

Glass Noodle Salad Wraps

Glass noodles (aka cellophane noodles) are available at many grocery stores and Asian markets. Ramen noodles may be substituted.

Makes 8 Wraps; Total Time: 20 Minutes

Soak, Drain, and Chill:
1 bundle (2 oz.) glass noodles
Prepare:
1/2 cup carrot, julienned
1/3 cup red bell pepper, diced
1/4 cup coarsely chopped cilantro
Blend; Toss Salad with:
1/4 cup rice vinegar
3 t. sugar
1/2 t. dark sesame oil
Pinch salt
Divide Salad Among:
8 Bibb lettuce leaves
Sprinkle with; Wrap:
Chopped peanuts
Serve with:
Cucumber Dipping Sauce

Soak noodles for 10 minutes in boiling water to cover. Drain and chill until ready to assemble salad.
Prepare carrot, bell pepper, and cilantro. Chill until salad assembly.
Blend vinegar, sugar, oil, and salt. Toss with noodles and vegetables.
Divide noodle salad among lettuce leaves.
Sprinkle salad with peanuts and fold sides of leaf over salad to enclose. Place wraps, seam side down, on serving plates.
Serve with dipping sauce.

Cucumber Dipping Sauce

Makes About 1 Cup

Puree:
1 cup cucumber, seeded, diced
1/4 cup plain lowfat yogurt
1/4 cup rice vinegar
1 T. sugar
2 t. minced fresh ginger
Salt and crushed red pepper flakes to taste

Puree all ingredients in a blender until smooth. Chill until ready to serve with wraps.

Shrimp and Plum Stir-fry

The most time you spend on this dish is in preparing the ingredients. Actual cooking happens in mere minutes.

Makes About 4 Cups; Total Time: 30 Minutes

▲ *Cut down the back of each shrimp and remove the dark vein.*

▲ *Cut "lobes" from plums around pits, then slice into half-moons.*

Prepare:

1 lb. shrimp, peeled, deveined
3/4 cup scallions, cut into 1" pieces
1 T. garlic, minced
1 T. fresh ginger, minced
2 ripe plums, sliced
3 dried red chiles

Combine:

2 T. dry sherry
2 T. brown sugar
2 T. ketchup
2 T. low-sodium soy sauce
2 T. fresh lime juice
2 t. dark sesame oil
2 t. cornstarch

Stir-fry in:

2 T. peanut or vegetable oil

Serve with:

Steamed white rice
Sauteed spinach

Garnish with:

Toasted sesame seeds

Prepare shrimp, scallions, garlic, ginger, plums, and chiles, keeping each separate. Set aside until ready to stir-fry.

Combine sherry, brown sugar, ketchup, soy sauce, lime juice, sesame oil, and cornstarch in a small bowl; set aside.

To stir-fry, heat oil in a large saute pan or wok over high heat until it shimmers. Stir-fry crumbled chiles 30 seconds, then add garlic and ginger. Cook, stirring constantly, until fragrant, 30 seconds. Add shrimp and stir-fry until opaque, 2–3 minutes. Add liquid mixture, scallions, and plums; simmer until liquid thickens, about 2–3 minutes.

Serve stir-fry with steamed rice and sauteed spinach.

Garnish with sesame seeds.

To stir-fry, the pan must be big enough to hold everything without crowding. And make sure that it's really hot when you start cooking. It cools down rapidly as things are added. ►

▲Crumble chiles into hot oil. Cook, then add garlic and ginger.

▲ Stir-fry shrimp until opaque. Add liquid, plums, and scallions.

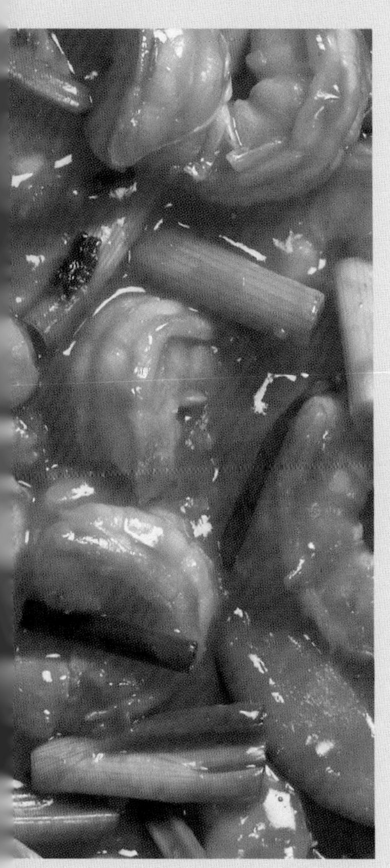

Summer Fruit in Ginger-Mint Syrup

Any summer fruit would be excellent here—try peaches, nectarines, or cherries. Serve with sugar cookies on the side.

Makes About 4 Cups; Total Time: 20 Minutes

Simmer:

- 1 cup sugar
- 3/4 cup water
- 1/4 cup fresh mint, coarsely chopped
- 3 T. fresh ginger, coarsely chopped
- Zest and juice of one lime

Strain Over:

- 1 cup watermelon balls
- 1 cup cantaloupe balls
- 1 cup honeydew balls
- 1 cup fresh pineapple, peeled, cut into chunks
- 1 pint blueberries
- 1 pint raspberries

A small ice cream scoop is great for melon balls. Chunks of melon are fine too! ►

Simmer sugar, water, mint, ginger, lime zest, and juice in a small saucepan over medium heat until reduced by half, about 10 minutes. Do not overcook or syrup will become thick and bitter. **Strain** syrup over fruit and stir gently to coat. Chill at least 30 minutes, or until ready to serve.

from our readers

Q&A questions & answers

CORK VS. SYNTHETIC

Are synthetic corks harmful to wine?

Gary Rahons
Portland, OR

I talked with Andrea Immer, Master Sommelier and the winner of the 2002 James Beard Outstanding Wine and Spirits Award. She assured me that synthetic corks do not negatively affect wine. Because synthetic corks have only been around the last few years, there's not a lot of information on the *long-term* aging effects. But since most people don't age wine, and most wine doesn't *need* to be aged, it's a legitimate alternative to natural cork and also screw caps.

In recent years wine sales have increased and there has been a combination of a cork shortage and quality control issues. Inferior cork can produce "corked" or spoiled wine that has a musty, moldy taste. Spoiled wine is frustrating, no matter the cost. Synthetic corks are intended to counteract this problem.

Methods of bottle closure (natural cork, synthetic cork, or screw caps) are a hot debate in the wine world. Whatever the future holds, it's clear that cork is no longer the only player.

Look for the new book ***Andrea Immer's Wine Buying Guide for Everyone*** *at bookstores or order from* ***amazon.com***

WHITE CRANBERRIES

I've seen the new white cranberry juice, but I've never seen a white cranberry. What is it?

Mary Ann Berning
Lindenwold, NJ

Mild white cranberries are the very same berries as red. They're just harvested a few weeks earlier. Unripe green berries turn white as they ripen. The longer these berries are on the vine, the redder and tarter they become.

Ocean Spray nationally debuted the first white cranberry juice drink in January 2002.

COFFEE BEAN ROASTING

Is it possible to roast my own coffee beans at home?

Sam Ball
Lincoln, NE

Absolutely. Roasting your own coffee beans is definitely doable and quite possibly addictive! Fans of the method enjoy the incomparable freshness of their brewed coffee, along with the satisfaction derived from the roasting process. Of course there are roasting machines available (ranging in price between \$60–\$275), but roasting can also be done on the stovetop, in the oven, and even in some corn poppers. The process emits a distinct smell similar to burned toast.

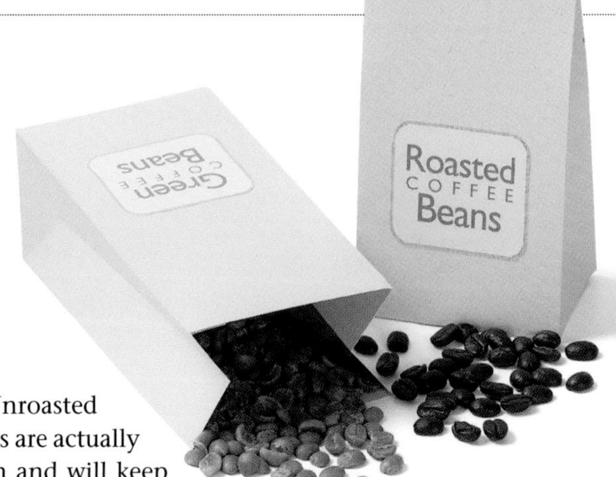

Unroasted beans are actually green and will keep for a couple of years—far longer than roasted beans. You may be able to purchase green beans at a local coffee shop that roasts their own beans. The price should be about half their roasted price. To order green coffee beans, see the sidebar, *left*.

While roasting is accessible, don't head into it uninformed. Kenneth Davids' book *Home Coffee Roasting* is the map to guide you through the details of process and equipment, as well as provide inspiration.

Order green coffee beans and view an online video (for a visual taste of the roasting process) at ***coffeeproject.com (800) 779-7578***

For a preview of Kenneth Davids' roasting book, click "About Coffee" at ***lucidcafe.com***

PRODUCE WASHES

What are fruit and vegetable washes supposed to do? Are they more effective than plain water? And is the brand Fit *still available?*

Pat Wistrom
Carlisle, IA

There are several brands of fruit and vegetable washes available. Their purpose is to remove wax and any residual pesticides and chemicals that may linger on produce. However, *Fit* is no longer on the market.

The potential problem with rinsing with just water is twofold. First, some pesticides are water resistant. Second, any residue is often buried under a coating of wax that water alone can't permeate. For these purposes, a wash containing a natural solvent (like Veggie Wash) is more effective than water.

CRUSTY LOBSTER SHELL

Is it true that the crustiest-looking lobster, with barnacles on it, is probably the best one in the tank?

Charlotte Klise
Topeka, KS

It may sound like an old wives' tale, but Bob Bayer, Executive Director of the Lobster Institute at the University of Maine, says it's true. Lobsters molt, or shed their outgrown hard shell, then grow and fill their new shell. A dark, scratched up shell with barnacles growing on it is a sign that it's been a while (at least six months) since the lobster has shed. And this means it's likely to have a high meat yield.

DRIED PLUMS OR PRUNES?

I've noticed dried plums at the market. Aren't they really prunes?

Donna Thompson
Lakeland, FL

Yes, they are one and the same. But you may find them packaged under either or both names.

In June 2000, the FDA approved renaming prunes as dried plums. The goal was to enhance consumer appeal and reach a younger target audience. The updated image is working and industry sales are up. Now that they're at the end of a two-year transition period, the name "prunes" may actually disappear from packaging.

While the fiber benefits of prunes have long been understood by consumers, this name campaign stresses added health benefits, like high antioxidants, potassium, and vitamin A.

resources

AMAZON.COM
Pedrini Salad Spinner,
Item #B00005U2FD
amazon.com

KITCHEN ETC.
Zyliss Salad Spinner,
Item #115529
(800) 232-4070
kitchenetc.com

TUPPERWARE
Tupperware Salad Spinner,
Item #0620
tupperware.com

FANTE'S KITCHEN WARES SHOP
Oxo Salad Spinner,
Item #97177
(800) 443-2683
fantes.com

COOKING.COM
Emsa Salad Spinner,
Item #126769
(800) 663-8810
cooking.com

TARGET STORES
Copco Turbo
Salad Spinner

Tart Pans
The April issue of Cuisine at home *features a recipe for Lemon Tartlets using eight 4" tartlet pans with removable bottoms. They are available from* ***Sweet Celebrations*** *for $1.45 each, plus shipping.*

Sweet Celebrations,
Item #18201
(800) 328-6722
sweetc.com

Q&A

Do you have a question for *Cuisine at home*?

If you have a question about a cooking term, procedure, or technique, we'd like to hear from you. We'll consider publishing your question in one or more of our works. Just write down your question and mail it to *Cuisine at home*, Q&A Editor, 2200 Grand Ave., Des Moines, IA 50312, or contact us through our email address shown below. Please include your name, address, and daytime phone number in case we have questions.

Email: CuisineAtHome@CuisineAtHome.**com**
Web address: CuisineAtHome.**com**

baby Burgers

Want to see people make a fuss? Put out a platter of these baby burgers.

Normally I like things big, but these mini burgers were so popular in the test kitchen, I just had to show them to you. Besides the neat presentation, piled high on a platter, they're easy to make, and ideal for anyone with a small appetite.

The trick is finding little burger buns. My supermarket has small soft rolls ("cocktail buns")—about $2^1/_2$" across.

Mix the ground meat just like you did on Page 7. Then gently shape the meat in a biscuit cutter that's slightly larger than the bun (this allows for shrinkage). You can also shape them free-form. Grill according to instructions on Page 8—they just won't take as long. Serve with Roma tomato slices, leaf lettuce, and a little blue cheese dressing.

REAL ITALIAN MEATBALLS—ONE RECIPE, THREE MEALS

Cuisine at home®

Shrimp that rocks

Restaurant recipes you can do at home

Plus:

Parmesan Crusted Chicken

simple technique, dynamite flavor

Issue No. 35 October 2002
A publication of August Home Publishing

Cuisine at home

Publisher
Donald B. Peschke

Editor
John F. Meyer

Senior Editor
Susan Hoss

Assistant Editor
Sara Ostransky

Test Kitchen Director
Kim Samuelson

Photographer
Dean Tanner

Art Director
Cinda Shambaugh

Assistant Art Director
Holly Wiederin

Graphic Designer
April Walker Janning

Image Specialist
Troy Clark

Contributing Food Stylist
Jennifer Peterson

AUGUST HOME PUBLISHING COMPANY

Corporate:
Corporate Vice Presidents: Mary R. Scheve, Douglas L. Hicks • *Creative Director:* Ted Kralicek • *Professional Development Director:* Michal Sigel *New Media Manager:* Gordon C. Gaippe • *Senior Photographer:* Crayola England *Multi Media Art Director:* Eugene Pedersen • *Web Server Administrator:* Carol Schoeppler • *Web Content Manager:* David Briggs • *Web Designer:* Kara Blessing *Web Developer/Content Manager:* Sue M. Moe • *Controller:* Robin Hutchinson *Senior Accountant:* Laura Thomas • *Accounts Payable:* Mary Schultz • *Accounts Receivable:* Margo Petrus • *Production Director:* George Chmielarz • *Pre-Press Image Specialist:* Minniette Johnson • *Electronic Publishing Director:* Douglas M. Lidster • *Systems Administrator:* Cris Schwanebeck • *PC Maintenance Technician:* Robert D. Cook • *H.R. Assistant:* Kirsten Koele • *Receptionist/ Administrative Assistant:* Jeanne Johnson • *Mail Room Clerk:* Lou Webber

Customer Service & Fulfillment:
Operations Director: Bob Baker • *Customer Service Manager:* Jennie Enos *Customer Service Representatives:* Anna Cox, Kim Harlan, April Revell, Deborah Rich, Valerie Jo Riley, Tammy Truckenbrod • *Technical Representative:* Johnny Audette • *Buyer:* Linda Jones • *Administrative Assistant:* Nancy Downey • *Warehouse Supervisor:* Nancy Johnson • *Fulfillment:* Sylvia Carey

Circulation:
Subscriber Services Director: Sandy Baum • *New Business Circulation Manager:* Wayde J. Klingbeil • *Multi Media Promotion Manager:* Rick Junkins • *Promotions Analyst:* Patrick A. Walsh • *Billing and Collections Manager:* Rebecca Cunningham • *Renewal Manager:* Paige Rogers • *Circulation Marketing Analyst:* Kris Schlemmer • *Associate Circulation Marketing Analyst:* Paula M. DeMatteis *Art Director:* Doug Flint • *Senior Graphic Designers:* Mark Hayes, Robin Friend

www.CuisineAtHome.com

talk to ***Cuisine at home***
Questions about Subscriptions and Address Changes? Write or call:

Customer Service
2200 Grand Avenue,
Des Moines, IA 50312
800-311-3995,
8 a.m. to 5 p.m., CST.

Online Subscriber Services:
www.CuisineAtHome.com
Access your account • Check a subscription payment • Tell us if you've missed an issue • Change your mailing or email address • Renew your subscription • Pay your bill

Cuisine at home® (ISSN 1537-8225) is published bi-monthly (Jan., Mar., May, July, Sept., Nov.) by August Home Publishing Co., 2200 Grand Ave., Des Moines, IA 50312.
Cuisine at home® is a trademark of August Home Publishing Co.

Subscriptions: Single copy: $4.99. One year subscription (6 issues), $24.00. (Canada/Foreign add $10 per year, U.S. funds.)

Periodicals postage paid at Des Moines, IA and at additional mailing offices. "USPS/Perry-Judd's Heartland Division automatable poly".
Postmaster: Send change of address to **Cuisine at home**, P.O. Box 37100 Boone, IA 50037-2100.
Cuisine at home® does not accept and is not responsible for unsolicited manuscripts. **PRINTED IN SINGAPORE.**

editor's letter

Ahhh ... September and October. These months rate at the top as my favorite time of year. August just about burned up my lawn and watering has grown tedious. My legs have tanned enough—if you can believe it, the novelty of wearing shorts has worn off. And what can I say about family vacations? The memories last a lifetime, but "in the moment," they can be trying at best. Grilling has become just a way to cook rather than a way to express myself. I want to spend time in the kitchen. As the seasons change, so do the foods I crave. I want (and need) comfort.

This issue is jam-packed with recipes that can warm some of those chilly nights. Like the fall fruit cobbler, crisp, and buckle—bubbling over, then down the sides of their dishes, they perfume the entire house with autumn. Or the aroma of Italian meatballs filled with fresh garlic and herbs simmering away in a zesty tomato marinara sauce. Fall is here!

But don't think for a minute that just because summer is over, the farmer's markets are waning. Explore the fall harvest of the markets and your garden with recipes from our guest chef, Deborah Madison. Winter Squash Risotto or the quick Chard and Cilantro Soup with Noodle Nests remind us that vegetables can be more than just side dishes on a plate.

However, if you feel compelled to eat a little meat, any of Deborah's recipes go perfectly with crusted chicken. Parmesan cheese or chopped pecans make a great crust, but there's more to it. We've uncovered the secrets to coating chicken so you can get a perfectly golden crust with restaurant looks—with even better taste. It's a dinner party waiting to happen, yet easy enough to make on a Wednesday night.

So enjoy the fall. It's the calming season resting between those family vacations and hectic holidays. And find a good pile of leaves and fall into them—simple can be comforting too.

John

table of contents

Issue No. 35 October 2002

departments

features

from **our** readers

tips
and techniques

Tip from the Test Kitchen
Shrimp shells make a great seafood stock. After peeling shrimp, save and freeze the shells. The next time a recipe calls for a fish stock (like clam or seafood chowder), put the shells in water and simmer for 20 minutes.

Mini Job

Use a pastry bag when putting batter (such as muffin, quiche, or cheesecake) into mini muffin pans. It's much easier and a lot less messy than using a spoon.

Kathy Sayler
Hagerstown, MD

Standing Tall

Some cooking utensils are too short to fit in my utensil crock. To keep the smaller utensils from slipping down too far, I put a couple inches of stones or marbles in the bottom of the container (glass decorative gardening stones work great).

The smaller utensils rest on top of the stones and remain at a visible height. The longer utensils can be pushed down between the stones to the bottom of the crock for stability.

Mary C. Goldman
Berkeley, CA

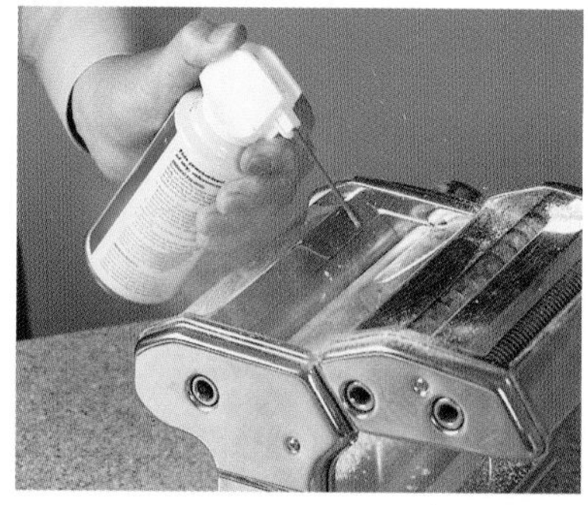

Air Spray Cleaner

I've found a great way to clean my pasta machine. I use a can of compressed air spray for cleaning dust off computer keyboards. It works really well and gets out all the flour and pasta dough particles.

Dorothy Chilson
Elmira, OR

Custom Bowl Scraper

I do a lot of baking and, consequently, have a lot of bowl scraping to do. Here's my solution for cleaning sticky dough from mixing bowls—create your own custom-sized (and shaped) bowl scrapers from the plastic lids of coffee cans. They are flexible enough to conform to the bowl, and are easy to clean.

Not only can you make your scraper as large as you like, but you can also trim it to any curvature.

R.B. Himes
Vienna, OH

Easy Tomato Seeding

To seed tomatoes, slice them in half, then use a grapefruit spoon to scoop the seeds. The spoon is just the right size, and its serrated edge works great for scraping.

Janice Tocchio
Plymouth, MA

Sticky Situation

Bottles with "sticky" contents (corn syrup, honey, maple syrup, etc.) can be a hassle to keep reopening. So before using the bottle for the first time, wipe the threads with a light coating of oil. The lid will never stick and won't be difficult to open!

Mary Arris
Virginia Beach, VA

Instant Soft Butter

I bake cookies all the time, but usually forget to take the butter out of the fridge to soften. I've used a microwave, but if I turn my back—instant butter puddle! To soften butter quickly, unwrap a stick of butter, place it in a resealable plastic bag, and use a rolling pin to beat and flatten the butter out.

Ching-Yee Hu
Mountain View, CA

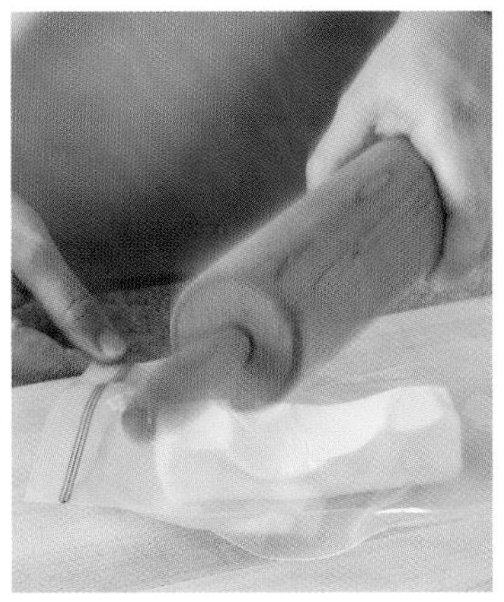

Freezing Tortillas

Before freezing extra tortillas, place waxed paper between each one. This allows you to easily and quickly remove as many as needed without damaging the tortillas or having to thaw the entire package.

Carolyn Stratton
Grand Junction, CO

Roll Out The Salad...

Salad dressing is not much good when tossed with a bowl full of wet greens. Here's my solution: I wash the greens, separate them into leaves, lay them on a large, clean kitchen towel, and roll them up like a jelly roll. Stored in the refrigerator, the towel will absorb the water and then slowly feed it back to the leaves, keeping them fresh for a week. The result is crisp, clean, dry salad greens that won't get rust spots and or dilute the salad dressing.

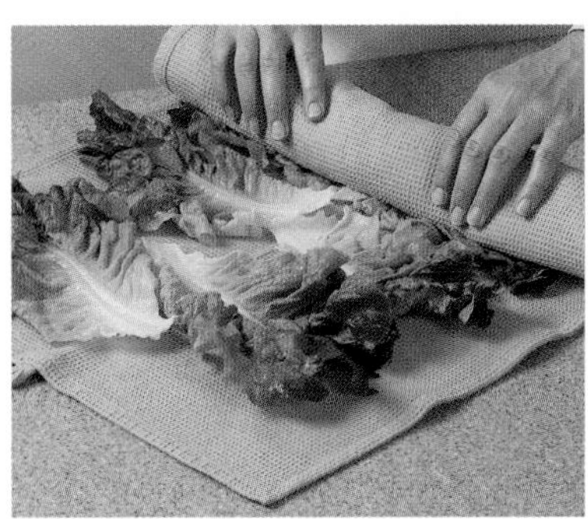

Lillian Kayte
Gainesville, FL

Easy Chile Seeding

To seed jalapeños (without gloves!), cut off both ends of the chile. Stand it on a cutting board and slice down its sides, removing the flesh around the core. Discard the core with the seeds.

Ann Marie Mattioli
New York, NY

Measuring Honey

Honey can be tough to remove from measuring cups and spoons. One technique is to oil the utensil before measuring—the honey will slide out cleanly. Another trick is to use heat. Simply dip the measuring spoon in hot water. Honey will not stick to a heated spoon.

Chocolate Grating

Whenever you need just a bit of chocolate for sauces, ganache, or a quick topping, try using a grater (large holes work best). Hold the chocolate by the wrapper to keep it from melting. To store, seal the grated chocolate in a plastic bag and keep in a cool, dark place—not the fridge or freezer.

Mark Montgomery
Wheeling, WV

share your tips *and techniques* **with *Cuisine at home***

If you have a unique way of solving a cooking problem, we'd like to hear from you, and we'll consider publishing your tip in one or more of our works. Just write down your cooking tip and mail it to *Cuisine at home*, Tips Editor, 2200 Grand Ave., Des Moines, IA 50312, or contact us through our email address shown below. Please include your name, address, and daytime phone number in case we have questions. We'll pay you $25 if we publish your tip.

Email: CuisineAtHome@CuisineAtHome.com

Web address: CuisineAtHome.com

cuisineclass

a guide to buying shrimp

How many shrimp should you buy for six people? You see different kinds of shrimp for sale—is one as good as another?

You're pumped to try a new shrimp recipe, so you go to your grocery to pick up some of the sweet crustaceans. Then you hit the roadblock—shrimp come in all different varieties and sizes. This could be a problem, but here is some information that will clear up a little of the mystery.

Common types of shrimp

There are three kinds of shrimp commonly sold in our markets.

Gulf Shrimp: This is what you probably eat most of the time. They're from the Gulf of Mexico and Atlantic coast, and are named by their color although it's hardly discernable. *White* shrimp are firm and sweet, and considered to be the best. *Pinks* are similar to whites in flavor and texture. They are also considered to be top quality. *Browns* are inferior shrimp. They are less flavorful and not as firm as whites and pinks. They have a slight iodine flavor since they feed on iodine-rich kelp found off the coast of Texas.

Tiger Shrimp: Tigers are farm-raised Asian shrimp with very distinctive markings—black and yellow stripes. While less expensive than Gulf shrimp, they tend to be inconsistent in quality—I stay away from them.

Rock Shrimp: A cold-water shrimp that has an outstanding lobster-like flavor. Their shells are hard and tough to remove so they're often sold already peeled. Do yourself a favor and try these tasty jewels if you can find them.

Storing: The best way to store shrimp is in a resealable plastic bag on ice. You don't want shrimp standing in water, so place the bag in a colander and surround it with ice. Put the colander in a bowl to catch the melting ice.

Sizing up shrimp

In many stores, shrimp are mislabeled by sizes with names like jumbo, large, or medium. But these are market terms and differ between stores.

The best way to buy shrimp is to ask for them by count. This count is the number (actually the range) of shrimp it takes to make one pound. The smaller the number, the bigger the shrimp.

If you are told that they are 16–20s, that means there are 16 to 20 shrimp per pound (I take the average—for this size, it would be 18). Using a count like this is useful in recipes because you can easily interchange pounds and numbers.

Shrimp come in all sizes, again, measured by the pound using a typical range of numbers just described. I've also seen them marked U/5s meaning there are *under* five shrimp per pound—those are some big shrimp and great for grilling. Then I've bought some marked ov/80s, meaning there are *over* 80 shrimp per pound—they're small and best for shrimp salad.

So, for recipe success, use a count rather than a name.

General guideline
Market terms are on the left and shrimp count (to make one pound) are on the right.

Colossal ....10 or less
Jumbo 11–15
Extra large 16–20
Large.............21–30
Medium 31–35
Small 36–45

Cleaning shrimp

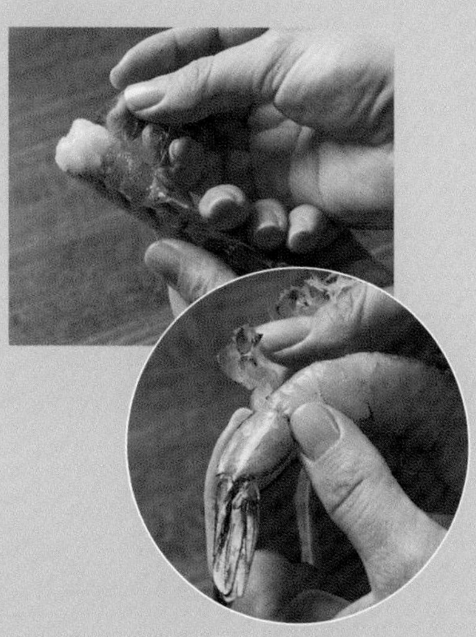

▲*To peel shrimp, remove legs and peel off shell. Leave the tail segment on if you want (see inset).*

▲*To devein, cut a slit down the back to expose dark vein.*

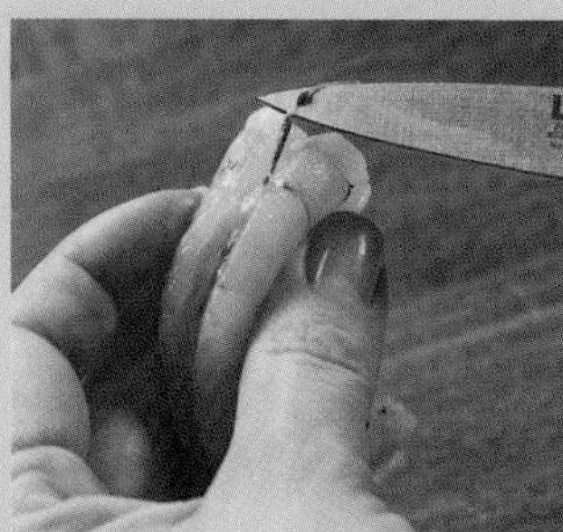

▲*Lift out vein and rinse the shrimp thoroughly under cold, running water.*

Quality checklist

When buying shrimp, you are already equipped with the best tools to make good choices—your senses.

Smell

First and foremost, use your nose when buying shrimp. All you should smell is the sweet, mild aroma of clean ocean. If there is a bad odor or ammonia smell, stay away. This indicates that the shrimp are beginning to spoil.

Texture

After your nose, rely on your sense of touch. Good shrimp should be firm, not mushy. The shells don't necessarily have to be firm. Shrimp periodically shed their shells, and the new shells that form tend to be soft. But you don't want the shells to be slimy at all—another indication of spoilage.

And one last thing: If you touch the shell and it feels gritty like sandpaper, stay away from these shrimp. This indicates they've been improperly treated with too much sodium bisulfite—a chemical used to prevent black spots along the sides of the shrimp (a sign of deterioration).

Color

Finally, use your eyes to pick good shrimp. Look out for black spots or rings on the shell or meat (except tiger shrimp)—an indication of deterioration.

Also avoid meat or shells that are yellow. This is another result of too much sodium bisulfite.

Picking out good quality shrimp isn't that hard as long as you use your good sense(s).

Headless?
Most shrimp come with their heads removed. Acids from the head cause the body to deteriorate faster.

shrimp & grits

Don't blow off this recipe until you try it. This is the perfect dish to introduce yourself to a great Southern staple—grits.

menu

Shrimp and Grits

Sauteed Mustard Greens

That's right. You're going to buy grits (hopefully not quick grits), cook them and eat them with a wonderfully spicy dish of shrimp and smoked sausage. Then, you're going to wonder why you have made fun of grits all these years.

Southerners have known forever that grits are something special. Now, many of the big city restaurants are realizing the same thing too—grits make a great-tasting side dish.

What's nice about this dish is how quick it is to make. Cutting up the vegetables (can be done a day ahead) and cooking the grits (about 20 minutes) are the only things that take any time. Actual cooking only takes about 10 minutes—any longer and the colorful vegetables turn dull and flavorless.

Do yourself a favor and try this traditional Southern combination. You'll be glad you did.

Understanding grits

Grits are simply ground corn, so the flavor shouldn't be foreign to you at all. To produce grits, hard corn kernels are soaked in a lye solution to remove the hull and germ. This is now called hominy. It can be dried and ground into two corn products: grits (coarse ground) and cornmeal (fine grind).

Old fashioned, stone-ground cornmeal and grits are still made and are the most flavorful to me. Check out Page 43 for a source. Store bought grits tend to be a little more processed. They're either quick (cook in 5 minutes) or instant (pour boiling water over them and stir). No matter which variety you use, consistency in this dish is important. The grits need to be thick and firm so they hold their shape, not run on the plate.

You can thicken the grits by cooking them longer than package directions indicate, or by simply adding extra grits at the beginning. Be sure to keep stirring them as they thicken to prevent any scorching.

For Creamy Grits: Grits are usually made with water, but for creamy grits, use half milk, half water. Cook until thick and firm.

Prepare all the ingredients before cooking—this is called "mise en place."

Shrimp and Grits

Makes 2–4 Servings
Total Time: 40 Minutes

For the Grits—
Prepare:
2 cups grits, *see left*
For the Shrimp—
Dust with Flour:
10 large shrimp (16–20 count), peeled and deveined
Saute in 2 T. Vegetable Oil:
Floured shrimp
1 cup kielbasa, 1/4"-thick slices
Add with 1 T. Butter:
1/2 cup yellow pepper, diced
1/2 cup red pepper, diced
1/2 cup celery, diced
Stir in:
1 cup tomatoes, seeded and diced
2 t. garlic, minced
2 t. Old Bay seasoning
1 t. dried oregano
1/2 t. crushed red pepper flakes
Add; Reduce:
1/2 cup low-sodium chicken broth
1 T. heavy cream
Stir in:
Sauteed shrimp and kielbasa
1/2 cup scallions, chopped (green part only)
Serve Over:
Sauteed mustard greens
Prepared grits
Garnish with:
Lemon wedge

Prepare grits according to package directions using half milk and half water.
Dust peeled and deveined shrimp with flour; set aside.
Saute shrimp and kielbasa in pan over medium heat for 3–4 minutes. Remove and set aside.
Add 1 T. of butter to pan with peppers and celery. Saute 2–3 minutes, scraping bottom of pan.
Stir in tomatoes and seasonings. Cook 3–4 minutes.
Add broth and cream. Reduce until liquid thickens, about 4–5 minutes.
Stir in reserved shrimp and kielbasa, and chopped scallions. Simmer 2–3 minutes.
Serve over sauteed mustard greens and prepared grits.
Garnish each serving with a wedge of lemon.

▲ *Saute shrimp and kielbasa for 3–4 minutes. Remove and set aside.*

Add butter to pan and saute peppers and celery for 2–3 minutes. ▼

▲ *Stir in tomatoes and seasonings. Cook just until you smell the spices.*

◄ *Stir in shrimp, kielbasa, and scallions; simmer 2–3 minutes. Serve over sauteed mustard greens and grits. Garnish with lemon.*

Coconut shrimp

Resurrected flavors! Coconut shrimp have been around a while but now enjoy a rebirth of popularity.

The perfect combination of sensations: sweet, sour, hot, cool. These crispy fried shrimp blend many characteristics of good food into one dish. But for best results, pay attention to two key ingredients—panko bread crumbs and unsweetened coconut.

Make an effort to find panko bread crumbs—they make a great crispy crust. If your grocer does not carry them, an Asian market certainly will. Then, use only unsweetened coconut. This, too, makes a good crust that's not overwhelmingly sweet.

Coconut Shrimp

Makes 16 Shrimp; Serves 4
Total Time: 25 Minutes

Prepare:
16 large shrimp (1 lb. 16–20 count), peeled and deveined
Combine; Dredge Shrimp in:
1/2 cup cornstarch
1 t. kosher salt
1/2 t. cayenne
Whisk; Dip Shrimp in:
2 egg whites
1/4 cup water
Combine; Bread Shrimp in:
1 1/2 cups shredded unsweetened coconut
3/4 cup panko bread crumbs
1 t. kosher salt
Heat; Fry Shrimp in:
Vegetable oil
Serve with:
Red Pepper Sauce, *right*
Sweet Cilantro Sauce, *right*

Prepare shrimp as on Page 7.
Combine cornstarch, salt, and cayenne in a plastic bag. Dredge shrimp in mixture.
Whisk together egg whites and water until frothy. Dip dredged shrimp into egg white mixture.
Combine coconut, panko, and salt in another plastic bag. Add shrimp, a few at a time, and shake to coat. Place coated shrimp on a rack. Fry shrimp at this point or chill 2–3 hours.
Heat 1/2" vegetable oil in a saute pan over medium heat to 365°. Fry shrimp 1–2 minutes per side; remove to a cooling rack.
Serve hot with Red Pepper Sauce and Sweet Cilantro Sauce.

▲*Dredge shrimp in cornstarch mixture, then dip in frothy egg whites.*

◄*Combine coconut breading in a bag. Add shrimp and shake well to coat.*

▲*Heat vegetable oil to 365°. Fry shrimp until golden, 1–2 minutes per side.*

▲*Remove fried shrimp to a cooling rack. Serve immediately with chilled sauces.*

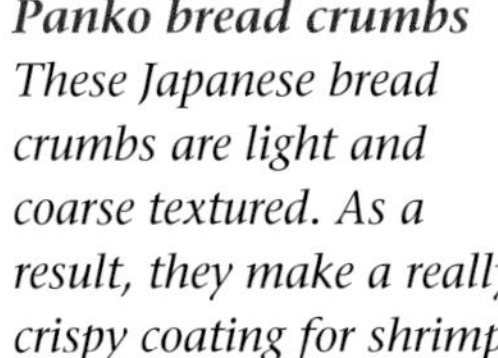

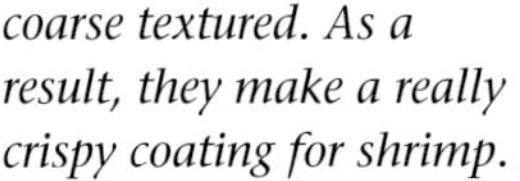

Panko bread crumbs
These Japanese bread crumbs are light and coarse textured. As a result, they make a really crispy coating for shrimp.

Red Pepper Sauce

Makes 2 Cups

Blend; Simmer:
2 cups red bell pepper, seeded and chopped
1 cup sugar
1/2 cup white wine vinegar
2 t. crushed red pepper flakes
2 t. fresh ginger, chopped
Salt to taste
Combine; Add and Simmer:
1 T. cornstarch
1 T. water

Blend the pepper, sugar, vinegar, pepper flakes, and ginger in a processor or blender until smooth. Simmer over medium-high heat in a saucepan for 4–5 minutes. Season with salt to taste.
Combine cornstarch and water. Add to bell pepper mixture; simmer until thickened, about 2 minutes. Chill sauce before serving.

Sweet Cilantro Sauce

Makes About 1 1/2 Cups

Simmer:
1 cup white wine or rice vinegar
1/4 cup sugar
1/4 cup water
2 T. fresh lime juice
1 t. crushed red pepper flakes
Salt to taste
Combine; Add and Simmer:
1 T. cornstarch
1 T. water
Before Serving, Stir in:
1/4 cup scallions, minced
1/4 cup chopped fresh cilantro

Simmer vinegar, sugar, water, lime juice, pepper flakes, and salt in a saucepan for about 5 minutes.
Combine cornstarch and water. Stir into sauce and simmer to thicken, about 2 minutes; chill.
Before serving, stir in scallions and cilantro.

Crusting chicken

Finally! A crusted chicken breast that's crisp on the outside, juicy on the inside. Read on for the secrets.

I'm picky about crusted chicken. Way too much of it has been dredged in powdered, pulverized bread crumbs and dull, dried herbs. As if that weren't enough, it's often baked—to death.

So developing a recipe for chicken with a flavorful crust and juicy interior was just the kind of challenge I like. The keys are in the four "Cs": the chicken, crumbs, coating, and cooking.

The chicken

Boneless, skinless breast halves are the way to go—they're convenient and cook quickly. Whole breast halves are too big, so first, halve each one lengthwise, *see Figure 1*. Doing this ensures that the coating doesn't burn before the chicken is cooked through. If you double this recipe, just be sure to saute the chicken in two pans to avoid crowding.

Now, lightly pound the pieces to an even 1/2" thick, *see Figure 2*. You aren't tenderizing or creating a cutlet for scaloppine here, so be gentle. Pounding them in a slightly damp plastic bag helps prevent sticking and tearing.

1 Trim excess skin and fat from chicken. Slice each breast half lengthwise down the center.

2 Lightly pound each piece (in a plastic bag with a little water inside) to an even thickness.

Crusted Chicken Breasts

Makes Four 2–3 oz. Pieces
Total Time: About 1 Hour

Prepare:
2 boneless, skinless chicken breast halves (6–8 oz. each)

For the Dipping Mixture—
Blend:
2 egg whites
2 t. cornstarch
Juice of 1/2 lemon

For the Crusting Mixture—
Combine:
1 cup coarse dry bread crumbs, *see right*
1 T. chopped fresh parsley
1 t. kosher salt
1/4 t. ground black pepper
Zest of one lemon, minced

Saute Chicken in:
3 T. olive oil

Preheat oven to 450°.
Prepare chicken breasts, cutting and pounding, *Fig. 1 and 2.*
Blend egg whites, cornstarch, and lemon juice with a fork in a wide, shallow dish; set aside.
Combine bread crumbs, parsley, salt, pepper, and zest in a second wide, shallow dish.
Crust chicken breasts, *Fig. 3 and 4.* Let chicken rest at room temperature on a rack for 20–30 min. to set crust.
Saute chicken in oil in a large, nonstick, ovenproof skillet over medium-high heat for about 3 minutes, or until golden brown and crisp, *Fig. 5.* Carefully turn with a spatula, *Fig. 6*, and transfer the skillet to the oven to finish cooking. Roast chicken just until done, about 8 more minutes, *Fig. 7.*

The crumbs

Crumbs are the most important "C" in this equation. Besides adding great flavor, they're essential for the right texture. They create a crouton-like crust on the chicken, not a dry, crumbly one.

For the best crumbs, you need the right bread. A rustic-type loaf with a chewy, yet fairly soft crust (like *ciabatta*) is ideal. Bread with a holey interior makes crumbs that vary in size—that's good. Stay away from loaves having dense, hard crusts. These crumbs would make chewing painful!

Cut bread into cubes (leave crust on) and process to crumbs. Work in batches and don't overfill the bowl. The crumbs will be different sizes—from powdery to the size of peas. That's fine. Uniformity is not the goal here.

Dry the crumbs on a baking sheet for 10–15 minutes in a 200° oven until they're completely dried but not toasted. Freeze any extra crumbs in a resealable bag.

Coating and cooking

To coat, you need to dip the chicken into something wet (egg whites), then roll it in something dry (crumbs). Even if the meat feels moist, it's not enough for crumbs to stick and stay stuck. Egg whites are the natural "glue."

Dip the chicken in the egg, then the crumb mixtures, *see Figures 3 & 4*. Because the crumbs are fairly coarse, they won't adhere well—don't worry. Scoop handfuls of crumbs, piling them on each piece, then transfer the chicken to a rack set over a baking sheet. Air-dry chicken 20–30 minutes to help set the crumbs.

To cook, first saute the chicken on the stove in an ovenproof, nonstick skillet. As you put the chicken in the pan, lay it *toward* you, *see Figure 5*. This way, it rests on top of any crumbs that fall off. Saute until the chicken is golden and crisp on one side, then carefully flip the pieces over (use your hand to help gently guide them), *see Figure 6*. Finally, transfer the whole pan to a 450° oven to finish, *see Figure 7*. Eight to 10 more minutes is all it takes.

3 Dip both sides of prepared chicken into egg white-cornstarch mixture. Transfer the chicken to the crumb dish.

4 Pat crumbs on both sides of chicken—it's okay if some crumbs fall off. Air-dry on rack 20–30 minutes.

5 Heat oil in large nonstick pan. Lay chicken *toward* you in the pan—the loose crumbs will form a "bed" for chicken to lay on.

6 Saute chicken until golden, 3 minutes. Carefully flip chicken, then transfer pan to oven.

7 Roast chicken in the pan in the oven 8–10 minutes, or until cooked through.

Parmesan crusted chicken
with sage-butter sauce

Don't think crusted chicken is "upscale" enough for company? Well, it is when it's with a rich butter sauce and crispy roasted potatoes.

It's true, the crusted chicken on Page 13 is *really* good. But for something a tad more fancy (without a whole lot more work), try this—Parmesan crusted chicken with sage sauce and roasted potatoes. You'd pay money for this meal in a restaurant (but it wouldn't be as good).

Making a full dinner like this isn't as hard as you think. The chicken is prepared just like it is on Page 13 except that Parmesan is added to the crumb recipe. Follow the crusting steps for the chicken on Page 13, then prepare the potatoes and start roasting them while the chicken air-dries (but before it's sauteed).

After that, make the sage sauce and keep it warm in a water bath—it will hold just fine like that for at least an hour. Then, once the potatoes have roasted for 15 minutes, saute and roast the chicken.

Parmesan Crusted Chicken

Makes 4 Servings; Total Time: About 1 Hour

Prepare:
2 boneless, skinless chicken breasts halves, *Page 12*
Whisk:
Dipping Mixture, *Page 12*
Add to Crusting Mixture, Page 12:
½ cup Parmesan cheese, grated
Serve Chicken with:
Sage-Butter Sauce
Roasted Potatoes with Garlic and Rosemary

Preheat oven to 450°.
Prepare chicken breasts by halving and pounding.
Whisk egg whites, cornstarch, and lemon juice in shallow dish for Dipping Mixture.
Add Parmesan to the Crusting Mixture. Crust prepared chicken, let rest, saute, and roast, *Page 13*.
Serve chicken with Sage-Butter Sauce and Roasted Potatoes with Garlic and Rosemary.

Sage advice
Dried or fresh, a little sage goes a long way. Fresh is preferable here, but ½ t. dried sage will do.

Gradually whisk cold butter into simmering sauce base. ▼

◄*Keep sauce warm in a cup set inside a bowl of hot (not boiling) water. Stir sauce often.*

Sage-Butter Sauce

Makes About 1 Cup
Total Time: 20 Minutes

Saute in 1 T. Unsalted Butter:
3 T. shallot, minced
Add and Reduce:
½ cup dry white wine
½ cup heavy cream
½ cup low-sodium chicken broth
1 t. fresh lemon juice
Whisk in:
4 T. (½ stick) cold unsalted butter, cubed
Finish with:
1–2 t. minced fresh sage
Salt, white pepper, and cayenne to taste

Saute shallot in butter in a small saucepan over medium heat just until soft, 2–3 minutes.
Add wine, cream, broth, and lemon juice. Simmer until reduced by half, 8–10 minutes.
Whisk in butter, 1 T. at a time, stirring constantly. Do not add more butter until previous addition has melted completely.
Finish sauce with sage and seasonings. Keep warm in a water bath until ready to serve.

make it a menu

Roasted Potatoes with Garlic and Rosemary

Makes About 3 Cups
Total Time: 30–45 Minutes

Heat:
¼ cup olive oil
4–5 cloves garlic, smashed
1 T. chopped fresh rosemary
Boil:
2 lb. Yukon gold and/or red skinned potatoes, unpeeled, cut into large chunks
Roast; Season with:
Coarse sea salt and freshly ground black pepper to taste

Preheat oven to 450° with rack in lower third. Bring 6 quarts salted water to a boil in a large saucepan.
Heat oil, garlic, and rosemary on a large baking sheet (with sides) on stovetop over medium-low heat. Do not allow garlic to brown.

◄*To heat oil, place the pan directly on the stovetop.*

Boil potatoes in water for one minute. Transfer to the baking sheet on the stove with a slotted spoon; stir to coat with oil.
Roast potatoes in oven on lower rack for 20 minutes. Carefully toss them with a spatula, then roast another 10 minutes, or until cooked through, browned, and crisp. Season with sea salt and freshly ground black pepper.

35

online **extra**

Want another potato recipe?
Visit **www.CuisineAtHome.com** for Mashed Potatoes and Root Vegetables.

pecan crusted chicken salad

with honey-mustard dressing

Salads like this one don't come along very often. Its full flavor and crunchy texture are sure to satisfy.

My big complaint about a lot of salads is their narrow-mindedness. Lettuce, cucumbers, and tomatoes are the accepted norm. But there's plenty more out there to build a better salad.

Like chicken. You're already familiar with crusted chicken. The pecans and spices in this crumb mixture add more flavor.

Add onion and goat cheese for a pungent bite. Bitter greens, like arugula and radicchio, offset the sweet-tart dressing, but some romaine leaves tossed in there helps balance out the equation.

But you know the best part? The crumbs left in the saute pan! Sprinkle them on top of the salads. *Voilà*—instant croutons!

Pecan Crusted Chicken

Makes 4 Servings; Total Time: About 1 Hour

Prepare:
2 boneless, skinless chicken breast halves, *Page 12*

Whisk:
Dipping Mixture, *Page 12*

Add to Crusting Mixture, Page 12:
3/4 cup finely chopped pecans
1/2 t. dried oregano
1/2 t. dried thyme
1/2 t. paprika
1/4 t. cayenne

Slice Chicken; Serve with:
Salad Greens with Honey Mustard Dressing

Preheat oven to 450°.
Prepare chicken breasts by halving and pounding.
Whisk egg whites, cornstarch, and lemon juice in shallow dish for Dipping Mixture.
Add pecans, herbs, and spices to the Crusting Mixture. Crust prepared chicken, let rest, saute, and roast, *Page 13*.
Slice chicken and serve fanned over salad greens tossed with Honey-Mustard Dressing.

Salad Greens with Honey-Mustard Dressing

For the Dressing, Combine:
1/4 cup honey
3 T. Dijon mustard
3 T. extra-virgin olive oil
1 T. shallot, minced
1 T. apple cider vinegar
Juice of 1/2 lemon
Salt and pepper to taste

Toss Dressing with:
8 cups mixed greens such as arugula, radicchio, curly endive, romaine, and leaf lettuces
1/2 cup red onion, thinly sliced
4 oz. mild goat cheese, crumbled

Top with:
Sliced Pecan Crusted Chicken
Toasted crumbs from pan

For the dressing, combine all ingredients until blended.
Toss dressing with greens, onion, and goat cheese (you won't need all the dressing). Arrange greens on four plates.
Top greens with sliced chicken. Sprinkle any toasted crumbs left in the pan on the salads. Serve with extra dressing on the side.

▲ *Toss greens, onion, and goat cheese with some of the Honey-Mustard Dressing.*

Slice crusted chicken on bias and fan out on beds of greens. ►

▲ *Sprinkle some of the toasted crumbs from the saute pan on top of each salad.*

option

Baked Sweet Potatoes with Maple-Jalapeño Sour Cream

These potatoes are a nice change from gooey Thanksgiving-like sweet potato preparations.

Makes 4 Potatoes
Total Time: 40–45 Minutes

For the Sweet Potatoes—
Rub with Oil and Salt:
4 sweet potatoes, scrubbed, dried

For the Topping—
Combine:
1/2 cup sour cream or plain yogurt
1 T. pure maple syrup
2 t. jalapeño, seeded, minced
1 t. fresh lime juice
Salt and Tabasco to taste

Serve Potatoes with:
Maple-Jalapeño Sour Cream
Bacon bits
Sliced scallions

Preheat oven to 450° with rack positioned in the center.
Rub scrubbed, dried sweet potatoes with oil and salt. Bake directly on rack for 40–45 minutes, or until soft when pierced.
Combine all topping ingredients; chill until ready to serve.
Serve potatoes with Maple-Jalapeño Sour Cream, bacon bits, and scallions.

allabout honey

Honey—it's liquid gold, sweeter than sugar, and the only food humans eat that is insect-generated. So dig in and get your hands sticky. Honey is neat stuff!

The closest most people get to honey is on a biscuit or in tea. But it's the center of a bee's life. Here's what the buzz is all about.

What is honey?

Honey is simply bee food that bees make from flower nectar. A bee colony (population: tens of thousands) needs a large, reliable food source in order to sustain its residents. Honey is the answer.

Even with all those mouths to feed, a colony's average annual honey yield of 77 pounds is way more than enough to keep it going. A bee, fueled by a mere *one ounce* of honey, could fly around the world! Any extra is what we get to enjoy.

Honey Color and Flavor

The color and flavor of honey is largely determined by the type of flower the nectar was drawn from. Sage honey is very pale and light in flavor. On the other hand, buckwheat honey is a few shades lighter than molasses and has a similar spicy, deep flavor.

How is honey made?

To make honey, bees gather nectar (a clear, sweet liquid) from flowers. Back at the hive, the nectar goes through several stages before being stored in the hexagonal cells of the honeycomb. There it ripens for a few days before the comb is "capped" with a layer of wax. The honey stays in the hive for the bees to use as needed, or until it's taken out (very carefully!) by a beekeeper.

Nectar gathering isn't just for honey—it's critical for pollination, ensuring better quality crops with higher yields. As bees search for nectar, they collect pollen on their bodies, then deposit it as they move in and out of flowers.

Forms of honey

Thick, amber liquid is the most recognizable form of honey—it's the stuff that's extracted from the comb, then heated, filtered, and packed. *Comb* or *cut comb* honey is packaged along with some of the waxy honeycomb (which is edible). *Creamed* or *spun* honey has been mechanically crystallized; its pearly white look is from super-fine crystals. *Raw* honey isn't measured against any regulatory guidelines—it's whatever the packer wants it to be.

Honey's flavor depends on its nectar source. Floral honeys (like lavender, orange blossom, and clover) are required by the USDA to be comprised of at least 80% of those specific flowers. "Mixed flower" or "wildflower" honey is made with nectar from many flower sources. As a rule, taste honey before using it. Some have distinct flavors that may not be best for what you're making.

Honey handling

Store honey at room temperature—don't chill it. That speeds crystallization, a common occurrence in most honeys. Due to its natural preservatives, honey is not susceptible to spoiling.

If your honey has crystallized, reliquefy it by heating it gently, placing the jar either in a pan of simmering water or the microwave. It'll stay fluid for a while, but repeat the process if needed.

Go ahead, eat cookies for breakfast! These are crammed full with the same good things as your granola. All you supply is the milk (or tea—with honey).

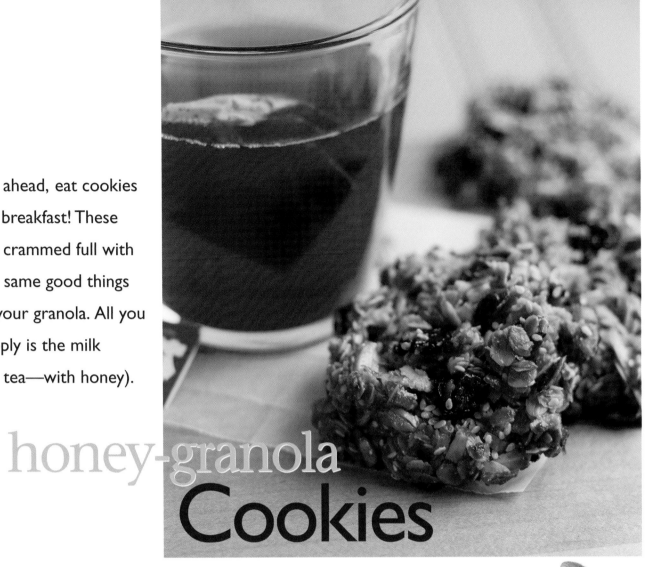

honey-granola Cookies

Honey-Granola Cookies

Makes 14–16 Cookies; Total Time: 1 Hour

Combine:
3/4 cup brown sugar
1/2 cup (1 stick) unsalted butter
1/2 cup clover honey
1/4 cup water
1/2 t. kosher salt

Off Heat, Stir In:
2 t. vanilla extract

Combine; Add:
3 cups old-fashioned oats
2/3 cup (3 oz.) dried tart cherries
1/2 cup toasted wheat germ
1/2 cup slivered almonds
1/2 cup sweetened coconut
1/3 cup sunflower seeds
1/3 cup sesame seeds
1/3 cup pepitas, *see sidebar*
1/2 t. kosher salt
1/2 cup semisweet chocolate chips, *optional**

Preheat oven to 350°.
Combine brown sugar, butter, honey, water, and salt in a large saucepan. Warm over low heat until sugar and honey melt.
Off heat, stir in vanilla.
Combine dry ingredients and add to honey mixture; stir to coat. Fill a #16 scoop (or 1/4 cup measuring cup) with dough, pressing it against side of pan to level. Drop dough 4" apart onto baking sheets lined with parchment; flatten slightly with scoop. Bake 13–15 min., or until set and golden. Transfer to a rack and cool 20 min. before serving.

** Optional chocolate chips must be added to cooled dough only.*

Pepitas
These green, hulled pumpkin seeds are popular in Mexican cooking. Use white ones (or omit) if you can't find them.

honey-lime Chicken Wings

Honey-Lime Chicken Wings

Brine these wings for at least an hour to deeply seasons the meat. If brining for 10–12 hours, omit the salt from the sauce. The wings will leach some of the salt brine into the sauce during simmering.

Makes 5 Lb. Wings; Total Time: 1 Hour + Brining

For the Chicken and Brine—

Prepare:

5 lb. chicken wings, tips removed

Dissolve:

2 cups boiling water
1/2 cup brown sugar
1/2 cup kosher salt

Add to Brine:

6 cups ice water
Prepared chicken wings

For the Sauce—

Whisk Together:

1/2 cup clover honey
1/2 cup fresh lime juice
3 T. white sesame seeds
1 T. fresh ginger, minced
2 t. cayenne
2 t. kosher salt
1 t. garlic, minced
1 t. freshly ground black pepper

Prepare chicken wings by first cutting off the wing tips (discard tips or save for stock); set aside.
Dissolve boiling water, sugar, and salt in a 2-gallon resealable plastic bag.
Add ice water to cool, then the wings. Seal bag and chill for at least one hour, or up to 12 hours.
Whisk together all sauce ingredients. When ready to prepare wings, preheat oven to 450° and line two baking sheets with double layers of parchment paper. Place sauce in a large saute pan and bring to a simmer over medium-high heat. Remove wings from brine, add to the sauce, and simmer for 20 minutes, turning wings often to coat with sauce. Transfer chicken to prepared baking sheets (do not crowd the pans or wings will not brown as well) and roast for 10 minutes. Brush wings with some of the remaining sauce left in the saute pan and roast for 10 more minutes. Brush again with sauce and any accumulated pan juices; roast another 5 minutes. Remove from pans while hot or wings will stick.

35

online **extra**

Want a wing option? Visit www.CuisineAtHome.com for a recipe to make Spicy BBQ Chicken Wings.

honey-grapefruit Sorbet

It's time grapefruit was given more attention than at the breakfast table. A little honey makes this deal even sweeter.

The word "sorbet" can make people uncomfortable. It sounds too fancy or something. But sorbet is simply sweetened, frozen fruit juice or puree—it's just like a Popsicle, but in a different shape.

As simple as it sounds, there's a lot going on that could affect the end result. For example, too much sweetener will make the sorbet too soft to scoop. But if there's not enough sweetener, the mixture will freeze rock hard. It's like scooping cement—and about as pleasant to eat.

This recipe is perfectly balanced. It's tart, but in a good, refreshing way. If you'd prefer something sweeter, however, *do not* up the honey. You'll get slush.

Instead, try the sherbet featured in the Online Extra. It's still tart, but a bit more subdued than this sorbet. Sherbet is a cousin of sorbet—it has the same sweetened fruit juice, but also has added dairy, like milk, yogurt, or egg whites. The yogurt in this sherbet cuts some of the grapefruit's tanginess.

Honey-Grapefruit Sorbet

Serve this ultra-tangy sorbet as a light, refreshing dessert or even for brunch with fresh fruit.
Makes About 2 Cups

Combine:

1 cup fresh pink grapefruit juice, strained
1/2 cup water
1/3 cup clover or orange blossom honey
2 t. grapefruit zest, minced
1 t. maraschino cherry juice (for coloring, optional)
Pinch salt

Combine all ingredients, stirring until honey dissolves. Process mixture in ice cream maker according to manufacturer's directions until it becomes firm. Transfer sorbet to a freezer container and press waxed or parchment paper directly on top. Cover tightly with a lid and freeze sorbet until firm and scoopable, at least 2 hours.

Maraschino cherry juice *Instead of using straight red food coloring, a little cherry juice adds color to the sorbet.*

35 *online* **extra**

Want sherbet? Visit www.CuisineAtHome.com for a recipe to make Honey-Grapefruit Sherbet.

making great meatballs

Juicy, aromatic, and packed with flavor, these homemade Italian meatballs have a lot more talent than just being able to sit on top of pasta.

With schedules the way they are, it's good to run across a dish that can serve several menus. These meatballs do just that.

Saucy Meatballs with Pasta: As common as this might seem, this dish has plenty of fans. Of course the meatballs are sensational tasting, but what's fun is making them any size you want. Two giant meatballs sitting on a mound of pasta looks pretty cool.

Italian Wedding Soup: A quick soup that makes a perfect main course. Although you use canned chicken broth, the fresh vegetables combine with the beans and tiny meatballs to make an unusually rich stock.

Meatball Sub: Check out the Back Cover for a hero of a lunch. Crusty hoagies filled with spicy meatballs and oozing cheese will warm any fall day.

Some recipes fry meatballs for extra flavor and firm texture. In my opinion, this isn't necessary. You can retain *plenty* of flavor and texture by baking them at a high temperature. The best part—there's no mess!

Mixing: Mixing meatballs is a two step process. Before adding the meat, blend other ingredients thoroughly then add the meat and mix with a fork, *see Figure 1*. Using a fork prevents overmixing and compacting which can toughen meatballs.

Shaping: The best way to shape meatballs is to use a disher, *below*. Scoop out the meat mixture (with the disher) onto a baking sheet, and then roll the scoops into balls, *see Figure 2*. To prevent sticking, dip your hands in water.

Cooking: Once all the meatballs are rolled and placed on the baking sheet, pour beef broth to cover the bottom of the pan, *see Figure 3*. This keeps the meatballs juicy. Be sure to save the drippings after baking—you'll want to put this into your tomato sauce for knockout flavor.

Basic Meatballs

You can cook these meatballs ahead and then freeze by placing them on a baking sheet. When hard, remove and store in a freezer bag.

Makes 30–33 (1 1/2 oz.) Meatballs; Total Time: 50 Minutes

Stir Together:

- 1 cup unseasoned bread crumbs
- 3/4 cup Romano or Parmesan cheese, finely grated
- 1/2 cup whole milk
- 1/2 cup low-sodium beef broth
- 1/2 cup chopped fresh parsley
- 3 eggs, beaten
- 2 T. dried oregano
- 1 T. garlic, minced
- 1 T. kosher salt
- 1 T. ground black pepper
- 2 t. dried basil
- 1 t. crushed red pepper flakes
- Pinch nutmeg

Add; Shape:

- 2 lb. ground chuck

Cover Bottom of Pan with:

- 1 cup low-sodium beef broth

Preheat oven to 450°.

Stir together all ingredients (except the ground meat) in a large mixing bowl.

Add the ground chuck and mix together thoroughly. Using a portioning scoop or 2 spoons, shape the meat mixture into balls (about 2" in diameter or 1 1/2 oz. each). Coat a baking sheet or shallow roasting pan with nonstick cooking spray. Space the meatballs on the pan so they're not touching or crowded together.

Cover bottom of pan with beef broth. Bake for 25 minutes, or until the meatballs are just cooked through. Reserve pan juices for sauce.

1 Combine the ground chuck with the bread crumb mixture. Stir thoroughly with a fork.

2 Scoop out meat to form golf ball-sized portions. Roll and place on pan so they're not touching.

3 Cover the bottom of the pan with beef broth. Bake about 25 minutes.

Easier Ways to Scoop

You might want to consider utilizing one of the tools below for making meatballs a consistent size. The first is simply a large melon baller—it works just fine, but meat tends to stick in its bowl. The next two scoops are different sized "portioning scoops," or dishers. These work best as they have retracting blades that release the meat or other foods (like cookie dough). Finally, you can use two spoons to form an oval which can then be shaped into a ball.

melon baller

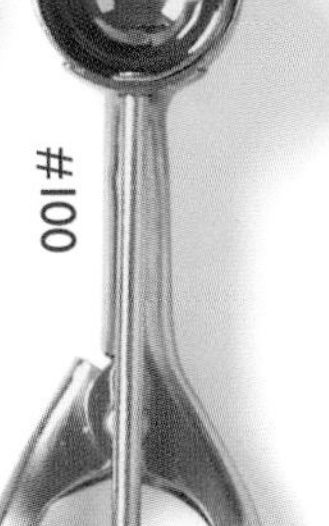

#30

saucy meatballs *with pasta*

▲ *The pan drippings from the meatballs add extra flavor to the sauce.*

▼ *Add the cooked meatballs to the sauce to heat through.*

▲ *Stir in the pasta and toss well to coat with the sauce.*

Meatballs in Fresh Tomato Sauce

Serves 4–6; Total Time: 40 Minutes

Saute in 1/4 Cup Olive Oil:
1 1/2 cups yellow onion, diced
Stir in:
2 t. garlic, minced
Add and Simmer:
3 cans (14 1/2 oz. each) whole plum tomatoes, crushed
1/2 cup reserved meatball pan drippings, *Page 23*
1/2 cup minced fresh parsley
1 T. sugar
1 t. crushed red pepper flakes
Salt to taste
Add and Simmer:
12 cooked meatballs
Stir in:
1 lb. cooked pasta
Before Serving, Add:
1/4 cup fresh basil, cut in strips
Garnish with:
Parmesan cheese, grated

Saute onions in oil over med.-high heat in a large pan until translucent, about 4 min.
Stir in garlic. Cook just until you smell it, about 30 seconds.
Add tomatoes, pan drippings, parsley, sugar, pepper flakes, and salt. Simmer 15 minutes. Start boiling the water for pasta.
Add cooked meatballs to the sauce and simmer, uncovered, for 10 minutes to heat through. Meanwhile, cook pasta according to package directions; drain.
Stir in the cooked pasta and toss well to coat.
Before serving, add the fresh basil strips.
Garnish pasta and meatballs with grated Parmesan cheese.

Italian wedding soup

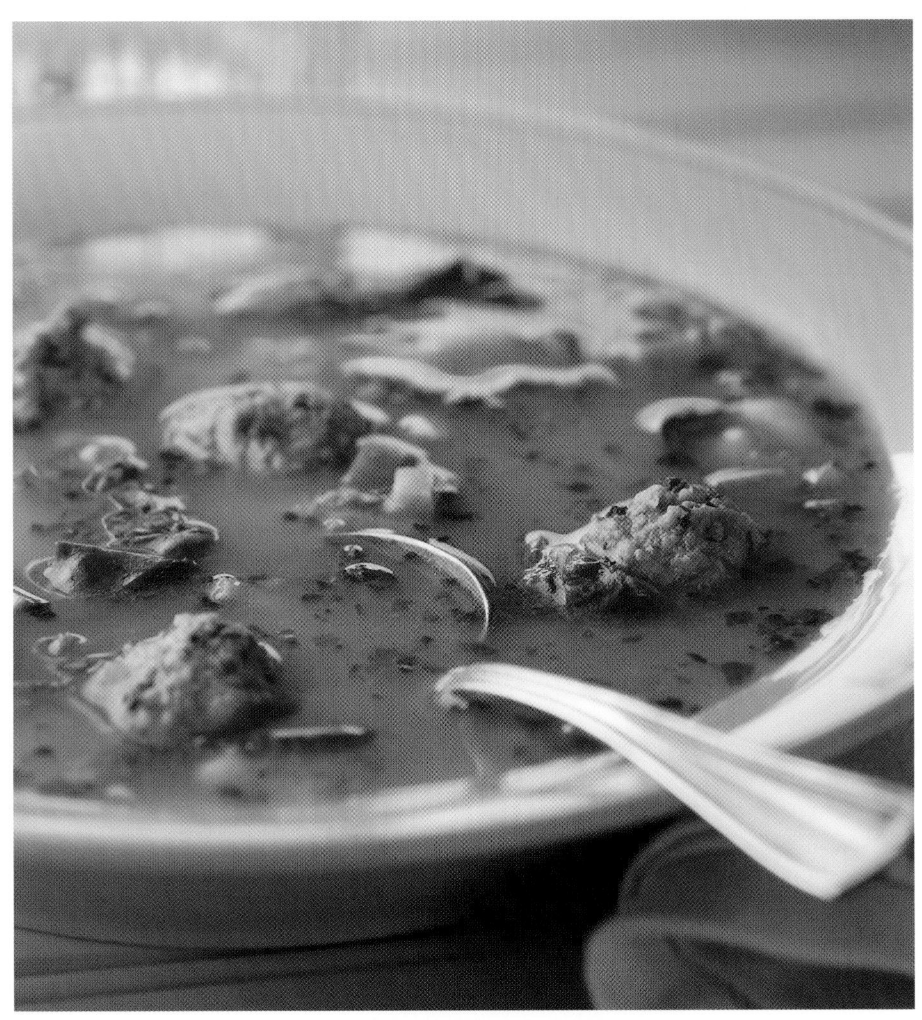

Italian Wedding Soup

We used 12 ounces of the meatball mixture from Page 23 and a #100 scoop to make the tiny meatballs for this classic soup.

Makes 12 Cups
Total Time: 45 Minutes

Sweat in 2 T. Olive Oil:
1 cup yellow onion, diced
1 cup celery, diced
1 cup carrot, diced
1 cup ham, diced
1 T. garlic, minced

Add and Simmer:
6 cups low-sodium chicken broth
2 t. dried oregano
2 t. crushed red pepper flakes
1 bay leaf

Drop in:
30 uncooked marble-sized meatballs, *Page 23*

Stir in:
1 can (15 oz.) white beans, drained and rinsed
2 cups whole spinach leaves
1/2 cup chopped fresh parsley

Combine; Off Heat, Add:
2 eggs, beaten
1/2 cup Parmesan, grated

This is one of the richest soups you'll ever make in 45 minutes using canned broth. The fresh vegetables totally take away any prepackaged taste you might get from canned broth. The meatballs add depth because you're actually cooking them in the broth. And finally, the soup reaches "full-bodied" status by swirling in a Parmesan-egg mixture just before serving.

◄ Use a small scoop or a melon baller, to drop the raw meatballs into the soup.

Whisk together the eggs and Parmesan. Off heat, stir mixture into the soup. ►

Sweat vegetables, ham, and garlic in oil in a stockpot over medium heat until softened. **Add** chicken broth and seasonings; simmer 15–20 minutes. **Drop** meatballs into simmering soup with a small scoop or a melon baller. Cook until they float to the top, 3–4 minutes. **Stir in** beans, spinach, and parsley. Cook just until spinach wilts, about 2 minutes. **Combine** eggs and Parmesan with a whisk. Off heat, stir egg mixture into soup.

wares
peelers

Need a better peeler? Most of us do. But you probably haven't put a lot of thought into the subject. Consider all the options and you'll be able to choose one that's comfortable for your hand, style, and budget.

I'm almost embarrassed to tell you that we tested 38 peelers. While the best ones were quickly evident, each staff member chose a different winner. Not surprising given the dizzying array of choices that came into play.

There's a lot to consider, but it doesn't have to be complicated. Just ask yourself a few questions. What kind of blade do you prefer? Do you like to peel toward or away from yourself? What style choice and weight are comfortable in your hand? And finally, how often do you use a peeler and what foods do you usually peel? Your unique combination of answers will guide your peeler choice.

No matter what peeler you choose, the blade absolutely *must* swivel. If it does not, your hand and wrist will be doing all the swiveling.

Blade options

Peeler blades are made of three materials: carbon steel, stainless steel, and ceramic.

Carbon is what Grandma's peeler blade was made of. A good carbon blade will likely keep a sharp edge longer than stainless. But it needs to be hand-washed and dried or it develops a light dusting of rust (easily washed and wiped away). A good stainless blade offers low maintenance while still providing a sharp edge.

Ceramic blades are made of zirconium oxide, an extremely hard surface (only a diamond is harder). Although we couldn't test longevity, ceramic blades are reported to keep a sharp edge far longer than either of the steels.

Style options

Peelers come in three styles: vertical, Y-shape, and harp-grip. The vertical peelers are the most traditional. They're right- and left-hand friendly, with double-edged blades that peel in two directions. Y-shapes have single-sided blades and allow peeling toward yourself and to the side. Harp-grip blades vary and peeling can be toward yourself or to the side.

Extra option

Some peelers offer a "digger" for removing eyes from potatoes. If designed well, it's a bonus. But its absence is irrelevant—unless you peel potatoes by the bushel.

The choice is yours

Now that you're educated, you need a little hands-on experience. Go to your kitchenware store, pick up the peelers, and see what feels best. If you can't get to a store, see Resources, *Page 43*, for ordering information.

These peelers were all rated "four-star and above" in the Cuisine Test Kitchen

Kuhn Rikon Y *price: $12.99*

Ultra-smooth strokes produce *very* thin peels of moderate width from this stainless steel blade. A solid, medium-weight grip comes from the cement-filled handle. On the market for about a year, this Kuhn Rikon model is dishwasher safe, and offers their standard lifetime warranty. Does not have a digger option.

Kuhn Rikon Harp *price: $9.75*

This single-edged, stainless steel blade glides with unbelievable smoothness and an incredibly light touch. It deftly shaves off paper-thin, fairly narrow peels. The lightweight (some say flimsy) model is made in Switzerland and has a lifetime warranty. Is there a downside? The digger's a dud.

Rösle Y *price: $25.95*

Made in Germany, this weighty model peels with command. The hardened stainless steel blade smoothly cuts a thick, extra-wide swath. Rösle recommends hand washing to retain the sharp blade edge. Besides a lifetime warranty, Rösle will send a replacement blade at no charge if it's ever needed. The digger is clumsy.

Pedrini Acciaio *price: $12.99*

Thin, narrow strips roll off this traditional style vertical peeler with ease. The double-edged, stainless steel blade makes it both right- and left-hand user friendly. Made in Italy, the Pedrini has a medium-weight, ribbed handle, is dishwasher safe, and boasts a lifetime warranty. Does not include a digger option.

Sima Harp *price: $1.95*

Featherweight but exceptionally capable, this double-edged carbon steel blade easily removes wide peels that are medium-thick. French-made, the Sima is available only from Bridge Kitchenware (see Resources, Page 43). Since shipping charges overshadow the low price, order extras for friends—for the same $7.50 fee.

KitchenAid Euro *price: $8.99*

The chunky KitchenAid has a double-edged blade made of stainless steel with carbon added for lasting sharpness (but it's still dishwasher safe and won't rust). Available in eight colors, it peels with a slightly heavy pull as it removes medium-wide, medium-thick peels. Carries a one year hassle-free and limited lifetime warranty. No digger.

Kuhn Rikon Swiss *price: $6.99*

Realizing no single style is right for everyone, Kuhn Rikon offers yet another line. Their compact carbon steel Swiss peelers have soft-grip handles, are lightweight, and available in two styles. The vertical version is double-edged, while the Y-model has a single-edge blade. Both styles scrape medium-wide, medium-thick peels, and carry lifetime warranties. Bonus: The hard plastic diggers cut out impressively tidy rounds.

Kyocera Ceramic *price: $13.99*

Kyocera has been making ceramic knives for four decades, so it should come as no surprise that they also make peelers with ceramic blades. Almost impossible to chip, the hard blades cut fairly wide, medium-thick peels. The lightweight resin handles are shaped into harp and Y-styles for individual comfort options. Kyocera offers a five-year limited warranty. Double diggers on the harp model work remarkably well for removing potato eyes.

chef**at**home: *Deborah Madison*

farmer's market vegetables

Have you visited a farmer's market lately? Deborah Madison has—and she's got something to tell you.

Photograph ©Patrick McFarlin

I can't think of a better person to talk in-depth about vegetables than award-winning author and chef, Deborah Madison. Her latest book, ***Local Flavors: Cooking and Eating from America's Farmers' Markets*** *(Broadway, 2002), is full of information, recipes, and stories. And her knowledge is first-hand—she's the former market manager of the Santa Fe Area Farmer's Market. Deborah's other books include* ***Vegetarian Cooking for Everyone*** *(Broadway, 1997) and* ***The Greens Cookbook*** *(Bantam, 1986; reprinted by Broadway, 2001).*

Nowadays, it's hard *not* to find a farmer's market in most cities and towns. Deborah Madison likes it that way. Her book, *Local Flavors,* is a showcase of America's farmer's markets, their produce, its growers, plus simple, great-tasting recipes.

"I believe in enjoying what I cook and enjoying the process of cooking it," says Deborah. "When the farmer's market is on, that's the time I like best. The food is so alive, and, honestly, it tells *me* what to do more than I tell *it.*"

These three recipes are prime examples of just that—simple, yet flavorful. Of course, for optimal results, they rely on seasonal produce. What a perfect reason to support your farmer's market!

chard and cilantro soup
with noodle nests

Chard talk

It's easy to pick up on Deborah's love of vegetables just by talking to her. "Their colors and forms, their luxurious foliage, the way they glisten when new, their delicate scent—I love everything about them."

She must've been thinking about chard when she said that. Red- and white-stemmed chard, *below*, are common in grocery stores, and fine for this recipe. But if you find the "Rainbow" or "Bright Lights" variety with pastel colored stems, try it in this light soup.

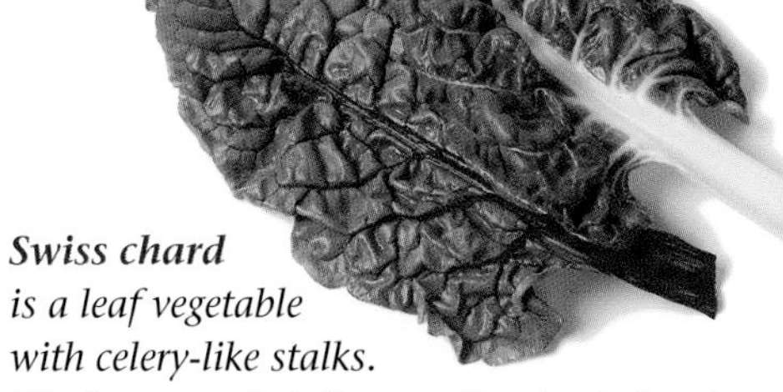

Swiss chard *is a leaf vegetable with celery-like stalks. The leaves and stalks are often treated as two different vegetables—the stems may be braised, while the leaves are tender like spinach. Most bunches weigh about a pound, yielding about 12 cups chopped, uncooked leaves.*

Chard and Cilantro Soup with Noodle Nests

"Cool-weather markets see steady supplies of chard and cilantro, which get together in this pretty soup. Mexican cooking expert Diana Kennedy is responsible for the noodle nests. I would never have come up with them myself, but they're a great addition, giving the soup texture and substance."

Makes 8 Cups Soup and 4–6 Noodle Nests; Total Time: 45 Minutes

For the Noodle Nests—

Beat:

2 egg whites

Stir in:

2 egg yolks

3 oz. (1 3/4 cups) fresh angel hair pasta

1/3 cup Monterey Jack cheese, grated

2 T. chopped fresh cilantro

Sea salt to taste

Heat; Fry Nests in:

Peanut oil

Beat the egg whites in a clean bowl until they hold firm peaks.

Stir in the yolks, pasta, cheese, and cilantro. Season with salt, then combine the mixture with your hands. The mixture will seem very dry.

Heat enough peanut oil in a medium skillet over medium-high heat to float the noodle nests by at least 1/4". When hot, drop the batter into the oil, dividing it by eye into 4–6 nests. Fry until golden, 1 minute per side. Set aside to drain on paper towels.

For the Soup—

Saute in 1 T. Olive oil:

2 bunches scallions, including green, finely chopped

1 celery rib, diced

Add:

1 cup finely chopped cilantro, stems and leaves, packed

1/2 cup vegetable or chicken stock, or water

6 cups Swiss chard leaves, chopped and tightly packed

1 t. sea salt

Stir in:

6 cups vegetable or chicken stock, or water

Freshly ground pepper

Warm the olive oil in a soup pot.

Saute the scallions and celery over medium-high heat for 2–3 minutes, stirring occasionally.

Add the cilantro and 1/2 cup stock after a few minutes—the vegetables should stew rather than fry. Add the chard leaves, sprinkle with sea salt, then cover and cook until chard has wilted down, about 1–2 minutes.

Stir in the stock or water. Bring to a boil, lower the heat, and add the noodle nests to the pot. Simmer soup until chard is tender, about 10 minutes. Taste for salt and season with pepper. Ladle into bowls and garnish with a sprig of cilantro.

◄ Use uncooked fresh angel hair pasta for the noodle nests. Add remaining ingredients, combining with your hands.

Drop batter into hot oil. Gently spread the strands with a fork so they're loose and lacy. Fry until golden on both sides, about 1 minute per side. ►

▲ To chop chard, trim the stalks from the leaves. Roll leaves together and chop into strips.

Add the noodle nests to the soup pot. Simmer with the chard, about 10 minutes. Taste for salt and season with pepper.▼

chef**at**home: *Deborah Madison*

roasted peppers and tomatoes
with herbs & capers

"With its silky texture and summery fragrance, this is one of the most pleasurable dishes to make. Baking melds everything together, transforms the flavors, and yields juices so delicious they invite dunking. Serve cold as a salad, inside a sandwich, on a frittata, or as a topping for grilled garlic toasts."

Roasted Peppers and Tomatoes Baked with Herbs and Capers

Makes 4–5 Cups; Total Time: 1 Hour

For the Vegetables—
Roast; Cut into Strips:
4 bell peppers (red, orange, and yellow)
Prepare:
1 large beefsteak-type tomato (or 1 3/4 lb. ripe tomatoes)
2 small yellow tomatoes

For the Sauce—
Chop:
1/2 cup flat leaf parsley leaves
12 large basil leaves
1 clove garlic
Add:
2 T. capers, rinsed
12 Niçoise olives, pitted
3 T. olive oil
3/4 t. sea salt
Pepper to taste
Toss with; Bake:
Prepared peppers and tomatoes

Roast peppers until charred; cool. Wipe off the blackened skin, pull out the seeds and core, and cut into strips.
Prepare tomatoes by scoring bottom, blanching, then removing skins, *see right*. Halve them crosswise, gently squeeze out seeds, and cut into wide pieces.
Chop parsley, basil, and garlic.
Add herbs to capers, olives, oil, salt, and pepper. Preheat oven to 400°. Lightly oil a gratin dish; pour sauce into the dish.
Toss tomatoes and peppers with sauce. Cover with foil and bake for 20 minutes. Let cool before serving.

Drop charred peppers into a bowl, cover, and set aside while preparing everything else. Then wipe off the blackened skin, pull out seeds and core, and cut into strips. ►

◄ *Score ends of the tomatoes, then drop them into boiling water for 10 seconds. Cool, then remove the skins.*

In a lightly oiled gratin dish, gently hand-toss peppers and tomatoes in the herb-garlic sauce. Cover and bake. ►

winter squash risotto

"Blue Hubbard squash is rich and meaty. You'll do well with it here, but also try Butter-cup, Hokkaido, Queensland Blue, or any other small, squat, green-skinned variety. Butternut, as always, works well. Except for a few smooth varieties, winter squash is hard to peel. Bake unpeeled, then scoop out flesh."

Winter Squash Risotto

Makes 5–6 Cups; Total Time: 45 Min.

Keep at a Simmer:

6 cups chicken or vegetable stock

Saute in 3 T. Butter:

1 yellow onion, finely diced

Add:

1½ cups arborio rice

Gradually Add:

Simmering stock

Stir in:

1 cup winter squash, baked, then mashed with a fork

Off Heat, Add:

1 cup Parmesan cheese

¼ cup chopped fresh sage, *OR*

1 head radicchio, cut into wedges and seared, *below*

Keep chicken or vegetable stock at a simmer.

Saute onion in butter in skillet over med. heat until wilted and lightly colored, about 5 minutes.

Add rice, stir to coat, and cook for 1 minute. Turn heat to high.

Gradually add 2 cups hot stock and cook at a boil, stirring just a few times. When first batch of liquid is fully absorbed, add more stock ½ cup at a time, stirring constantly. Continue until you've used all the stock.

Stir in cooked squash. Continue cooking until rice is tender and the sauce is creamy.

Off heat, add Parmesan and sage, or seared radicchio. Season with salt and pepper, and divide among heated plates.

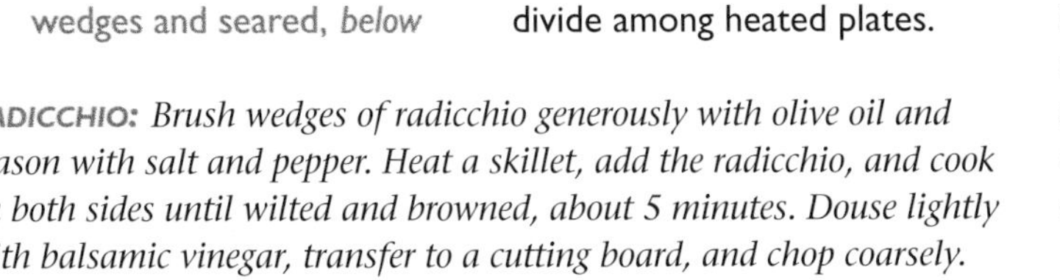

Radicchio: *Brush wedges of radicchio generously with olive oil and season with salt and pepper. Heat a skillet, add the radicchio, and cook on both sides until wilted and browned, about 5 minutes. Douse lightly with balsamic vinegar, transfer to a cutting board, and chop coarsely.*

Cut squash in half and scoop out seeds. Brush cut surface with oil and set squash, cut side down, on a baking sheet. Bake at 375° until very soft when pressed with a finger, 30 min. ►

◄*After first 2 cups of stock are absorbed, begin adding more, ½ cup at a time, stirring constantly.*

When all of the stock has been absorbed by the rice, stir in the mashed squash. Continue cooking until rice is tender. ►

Cobblers are mixtures of fruit with a layer of pastry dough or biscuits baked over the top. The "cobbled" look of the biscuits is what gives the dessert its name.

peach berry cobbler with pecan biscuits

Old fashioned desserts are never out of style. This cobbler gets a contemporary touch with fresh berries and pecan biscuits.

Traditional desserts like cobblers, crisps, and buckles seem a little out of step in our cell phone, high-speed Internet dependent world. Their "home spun" feel doesn't feel quite comfortable—unless they're intended for a family picnic or Sunday dinner.

But for times when a little familiarity is needed, these are the recipes to turn to. The fruit combinations are unique with deep, distinct flavors. So when nostalgia hits this fall, feature the last of summer's finest fruits right here in these desserts.

Build a better cobbler

The fruit and biscuits are the two big players in this cobbler—here is what to do with them.

Fruit: Fresh peaches are best, but if they aren't available (or ripe) try making the cobbler with thawed frozen peaches. I leave the skins on fresh peaches—it takes too much time to peel, and the skins flavor and color the cobbler. But if you don't want peach peel in there, peel away.

The fruit is partially baked before the biscuits go on in order to start the juices flowing. This helps the tapioca begin to thicken. If the biscuits went on top of cold fruit, the tapioca would not dissolve thoroughly, leaving small, chewy bits in the cobbler.

Biscuits: For tender biscuits, *gently* work the dough. Use a fork to mix, then pat the dough out with your hands (no rolling pin). Reroll any scraps, but be gentle about gathering them together—don't knead! You should get nine or ten biscuits from the batch.

Ground tapioca *So it dissolves thoroughly, grind instant tapioca to a powder in a coffee grinder. Or use an equal amount of tapioca starch.*

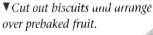

▲*Toss peaches and lime juice with sugar, tapioca, and salt.*

▲*For the biscuits, cut cold butter into dry ingredients until butter is size of peas.*

Peach Berry Cobbler with Pecan Biscuits

Makes 4–6 Servings
Total Time: About 1 Hour

For the Fruit—

Combine:

- 1/2 cup sugar
- 2 T. instant tapioca, ground
- Pinch salt

Slice:

- 2 lb. ripe fresh peaches, peeled (if desired) and pitted
- Juice of one lime

Sprinkle over Peaches:

- 1/2 cup fresh or frozen raspberries
- 1/2 cup fresh or frozen blueberries

For the Biscuits—

Combine:

- 1 1/2 cups all-purpose flour
- 1/4 cup sugar
- 1/4 cup pecans, finely chopped and toasted
- 1 1/2 t. baking powder
- Pinch salt

Cut in:

- 4 T. (1/2 stick) cold unsalted butter, cubed

Blend; Stir in:

- 4–5 T. buttermilk
- 1 egg

Brush and Sprinkle Biscuits with:

- Milk
- Sugar

Serve with:

- Vanilla ice cream

Preheat oven to 400°. Butter a 4-cup shallow baking dish.

Combine sugar, tapioca, and salt in a large bowl.

Slice peaches about 1/2" thick, add to sugar mixture along with lime juice, and toss. Transfer fruit to prepared baking dish; set dish on a baking sheet to catch drips.

Sprinkle berries over peaches and bake fruit for 15 minutes, or until juices start to bubble.

Combine flour, sugar, nuts, baking powder, and salt for the biscuits in a large bowl.

Cut in butter with pastry blender or two knives until mixture resembles coarse meal.

Blend together buttermilk and egg. Stir into flour mixture just until moistened (add more buttermilk if mixture seems dry). Turn out onto a lightly floured surface and pat into a 1/2"-thick round. Cut out 3" biscuits with a cutter and place on top of hot fruit mixture, slightly overlapping the edges. Gather scraps and gently reroll. Cut additional biscuits as needed.

Brush biscuits with milk and sprinkle generously with sugar. Bake 25–30 minutes, or until biscuits are golden and fruit juices are bubbling and thickened. Cool 15–20 minutes before serving. Serve cobbler warm with ice cream.

◄*Mix in buttermilk and egg. Gently pat dough into a circle.*

▼*Cut out biscuits and arrange over prebaked fruit.*

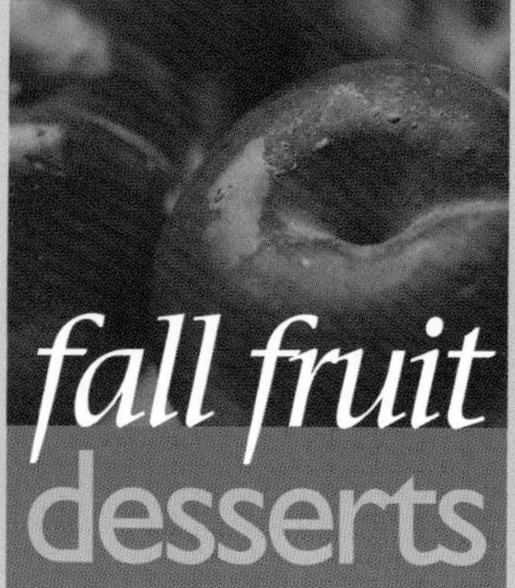

Crisps consist of fruit baked with a crumb topping (often made with oats and nuts). A "crumble" is a crisp with an English heritage—to the British, "crisps" are potato chips.

nectarine plum crisp with almond topping

Who wouldn't like this crisp? It's juicy, crispy, soft, chewy all at once. One more thing—it's *really* easy.

Of these three desserts, crisps are the most laid back. Assembling them is a snap, and even the choice of fruit is up for grabs. Peaches, tart cherries, and berries, fresh or frozen, all taste great under the almond topping. Try them in different combinations.

Crisps are an ideal candidate for small ramekins—the ratio of topping to fruit is high, making each bite a little fruity and a little crispy. No ramekins? Use a shallow 9 x 9" baking dish. It will look different but taste the same.

Creating the crisp

This crisp, like cobbler, has two components: fruit and topping. Here are the details of each one.

Fruit: Nectarines and plums taste so good fresh that they're not typically thought of as baking fruits. But this recipe is a good reason to think differently. Baked together, nectarines and plums are the ultimate sweet-tart flavor combination.

For this, definitely leave the skins on both fruits. They create a gorgeous sunset color in the fruit juices. Plus, they enhance the crisp's overall flavor (especially the tart plum skins). And I don't have to tell you that *not* peeling cuts prep time!

Fill the ramekins as full as possible with fruit—it will shrink by at least half during baking. It's a good idea to have extra plums or nectarines on hand to bulk things up if needed.

Topping: This crisp topping is a little bit like a chewy almond macaroon. Almond paste (not marzipan—it's too sweet) is critical for the macaroon-like flavor and texture. Find it in the baking aisle of your grocery store.

▲ *To "pit" stone fruits easily, simply slice down the fruit's four sides. Then cut the sides into chunks.*

Nectarine Plum Crisp with Almond Topping

Makes Six 6-oz. Crisps
Total Time: About 1 Hour

For the Fruit—

Combine:

1 cup sugar
2 T. instant tapioca, ground, *Page 33*
Pinch salt

Prepare:

1½ lb. nectarines, pitted, cubed
1½ lb. red plums, pitted, cubed
Juice of one lemon

For the Topping—

Blend:

1 cup all-purpose flour
½ cup sugar
½ t. baking powder
Pinch salt

Cut In:

4 T. (½ stick) unsalted butter, cubed
3 T. almond paste

Combine; Add:

1 egg
¼ t. almond extract

Sprinkle With:

⅓ cup sliced almonds

Preheat oven to 400°. Butter six 6-oz. ceramic ramekins.
Combine sugar, tapioca, and salt in a large mixing bowl.
Prepare nectarines and plums by lobing off sides around pits and cutting flesh into chunks, *see above right.* Add fruit to sugar mixture, drizzle with lemon juice, and toss together. Divide fruit among prepared ramekins, place them on a baking sheet to catch drips, and bake 15 minutes, until fruit begins to release its juices.
Blend flour, sugar, baking powder, and salt for the topping in a mixing bowl.
Cut in butter and almond paste until it looks like coarse meal.
Combine egg and extract in a small bowl. Add to the butter mixture and stir just to blend. Mixture should be clumpy and somewhat dry. Divide topping evenly among each ramekin.
Sprinkle almonds on top of crisps and bake an additional 20–30 minutes, or until topping is golden and fruit juices are bubbly and thickened. Cool 15–20 minutes before serving.

▲ *Combine both fruits with sugar mixture. Toss to mix thoroughly.*

▲ *For the topping, cut butter and almond paste into dry ingredients. Add egg mixture and blend.*

Divide fruit among ramekins and prebake. Pack crisp topping over fruit. ►

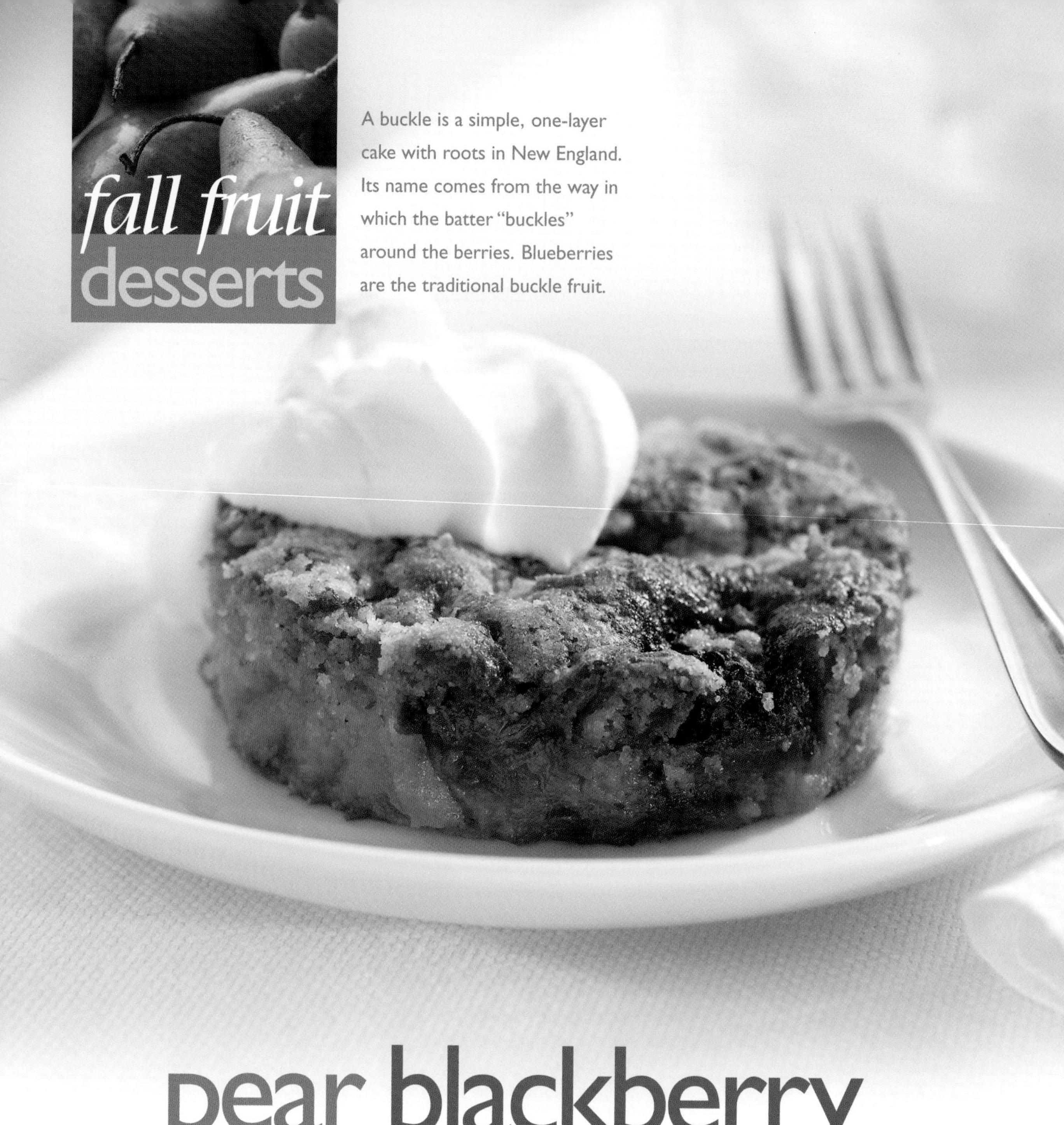

fall fruit desserts

A buckle is a simple, one-layer cake with roots in New England. Its name comes from the way in which the batter "buckles" around the berries. Blueberries are the traditional buckle fruit.

pear blackberry buckle

I'll bet you've never had a buckle. Once you try this moist, fruit-filled cake, you'll wonder why not.

Yes, the name is a little odd, but a buckle doesn't pull any punches. It's just cake, and a casual one at that—no layers to slice or frosting to spread. And since there's fruit in it, buckle makes a great dessert or brunch item. Serve it as coffee cake this weekend!

Pears aren't typical buckle fruit, but they work well—as long as they're not too ripe. The pears should give *slightly* when pressed. Overripe pears will give off a lot of juice and make the cake wet. Boscs are good because they're quite firm and somewhat dry.

Making the buckle

Sauteing the pears before mixing them with the cake batter is a critical step. As tempting as that step might be to skip, don't do it.

Why? Sauteing releases some pear juices so the cake won't be too wet. If the pears are *really* juicy after sauteing, don't add all the cooking liquid to the batter.

Fresh or frozen blackberries work fine here (raspberries are also good, as are cranberries). If you opt to use frozen berries, you don't need to thaw them before sprinkling over the cake batter.

I like to bake the buckle in a small jelly roll pan, then cut out rounds for serving—it makes for a nice presentation. If you don't have this size pan, simply use a 9 x 9" baking pan instead. But bear in mind that the buckle may need to bake longer since the baking pan is much deeper.

Saute pears just to soften slightly and bring out flavors. ►

▲Fold the sauteed pears into the cake batter.

Top batter with blackberries then sprinkle topping evenly over cake batter. ►

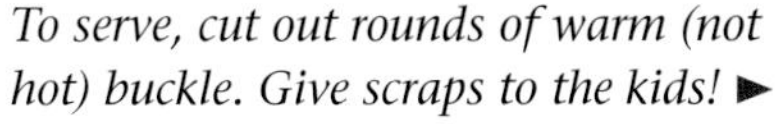

To serve, cut out rounds of warm (not hot) buckle. Give scraps to the kids! ►

Pear Blackberry Buckle

Makes One 9 x 13½" Pan; Total Time: About 1 Hour

For the Fruit—

Prepare:
- 2 lb. ripe, firm Bosc pears

Saute in 1 T. Unsalted Butter:
- Prepared pears
- ¼ cup sugar
- 1 T. dark rum
- 1 vanilla bean, split, scraped
- Zest of one lemon
- Pinch salt

Off Heat, Add:
- 1 t. vanilla extract

For the Cake Batter—

Beat:
- ½ cup (1 stick) unsalted butter, softened
- ½ cup sugar
- ½ t. vanilla extract

Add:
- 2 eggs

Combine; Add:
- ¾ cup all-purpose flour
- ¾ t. baking soda
- ¼ t. kosher salt

Sprinkle over Batter:
- 1 cup fresh or frozen blackberries

For the Topping—

Blend:
- ⅓ cup sugar
- ⅓ cup all-purpose flour
- ¼ cup (½ stick) cold unsalted butter, cubed
- ¼ cup chopped hazelnuts or walnuts
- ¼ t. ground cinnamon
- ¼ t. ground nutmeg

Serve with:
- Whipped cream

Preheat oven to 375°. Butter a 9 x 13½" jelly roll pan with 1" sides.

Prepare pears by peeling, coring, and cutting into chunks.

Saute pears with sugar, rum, vanilla bean, lemon zest, and salt in a large saute pan just until pears begin to release juices. Depending on ripeness, this takes about 5 minutes. Do not overcook. Remove from heat.

Off heat, add vanilla extract. Set pears aside to cool slightly.

Beat butter, sugar, and vanilla for the cake batter in a large mixing bowl until light and fluffy. Scrape down sides of bowl.

Add eggs, one at a time, beating after each addition. Scrape sides again after each egg is blended.

Combine flour, soda, and salt; mix into butter mixture just until blended. Remove and discard vanilla pod from pears; fold pears into batter, then spread it into the prepared pan.

Sprinkle blackberries over top of cake batter. If using frozen berries, do not thaw them first.

Blend all ingredients for the topping in a mixing bowl. Mixture will be dry, crumbly, and slightly flour-like. Sprinkle all the topping over batter and bake buckle 35–45 minutes, or until set in the center. Let cool 15 minutes; cut into rounds.

Serve buckle warm with whipped cream.

faster **with** fewer

the perfect breakfast

Here's a breakfast that's more elegant than a toasted bagel and only slightly more difficult to prepare. Give it a try this weekend!

Leisurely breakfasts have a lot going for them—civility, tranquility, and orderliness that few other daily activities can match.

But let's be realistic here: breakfast needs to be made by *someone*. And that usually means *you* getting up *early*, am I right?

Well, this menu is different. It's super-simple to put together, and you even have a chance to get a head start on it the day before. Mix the sausage, pancake batter, and cocoa, then chill them overnight. After that, it's all downhill—just bake (fruit and

menu

Puff Pancakes with Maple Baked Fruit

Breakfast Sausage

White Chocolate Cocoa

pancakes), fry (sausage), and reheat (cocoa). Talk about a perfect way to ease into the day!

And don't think that morning is the only time to enjoy the simplicity of this meal. Try it some Sunday evening—especially as the nights get cooler.

making your own breakfast *sausage*

Breakfast Sausage

After making your own homemade sausage, you may never go back to store-bought.

Makes 12–14 Patties
Total Time: 10 Minutes + Chilling

Combine and Shape:
1 lb. unseasoned ground pork
2 t. paprika
2 t. fresh ginger, minced
1 t. lemon zest, minced
1 t. fennel seed, crushed
1 t. ground sage
1 t. kosher salt
1/2 t. crushed red pepper flakes
1/4 t. ground nutmeg

Slice and Fry:
Refrigerated sausage, cut into patties

Combine all ingredients in a large bowl, using your hands to gently blend the mixture. Divide sausage in half and mound one half in the center of a piece of plastic wrap. Shape sausage into a cylinder by wrapping the plastic around the meat and rolling it back and forth. Twist the ends tightly and freeze until slightly firm, about 1 hour (or chill overnight). Repeat process with remaining sausage.
Slice sausage into 1/2"-thick patties and fry in a heavy nonstick skillet over medium-high heat. Brown on both sides, frying just until cooked through, about 10 minutes total. Drain sausage patties on a paper towel-lined plate before serving.

▲ To shape, wrap half of mixture in plastic. Roll into a cylinder.

◄ Twist ends to seal, then chill. Shape remaining sausage in the same manner.

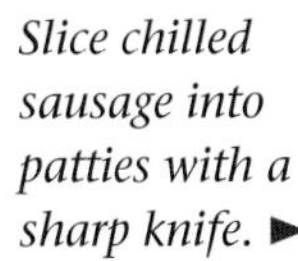

Slice chilled sausage into patties with a sharp knife. ►

◄ Fry in a dry, nonstick skillet, browning the patties on both sides.

puff pancake *with maple baked fruit*

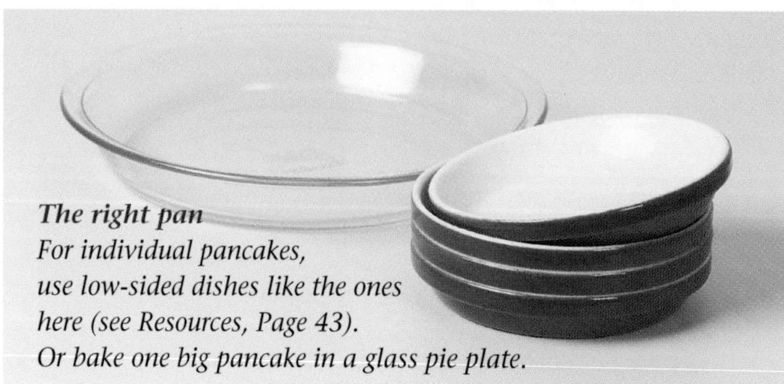

The right pan
For individual pancakes, use low-sided dishes like the ones here (see Resources, Page 43). Or bake one big pancake in a glass pie plate.

Puff Pancakes

Maple Baked Fruit is perfect with these pancakes. But they're also good with a little lemon juice and a lot of cinnamon sugar!

Makes Four 6" or One 10" Pancake
Total Time: About 35 Minutes

Melt:
4 t. unsalted butter

Whisk Together; Pour into Dishes:
1/2 cup all-purpose flour
1/2 cup whole or 2% milk
2 eggs
3 T. sugar
1/2 t. vanilla extract
Pinch salt

Serve with:
Maple Baked Fruit, *right*

Sprinkle with:
Powdered sugar

Preheat oven to 425° with rack in the center.

Melt 1 teaspoon butter in each of four 6" individual low-sided dishes (or 4 t. butter in one 10" glass pie plate) by placing in heated oven. Remove dishes from oven when butter has melted. Do not allow to cool.

Whisk the batter's remaining ingredients together until smooth. Pour 1/3 cup batter in each dish (or all into the pie plate). Do not stir batter in with melted butter. Bake until golden and puffed, 20–25 minutes for both the dishes or pie plate.

Serve pancakes right from the oven with Maple Baked Fruit.

Sprinkle with powdered sugar.

Maple Baked Fruit

If fresh fruit isn't available, frozen peaches and berries are a fine substitute. Thaw frozen fruit slightly before baking.

Makes About 4 Cups; Total Time: 20 Minutes

Pit and Slice:
1 lb. peaches or nectarines
1/2 lb. red plums
Pour Over; Bake:
1/2 cup pure maple syrup
Add:
1/2 cup fresh raspberries
1/2 cup fresh blueberries
Dollop With:
Sour cream

Preheat oven to 425°.
Pit and slice peaches and plums; spread in a shallow dish.
Pour syrup over fruit; toss gently to coat. Bake along with pancake until bubbly, 20 min.
Add berries and stir fruit gently. Spoon fruit inside puff pancakes; dollop with sour cream.

▲ *Add the berries after the peaches and plums have been baked. If the berries are baked along with the fruit mixture, they'll break down too much. This way, they heat through yet remain intact.*

▲ *Melt butter by placing dishes in preheated oven for 2–3 minutes.*

Pour batter into melted butter—do not mix the two together. ▼

▲ *Bake until pancakes are golden brown and puffed. Serve immediately—they fall very quickly.*

white chocolate cocoa

White Chocolate Cocoa

White chocolate chips won't melt properly here. Instead, look for Lindt or Ghirardelli brand chocolate bars.

Makes About 4 Cups
Total Time: 15 Minutes

Melt:
4 oz. good-quality white chocolate, finely chopped
Whisk In:
3/4 cup brewed coffee
1/2 t. vanilla extract
Add and Heat:
1 1/2 cups whole milk
1 1/2 cups half and half
Zest of one orange, minced
Pinch salt
Garnish With:
Grated nutmeg

Melt white chocolate in a heavy saucepan over low heat. Stir constantly to make a smooth mixture and prevent scorching.
Whisk in coffee and vanilla until blended.
Add milk, half and half, orange zest, and salt. Heat just until steam starts to rise from the surface—do not allow to boil. Divide cocoa among coffee cups.
Garnish each serving with a sprinkling of freshly grated nutmeg.

from **our** readers

Q&A
questions & answers

Mexican oregano

Mediterranean oregano

EVAPORATED MILK

What exactly is evaporated milk? And can I substitute regular milk in its place?

Susan Weintraub
Warren, MI

For recipes using Carnation evaporated milk, visit their website, ***verybestbaking.com***

Evaporated milk is unsweetened whole milk that has had 50–60% of the water removed through a heat and vacuum process. In effect, it has been concentrated so it has twice the fat and protein of an equal amount of whole milk. After canning, it's sterilized.

Because of the difference in water content, you should *not* substitute milk for evaporated. But you can reconstitute evaporated milk with an equal amount of water and use in place of milk.

OREGANO VARIETIES

How is Mexican oregano different from common oregano?

Jason Bigler
Plano, TX

The common oregano you're referring to is dried Mediterranean oregano. It's what you'll find at the grocery store labeled "oregano." Grown in southern Europe, it's a sweet, strong herb that's essential in Italian and Greek cooking.

Mexican oregano is more pungent and not sweet like the Mediterranean variety. Grown in Mexico, it's best suited to spicy, hot South American and Mexican dishes that can stand up to the stronger flavor. Don't substitute one for the other.

Order both varieties from Penzeys Spices at (800) 741-7787 or penzeys.com. Because their Mediterranean oregano is grown in Turkey, Penzeys also refers to it as Turkish oregano.

BAD SEEDS?

Should I remove the seeds from chipotle peppers in adobo sauce?

Linda Ledbetter
Huntsville, AL

We checked with Mexican cooking authority Rick Bayless. He said that it depends on how you plan to use the peppers. For most uses, they're blended and then strained, leaving the seeds behind. You'll still get heat—it's carried by the veins, not seeds.

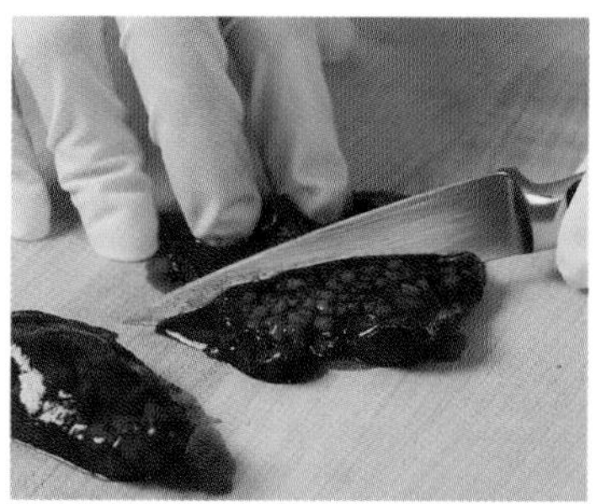

If using strips or chopped chipotle, it's easy to remove the seeds. Just cut the pepper open and scrape clean with a knife.

APPLE OPTIONS

What apples can I substitute for Jonagold and Braeburn to make the pies in Cuisine *#29?*

Karen Roy
Richmond Hill, Ontario, Canada

The best apple pies use a combination of varieties to achieve a balance of flavor and texture. You want to mix tart, flavorful apples with ones that will hold their shape while baking.

So how do you know which varieties to choose? Here's a loose guide. Granny Smith is tart, and Ida Red and Jonagold are a nice combination of sweet and tart. Any of those tasty apples would pair well with Empire, Gala, Fuji, Braeburn, or Golden Delicious varieties. For example, Golden Delicious will hold its shape but doesn't offer much flavor, so pair it up with tart Granny Smith.

This is a great time of year to check out your local farmer's market and find varieties not usually available at the supermarket. Then taste for yourself. If an apple is mealy or bland, don't use it. Once you taste what's available, you'll never want to go back to Red Delicious for *any* reason.

TAPIOCA STARCH/FLOUR

Are tapioca starch and tapioca flour the same thing? How are they used?

Mary Tyrrell
Long Beach, CA

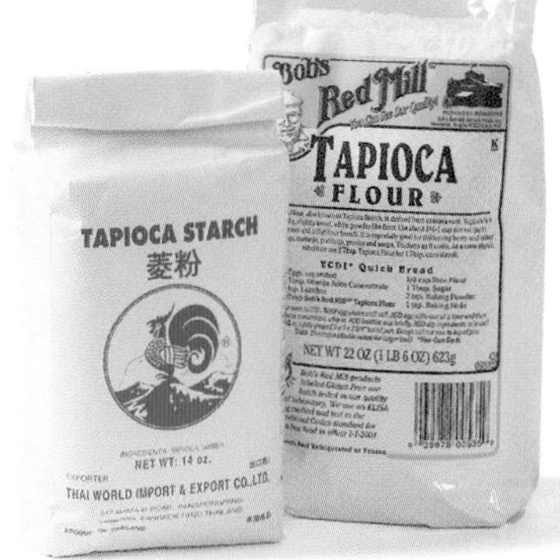

Tapioca, derived from the root of the tropical cassava plant, is available in several forms. It's most commonly used in the form of tapioca pearls. Tapioca starch and flour are another form. And yes, the starch and flour are the very same product, but marketed using both names.

Tapioca starch is most often found in Asian stores and is used to thicken sauces in Asian cooking. The tapioca flour label targets consumers interested in gluten- or corn-free products. It can be used in conjunction with other gluten-free flours for bread, or as an alternative to cornstarch for thickening. Use 2 T. tapioca flour for every 1 T. cornstarch.

The fruit cobbler and crisp on Pages 32–35 use ground instant tapioca as the thickener. You can substitute 2 T. tapioca starch or tapioca flour.

TO BLANCH OR PARBOIL

What's the difference between blanching and parboiling?

Juanita Graves
Findlay, OH

The terms blanching and parboiling are very closely related and often used interchangeably. Both terms refer to partial cooking (that's where we get *par-*) in boiling water.

But blanching includes a final step of plunging the briefly cooked food into cold water to stop the cooking process. This helps vegetables retain their bright colors and makes for easier peeling of items like peaches and tomatoes.

Parboiling usually requires a slightly longer cooking time than blanching. Its common purpose is to precook a food that will be combined with other ingredients which require different cooking times—like in stir-fries or casseroles. It may or may not include a plunge in cold water.

WHAT IS PERNOD?

What is Pernod and where can I find it? Would it be essential to a recipe or could it be omitted?

Linda Young
Des Moines, IA

Pernod (pronounced pair–NOH) is a greenish-yellow French liqueur. It's flavored primarily by star anise, which has a strong licorice taste. Look for it in liquor stores.

Because of its distinct anise taste, Pernod is usually an important part of the intended flavoring in a recipe. But you could substitute another liqueur (for an alternate flavoring) or water.

resources

SUR LA TABLE
Dishes for Puff Pancake, Item #115329
Rösle Y peeler, Item #107110
(800) 243-0852
surlatable.com

BRIDGE KITCHENWARE
Sima Harp peeler, Item #BHRP
Kuhn Rikon Harp peeler, Item #BHRP-S
(800) 274-3435
bridgekitchenware.com

CHEF'S CATALOG
Kuhn Rikon Y peeler, Item #3662
(800) 338-3232
chefscatalog.com

AMAZON.COM
Pedrini Acciaio peeler, Item #B00004VWTO
KitchenAid Euro peeler, Item #B00005KIC7
amazon.com/kitchen

CULINARY PARTS UNLIMITED
Kuhn Rikon Swiss peelers, Item #KU2695 (Y)
Item #KU2697 (vertical)
(800) 543-7549
culinaryparts.com

PROFESSIONAL CUTLERY DIRECT
Kyocera Ceramic peelers, Item #2CM2K01 (Y)
Item #2CM2K02 (harp)
(800) 859-6994
cutlery.com

To order white or yellow Southern Style Grits from ***Old Mill of Guilford****, call* ***(336) 643-4783****, or go to* ***oldmillofguilford.com***

Q&A

Do you have a question for *Cuisine at home*?

If you have a question about a cooking term, procedure, or technique, we'd like to hear from you. We'll consider publishing your question in one or more of our works. Just write down your question and mail it to *Cuisine at home*, Q&A Editor, 2200 Grand Ave., Des Moines, IA 50312, or contact us through our email address shown below. Please include your name, address, and daytime phone number in case we have questions.

Email: CuisineAtHome@CuisineAtHome.**com**
Web address: CuisineAtHome.**com**

meatball subs

Meatball Sub Sandwiches

Makes 4 Sandwiches
Total Time: 20 Minutes

Prepare:
4 6" hoagie buns, hollowed
Brush with:
2 T. olive oil
Fill with; Bake:
Mozzarella cheese
Fill with:
Tomato Sauce and Meatballs, *Page 24*
Top with:
Tomato Sauce, *Page 24*
Grated Parmesan

Preheat oven to 450°.
Prepare buns by shaving a thin layer off the top of each roll. Remove some of the bready interior so you're left with a "submarine."
Brush inside of hollowed-out buns with olive oil.
Fill bottom of each bun with mozzarella and place them on a baking sheet. Bake until buns are lightly browned and cheese melts.
Fill subs with hot tomato sauce, then 2–3 meatballs.
Top subs with more sauce, then sprinkle with cheese.

CLASSIC HOLIDAY PIES PLUS CHOCOLATE MINT BROWNIES

Cuisine at home®

easy & delicious holiday dinners

peppered **pork tenderloin**

maple-glazed **turkey**

Issue No. 36 December 2002
A publication of August Home Publishing

Cuisine at home

Publisher
Donald B. Peschke

Editor
John F. Meyer

Senior Editor
Susan Hoss

Assistant Editor
Sara Ostransky

Test Kitchen Director
Kim Samuelson

Photographer
Dean Tanner

Art Director
Cinda Shambaugh

Assistant Art Director
Holly Wiederin

Graphic Designer
April Walker Janning

Image Specialist
Troy Clark

Contributing Food Stylist
Jennifer Peterson

AUGUST HOME PUBLISHING COMPANY

Corporate:

Corporate Vice Presidents: Mary R. Scheve, Douglas L. Hicks • *Creative Director:* Ted Kralicek • *Professional Development Director:* Michal Sigel *New Media Manager:* Gordon C. Gaippe • *Senior Photographer:* Crayola England *Multi Media Art Director:* Eugene Pedersen • *Web Server Administrator:* Carol Schoeppler • *Web Content Manager:* David Briggs • *Web Designer:* Kara Blessing *Web Developer/Content Manager:* Sue M. Moe • *Controller:* Robin Hutchinson *Senior Accountant:* Laura Thomas • *Accounts Payable:* Mary Schultz • *Accounts Receivable:* Margo Petrus • *Research Coordinator:* Nick Jaeger • *Production Director:* George Chmielarz • *Pre-Press Image Specialist:* Minniette Johnson • *Electronic Publishing Director:* Douglas M. Lidster • *Systems Administrator:* Cris Schwanebeck *PC Maintenance Technician:* Robert D. Cook • *H.R. Assistant:* Kirsten Koele *Receptionist/ Administrative Assistant:* Jeanne Johnson • *Mail Room Clerk:* Lou Webber • *Office Manager:* Natalie Lonsdale • *Facilities Manager:* Kurt Johnson

Customer Service & Fulfillment:

Operations Director: Bob Baker • *Customer Service Manager:* Jennie Enos *Customer Service Representatives:* Anna Cox, Kim Harlan, April Revell, Deborah Rich, Valerie Jo Riley, Tammy Truckenbrod • *Technical Representative:* Johnny Audette • *Buyer:* Linda Jones • *Administrative Assistant:* Nancy Downey *Warehouse Supervisor:* Nancy Johnson • *Fulfillment:* Sylvia Carey

Circulation:

Subscriber Services Director: Sandy Baum • *New Business Circulation Manager:* Wayde J. Klingbeil • *Multi Media Promotion Manager:* Rick Junkins • *Promotions Analyst:* Patrick A. Walsh • *Billing and Collections Manager:* Rebecca Cunningham *Renewal Manager:* Paige Rogers • *Circulation Marketing Analyst:* Kris Schlemmer *Circulation Marketing Analyst:* Paula M. DeMatteis • *Art Director:* Doug Flint *Senior Graphic Designers:* Mark Hayes, Robin Friend

www.CuisineAtHome.com

talk to ***Cuisine at home***

Questions about Subscriptions and Address Changes? Write or call:

Customer Service
2200 Grand Avenue,
Des Moines, IA 50312
800-311-3995,
8 a.m. to 5 p.m., CST.

Online Subscriber Services:
www.CuisineAtHome.com
Access your account • Check a subscription payment • Tell us if you've missed an issue • Change your mailing or email address • Renew your subscription • Pay your bill

Cuisine at home® (ISSN 1537-8225) is published bi-monthly (Jan., Mar., May, July, Sept., Nov.) by August Home Publishing Co., 2200 Grand Ave., Des Moines, IA 50312.
Cuisine at home® is a trademark of August Home Publishing Co.

Subscriptions: Single copy: $4.99. One year subscription (6 issues), $24.00. (Canada/Foreign add $10 per year, U.S. funds.)

Periodicals postage paid at Des Moines, IA and at additional mailing offices. "USPS/Perry-Judd's Heartland Division automatable poly". Postmaster: Send change of address to **Cuisine at home®**, P.O. Box 37100 Boone, IA 50037-2100.
Cuisine at home® does not accept and is not responsible for unsolicited manuscripts. **PRINTED IN SINGAPORE.**

editor's letter

Hectic holidays. Too much shopping, too much cooking, too much company. We've all experienced it year after year and it shouldn't be this way. Everyone needs to enjoy this time—especially you. That's why I've made some simple, yet festive, recipes that can serve both family and company so you can treasure this time too. These dishes combine plenty of pizzazz with a whole lot of simplicity.

Two recipes in particular achieve this "long time in the kitchen" look—the phyllo-wrapped salmon and the peppered pork tenderloin. Both are simple to prepare, but also hit that "good enough for the holiday" mark.

Phyllo can be a little fussy to work with, but with the detailed instructions on Page 16, you'll be wrapping your salmon in no time. Once it's baked, you'll have towers of flavor rising from a delicious coconut sauce that'll thrill the most discerning guest. And you thought only chefs could make food look this good!

For the meat lovers, the peppered pork tenderloin is just the ticket for the holidays. Do-ahead ease along with great results makes this a great choice for company. This full dinner is even more special because it all cooks in under 45 minutes—not a bad option to have in your back pocket this season.

And finally, holidays and sweets are practically synonymous. For a special twist, I've reinvented some of your favorite pies, bringing each one up to a "special" level. The marshmallow meringue is the perfect topper to an already terrific sweet potato pie. The flavor of eggnog and caramelized sugar topping liven up an ordinary creamy custard pie. And the ubiquitous pecan pie is transformed into a chocolate lover's dream dessert.

Hopefully, *Cuisine* can make the holidays a little easier for you. Have a wonderful season and be sure to take time for yourself.

table of contents

Issue No. 36 December 2002

departments

features

from **our** readers

tips *and techniques*

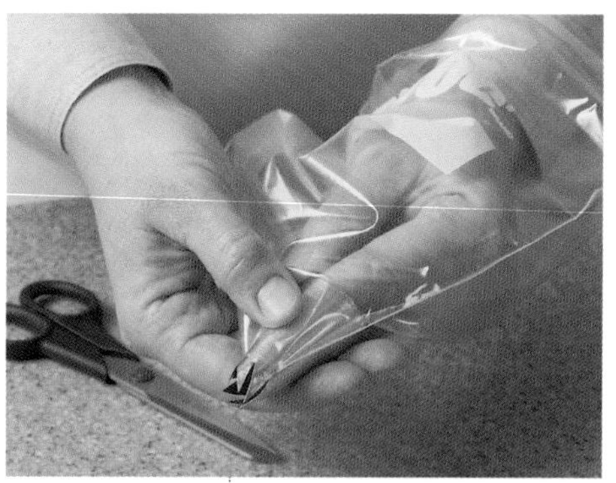

Great "Tip"

If you don't have a pastry bag, cut off a corner of a resealable freezer bag and place a pastry tip in the corner. Fill the bag with icing and squeeze it into the tip—instant pastry bag! If I'm decorating with more than one tip or color of icing, I just use two bags. It makes cleanup a snap.

Krista Sant
Anchorage, AK

Level Headed

A chopstick is a perfect leveling tool when measuring dry ingredients. I keep one right in my flour canister so I can aerate the flour and then level the measure with the chopstick. Just save a pair of disposable chopsticks from your next take-out—very practical and inexpensive.

Jerrold Jacks
Gurnee, IL

Nonstick Wraps

The next time you need to cover rising dough (bread, pizza, etc.), give the plastic wrap a quick blast of nonstick cooking spray before covering the dough. Now your dough will rise with ease.

Pete Auh
Albuquerque, NM

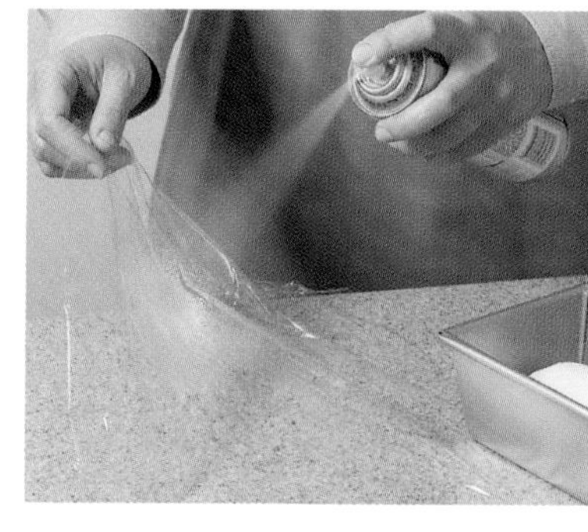

Raising Dough

Heat one cup water to boiling in a microwave. Leave the hot water in the microwave and place the prepared dough inside the microwave, either in a bowl or baking pan as directed. Cover the dough, close the microwave door, and let the dough rise.

Madeline Meade
Cartersville, GA

The Party's Over!

What to do with that tired, leftover vegetable tray? Rinse, dice, and toss the vegetables in a pot with a can of spiced, diced tomatoes (or spice your own). Simmer until vegetables are tender, then use as a filling for a Spanish omelet. Top with grated cheese and run it under the broiler.

Or chop the vegetables and use them in an Asian stir-fry or a homemade vegetable soup. See? Leftovers aren't so bad after all!

Mary Carson
Durham, NC

Easy Blanch

I found an easy way to blanch spinach. Put the leaves into a colander that's set inside a bowl. Heat water in a tea kettle and when the water is hot, pour it over the spinach. Then just lift out the colander with the perfectly blanched spinach.

Sean Rice
Denver, CO

Seed Saver

I loathe fishing lemon seeds out of my vinaigrettes, so I came up with a great solution. Cut a double thickness of cheesecloth, just large enough to cover half a lemon. Wrap the cheesecloth over the cut side. Now squeeze the lemon to release the juice—the seeds will remain behind. This works with any citrus.

Jim Thomson
Palm City, FL

Nonskid Boards

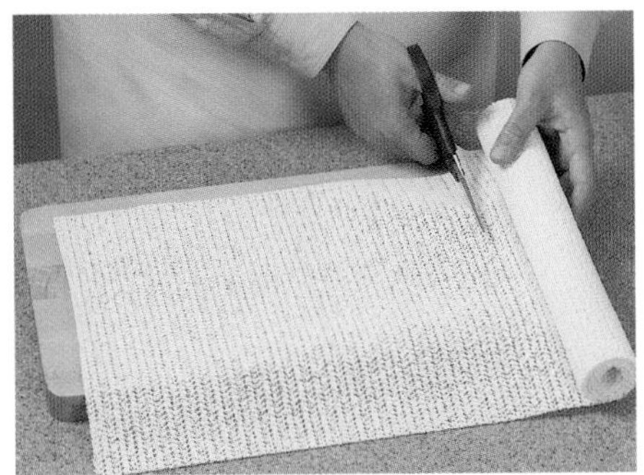

For a long time, I spread damp towels underneath my cutting board to hold it in place while I chop. But I found a better solution by using cushioning nonadhesive shelf and drawer liner—it's a mesh of soft plastic nubs. I cut sections that are a little smaller than my cutting boards, and keep them rolled up in a drawer. Now I don't have to use good towels under my boards, or deal with damp towels after I finish cooking. The lining cleans up nicely too.

Mary Brinig
Los Altos, CA

Saving Paste

Whenever you have leftover tomato paste or canned chipotles in adobo sauce, put any unused portion in a small resealable freezer bag. Flatten out the contents to remove the air, then place the bag in the freezer. When a recipe calls for a small amount of paste or chiles, simply open the bag and break off a piece from the frozen slab. No more waste!

Mary C. Goldman
Berkeley, CA

Sticky Situation

Here's a way to limit messes when measuring sticky foods like peanut butter. Line the measuring cup with a piece of plastic wrap and measure the food into the cup. Remove the sticky food by pulling up on the plastic wrap. Scrape the food off the wrap and into the mixing bowl. There's no mess to clean up—throw the plastic wrap away!

Darcy Maulsby
Granger, IA

Fast Cleanup

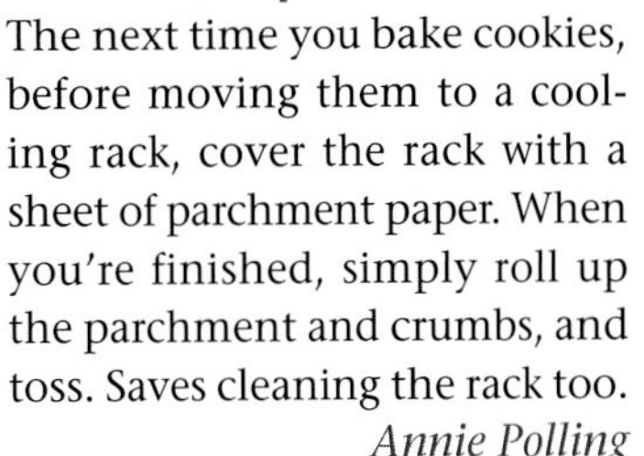

The next time you bake cookies, before moving them to a cooling rack, cover the rack with a sheet of parchment paper. When you're finished, simply roll up the parchment and crumbs, and toss. Saves cleaning the rack too.

Annie Polling
Moline, IL

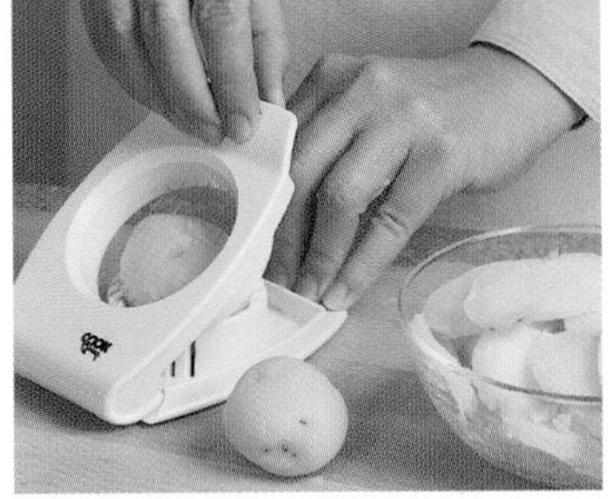

Potato/Egg Slicing

When preparing potatoes for potato salad or fried potatoes, make the slicing easy. Boil small red or white potatoes, cool, then peel. Then use an egg slicer. The potatoes slice easily and evenly, and it really is a time saver.

Paula Coomes
Ravensdale, WA

Test Kitchen Tip

For slicing cheese, a warm, dull knife works much better than a sharp one. Warm the knife in hot water before using—you'll find it cuts like butter. Cheese grates easier, too, if you set it in the freezer for about 5 minutes before grating.

share your tips and techniques with Cuisine at home

If you have a unique way of solving a cooking problem, we'd like to hear from you, and we'll consider publishing your tip in one or more of our works. Just write down your cooking tip and mail it to *Cuisine at home*, Tips Editor, 2200 Grand Ave., Des Moines, IA 50312, or contact us through our email address shown below. Please include your name, address, and daytime phone number in case we have questions. We'll pay you $25 if we publish your tip.

Email: CuisineAtHome@CuisineAtHome.com

Web address: CuisineAtHome.com

cuisineclass

roasting a turkey breast

Tired of traditional dry, overcooked turkey? The convenient solution is a brined, fresh turkey breast.

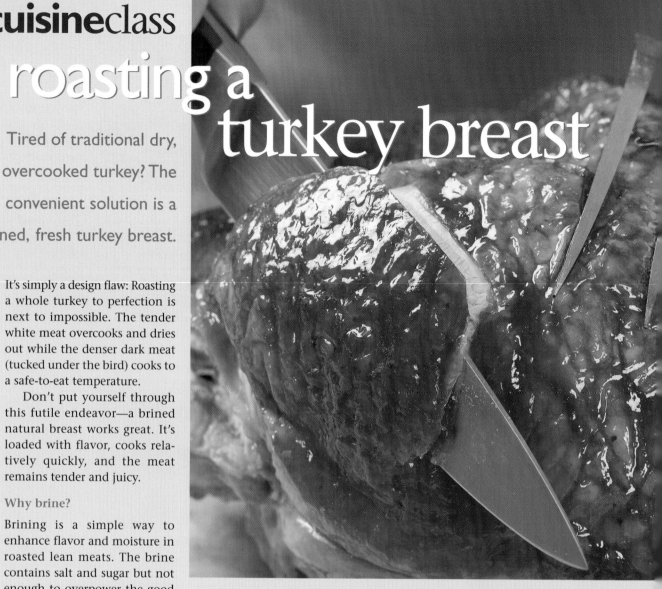

It's simply a design flaw: Roasting a whole turkey to perfection is next to impossible. The tender white meat overcooks and dries out while the denser dark meat (tucked under the bird) cooks to a safe-to-eat temperature.

Don't put yourself through this futile endeavor—a brined natural breast works great. It's loaded with flavor, cooks relatively quickly, and the meat remains tender and juicy.

Why brine?

Brining is a simple way to enhance flavor and moisture in roasted lean meats. The brine contains salt and sugar but not enough to overpower the good taste of the turkey. And brining does not have to take long—two hours is sufficient. This short time makes brining the perfect solution to an otherwise dry, overcooked holiday turkey.

1 Dissolve salt and brown sugar in hot water. Cool the brine thoroughly with ice before adding the breast.

Roasted Turkey Breast

Makes One 6–8 lb. Turkey Breast
Total Cook Time: 1½–2 Hours

For the Brine—
Dissolve:
½ cup kosher salt
½ cup brown sugar
2 cups hot water
Stir in:
2 cups apple juice
4 cups ice

For the Turkey—
Trim; Submerge in Brine:
1 6–8 lb. turkey breast, bone in
Roast; Baste with:
¼ cup maple syrup
¼ cup butter, melted

Dissolve salt and brown sugar in hot water in a 2-gallon resealable plastic bag.
Stir in apple juice and ice.
Trim excess rib and wing sections from the breast (save for making turkey stock). For easy carving, remove the wishbone. Submerge the breast in the brine and refrigerate until ready to roast, about 2 hours. Preheat oven to 375°.
Roast turkey breast side up on a rack over a shallow roasting pan. After one hour, baste breast with the maple-butter mixture. Baste every 15 minutes until the temperature of the breast reaches 165°. Remove the breast from the oven, tent with foil, and let rest 15–20 minutes before slicing.

The turkey breast

Roasting a turkey breast is more involved than just slapping it in the oven. Selecting, preparation, and brining are just as important as the actual roasting process.

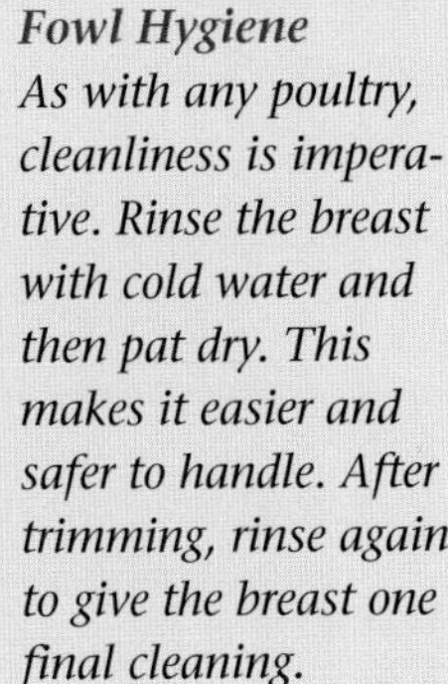

Fowl Hygiene

As with any poultry, cleanliness is imperative. Rinse the breast with cold water and then pat dry. This makes it easier and safer to handle. After trimming, rinse again to give the breast one final cleaning.

Selecting

To pick out the best breast, select one labeled USDA Grade A. Then, try to buy a natural breast—one that hasn't been injected with chemical solutions that enhance flavor (called *self-basting)*. If it is self-basting, brining the breast is a waste of time since it's already saturated.

And finally, don't waste your time with a breast that has a pop-up timer. They're set to "pop up" at 180–185° (USDA standards). This is 15° too high, resulting in overdone, dry white meat. Take yours out at about 165°.

Trimming

Trimming is quick and easy. First, cut off the ribs and wing bones using a pair of kitchen shears, *see Figure 2*. This stabilizes the breast when carving. Then remove all the excess skin, *see Figure 3* since the flabby skin adds no real flavor to the breast.

Removing the wishbone

Carving is much easier if you remove the wishbone before roasting. Lift up the skin around the wishbone (clavicle). Then scrape and cut the meat from around the bone. Now, gently pull the wishbone out using your hands, *see Figure 4*. If the bone is hard to grasp, use a paper towel to get a better grip.

Brining

Brine enhances the flavor of turkey. While the brine is made with hot water to dissolve the salt and sugar, it's important to chill it thoroughly before adding the meat to prevent bacteria.

The best part is that it does not take much time to brine. Most of the flavor is absorbed in the first two hours. After that, the results are negligible.

2 Trim away the ribs and wing bone. This stabilizes the breast for both roasting and carving.

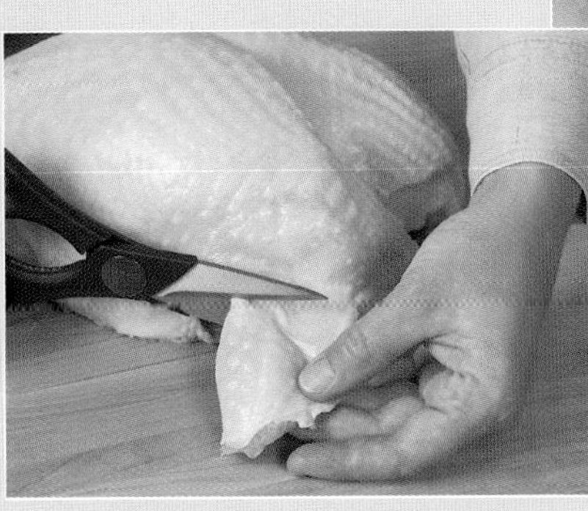

3 Trim away any excess skin around the breast. Leave about 1/2" overhang as it shrinks during roasting.

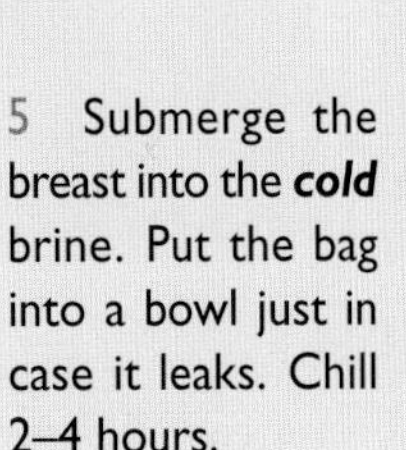

4 To remove wishbone, run a knife along the inside and outside to define it. Use your hands to pull it out.

5 Submerge the breast into the ***cold*** brine. Put the bag into a bowl just in case it leaks. Chill 2–4 hours.

cuisineclass

roasting a turkey breast

The best part about a turkey prepared this way is it's practically fool-proof. Golden brown on the outside, a perfectly cooked inside (no pink), meat that's so moist, it couldn't possibly belong to a turkey, and all cooked in under two hours. If you're a cooking rookie, it's the perfect recipe to cut your teeth on.

Roasting tip
Since cooking time is short, I found that roasting the breast in the upper third of the oven gave it the best color and cooked it more evenly.

Roasting

Place the breast on a rack so it's slightly elevated from the roasting pan, *see Figure 6*. This allows hot air to circulate easily around the breast. You also want the roasting pan to be fairly shallow. A high-sided pan inhibits air flow and tends to steam the meat rather than roasting it.

Roast the breast in a fairly hot oven. Many recipes call for a slow 325° oven, but I use 375° because it delivers more of a "roasted" flavor. Lower temperatures are used for a whole turkey to cook dark meat all the way through.

Basting

Because the breast is in the oven for a relatively short period (as opposed to a whole turkey), it doesn't have the benefit of slow browning. You'll need to hasten this process with a baste made from maple syrup and butter, *see Figure 7*. Both provide flavor but sugar in the syrup promotes browning. Start basting halfway through cooking (after an hour) and baste every 15 minutes.

Cook the breast until your thermometer hits 165°, *see Figure 8*. At this temperature, all the pink is gone but the meat remains very moist.

Carving

Since you've already removed the wishbone, carving should be easy. Using a sharp knife, cut *thin* slices parallel to the breast bone, *see Figure 9*. Cutting this direction makes long, tender slices that make a nice looking presentation on the plate.

8 Probe in thickest part of the breast. When internal temperature hits 165°, remove breast and tent.

6 Place breast on a rack and then into a shallow roasting pan. Roast at 375° in the upper third of your oven.

7 About an hour into cooking begin basting the breast every 15 minutes with the maple syrup and butter mixture.

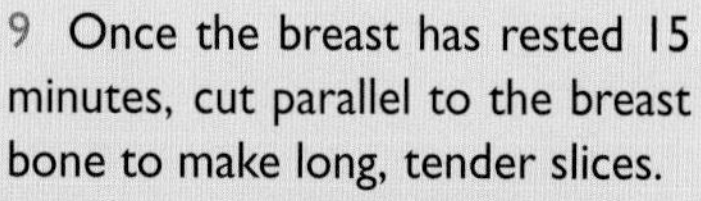

9 Once the breast has rested 15 minutes, cut parallel to the breast bone to make long, tender slices.

creamy gravy

You don't need a whole turkey to make gravy. Some of the best can be made ahead eliminating last minute gravy anxiety.

Yes, you have to slow-roast turkey to get good gravy. No, you don't have to use the whole bird.

The secret is to buy turkey wings at your grocery store and slowly roast them with plenty of celery and onion. Wings are cheap and easy to find. You can even do this months ahead and freeze the broth.

And talk about easy—the onions don't even need to be peeled, and you can use every part of the celery stalk. They're all loaded with flavor.

◄*Roast turkey wings and trimmings, onions, celery, and garlic at 375° for 2½ hours.*

Remove from oven and add water. Simmer on the stove for one hour, scraping pan often. ►

Strain the rich broth into a container for chilling so the fat can float to the top. Here, I'm using a fat separator. ►

◄*For gravy, make a roux and whisk in defatted stock. Finish with milk, vinegar, and, salt.*

Creamy Gravy

Milk is added to the gravy to give it a deep, rich flavor. It's a natural with the cornbread and country ham dressing.

Makes: 2¼ Cups
Total Time: 3–4 Hours

For the Turkey Stock—

Roast:

- 2 turkey wings, including trimmings from turkey breast
- 4 ribs celery, roughly chopped
- 1 onion, cut into chunks
- 4 cloves garlic, smashed

Add:

- 6 cups water

For the Turkey Gravy—

Make a Roux of:

- 4 T. unsalted butter, melted
- 4 T. all-purpose flour

Whisk in:

- 2 cups turkey stock, strained
- ½ cup whole milk
- 1 t. apple cider vinegar
- 1 t. kosher salt

Preheat oven to 375°.

Roast turkey wings and trimmings, celery, onion, and garlic in a large saute or roasting pan for 2½ hours. Remove from oven.

Add water and simmer gently over burner for 1 hour, allowing stock to reduce. Strain and defat.

Make a roux of melted butter mixed with flour. Cook, stirring over medium heat 2–3 minutes to cook out the flour taste.

Whisk in turkey stock. Cook until thickened. Add milk, cider vinegar, and salt to taste.

make it a **menu**

Roast Turkey Breast

Country Ham Dressing

Creamy Gravy

Cranberry Sauce

Sweet Potato Pie

country ham dressing

Cornbread dressing sounds so good but it's usually dense and bland. No more! Here's one that's moist and packed with flavor.

Most of the cornbread dressings I've had in the past have been dry and flavorless. Oh sure, they tasted like cornbread, but no amount of gravy could salvage their grainy, dry qualities. Since these two words, "cornbread" and "dressing," sound like they belong together, I was determined to make one that worked.

I discovered three things to making good cornbread dressing. The first is to use plenty of white bread. The second is to add more liquid than you think necessary. The third is to inundate the mixture with flavor. But don't fret. If country ham isn't on your favorite list, you can still make a good dressing without it.

Making dressing

Before actually making dressing, you have to stale the bread at least a day ahead. You want to dry up the starch cells so they can refill with flavorful liquids.

Staling: Tear bread into small pieces before staling, *see Figure 1.* White bread can turn rock-hard making it almost impossible to cut or tear. Put both breads into a 200° oven for an hour, then turn off oven and let the bread sit at least 12 hours.

Flavor: Now start to build the flavor by sauteing celery, onions, and ham, *see Figure 2.* Cook until onions turn translucent.

Rehydrate: With the bread *completely* dry, add milk to rehydrate, *see Figure 3.* Milk gives the dressing depth and body. Add all of the remaining ingredients including the eggs and broth. While it may seem a little runny, it will firm up once it bakes.

Bake for 45 minutes at 375° (same temperature as the turkey) in the lower third of your oven.

Country Ham & Cornbread Dressing

Country ham is dry-cured with salt. Don't adjust your seasoning like you normally would as the ham will add the necessary salt.

Makes: 10 Cups; Total Cook Time: 1 Hour

Saute in 4 T. Unsalted Butter:

2 cups celery, diced
2 cups yellow onion, diced
1/2 lb. center-cut country ham, diced

Combine:

6 cups cornbread, torn into pieces, staled
4 cups French bread, cut into pieces, staled
3 cups milk

Add:

Sauteed celery mixture, above
2 cups low-sodium chicken broth
3 eggs, beaten
2 t. dried thyme
1/4 t. cayenne

Preheat oven to 375°. Spray a 3-qt. baking dish with nonstick spray; set aside.
Saute celery, onion, and ham in butter until onion softens and ham tightens.
Combine milk and staled bread in a bowl, folding gently with your hands to thoroughly incorporate.
Add the sauteed celery mixture, broth, eggs, thyme, and cayenne; stir to combine. Spoon mixture into prepared baking dish and bake for 45 minutes or until dressing is cooked through.

Country Ham Sources

Burgers' Smokehouse
(800) 624-5426
www.smokehouse.com

Virginia Traditions
(800) 222-4267
www.vatraditions.com

Purchase center-cut slices. They taste best and are easier to handle than other cuts. ▼

1 Cut or tear bread into small pieces. Place on baking sheets (in single layer) and stale in 200° oven for at least 12 hours.

3 Add milk to the dried bread. Toss until all the liquid is absorbed completely and the bread is moist.

4 Coat baking dish with nonstick spray to prevent sticking. Bake dressing 45 minutes at 375° in lower third of your oven.

2 Saute celery, onions, and country ham until onions turn transparent. If you don't have or want to use country ham, substitute traditional city ham.

online **extra**

Cranberry Sauce too? Visit www.CuisineAtHome.**com** for *Cuisine's* step-by-step recipe guide.

faster **with** fewer

pork tenderloin *dinner*

Overlooked, underused, and ignored, yet perfect in every way. You might say pork tenderloin is the Cinderella of the food world.

When most of us think of pork, chops and roasts come to mind. Well, next time you're craving pork, think tenderloin. It's flavorful, a breeze to work with, and cooks in a snap. You just can't say enough good things about it.

It only stands to reason that pork tenderloin is the perfect cut for a quick weeknight dinner. This tender cut of meat is enhanced with a spicy peppercorn and rye bread crumb rub that's easy to make and apply.

buttermilk roasted potatoes

menu

Peppered Pork Tenderloin with Mustard Sauce

Buttermilk Roasted Potatoes

Green Beans

Roasted-Mashed Buttermilk Potatoes

Yukon gold potatoes work great for this recipe because of their color. If you can't find Yukon golds, regular russets work fine.

Makes 6 Cups
Total Time: 50 Minutes

Prepare and Roast:

6–7 cups Yukon gold potatoes, ($2\frac{1}{4}$ lb.), peeled and cut into large chunks
2 T. olive oil

Mash and Add:

$1\frac{1}{2}$ cups buttermilk, warmed
2 T. unsalted butter
1 T. minced chives
Salt and pepper to taste

Prepare potatoes for roasting by peeling and cutting into large chunks. Toss with oil. Place in 425° oven on lowest rack for best browning. Roast for 40–45 minutes, turning at least once.

Mash potatoes in large bowl, leaving them slightly chunky. Stir in buttermilk, butter, and chives. Season with salt and pepper.

And try the roasted mashed potatoes that cook along with the pork. These mashed potatoes get a boost of flavor from both the acidic buttermilk and the roasting process. As strange as it may sound, most foods benefit from acid—it tends to "pop" the flavor. This meal may be designed for weeknight speed but works well for a weekend dinner.

faster **with** fewer

peppered pork tenderloin

Peppered Pork Tenderloin

Makes Six 4-oz. Servings
Total Time: 1 Hour

For the Coating—
Grind in Spice Mill:
¼ cup assorted peppercorns
Combine with:
1 cup coarse rye bread crumbs
½ cup chopped fresh parsley
2 T. olive oil
1 t. kosher salt

For the Pork Tenderloin—
Trim and Tie:
2 pork tenderloins
Brush with:
¼ cup Dijon mustard

Preheat oven to 425°.
Grind peppercorns in spice mill until coarse.
Combine with rye bread crumbs, parsley, olive oil, and salt.
Trim fat and silverskin from the tenderloins. Fold the smallest end of the tenderloin under. Tie tenderloin with heavy duty cotton kitchen string.
Brush tenderloins with Dijon mustard—this adds flavor and helps coating stick. Spread the peppercorn coating mixture out on parchment paper. Roll tenderloins in coating. Place each piece of meat on a rack and roast for 30–40 minutes, until internal temperature reaches 140–145°.

Pork tenderloin is a mildly flavored cut of meat. Adding a mixture of mustard, peppercorns, and rye bread crumbs really pumps up the taste.

First, remove all the silver membrane from the tenderloin. If it's not removed, it will make the meat curl when heated. Tie the meat then brush with Dijon mustard for flavor and to help the coating mixture stick.

Now roll each tenderloin in the peppercorn mixture so it's coated completely (there is enough mixture to coat two tenderloins). Finally, place the meat on a rack and roast at 425° for about 30 minutes. The meat should register an internal temperature of about 140° (it'll be slightly pink inside). Let rest for 10 minutes before cutting into ½"-thick slices.

▲ *Run the blade of your knife under the silverskin to remove it.*

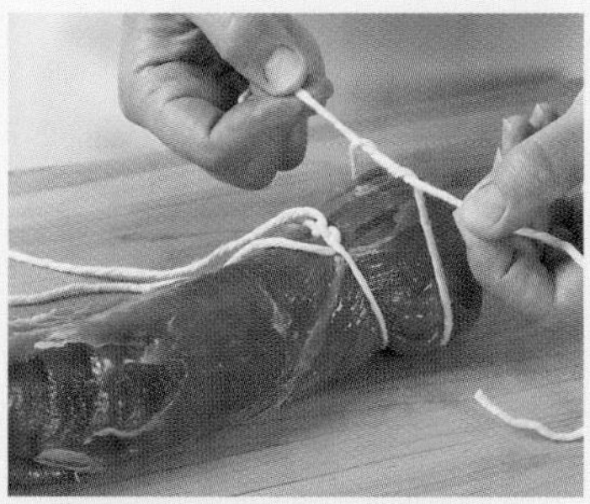

▲ *To make meat a consistent size for roasting, fold flat tail under and tie with cotton kitchen string.*

▼ *Brush meat with Dijon mustard—this adds flavor and helps the coating stick.*

▲ *Spread half of the bread crumb mixture on a sheet of parchment paper. Roll and press to coat.*

mustard sauce

Multi-Mustard Sauce

Makes 2 ¼ Cups
Total Time: 20–30 Minutes

Boil and Strain:

- 2 cups white wine
- 2 cups low-sodium chicken broth
- ½ cup shallots, chopped (3–4 shallots)
- ⅓ cup Dijon mustard
- 2 t. dry mustard

Add and Reduce:

- ⅔ cup heavy cream
- 2 T. mustard seeds
- ¼ cup prepared yellow mustard
- Salt and cayenne to taste

Finish Sauce with:

- ¼ cup (4 T.) unsalted butter, cold

Boil wine, broth, shallots, and mustards in a medium saucepan over medium-high heat until reduced by half (15–20 minutes). Strain liquid, return to a clean pan, and reduce heat to medium-low.

▲ *Strain liquid and return it to a clean pan.*

Add cream, mustard seeds, yellow mustard, salt, and cayenne. Simmer to reduce to a sauce consistency (about 10 minutes).

Finish sauce with butter before serving.

Just before serving, whisk in butter to finish sauce. ►

36 *online* **extra**

Want more info? Visit www.CuisineAtHome.com for a step-by-step photo guide on green beans.

working with phyllo

If you've always been curious about this classic Greek pastry dough but never had the guts to try it, then this article is for you. Read on, then wrap your heart out!

▲ *The secret to working with phyllo is keeping the sheets from drying out as you work with it. "Sandwich" the sheets between pieces of parchment and slightly damp towels.*

If you have worked with phyllo [FEE-loh] before, then you know that using it is, well, a challenge. But a few pointers are all you need to face the ins and outs of it. Once you give it a try and see how versatile it is, you'll be looking for all kinds of ways to use it.

What is phyllo, anyway?

Phyllo (also spelled "filo" and "fillo") is paper-thin sheets of pastry dough used in Greek and Middle Eastern cooking. One popular dish made with phyllo is a Greek pastry called baklava—layers of phyllo, nuts, honey, and a lot of melted butter.

But phyllo adds an elegant touch to everyday cooking too. A few sheets layered with butter can create a crisp, flaky wrap for many different things.

How do I make phyllo?

You don't need to! Making it requires stretching a simple dough (flour, water, oil) so thin that a newspaper can be read through it. Luckily for us, phyllo sheets are available in the frozen food section of many grocery stores. Athens widely distributes 1-pound boxes with 14 x 18" sheets. That's what was used in the recipes on Pages 18–21.

Are there any secrets to it?

There is one thing that's key: Never, *ever* use phyllo straight out of the freezer. Frozen sheets are not pliable and will break into shards if unfolded. It's imperative to thaw phyllo overnight in the refrigerator before using it. Shortcuts (microwave, thawing on a heater, etc.) don't work either. They cause moisture build-up, making the sheets gum together. You must plan ahead.

And one more thing: When you start to work with phyllo, keep any unused sheets covered with damp towels and parchment *at all times*. Phyllo dries out in a heartbeat and once it's dry, it's impossible to use.

Phyllo dough

▲ *Athens brand phyllo comes frozen so it must be thawed in the refrigerator overnight (no exceptions!). If possible, bring it to room temperature before using. These recipes were developed using 14 x 18" sheets.*

◄ *The stack of phyllo sheets should be stored in between layers of parchment and damp towels.*

Peel a sheet off the stack and lay it on a large piece of parchment. ►

Using phyllo

With a thawed box of phyllo, the right equipment, and good technique, you're ready to go!

Equipment

Have these things ready *before* even opening the package.

Damp towels and parchment: Use two barely damp tea towels to "sandwich" the phyllo sheets. And I mean *slightly* damp. Wad up each towel and quickly pass them under the water twice, no more. Too wet, they'll make the sheets gummy. If you wring out *any* water, start with new towels.

Use two sheets of parchment, wax paper, or plastic wrap as buffers between the phyllo and the towels. A third sheet of parchment or wax paper is also needed for assembly.

Hold phyllo by short edge and position it over the buttered sheet below. Don't pick it up to reposition.▼

Smooth sheet into position and patch tears if possible. A few tears, wrinkles, or folds will not matter.▼

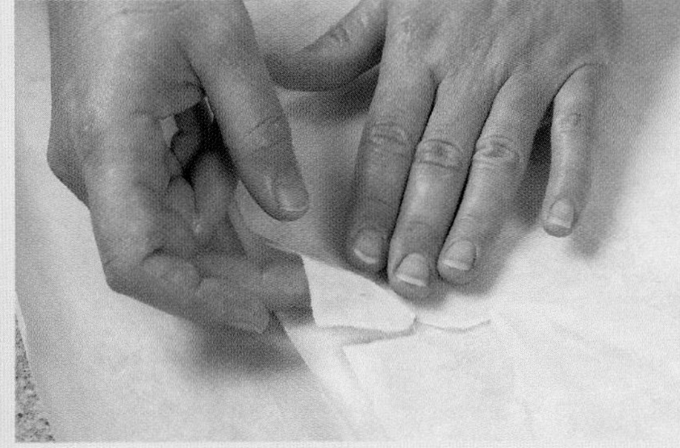

Pastry brush and pizza wheel: Use a wide, soft-bristled pastry brush for brushing—it's gentle on delicate phyllo sheets. A pizza wheel is nice for cutting, but a knife is fine too.

Butter and fillings: Equal parts of butter and oil is best for brushing on the sheets. Avoid using margarine (too watery) or oil sprays such as Pam (bad flavor). The fillings should be made and at room temperature (not hot).

Technique

Lay a damp towel on your work surface and top with a piece of parchment. Remove the thawed phyllo from its plastic wrap and carefully unroll the sheets onto the parchment. Don't panic if the top sheets are cracked—it's typical. Cover the sheets with parchment, then the other towel.

Now, peel back the top towel and parchment. At a corner, carefully separate the first phyllo sheet from the stack and gently lift it off, taking care not to rip existing cracks any further. If it does occur, it's okay—phyllo is so fragile, tears happen. The first few sheets are often pretty torn up, so just throw them out. There is plenty of phyllo in a package for these recipes.

Place the sheet on a third piece of parchment (don't forget to re-cover the stack of sheets!). With light brush strokes, coat the sheet with the butter-oil mixture. It's not necessary to cover the entire sheet, but do get the edges so they stay pliable. Don't go overboard on the butter, though, or the dough will be greasy.

◀*Brush butter-oil combination on sheets starting from the edges—it prevents them from cracking.*

Remove a second phyllo sheet and lay it over the buttered sheet. Try to match up the edges, but don't get too fussy. And once it's down, don't lift and adjust the sheet—it will tear. Smooth the sheet over the first, patching tears if you can, but a little imperfection is fine. Layer and butter as many sheets as specified in the recipe you're using.

Cut the stack with the pizza wheel, but use a ruler to measure dimensions given in the recipes. The proper size makes for easy filling and folding.

Storing

Roll any extra phyllo into a cylinder, then wrap that well in plastic. Store unused phyllo for up to a week in the refrigerator, but don't refreeze—it gets quite brittle and becomes even more difficult to use.

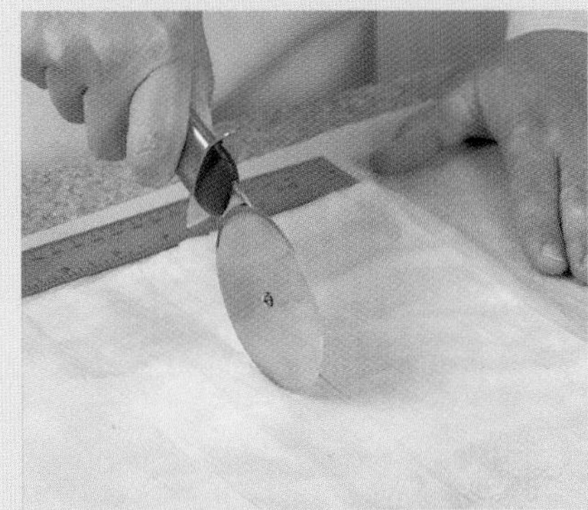

▲*For properly sized squares or strips, measure carefully before cutting.*

phyllo appetizers

Want to actually *enjoy* your own holiday party? These two appetizers are the ideal solution—assemble ahead, freeze, then bake when you need them!

We can all use a shortcut or two this time of year, and these appetizers are just that. Don't get me wrong, they *are* a little time consuming to put together. But once they're frozen, there's nothing to them but baking—and eating!

You can take some liberties with them. Fold the sausage stuffing into triangles (skip the mushrooms, of course). Or wrap the shrimp fillings into purses.

Sausage-Stuffed Mushroom Purses

The smaller the mushrooms, the better for these purses. They should be no larger than a ping pong ball.

Makes 24 Purses; Total Time: About 1 1/2 Hours + Freezing

For the Mushrooms—

Prepare; Season with:

24 small white mushrooms (reserve stems and scrapings)
Salt and pepper

For the Stuffing—

Saute:

1/2 lb. mild pork sausage

Add and Saute:

Reserved mushroom stems and scrapings, chopped
1/2 cup yellow onion, diced
1 t. garlic, minced
1/2 t. crushed red pepper flakes
1/2 t. whole fennel seed
1/4 t. dried basil
1/4 t. dried thyme
Salt to taste

Off Heat, Stir in:

2 oz. cream cheese, cubed
1 T. chopped fresh parsley

For the Phyllo—

Combine:

4 T. unsalted butter, melted
4 T. olive oil

Prepare:

12 sheets phyllo, *Pages 16–17*

Prepare mushrooms by removing stems and scraping out some of their interiors with a 1/4 tsp. measuring spoon. Season inside of mushrooms with salt and pepper; set aside. Chop reserved stems and scrapings, and set aside.

Saute sausage for filling in a large skillet over med.-high heat. Cook until no longer pink, 8 min. Add reserved mushrooms, onion, garlic, and seasonings; saute 3–4 min.

Off heat, stir in cream cheese and parsley; chill. Fill each mushroom with some of the stuffing.

Combine butter and oil for brushing over phyllo sheets.

Prepare 3 phyllo sheets, brushing each sheet with butter-oil mixture.

▲*Stem mushrooms, then scrape out some of their interiors to hold the stuffing.*

Cut phyllo and assemble purses, *below*. Prepare remaining sheets in the same way, then freeze purses on parchment-lined baking sheets. Bake frozen (not thawed) purses at 400° on the baking sheets until browned and heated through, 35–40 minutes. Serve hot.

The beggar's purse

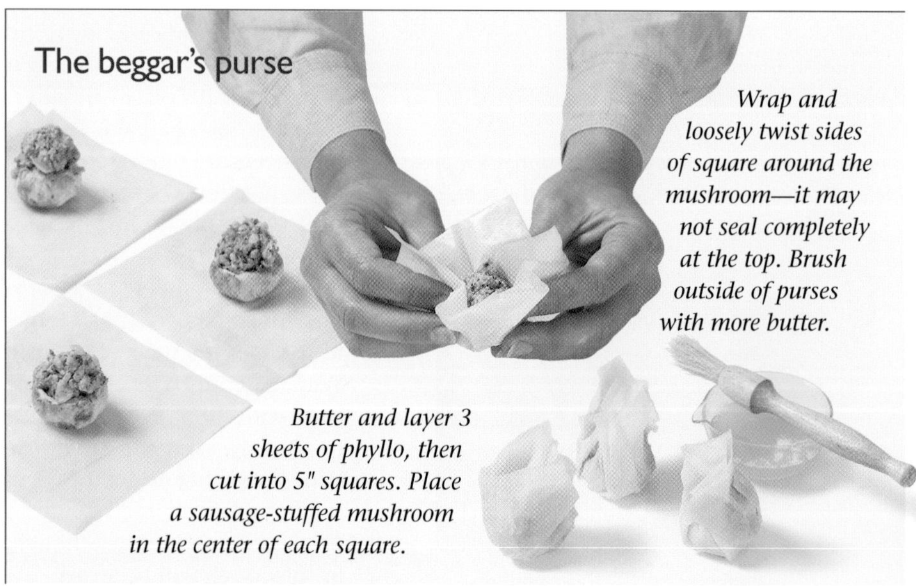

Butter and layer 3 sheets of phyllo, then cut into 5" squares. Place a sausage-stuffed mushroom in the center of each square.

Wrap and loosely twist sides of square around the mushroom—it may not seal completely at the top. Brush outside of purses with more butter.

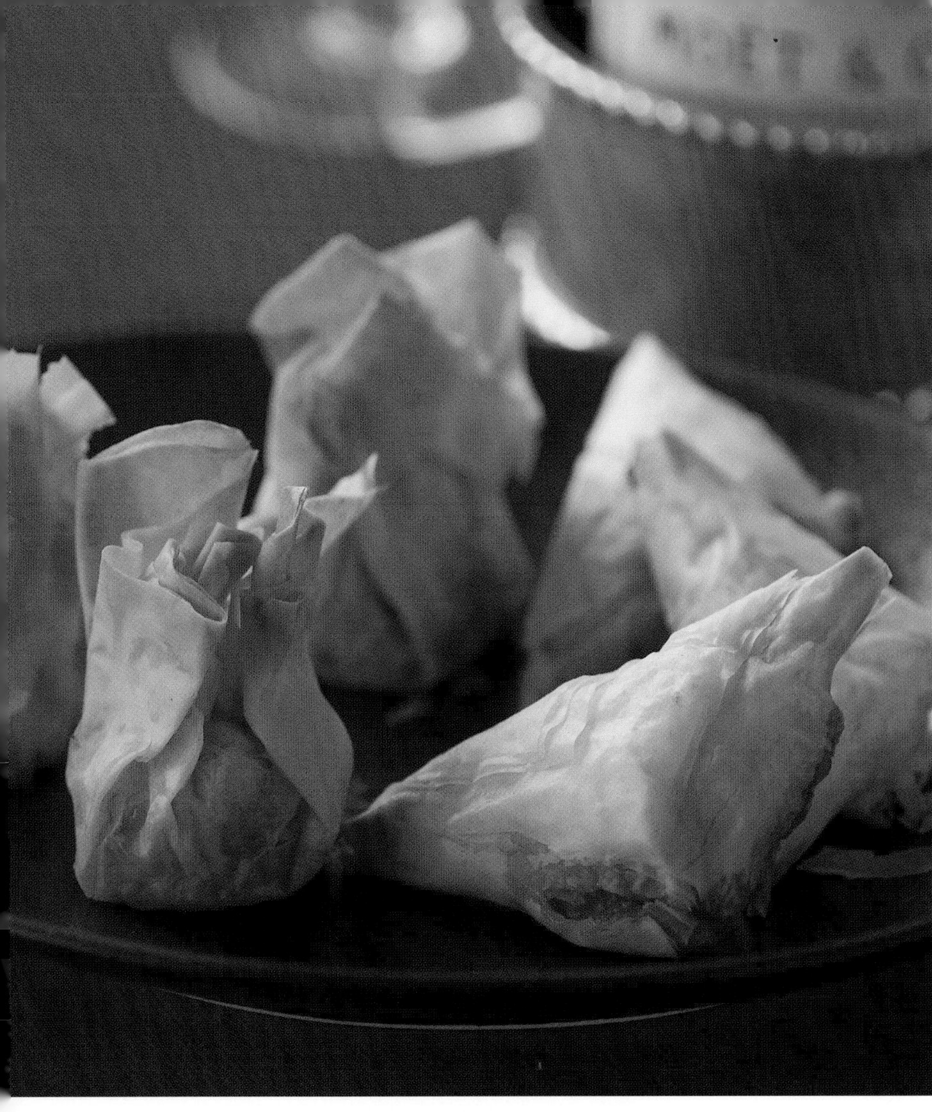

"Shrimp Cocktail" Phyllo Triangles

The cream cheese filling has a tendency to leak out of the triangle during baking—omit it if a neater look is desired.

Makes About 28 Triangles
Total Time: 1½ Hours + Freezing

For the Shrimp Filling—
Combine:
⅓ cup ketchup
2 t. prepared horseradish
1 t. sugar
1 t. Worcestershire sauce
½ t. lemon zest, minced
Juice of ½ lemon
Salt and pepper to taste
Stir in:
½ lb. cooked shrimp, coarsely chopped

For the Optional Cream Cheese Filling—
Combine:
4 oz. cream cheese, softened
2 T. scallions, minced
1 t. garlic, minced
Pinch salt
Dash Tabasco

For the Phyllo—
Prepare:
Butter-oil mixture, *Page 18*
12 sheets phyllo, *Pages 16–17*

Combine ketchup, horseradish, sugar, Worcestershire, lemon zest, juice, salt, and pepper.
Stir chopped shrimp into ketchup mixture until coated.
Combine ingredients for cream cheese filling, if using.
Prepare 3 phyllo sheets, brushing each sheet with butter-oil mixture. Cut and fill phyllo, then fold into triangles, *left*. Prepare remaining sheets the same way, then freeze the triangles in single layers on parchment-lined baking sheets. Bake frozen (not thawed) triangles at 400° on parchment-lined baking sheets until browned and heated through, 15–20 min. Serve hot.

The triangle

Butter and layer 3 phyllo sheets. With long side facing you, measure 2¼" wide strips and cut with a pizza wheel. You should get 7 strips from 14 x 18" sheets, with a small strip leftover.

Place 1 tsp. of cream cheese mixture (if using) on the lower right hand corner of each strip. Then spoon a small amount of shrimp mixture onto the cheese.

To fold triangles, bring the lower right corner up and over the filling until the corner meets the left side of the strip. Now bring the bottom tip up and over. Continue folding at right angles to the end, as if folding a flag.

Seal excess phyllo at the end of the strip to the triangle, then brush entire triangle with butter.

phyllo-wrapped Salmon

This dish has it all—bright flavors, knock-out looks, and ease. Good cooking doesn't get much better than that!

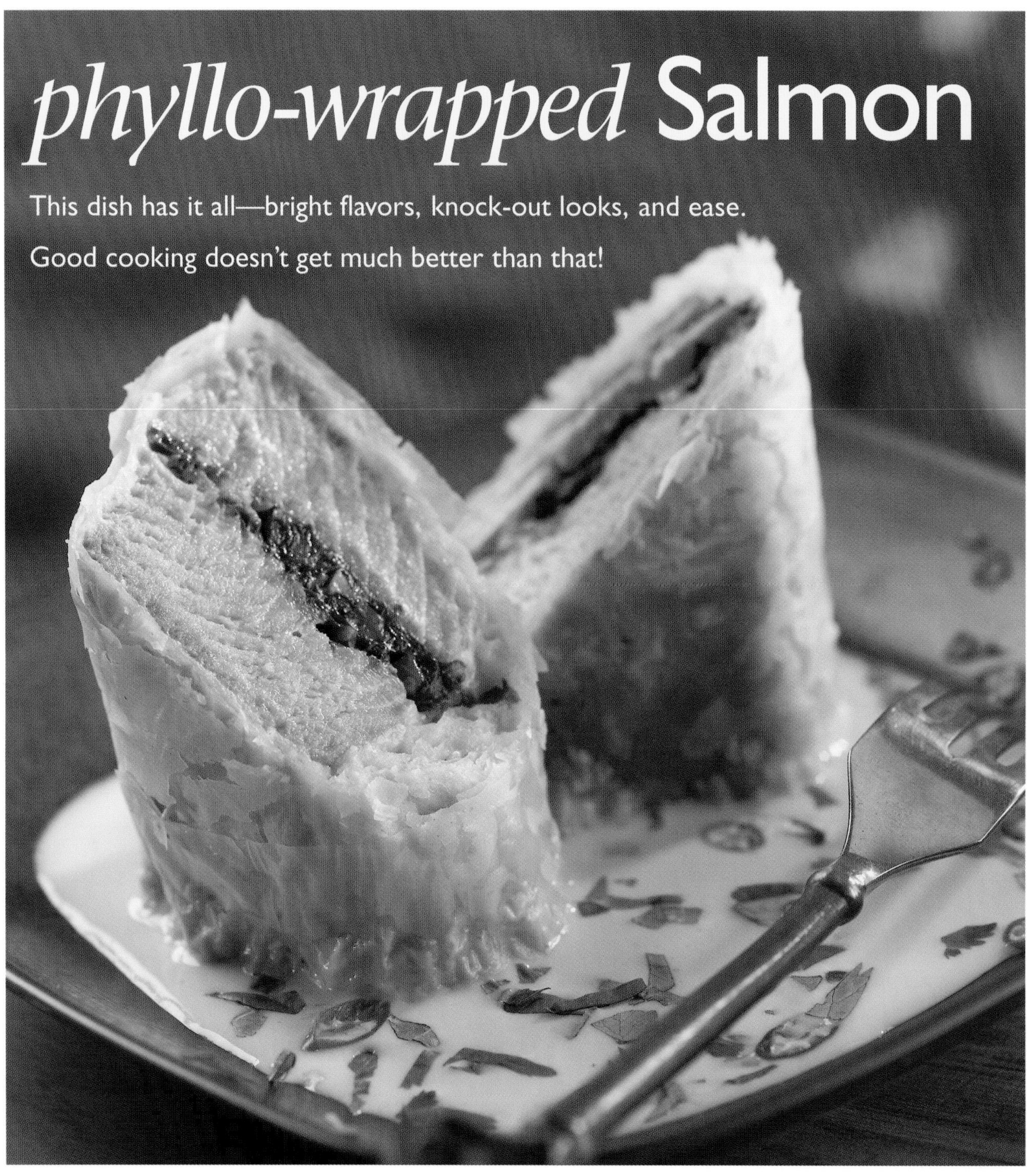

A few sheets of phyllo can work magic on ordinary ingredients like salmon and spinach. Then throw in an Asian flavored coconut-herb sauce, and you've got the ticket to one swanky dinner! With not much effort at all. I'm not kidding.

Again, by working ahead, just about all that's needed to get dinner on the table is preheating the oven. You can wrap the fish in phyllo and chill it four or five hours before baking. The sauce can be made in advance, too, and rewarmed while the fish is in the oven. But for optimal looks and flavor, don't chop the herb-chile garnish for the sauce until it's time to serve.

Use the freshest salmon available. If another thick-filleted fish (halibut, sea bass, etc.) is fresher, it's fine to substitute. But the cooking time may need to increase 2–3 minutes—their flesh is a bit denser.

Phyllo-Wrapped Salmon with Gingered Spinach Filling

Makes 4 Servings
Total Time: 1 Hour

For the Filling—
Heat:
2 T. vegetable oil
2 T. shallot, minced
1 T. garlic, minced
1 T. fresh ginger, minced
½ t. crushed red pepper flakes
Toss in Oil:
1 cup baby spinach leaves, coarsely chopped
Pinch of salt and sugar

For the Salmon—
Prepare:
Butter-olive oil mixture, *Page 18*
6 phyllo sheets, *Page 16–17*
1 T. sesame seeds, toasted
Assemble on Phyllo:
4 fillets (4 oz. each) salmon, skin removed, seasoned with salt and pepper
Prepared spinach

Heat oil for the filling in a small saute pan over medium-high heat. Add shallot, garlic, ginger, and pepper flakes. Cook just until fragrant, about 1 minute.
Toss hot oil with spinach; season with salt and sugar. Set mixture aside until ready to assemble rolls.
Prepare butter-oil mixture and brush some on 3 of the 6 phyllo sheets. Sprinkle sesame seeds on the first two buttered sheets.
To assemble, place one fish fillet about 1" from the bottom of a short side of the phyllo. Arrange half the spinach across the fillet. Top with a second fillet so the thick portion rests on top of the thin portion of the fillet below.

To roll, lift the bottom edge of the phyllo and roll the fillets one half turn (the top fillet is now on the bottom). Brush the exposed phyllo with butter, then fold the long sides in, all the way to the end of the sheet (as if folding a burrito). Brush these folds with butter, then roll to the end, brushing any uncoated phyllo with a little butter. Transfer to a parchment-lined baking sheet. Prepare remaining three sheets of phyllo and assemble second roll as the first.

Preheat oven to 425°. Bake wrapped fish 20 minutes; remove from oven and let rest 5 minutes before slicing. To serve, slice off about ½" from the ends of each roll using an electric knife or serrated slicing knife. Cut rolls in half, then cut each piece in half diagonally. To serve, stand two of the pieces upright on each serving plate.

Prepare phyllo as shown on Page 17. After brushing with butter, sprinkle sesame seeds over each sheet. ►

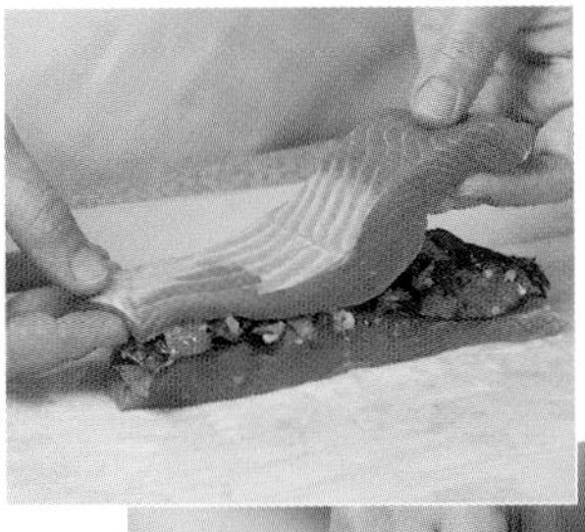

◄*For even shape, place the thicker section of the top fillet on top of the thinner section of the bottom fillet.*

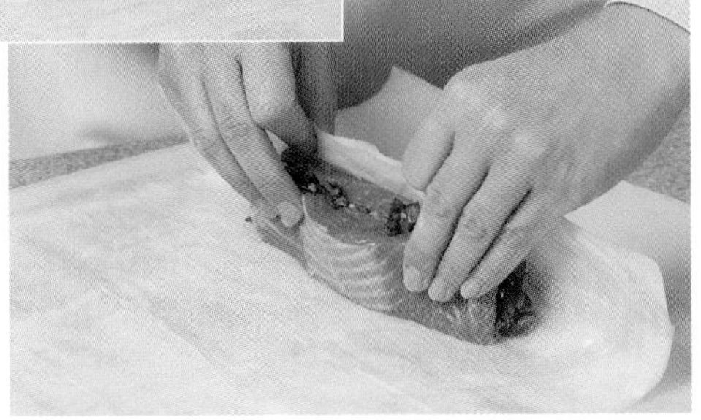

▲*Grab bottom of phyllo with thumbs and forefingers; keep top fillet in place with the tips of your other fingers. In one motion, roll fillet a half turn. Fold in sides and roll to the end, lightly brushing phyllo with butter as you go.*

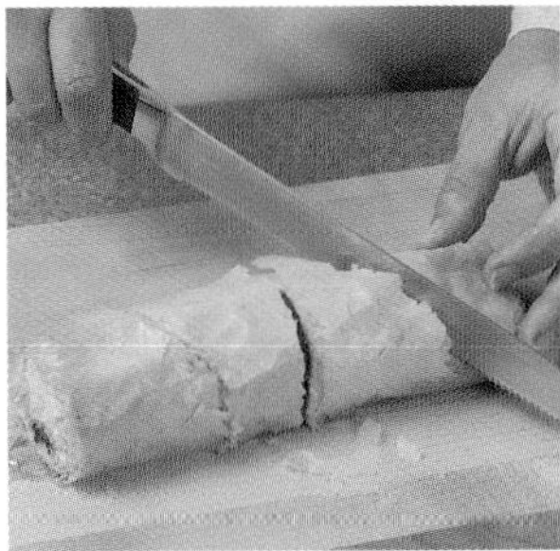

◄*Bake rolls until golden and crisp, 20 min. After resting, slice ½" off both ends. Cut rolls in half, then in half again at a diagonal. Arrange on plates.*

make it a **menu**

Herbed Coconut Sauce

Makes 1 Cup; Total Time: 25 Min.

Simmer, Reduce, and Strain:
1 cup unsweetened coconut milk
½ cup water
1 T. garlic, minced
1 T. fresh ginger, minced
1 T. shallot, minced
½ t. sugar
¼ t. crushed red pepper flakes
Combine; Whisk into Sauce:
1 t. fresh lime juice
½ t. cornstarch
Salt to taste
Garnish Plates with:
¼ cup chopped fresh cilantro
¼ cup chopped fresh basil
1 Thai chile, sliced into rings, *or* 1T. jalapeño or serrano chile, seeded and minced

Simmer coconut milk, water, garlic, ginger, shallot, sugar, and pepper flakes in a small saucepan over med.-high heat. Reduce to about 1 cup, about 15 minutes. Strain mixture through a fine mesh strainer and return liquid to a clean saucepan.
Combine lime juice and cornstarch in a small bowl. Bring sauce to a boil again and whisk in cornstarch mixture. Simmer about 1 minute, then season with salt to taste. To serve, spoon some of the sauce onto plates, then stand two pieces of the phyllo-wrapped salmon in the sauce.
Garnish with herb-chile mixture.

▲*Spoon sauce onto plates, top with pieces of phyllo-wrapped fish, then garnish generously with the herb mixture.*

allabout

blue cheese

If the only blue cheese you're familiar with is whatever's in the dressing on the salad bar, read on. You deserve better.

Let's face it. Blue cheese isn't for everyone. But if you like it, you owe it to yourself to know more about it.

And that means tasting. We tried a dozen blues from the world over, as well as grocery store "regulars." And we learned *a lot*—just by eating!

Types of blue cheese

There's a myriad of blue cheeses,but these four are the Big Blues of the cheese world. Sample them back to back if you can.

Roquefort is France's best known blue. Crafted for centuries in a region of southern France, this sheep's milk cheese is ivory colored with blue-green striations throughout. The flavor is pungent and often described as salty. Only cheese made in the region may be called Roquefort. Authentic Roquefort has a red sheep seal on the label.

English *Stilton* is from cow's milk and has been in production since the 1700s. It is characterized by a dry, brown natural rind surrounding a firm, yet slightly crumbly straw-colored interior. The blue-gray veins should reach to the edges. Stilton's flavor is strong, but with a bit less "bite" than Roquefort.

Gorgonzola is an Italian blue. This cow's milk cheese comes in two styles—*dolce* and *naturale*. Both are made the same way; naturale is just aged longer. The added aging makes naturale firmer, bluer, and more assertive in flavor than dolce.

Iowa-made *Maytag* is considered one of this country's cheese treasures. In production since 1941 (yes, by the appliance people), Maytag is creamy white punctuated by blue-green veins. It has a smooth texture and peppery taste that turns even more powerful the longer it ages.

Using blue cheese

These four cheeses are best as an appetizer or cheese course at meal's end—that way, you can appreciate their finer points and subtleties. Maytag or Roquefort, however, is a nice addition to a salad, *see right*. But in general, with recipes calling for many ingredients (like those on Pages 24–25), use a less expensive grocery store cheese, like Danish blue. The intricacies of a more complex cheese would be lost.

Storing blue cheese

As with all cheeses, blues are best stored in the vegetable bin of the refrigerator. Wrapped in plastic, foil, or wax paper, they'll be able to "breathe" without drying out. Each time you remove the wrapping, replace it with a fresh piece to ensure a tight seal. Never, *ever* freeze blue cheese—it destroys texture and flavor. And you'll know when blue cheese has gone bad if it becomes discolored with tinges of pink, brown, or grey.

blue cheese salad

This is not your typical lettuce-and-tomato salad. Wild with texture and flavor, it is an amazing eating experience.

Blue Cheese, Pear, and Pecan Salad with Warm Bacon Dressing

Makes About 12 Cups
Total Time: 45 Minutes

For the Pecans—

Toast:

1 cup pecan halves or pieces

Combine; Toss with Pecans and Roast:

2 T. sugar
1 T. vegetable oil
1/2 t. kosher salt
1/2 t. ground cinnamon
1/4 t. ground ginger
1/4 t. dry mustard
1/8 t. ground nutmeg
1/8 t. ground cloves
Pinch cayenne

For the Dressing—

Saute:

6 slices (8 oz.) thick-sliced bacon, diced

Add and Saute:

1/4 cup shallots, minced (about 3 shallots)

Stir In:

1 T. honey mustard
1 t. ground cinnamon

Whisk In:

1/2 cup apple juice concentrate
1/4 cup extra-virgin olive oil
1 T. apple cider vinegar
Salt and pepper to taste

For the Salad—

Toss Together:

12 cups mesclun salad greens
1 cup fennel bulb, thinly sliced
1 firm yet ripe Bosc pear, cored and thinly sliced
1/2 cup Maytag, Roquefort, or other good-quality blue cheese, crumbled
Prepared pecans and dressing

Preheat oven to 350°.
Toast pecans on a baking sheet in oven until golden, about 10 min.
Combine sugar, oil, salt, and spices in a small bowl while nuts toast. Toss hot pecans with sugar mixture until well coated. Return nuts to baking sheet and roast 8–10 more minutes, or until coating is dry. Do not overbake.

Saute bacon for the dressing in a medium skillet over medium-high heat until crisp. Spoon off excess fat; leave bacon in skillet.
Add the shallots to the skillet; saute until softened, about 3 min.
Stir in the mustard and cinnamon; cook another minute.
Whisk in the apple juice concentrate, oil, and vinegar. Season with salt and pepper. Keep dressing warm over low heat until ready to toss the salad.
Toss the greens, fennel, pear, blue cheese, and spiced pecans with some of the warm dressing (you may not use all the dressing). Serve salad immediately.

Nuts may be made 2 weeks ahead and stored in an airtight container. ►

◄ *Dressing may be made 2 days ahead and chilled. Gently rewarm before using.*

blue cheese hors d'oeuvre

▼*Stir eggs into dough. It won't seem like they'll incorporate, but they will.*

▲*Drop dough onto baking sheets; bake until dry and golden. (May be baked, frozen, and reheated at 350° until crisp.)*

Blue Cheese and Bacon Puffs

These puffs are great with cocktails, but they make a good accompaniment to salads too.

Makes About 5 Dozen 2" Puffs
Total Time: About 1 Hour

Saute; Drain and Set Aside:
3 slices (4 oz.) thick-sliced bacon, diced

Bring to a Boil:
1/2 cup milk
1/2 cup water
6 T. unsalted butter
1/2 t. kosher salt
1/4 t. black pepper
1/4 t. cayenne

Add:
1 cup all-purpose flour

Beat in:
4 eggs

Stir in:
4 oz. blue cheese, crumbled (about 2/3 cup)
1/4 cup Parmesan cheese, grated
1/4 cup scallions, sliced (green part only)
Reserved bacon pieces

Preheat oven to 425° with rack in the lower third.

Saute bacon in a small skillet over medium-high heat until crisp. Drain on paper towel-lined plate.

Bring milk, water, butter, and seasonings to a boil in a medium saucepan over medium heat.

Add flour and stir mixture with a wooden spoon until dough forms a ball around the spoon. Cook until it starts to stick slightly on bottom and sides of pan. Remove from heat and cool slightly.

Beat in eggs, one at a time, until completely incorporated.

Stir in both cheeses, scallions, and reserved bacon. Using a #100 scoop or a 1-teaspoon measure, drop dough 2" apart onto parchment-lined baking sheets. Bake 20–25 min., or until puffs are browned and crisp. Serve warm or at room temperature.

blue cheese appetizer

Blue Cheese Dip with Caramelized Onions

This is like French onion dip and blue cheese dip all in one!

Makes $1\frac{1}{2}$ Cups
Total Time: 30 Minutes

Caramelize in 1 T. Olive Oil:
2 cups yellow onion, chopped
Pinch of sugar and salt

Stir in:
1 T. tawny port, *optional*

Blend:
4 oz. blue cheese, crumbled (about $\frac{2}{3}$ cup)
$\frac{1}{2}$ cup plain lowfat yogurt
$\frac{1}{2}$ cup reduced calorie mayonnaise
$\frac{1}{2}$ t. Worcestershire sauce
Juice of $\frac{1}{2}$ a lemon

Add:
Caramelized onions
2 T. chopped fresh parsley, scallions, or chives
Salt and cayenne to taste

Serve with:
Fried pita triangles, potato chips, raw vegetables, etc.

Caramelize onion in olive oil with sugar and salt in a heavy skillet over medium-low heat. Stir occasionally to prevent scorching, but do not stir too often—they will brown better if left alone. After about 5 minutes of cooking, cover the pan (the lid keeps moisture inside so the onions won't burn as readily). Cook until brown and very soft, 20–25 min.
Stir in the port, scraping up any brown residue left on the bottom of the pan; cool onions slightly.
Blend cheese, yogurt, mayonnaise, Worcestershire, and lemon juice in a bowl.

▲*Add port to caramelized onions, scraping up browned bits.*

◀*Mix in onions. Chill before serving—24 hours is best.*

Add cooled onions, herbs, salt, and cayenne to taste; stir to blend. Cover and chill dip for at least 2 hours before serving.
Serve with fried pita triangles, potato chips, or raw vegetables.

36 *online* **extra**

To make fried pita triangles, visit our website, www.CuisineAtHome.com for instructions.

wares
steak knives

It may seem kind of obvious, but the way a knife cuts through meat is the primary consideration when choosing a steak knife.

We tested 56 knives to find which ones cut the best and determine what really counts in a steak knife. (Don't get steak envy—to make it a true test, we had to slice a lot of tough meat.)

Here's what you need to know before upgrading your wedding set or giving steak knives as a gift.

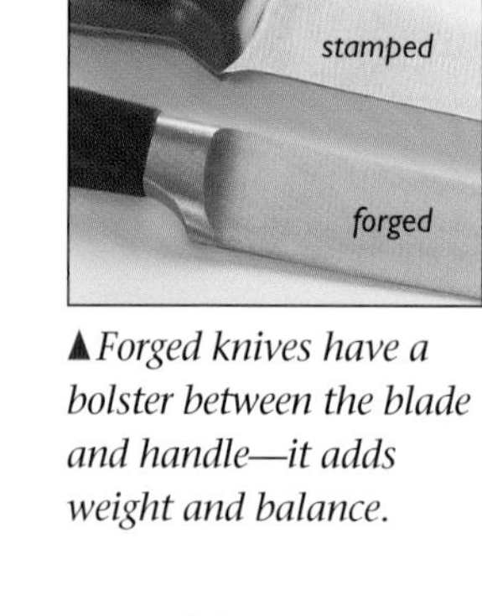

▲*Forged knives have a bolster between the blade and handle—it adds weight and balance.*

Forged or stamped?

There are two ways to form knife blades: by forging or stamping.

Forged: A single piece of steel is heated, then hammered into a knife that includes a bolster (the thick steel at base of blade), *see left*.

Stamped: The blade is stamped or cut from a flat sheet of steel—a less involved process than forging. It's lighter in weight, less expensive, and easy to spot because there's no bolster.

I have to tell you that if I was recommending a *chef's* knife, I'd steer you toward forged knives. Their quality and craftsmanship allow years of daily service. But steak knives are different. They don't routinely get that kind of a rigorous workout—they're usually pulled out a couple times a month at most. While the weight and balance of a forged steak knife may feel better in your hand, stamped knives often cut just as well. As far as steak knives go, forged is nice, but not critical.

What's a tang?

The tang is an extension of the blade that reaches through the handle. Although not always visible, it is important. Full and partial tangs provide balance and weight. They also make the blade less likely to snap off at the handle.

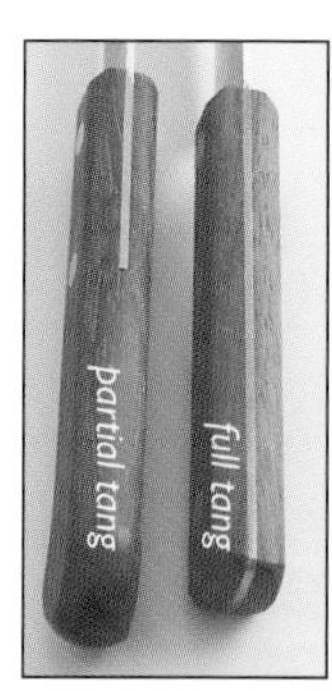

▲*Knives are often designed to reveal the tang running through the handle*

Cutting edges

Traditionally, Europeans use steak knives with straight edges, while Americans gravitate toward serrated.

Straight: Good straight edge knives make smooth, clean cuts. But sooner or later they need to be sharpened. Most manufacturers recommend regular maintenance with a honing steel to realign the edge and keep factory sharpness.

Serrated: Good serrated knives also make clean cuts. Serrations vary from tiny, barely noticeable indentations to big, deeply carved, almost scary teeth. The blades with extreme serrations tear the meat and even leave meat clinging to the knife.

Serrated steak knives are lower maintenance than straight knives because they can't be sharpened. But while they may keep their sharp edges longer, they'll eventually dull.

But with either blade, wash steak knives by hand—dishwasher detergent can harm or dull the edge.

The final cut

We are recommending nine knives that did a good job cutting meat. Interestingly enough, they include stamped and forged, straight edged and serrated! Consider how often the knives will be used, their style, and the investment you want to make in them. Then, shop your kitchenware or department store, or see Resources, *Page 43,* to order.

These steak knives are all rated four stars or above in the Cuisine Test Kitchen.

Victorinox/Forschner

set of 6: $99.99

This is the Swiss Army Knife company, so it's not surprising that their steak knife performs so well. The lightweight knife cuts through even tough steak like butter. That ultra-smooth slicing is a result of their blade polishing procedure. Both the rosewood and nylon ($29.95 for six) handles come with serrated or straight edges. Swiss made, all are stamped, with a 3/4 tang.

Messermeister *set of 4: $88.50*

We really like the entire line (both forged and stamped) of the German-made Messermeister steak knives. While all their knives are serrated, the stamped Park Plaza model is the only one with a wavy serration and it makes outstandingly easy cuts. If the knives dull, you can send them to Messermeister for free resharpening (you pay only the freight).

Fante's *set of 4: $35.99*

Fante's is a kitchen and cookware store in Philadelphia that has its own line of cutlery, made in Solingen, Germany to their specifications. While the rest of their Fante's Pro Cutlery line is forged, the steak knives are stamped. The full tang stainless steel blade has micro-serrations that allow fine cutting at an affordable price.

Wüsthof *set of 4: $219.99*

The forged straight edge Culinar is German-made Wüsthof's top of the line steak knife that looks at home with even the finest dishes. A beautiful combination of cutting ease and style, the Culinar settles into the hand with perfect balance. It owes its high-end price tag to the hand brushed stainless steel handle. The Classic and Grand Prix lines pair the same great blade with black handles for around $150.

Chef'sChoice *set of 4: $229.95*

Chef'sChoice has been making knives at their Pennsylvania plant for about 10 years. This forged, full tang, straight edge knife is made from their unique Trizor steel. It's so strong, it "pings" when tapped on a hard surface—a test bell makers use to gauge steel strength. The triple-bevel blade is designed to lengthen the life of the edge, and confidently cuts through meat.

KitchenAid *set of 4: $149.95*

Made in the classic style of traditional triple riveted knives, the Epicurean Series steak knife from KitchenAid has been on the market for just two years. Yet it still delivers the quality you've come to expect from the company. The curved, full handle offers comfort, while the forged, high carbon stainless steel straight edge blade makes clean cuts.

Chicago Cutlery *set of 4: $39.99*

Walnut Tradition steak knives have been made by Chicago Cutlery for 40 years. The straight edge blade curves up toward the tip to make cutting easier on the user. This sturdy knife is stamped, and the triple rivets secure a full tang to the wooden handle. The reasonable price tag makes this set a great deal. Their Walnut Signature steak knife (the blade is straight, not curved up) also cuts quite well.

J.A. Henckels *set of 4: $149.99*

Made in Germany, the Henckels Professional "S" steak knife offers classic handling and design. Forged, with full tang and triple rivets, the straight edge stainless steel blade makes strong cuts. Henckels also makes a less expensive International line that's made in China. It includes the stamped, serrated Fine Edge Pro that also does a good job.

LamsonSharp *set of 4: $49.95*

LamsonSharp produces the best jumbo steak knife we found. Seemingly meant for the biggest of steaks, this stamped knife makes a statement! Made in Massachusetts, the large blade has deep but effective serrations. The beefy handle is available in rosewood as well. The company also makes very good medium-sized, forged steak knives with a variety of handle styles.

candy bars for the holidays

The matriarch of modern baking, Maida Heatter never tires of it or of teaching others how to make desserts that turn out every bit as good as her own creations.

Known for everything from cheesecake to biscotti to Key lime pie, Maida says it's her Palm Beach Brownies that top the list of most requested recipes. She describes them as "the biggest, thickest, gooiest, chewiest, darkest, sweetest, mostest-of-the-most chocolate bars with an almost wet middle and a crisp-crunchy top." But when she nestles peppermint patties in the middle, they're pure holiday.

Maida shares the recipe and techniques for these and two more decidedly different bars, urging bakers to always follow instructions—and have fun!

Maida Heatter (pronounced May-da Hee-ter) is the author of eight dessert cookbooks, including a New York Times bestseller. She's won nearly every honor possible for a cookbook writer, including three James Beard Foundation Awards for excellence in cooking. Her ***Book of Great Desserts*** *was inducted into the James Beard Foundation Cookbook Hall of Fame. And she was one of the first inducted into* ***Chocolatier*** *magazine's Hall of Fame.*

Maida lives in Miami Beach, Florida, where she spends much of her time baking. Lucky baking recipients can be the FedEx person, her doctor, the ladies at the beauty parlor, neighbors, or any number of friends both near and far.

Palm Beach brownies

Preferred pan *Maida likes to use a Magic Line pan for these brownies. The straight sides and square corners means the edges don't have to be trimmed. See Page 42 to place an order.*

◄Pan Prep *It takes a little patience to fit the pan with foil, but doing so results in easy removal and effortless cleanup.*

Invert pan and center heavy duty foil over pan bottom. Press down sides and corners, shaping to the pan. Remove foil, turn pan right side up, and place foil inside. Carefully press into place.

Add 1 T. butter to pan and place pan in preheating oven. When butter is melted, spread it over the foil with a pastry brush.

▲Place whole peppermints in a single layer over the batter.

▲Pour remaining batter over the mints and smooth the top. The mints will not melt.

Palm Beach Brownies with Chocolate-Covered Mints

Refrigerate the pan of brownies for at least a few hours or overnight before cutting—they cannot be cut into bars fresh from the oven.

Makes 32 Brownies; Total Time: 1 Hour

Melt:
- 8 oz. unsweetened chocolate
- 8 oz. (2 sticks) unsalted butter

Beat:
- $3\frac{3}{4}$ cups sugar
- 5 eggs
- 1 T. + 1 t. instant espresso powder
- 2 t. vanilla extract
- $\frac{1}{2}$ t. almond extract
- $\frac{1}{4}$ t. table salt

Add:
- Chocolate mixture

Add:
- $1\frac{2}{3}$ cups sifted all-purpose flour

Stir in:
- 8 oz. walnuts, broken in large pieces (2 generous cups)

Layer with:
- 40 York chocolate-covered peppermint patties (about 20 oz.)

Preheat oven to 425° with rack one third up from the bottom. Prepare 9 x 13 x 2" pan as directed above left; set aside.

Melt the chocolate and butter in a double boiler over hot water on moderate heat, or in a 4- to 6-cup heavy saucepan over low heat. Stir occasionally until chocolate and butter are melted. Remove from heat; set aside.

Beat the sugar, eggs, espresso powder, extracts, and salt in a large bowl of an electric mixer set at high speed for 10 minutes.

Add the chocolate mixture (which may still be warm) with mixer on low speed. Beat just until blended.

Add the flour and beat again on low speed only until mixed.

Stir in the nuts. Spoon half the mixture (about $3\frac{1}{2}$ cups) into the prepared pan; smooth top.

Layer the peppermints over the chocolate layer. They should touch each other and come as close to the edges of the pan as possible (*do not* cut mints in half to fill in spaces—the filling will ooze and burn). Spoon remaining chocolate mixture over mints; carefully smooth top.

Bake for 35 minutes (and no longer), rotating the pan once during baking. Remove from oven and let stand in pan until cool. Invert pan and remove foil lining. Invert again so brownies are right side up. Refrigerate a few hours or overnight before cutting.

▲Use a long knife with a sharp blade to cut the brownies into quarters. Trimming the edges is optional.

▼Cut each quarter in half, then cut each eighth into four bars. This narrow shape shows off the mints.

chef**at**home: *Maida Heatter*

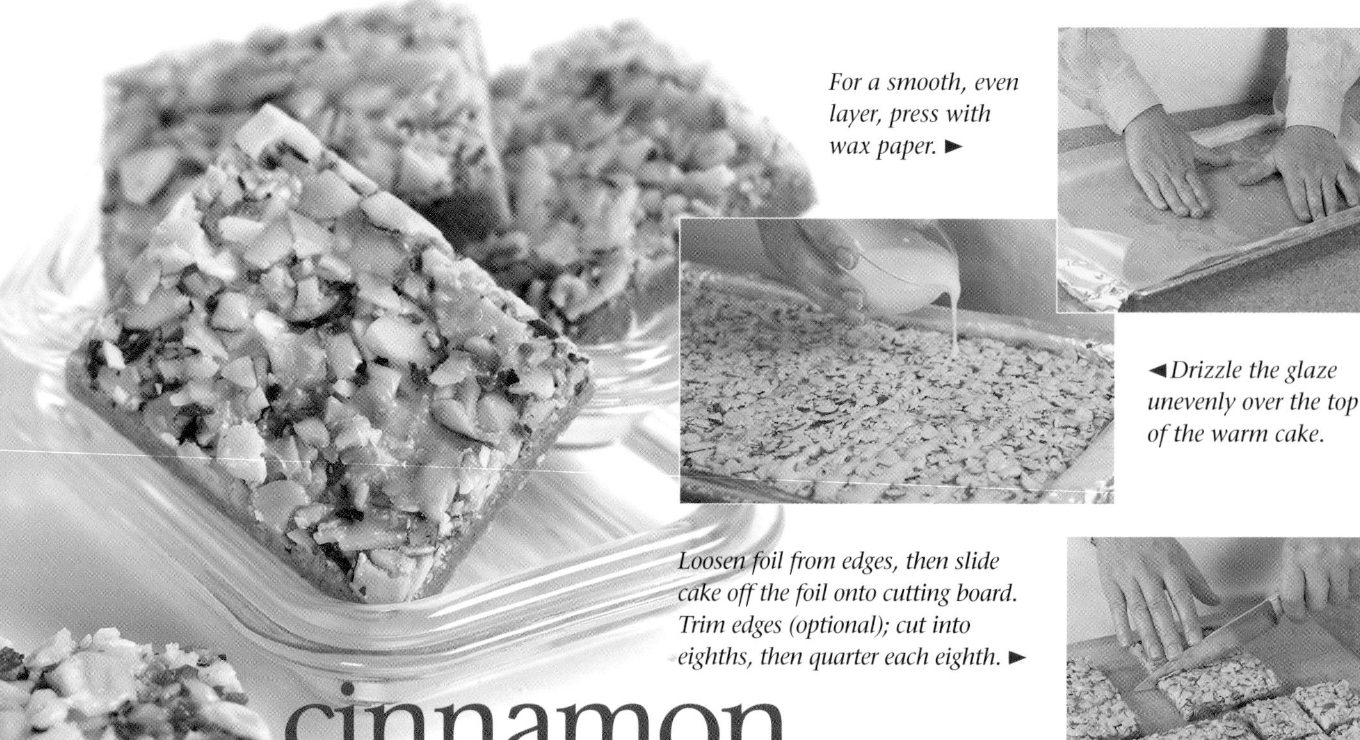

For a smooth, even layer, press with wax paper. ►

◄*Drizzle the glaze unevenly over the top of the warm cake.*

Loosen foil from edges, then slide cake off the foil onto cutting board. Trim edges (optional); cut into eighths, then quarter each eighth. ►

cinnamon almond bars

CINNAMON ALMOND BARS
MAKES 32 BARS
TOTAL TIME: 1 HOUR

CREAM:
8 oz. (2 sticks) unsalted butter, softened
ADD:
1 cup sugar
2 t. ground cinnamon
BEAT IN:
1 egg yolk (reserve white)
GRADUALLY ADD:
2 cups sifted all-purpose flour
BRUSH WITH:
Reserved egg white, beaten until foamy
SPRINKLE; BAKE:
1¾ cup sliced almonds, crumbled (6 oz.)
FOR THE GLAZE—
WHISK; DRIZZLE OVER:
1 cup powdered sugar, sifted
1 T. unsalted butter, melted
1 T. boiling water
1 T. lemon juice

Preheat oven to 300° with rack in center. Line a 10 x 15" jelly roll pan with foil (see note below). Grease foil with a little soft butter and set pan aside.

Cream the butter in a large bowl with an electric mixer.

Add the sugar and cinnamon; beat to mix well.

Beat in the egg yolk.

Gradually add the flour with the mixer on low speed, scraping bowl with a rubber spatula. Beat just until thoroughly mixed; dough will be thick. Drop large spoonfuls of dough into the prepared pan and spread it to cover the bottom. Cover dough with a large piece of wax paper, then smooth it with your hands. Remove the wax paper.

Brush entire egg white over dough with a pastry brush.

Sprinkle almonds evenly over the egg white. Cover again with wax paper and press the almonds into the dough; remove wax paper. Bake for 40–45 minutes, until golden brown. A minute or so before removing from the oven, prepare the glaze.

Whisk sugar, butter, water, and lemon juice in a small bowl until completely smooth. The glaze should be the consistency of heavy cream. As soon as the cake is removed from the oven, drizzle glaze unevenly in a thin stream over the top. It will be shiny and transparent.

Cool cake in the pan 10–15 minutes, then carefully lift it from pan using the foil ends (it will still be warm). Loosen foil from the edges, then slide the cake onto a cutting board. Cut into bars as above and finish cooling on rack.

Note: *Do not substitute a different size pan or the outcome will be affected. Doughmakers makes a 10 x 15" aluminum jelly roll pan. See Resources, Page 42, to order.*

peanut bars

PEANUT BARS

The recipe for these thin caramel cookie bars comes together quickly, so be sure to have all of the ingredients ready.

MAKES 24 BARS; TOTAL TIME: 45 MINUTES

SIFT; SET ASIDE:
- 3/4 cup sifted all-purpose flour
- 1 t. ground cinnamon
- 1/2 t. ground ginger

MELT:
- 4 oz. (1 stick) unsalted butter
- 1 cup (6 oz.) butterscotch morsels

WHISK IN:
- 1 1/2 t. instant coffee

STIR IN:
- 1/4 cup sugar
- Sifted dry ingredients

ADD:
- 1 egg, whisked

SPRINKLE WITH:
- 3/4 cup (3 oz.) salted peanuts (preferably the dry-roasted type), coarsely chopped

Preheat oven to 325° with rack in the center of the oven. Turn a 10 x 15" jelly roll pan upside down (see note, Page 30). Cover pan with a piece of foil large enough to fold down on all four sides. Fold the edges just to shape them, remove foil, and invert the pan. Sprinkle drops of water in the pan (to stabilize the foil), then position foil in pan. Use a folded towel to press the foil firmly against the pan. Brush with soft or melted butter, then place pan in freezer. Chilling makes it easier to spread a thin layer of batter.

Sift together the flour, cinnamon, and ginger; set aside.

Melt the butter and butterscotch morsels in a heavy saucepan over moderate heat. Stir occasionally until smooth.

Whisk in the instant coffee. Remove from heat and whisk until smooth.

Stir in the sugar and sifted dry ingredients. Batter will be grainy.

Add the egg and stir until smooth. Quickly pour the batter into the chilled pan and evenly spread in a very thin layer.

Sprinkle batter with chopped peanuts. Bake for 25 minutes until top is golden and springs back when lightly touched. Remove from oven and cool 3 minutes.

Cover cake with a large baking sheet. Invert the cake, then remove pan and scroll back foil. Cover with another baking sheet and invert again so it's right side up. Carefully slide cake onto cutting board, cut into bars, then transfer them to a rack to cool.

◄Add egg to the batter, stirring quickly so the egg incorporates, but doesn't cook.

With the back of a spoon, quickly spread the batter as evenly as possible. ►

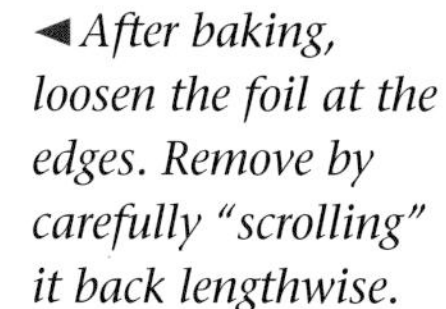

◄After baking, loosen the foil at the edges. Remove by carefully "scrolling" it back lengthwise.

▲For credit card sized bars, cut warm cake first in half, then cut each half into four narrow strips. Finally, cut lengthwise in thirds.

entree soups

chicken pot pie

Question: What's more satisfying than salad and less filling than dinner? *Answer:* An entree soup. It's a meal that fits just right after too many holiday feasts.

A good soup should be a perfect balance of flavor, nourishment, and satisfaction without being overbearing. Soups are ignored as a player in the entree world. And that's too bad because you can easily turn your favorite entree into a soup. Here are three of my favorite entrees transformed. They're a nice change from the usual holiday excess.

What's nice about the three entree soups is that they all use canned chicken broth—no long simmering process to make stock. Most of these full-flavored soups take less than 45 minutes from start to finish using leftovers and common kitchen ingredients. And don't just think about these soups during the season—they work well around the calendar.

Chicken pot pie in a bowl

You can have this Chicken Pot Pie Soup on the table in about 30 minutes. Pop the puff pastry shells in the oven, pick apart the chicken, and start chopping.

You can find puff pastry shells in the frozen food aisle of most supermarkets. Pepperidge Farms brand works well and only takes 20 minutes to bake, *see below.*

While the pastry shells are baking, pull the chicken from the bone. Since rotisserie chicken seems to be in most grocery stores, use it. If it's not available or convenient, no problem—just buy a whole chicken and cook it yourself in water. It'll take a little longer, but then you can use the stock in the soup.

Be sure not to cook the frozen vegetables too long or they'll turn a dull color. Actually, when I make this soup, I simply cut the heat, then add the corn and peas. The residual heat is enough to cook them through.

And finally, finish the soup with fresh parsley and a little cream. The cream will add body and enough richness to make it the perfect soup for a cold day.

Chicken Pot Pie Soup

Purchase rotisserie chicken and frozen puff pastry shells from your supermarket to make this a simple weeknight meal.

Makes 6 Cups; Total Time: 30 Minutes

Bake:
4 puff pastry shells

Sweat in 4 T. Unsalted Butter:
1 cup yellow onion, diced
3/4 cup celery, diced
3/4 cup carrot, sliced
1 1/2 cups red potatoes, diced

Whisk in:
1/4 cup all-purpose flour

Stir in:
4 cups low-sodium chicken broth
2 T. dry sherry
1 1/2 t. poultry seasoning
1 t. white pepper
3/4 t. kosher salt
1/8 t. ground nutmeg

Add:
2 cups cooked chicken
1/2 cup frozen corn kernels
1/2 cup frozen green peas

Finish with:
2 T. chopped fresh parsley
1/4 cup heavy cream

Serve with:
Baked Puff Pastry Shells

Bake pastry shells according to package directions; set aside.
Sweat vegetables with butter in soup pot over medium heat until softened, about 5 minutes.
Whisk in flour. Cook 2–3 mins.
Stir in broth, sherry, and seasonings. Increase heat to med-high and simmer until thickened, 10–15 minutes.
Add cooked chicken, corn and peas. Remove from heat.
Finish with parsley and cream.
Serve with puff pastry shells.

◄ *Sweat vegetables, then add the potatoes last—they will cook in the broth.*

Stir in broth, sherry, and seasonings. Cook to thicken, 10–15 minutes. ►

◄ *Add chicken and frozen vegetables. Remove from heat, and finish with parsley and cream.*

Puff Pastry

This wonderful French concoction is made by placing cold butter between layers of pastry dough. It's rolled out and folded into thirds then repeated many times. When baked, the moisture in the butter creates steam causing the dough to puff into many thin flaky layers.

shrimp creole

Shrimp Creole Soup

Add the shrimp right before serving to keep from overcooking and causing them to become rubbery.

Makes 6 Cups
Total Time: 45 Minutes

Peel and Devein; Chill:
1/2 lb. medium shrimp
Cook :
2 slices bacon, diced
Add:
1 cup yellow onion, diced
1 cup celery, diced
1 cup red bell pepper, diced
1 T. garlic, minced
Whisk in:
1/3 cup all-purpose flour
Stir in and Simmer:
4 cups low-sodium chicken broth
1 can (14.5-oz.) diced tomatoes
2 T. lemon juice
2 T. Worcestershire sauce
1–2 T. Tabasco
1 t. dried thyme
1 t. sugar
1/2 t. cayenne
1 bay leaf
Salt to taste
Add:
Prepared shrimp
Stir in:
1/4 cup chopped fresh parsley
1/4 cup scallions, minced
Serve with:
Cooked white rice

Peel and devein shrimp. Chill until ready to use.
Cook bacon in a large soup pot over medium–high heat until crisp.
Add onion, celery, bell pepper, and garlic. Cook 4–5 minutes.
Whisk in flour. Cook 2 minutes.
Stir in broth, tomatoes, lemon juice, Worcestershire, Tabasco, and seasonings. Simmer 10–15 minutes to thicken.
Add shrimp and cook 3 minutes.
Stir in parsley and scallions.
Serve with cooked white rice.

◄*Whisk in the flour and coat the bacon and vegetables. This will thicken soup.*

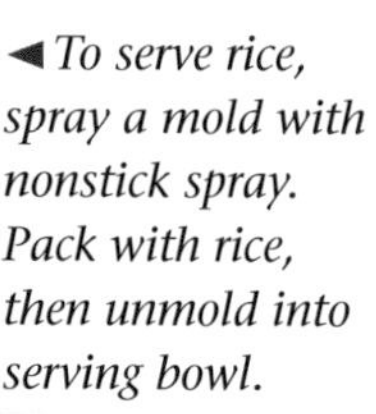

◄*To serve rice, spray a mold with nonstick spray. Pack with rice, then unmold into serving bowl.*

▲*Add the shrimp after the soup has cooked, right before serving.*

turkey tetrazzini

Turkey Tetrazzini Soup

Lots of sherry brings up the flavor of this favorite leftover turkey dish. Paprika gives it its rich color.

Makes 6 Cups; Total Time: 45 Minutes

For the Topping—

Toast in 1 T. Unsalted Butter:

1 cup fresh bread crumbs

Cool; Stir in:

2 T. Parmesan, finely grated
1 T. chopped fresh parsley
1 t. lemon zest, minced
Salt and pepper to taste

For the Soup—

Cook Al Dente; Set Aside:

4 oz. medium shell pasta

Saute in 4 T. Unsalted Butter:

$1\frac{1}{2}$ cup yellow onion, diced
8 oz. button mushrooms, stems trimmed, sliced

Whisk in:

$\frac{1}{4}$ cup all-purpose flour
2 t. paprika
$\frac{1}{2}$ t. dried thyme
$\frac{1}{2}$ t. kosher salt
$\frac{1}{2}$ t. black pepper
$\frac{1}{4}$ t. ground nutmeg

Stir in:

$\frac{1}{3}$ cup dry sherry
4 cups low-sodium chicken broth
1 T. fresh lemon juice

Add:

2 cups cooked turkey, diced
$\frac{1}{2}$ cup Parmesan, finely grated
$\frac{1}{4}$ cup pimientos, sliced
Reserved cooked pasta

Serve with:

Bread crumb topping

Toast bread crumbs for topping in butter over medium heat.
Cool the bread crumbs. Stir in the Parmesan, parsley, lemon zest, salt, and pepper. Set aside.
Cook pasta for soup according to package directions. Set aside.
Saute onions and mushrooms in butter over med.-high, 5 minutes.
Whisk in flour and seasonings.
Stir in sherry, broth, and fresh lemon juice.
Add turkey, pimientos, Parmesan, and cooked pasta.
Serve with bread crumb topping.

Toast bread crumbs, cool. Add Parmesan, parsley, lemon zest, and seasonings. ►

◄ *Add sherry and stir to combine. Allow the alcohol to cook out.*

Editors Note:
Pimientos are red sweet peppers that are smaller, sweeter, and more aromatic than a regular bell pepper. Most of the pimiento crops are used to make paprika.

Time for pie
new holiday classics

With all the hype over the turkey, potatoes, and cranberries, dessert often takes a back seat. These pies put it up front—so save room!

Sometimes it takes a lot for a holiday dessert to get noticed. No matter how good or gorgeous the grand finale is, it still can be tough to face after over-indulging on the Big Dinner.

But these three pies are different. They all taste vaguely familiar, yet there's something new and fresh about them. Sweet potato pie is a Southern staple that fits in just fine this time of year. But this one, loaded with marshmallow meringue, was inspired by those sweet potato side dishes that are served alongside the holiday bird but rarely eaten. For a good, simple pie crust for any of these pies, see Page 41, or use one of your favorite recipes.

This year, eggnog makes an appearance by way of a pie, not a milk carton! This pie is super-easy to make, but what sets it off is the brittle burnt sugar topping—just like crème brûlée from your favorite restaurant! Put the butane torch, *Page 39*, on your wish list this holiday.

Finally, chocolate turns an ordinary pecan pie around. Full of nuts and a rich, fudgey, pudding-like filling, you'll be glad you skipped seconds of turkey!

sweet potato pie
with marshmallow meringue

Weep no more *Beads of liquid often form on meringue. To avoid "weeping," spread the meringue on the pie while the filling is hot, then brown it. Weeping may still occur, but minimally.*

Making sweet potato pie is similar to making pumpkin pie. Here are key points to think about.

For the best pie, bake the potatoes yourself instead of opting for canned sweet potatoes. If you're short on time, canned potatoes (also labeled yams) will work, but at the expense of the filling's flavor, texture, and color.

While it is optional, spreading pineapple preserves on the pie shell adds a tangy contrast. But you'd be *crazy* not to top the pie with this meringue. Be sure to watch the meringue while it browns—it can burn if you're not careful. Just like marshmallows!

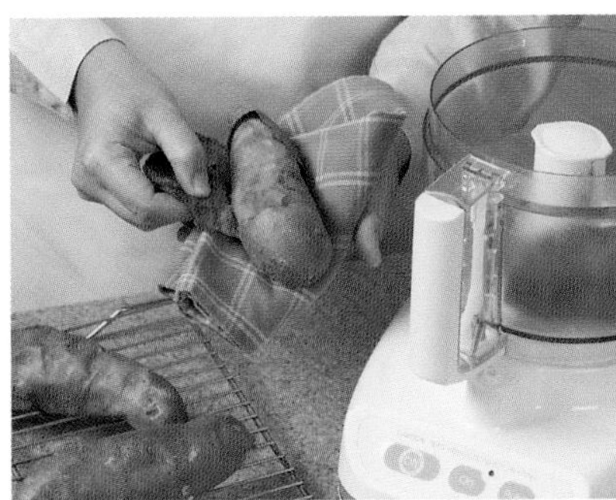

▲*Peel then process sweet potatoes while hot for a smoother puree. Blend 2 cups puree with remaining filling ingredients.*

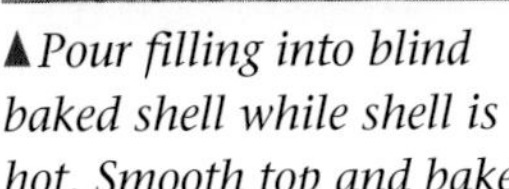

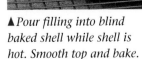

▲*Pour filling into blind baked shell while shell is hot. Smooth top and bake.*

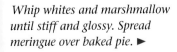

Whip whites and marshmallow until stiff and glossy. Spread meringue over baked pie. ►

Sweet Potato Pie with Marshmallow Meringue

Makes One 9" Pie
Total Time: About 1 1/2 Hours

For the Crust—
Prepare and Prebake:
One recipe Cream Cheese Pastry Dough, *Page 41*, (or your favorite dough recipe)

For the Filling—
Bake; Peel and Puree:
2–3 large sweet potatoes (to make 2 cups puree)
Add to Puree:
4 egg yolks (reserve whites for meringue topping)
3/4 cup sugar
1/4 cup brown sugar, lightly packed
1/4 cup evaporated milk
1 T. fresh lemon juice
1 t. vanilla extract
1 t. ground cinnamon
1/2 t. kosher salt
1/4 t. ground nutmeg
Zest of one lemon, minced
Spread:
1/4 cup pineapple preserves, *optional*

For the Meringue—
Beat:
4 reserved egg whites
Gradually Add:
10 oz. (2 1/2 cups) marshmallow creme

Preheat oven to 400°.
Prepare dough, line a pie plate, and blind bake crust, *Page 41*.
Bake sweet potatoes for the filling for 40 minutes, or until very soft. Peel while hot and place potatoes in food processor fitted with steel blade; puree until very smooth. Measure 2 cups potato puree into a mixing bowl.
Add egg yolks, sugars, milk, lemon juice, vanilla, spices, and lemon zest; whisk just to blend.
Spread optional preserves carefully over bottom of hot prebaked crust. Pour in filling, smooth the top, and bake 20 minutes. Reduce oven to 325°; continue baking pie until edges are puffed and a knife inserted 1" from the center comes out clean, 20–30 minutes. Remove pie, but leave oven on.
Beat reserved egg whites with a hand mixer in a clean metal or glass bowl until soft peaks form.
Gradually add marshmallow creme and continue beating until stiff peaks form, 5–7 min. Spread meringue over pie all the way to the edges, "spiking" it to make swirls and swoops. Return pie to the oven and bake 15–20 min., or until topping is golden, rotating it for even browning. Cool to room temperature before slicing. To cut, dip a sharp knife in hot water and gently slice through meringue—dip knife each time. Wrap leftovers loosely in plastic and chill.

▲*Cool pie to room temperature. Slice it using a knife dipped in hot water, but not dried.*

eggnog custard pie

'Tis the season for holiday cheer—and what better way to toast the festivities than with a piece of this pie.

Eggnog isn't just for drinking. The basic ingredients in eggnog (cream, eggs, and sugar) are the same ones that are in custard. The difference is that custard is baked, eggnog isn't.

Now, custards can be a little tricky to make on account of the eggs. They coagulate (get firm) at fairly low temperatures (160–180°) which means that baking must be closely monitored. If the pie is overcooked, the custard will turn grainy and watery. But if it's not cooked long enough to reach those coagulation temperatures, the custard will be runny and impossible to slice.

So, *be sure* to reduce the oven temperature after the crust is blind baked, before baking the pie. Then, *do not* leave the kitchen until the pie is out of the oven! It's done when the edges are set but the center is still wobbly. You'll want to leave it in longer, but don't. Carryover heat will finish the cooking, and chilling will help it firm up.

Caramelizing sugar on top is optional, but really festive. Don't try it, though, without a torch, *Page 39*. Oven broilers will curdle the custard before the sugar is caramelized.

Eggnog Custard Pie

Makes One 9" Pie

Total Time: About 1 Hour + Chilling

For the Crust—

Prepare and Prebake:

One recipe Cream Cheese Pastry Dough, *Page 41* (or your favorite dough recipe)

For the Filling—

Heat and Infuse:

1 cup heavy cream
1 cup half and half
2 T. bourbon, dark rum, or whiskey, *optional*
1 T. sugar
1/2 vanilla bean, split and scraped

Whisk:

5 egg yolks
1/2 cup sugar
1 t. vanilla extract
1/8 t. freshly ground nutmeg
Pinch salt

For the Optional Topping—

Sprinkle with:

Granulated sugar

Prepare dough, line a pie plate, and blind bake crust, *Page 41.*

Heat cream, half and half, optional liquor, sugar, and vanilla seeds and pod for the filling in small saucepan over medium heat. When steam begins to rise off the cream, remove from heat and let infuse 15 minutes.

Whisk together yolks, sugar, vanilla, nutmeg, and salt in a medium bowl. Remove vanilla pod from infused cream and gradually temper hot cream into egg mixture, stirring constantly. (Try not to froth the custard too much, or it will create a foamy layer on top of the pie.)

Remove partially baked pie crust from oven and reduce temperature to 325°. Carefully pour custard into the hot shell (again, try not to froth it too much or it'll foam). Return the pie to the oven and bake 15–25 minutes, or until custard is barely set. Do not overbake. It should still jiggle when removed from the oven—the filling will continue to set as it cools. Cool pie to room temperature, then chill until cold, at least 4 hours. To serve, cut pie with a thin, sharp knife and place slices on serving plates.

Sprinkle each slice with about 1/2 teaspoon sugar for caramelizing. Then use a butane torch to "burn" the sugar into a caramelized, crunchy shell (for safe handling, follow manufacturers' instructions). Wave flame 1–1 1/2" above sugared surface until sugar melts and browns. Let stand 2 minutes before serving to allow the caramelized sugar to harden.

▲*Slowly whisk some of the hot cream mixture into the yolk mixture to keep eggs from curdling.*

▼*Pour custard into hot baked shell to help prevent a soggy bottom crust.*

▲*Cut chilled pie into slices and sprinkle tops with a thin layer of sugar. "Burn" sugar with a torch until it caramelizes.*

Butane Torch

Restaurant kitchens use propane torches to caramelize sugar on crème brûlée. Now you can burn like the "big guns," too, but with a little less fire power. These butane-powered torches caramelize sugar without risk of overheating and curdling the delicate custard underneath (as oven broilers often do). This torch is easy to use, self-igniting, refillable, and safe when handled properly. See Resources, Page 43, for ordering info.

chocolate pecan pie

This year, buck traditional pecan pies with a chocolate one. It just might become a new favorite.

Chocolate doesn't *always* make a good recipe better. But in the case of pecan pie, it really does. This recipe is a perfect balance of chocolate and pecans, not too sweet or chocolatey. Yes, it *is* rich, but it's the holidays. Enjoy yourself *now*—scale back in January.

Pecans are integral to the visual and flavor impact of this pie. Even though pecan pieces are less expensive, don't settle for them. Splurge a little and get halves—you'll be glad you did. Use the full two cups, and be sure to include the toasting step. It adds a flavor dimension to the pie that untoasted nuts cannot.

Proper baking is one other key to this pie's success. If overcooked, the filling is grainy, like half-baked brownies. Not enough time in the oven makes it soft so it won't slice cleanly. The perfect piece of this pie is firm at the edges, pudding-like in the center, and *packed* with pecans.

Chocolate Pecan Pie

Makes One 9" Pie; Total Time: About 1 Hour + Cooling

For the Crust—

Prepare and Prebake:

1 recipe Cream Cheese Pastry Dough, *Page 41* (or your favorite dough recipe)

For the Filling—

Toast:

2 cups pecan halves

Melt:

1/3 cup semisweet chocolate chips
3 T. light corn syrup
2 T. cocoa powder
1 T. unsalted butter
1 T. espresso powder

Stir In:

1/2 cup brown sugar, lightly packed
1/2 cup sugar
1 T. dark rum, *optional*
1 t. vanilla extract
1/4 t. kosher salt
3 eggs

Prepare dough, line a pie plate, and blind bake crust, *Page 41*.
Toast pecans for the pie filling on a baking sheet at 400° until fragrant, 8–10 minutes.
Melt chocolate chips, corn syrup, cocoa, butter, and espresso powder for the filling in a glass bowl set in a pan of *barely* simmer water. Stir often to prevent scorching.
Stir in both sugars, rum, vanilla, salt, and eggs. Keep mixture warm over low heat, stirring often to dissolve sugar. The mixture should be hot to the touch, but *never* let the water boil, or the eggs may curdle.

After blind baking, scatter pecans over the bottom of the hot crust. Pour the hot chocolate mixture over the pecans, pressing the chocolate down into the nuts. Return pie to the oven and bake 15–18 minutes, or until edges are set but center is still gooey—do not overbake. Cool pie to room temperature before serving.

Stir both sugars, rum, vanilla, alt, and eggs into melted chocoate mixture. Keep warm until eady to pour into shell.

▲*Place nuts in partially baked shell; pour hot chocolate over. Bake until set, 15–18 minutes.*

cream cheese pastry dough

At the heart of a good pie is a good crust. But no matter what recipe you use, "blind bake" the crust first to avoid a soggy, underdone base for your pie.

To blind bake, line the pie pan with the dough, freeze, then line it with foil. Fill the pan with raw rice or dried beans, and bake. It may shrink a little—that's okay.

Cream Cheese Pastry Dough

Makes Enough for One 9" Pie
Total Time: 30 Minutes + Chilling

Blend:
1 cup all-purpose flour
1/4 cup powdered sugar
Pinch salt

Add and Mix:
1 stick (1/2 cup) unsalted butter, cold, cubed
4 oz. cream cheese, cold, cubed

Blend dry ingredients in food processor fitted with steel blade. **Add** butter and cream cheese; mix just until dough forms around blade. Wrap dough in plastic, flatten into a disk, and chill 30 min.

Roll dough on lightly floured surface to 14" in diameter and 1/4" thick. Flip and turn it often to prevent sticking. Fold into quarters, then unfold into a 9" pie plate. Adjust dough to fit, pressing it lightly against bottom and sides of pan (try not to stretch it or it'll shrink). Trim all but 1" of overhang with scissors, fold edge under, and crimp. Freeze until firm, 15 minutes.

Preheat oven to 400°. Line frozen shell with foil, pressing firmly against the sides and folding gently over the edges. Fill shell with raw rice or dried beans and "blind bake" until crust is set but not browned, about 20 minutes. Unfold foil at edges and carefully lift it out; return shell to oven and bake 5–10 minutes, or until pale golden. Fill as directed in recipes.

◄*Unfold rolled out dough in pie plate. Adjust dough, without stretching it, to fit inside plate.*

Trim any overhang from dough. Turn edges under and crimp. Freeze dough until firm. ►

◄*Line dough with foil, folding it loosely over crimped edge. Fill pie with 2–3 cups dry rice or beans.*

Blind bake crust 20 min. Loosen foil and carefully lift it out of the pan. Bake until light golden; fill. ►

from **our** readers

Q&A
questions & answers

Unripe

Approaching ripe

Nearly overripe

RED BANANAS

Recently I've seen small red bananas in the grocery store. Do they taste like regular bananas, and how can I tell when they're ripe?

Brenda Lawyer
Carmel, IN

Red bananas are shorter and chunkier than the familiar yellow (Cavendish) variety. Their flesh is very sweet, and both the color and texture are creamy.

As the fruit begins to ripen, the brownish-red peel will start to lighten to a dark reddish-purple and sugar spots (they look like freckles) will appear. The spots indicate that starch is converting to sugar and the fruit will be sweet to eat. When the spots are larger, the fruit is overripe.

Another ripeness test is touch—the banana should yield slightly when gently squeezed. Avoid extremely soft bananas and bunches with mold around the stem.

WHAT IS THIS?

I inherited a cast iron pan from my grandmother that has seven 2" holes. What is it for?

Evie Jensen
Jefferson City, MO

The pan you're describing is an aebleskiver [EH-bel-skee-ver] pan. Usually made of cast iron, its sole function is for making sweet, round, Danish pancake balls called aebleskivers.

To make them, oil is heated in each indentation before pouring in batter. When the bottom forms a crust, the puff is flipped with a skewer so the batter spills back into the cup, creating a ball.

For those without an inheritance, pans are available from **Sweet Celebrations** for $29.99, (Item #68632) at (800) 328-6722. Their website, **sweetc.com**, offers several recipes for aebleskivers. Always season cast iron before using: coat pan with shortening, then bake at 350° for one hour.

SHORT PASTRY

What is meant by a "short" pastry crust?

Cathy Newell
Cambridge, MA

The term refers to a rich, crumbly,tender pastry crust. Often a base for tarts, it has a shortbread cookie consistency due to a higher ratio of fat (butter) to flour. It's also blended more thoroughly than a classic flaky crust. As a result, a short dough is quite soft and hard to roll out. It's best to pat it into a tart pan rather than roll out like pie dough.

MAKING SENSE OF MINCEMEAT

Last year over the holidays, my aunt made mincemeat pie. What exactly was I eating?

Cindy Robertson
Adel, IA

Mincemeat is a rich preserve made with fruits, spices, and nuts. It's used especially around Thanksgiving for pies and other desserts.

Originally, mincemeat included beef suet and finely chopped, cooked meat (that's where it gets the name). Before refrigeration, this was a method of preserving meat. While some homemade versions still use meat, commercial varieties leave it out.

Q&A

Do you have a question for *Cuisine at home?*

If you have a question about a cooking term, procedure, or technique, we'd like to hear from you. We'll consider publishing your question in one or more of our works. Just write down your question and mail it to *Cuisine at home*, Q&A Editor, 2200 Grand Ave., Des Moines, IA 50312, or contact us through our email address shown below. Please include your name, address, and daytime phone number in case we have questions.

Email: CuisineAtHome@CuisineAtHome.**com**

Web address: CuisineAtHome.com

SWEET CREAM BUTTER

What does "sweet cream butter" mean? I see it on some butter packages and not others.

M. E. Rutter
Haddon Heights, NJ

All butter (both salted and unsalted) is technically sweet cream butter. It simply refers to butter made with regular cream instead of sour cream.

The practice of labeling butter "sweet cream" came about years ago when some butter was made with sour cream. To avoid confusing the two butters, the word "sweet" was added on packages made with sweet cream. Today some companies still use the term on their packaging while others do not.

FREEZING NUTS

I order a large amount of nuts this time of year for holiday baking. If I don't use them all, is it okay to freeze them?

Donald Connelly
Liberal, KS

Not only is it okay to freeze nuts, it's recommended. Because nuts contain high amounts of oil, they can turn rancid fairly quickly. To preserve their freshness, freeze nuts in a resealable plastic freezer bag for up to six months.

Always be sure to taste nuts (frozen or not) before baking or cooking with them. Rancid nuts have a harsh taste and will ruin the flavor of anything they're in.

resources

PROFESSIONAL CUTLERY DIRECT
(800) 859-6994

Wüsthof Culinar knife set, Item #2CM302

Victorinox/Forschner knife set, Item #2CM304

Messermeister Park Plaza knife set, Item #2CM301

LamsonSharp jumbo knife set, Item #2CM303

Pedrini salad spinner, Item #9282, $19.99

CHEF'S CATALOG
(800) 338-3232
chefscatalog.com

Henckels Professional "S" knife set, Item #5584

Doughmakers jelly roll pan, Item #3167, $19.99

FANTE'S KITCHEN WARES SHOP
(800) 443-2683
fantes.com

Fante's Pro knife set, Item #7535

Chef'sChoice knife set, Item #12323

YOU ASKED FOR IT
We've received numerous requests for catalog sources for two of our top-rated Wares items. Both are available at ***Fante's Kitchen Wares Shop****,* see above.

KITCHEN CONSERVATORY
(866) 862-2433
kitchenconservatory.com

Magic Line 9 x 13" pan, Item #POB9132, $14.95

Culinary butane torch, Item #torch, $31.95

GOURMET KITCHEN STORE
(888) 304-2922
gourmetkitchenstore.com
KitchenAid knife set, Item #KCESET4S

KITCHEN ETC.
(800) 232-4070
kitchenetc.com
Chicago Cutlery Walnut Tradition knife set, Item #90172

Taylor 9878 digital thermometer, Item #99054, $23.99

STATEMENT OF OWNERSHIP, MANAGEMENT, AND CIRCULATION (REQUIRED BY 39 USC 3685)

Publication title: Cuisine at home. 2) Publication number: 1537-8225. 3) Filing date: September 15, 2002. 4) Issue frequency: bimonthly. 5) Number of issues published annually: six. 6) Annual subscription price: $24.00. 7) Complete mailing address of known office of publication: 2200 Grand Avenue, Des Moines, Polk County, Iowa 50312-5306. 8) Complete mailing address of headquarters or general business office of publisher: 2200 Grand Avenue, Des Moines, Iowa 50312. 9) Full names and complete mailing address of publisher, editor, and managing editor: Donald B. Peschke, 2200 Grand Avenue, Des Moines, Iowa 50312; Editor: John Meyer, 2200 Grand Avenue, Des Moines, Iowa 50312. 10) Owner: August Home Publishing Company, 2200 Grand Avenue, Des Moines, Iowa 50312; Donald B. Peschke, 2200 Grand Avenue, Des Moines, Iowa 50312. 11) Known bondholders, mortgagees, and other security holders owning or holding 1 percent or more of total amount of bonds, mortgages, or other securities: none. 12) Does not apply. 13) Publication title: Cuisine at home. 14) Issue date for circulation data below: July/August 2002. 15) Extent and nature of circulation:

	Average no. copies each issue during preceding 12 months	Actual no. copies of single issue published nearest to filing date
A. Total number copies (net press run)	139,394	166,862
B. Paid and/or requested circulation		
1. Paid/requested outside-county mail subscriptions stated on Form 3541	105,066	127,351
2. Paid in-county subscriptions	0	0
3. Sales through dealers and carriers, street vendors, counter sales, and other non-USPS paid distribution	11,067	16,548
4. Other classes mailed through the USPS	0	0
C. Total paid and/or requested circulation	116,133	143,899
D. Free distribution by mail		
1. Outside-county as stated on Form 3541	268	274
2. In-county as stated on Form 3541	0	0
3. Other classes mailed through the USPS	0	0
E. Free distribution outside the mail	0	0
F. Total free distribution	268	274
G. Total distribution	116,401	144,173
H. Copies not distributed	22,993	22,689
I. Total	139,394	166,862
J. Percentage paid and/or requested circulation	99.77%	99.81%

16. This statement of ownership will be printed in the Nov/Dec 2002 issue of this publication.
17. I certify that the statements made by me above are correct and complete. (signed) John Meyer, Editor

grilled turkey sandwich
with blue cheese mayonnaise

GRILLED TURKEY SANDWICH WITH BLUE CHEESE MAYONNAISE

MAKES TWO 8" SANDWICHES
TOTAL TIME: 15 MINUTES

FOR THE MAYONNAISE—
WHISK TOGETHER:

- 1/4 cup mayonnaise
- 1/4 cup blue cheese, crumbled
- 2 T. apricot preserves

FOR THE SANDWICH—
PREPARE:

- 2 8" sourdough rolls

SPREAD EACH ROLL WITH:

- 1/4 cup Mayonnaise

FILL WITH; GRILL:

- 1 lb. roast turkey breast, sliced, divided
- 2 cups arugula, divided

Whisk together ingredients for Mayonnaise.
Preheat griddle.
Prepare rolls by slicing thin layer off the top and bottom of each roll. Slice lengthwise to make two halves.
Spread with Mayonnaise.
Fill each sandwich with half of the turkey and arugula. Grill on hot buttered griddle until golden brown. Slice and serve.

Volume 6 INDEX
Issues 31–36